GIORGIO AGAMBEN

FORDHAM UNIVERSITY PRESS   NEW YORK   2015

COMMONALITIES
Timothy C. Campbell, series editor

GIORGIO AGAMBEN

Beyond the Threshold of Deconstruction

KEVIN ATTELL

THIS BOOK IS MADE POSSIBLE BY A COLLABORATIVE GRANT
FROM THE ANDREW W. MELLON FOUNDATION.

Copyright © 2015 Fordham University Press

All rights reserved. No part of this publication may be reproduced, stored in a retrieval system, or transmitted in any form or by any means—electronic, mechanical, photocopy, recording, or any other—except for brief quotations in printed reviews, without the prior permission of the publisher.

Fordham University Press has no responsibility for the persistence or accuracy of URLs for external or third-party Internet websites referred to in this publication and does not guarantee that any content on such websites is, or will remain, accurate or appropriate.

Fordham University Press also publishes its books in a variety of electronic formats. Some content that appears in print may not be available in electronic books.

Library of Congress Cataloging-in-Publication Data

Attell, Kevin.
 Giorgio Agamben : beyond the threshold of deconstruction / Kevin Attell. — First edition.
     pages cm. — (Commonalities)
 Includes bibliographical references and index.
 ISBN 978-0-8232-6204-5 (cloth : alk. paper) —
 ISBN 978-0-8232-6205-2 (pbk. : alk. paper)
 1. Agamben, Giorgio, 1942– 2. Derrida, Jacques. 3. Deconstruction. I. Title.
 B3611.A44A88 2014
 195—dc23

                                                2014017794

Printed in the United States of America

17 16 15   5 4 3 2 1

First edition

This was a case of metaphysics, at least as difficult for Joe to deal with, as for me. But Joe took the case altogether out of the region of metaphysics, and by that means vanquished it.

—CHARLES DICKENS, *GREAT EXPECTATIONS*

CONTENTS

Acknowledgments ix
Abbreviations xiii

Introduction. Agamben and Derrida:
An Esoteric Dossier 1

PART ONE: FIRST PRINCIPLES

1 Agamben and Derrida Read Saussure 13

2 "The Human Voice" 40

3 *Potenza* and *Différance* 84

PART TWO: STRATEGY WITHOUT FINALITY OR MEANS WITHOUT END

4 Sovereignty, Law, and Violence 125

5 Ticks and Cats 167

6 A Matter of Time 213

Coda: Play 255

Notes 263
Works Cited 289
Index 297

ACKNOWLEDGMENTS

In these acknowledgments of the many people to whom I am indebted, my first is to Giorgio Agamben, whom I had the good fortune to meet while studying at Berkeley. I thank him for his personal and intellectual generosity over the years since then and, of course, for his extraordinary body of work.

This book was being set in page proofs when we all received the terrible and shocking news of Fordham University Press Editorial Director Helen Tartar's death. Helen supported this book and its author from early on—indeed, as early as my translation of Agamben's *The Open*—and I consider it a supreme privilege to have known and worked with her. It is a joyful honor—alas, now mixed with deep sadness—to have this book appear with Fordham University Press under her editorial directorship.

The idea for this book arose while I was an Andrew W. Mellon Postdoctoral Fellow in the English department at Johns Hopkins University. I would like to thank the Mellon Foundation as well as all those who made Gilman Hall such a happy and exciting academic home, especially Amanda Anderson, Sharon Cameron, Frances Ferguson, Richard Halpern, Allen Grossman, and Gabrielle Spiegel. And from Baltimore to Ithaca—that is to say, from the beginning to the completion of this book—Simon During and Neil Hertz have continuously offered kind support and sage advice. By a happy chance, Jesse Molesworth was also a Mellon fellow at Hopkins at the same time, and I have benefitted from his friendship and intelligence ever since.

One could hardly think of a better place than Cornell to think and write about contemporary philosophy, and deconstruction in particular. I must especially thank Cynthia Chase, Jonathan Culler, and Dominick LaCapra for being such patient, supportive, and—even in disagreement—generous interlocutors over the years I was working on this book. Satya Mohanty carefully read the manuscript when it was about half done and gave crucial advice that fundamentally influenced the shape the book ultimately took. For the many ways in which they have helped me in writing this book, I would also like to thank my extraordinary senior colleagues in the English department at Cornell, especially Mary Pat Brady, Laura Brown, Andy Galloway, Roger Gilbert, Ellis Hanson, Molly Hite, Tim Murray, Neil Saccamano, Paul Sawyer, and Dan Schwarz. I have also been fortunate to have Elizabeth Anker, Jeremy Braddock, Jason Frank, Peter Gilgen, Rayna Kalas, Philip Lorenz, Jenny Mann, Karen Pinkus, Dagmawi Woubshet, and Samantha Zacher as wonderful colleagues and friends in Ithaca. I would additionally like to thank the students who participated in my graduate seminar on Agamben and deconstruction.

Ingrid Diran and Lytle Shaw read large portions of the manuscript in progress, and their comments and suggestions improved virtually every page. Many thanks also to Tom Lay, Tim Roberts, and Susan Murray at Fordham Press.

Since well before he was the editor of the Commonalities series, Tim Campbell has been a supportive, incisive, and challenging interlocutor, not to mention a great friend. I am grateful for all he has helped me to think through over these years and I am deeply delighted to see this book appear in his series.

I would like to thank the Mellon Foundation, once again, for supporting the Modern Language Initiative, as well as Johns Hopkins University Press for permission to reprint material that first appeared the following articles: "An Esoteric Dossier: Agamben and Derrida Read Saussure," *ELH* 76:4 (2009), 821–46 © 2009 by The Johns Hopkins University Press. And "Potentiality, Actuality, Constituent Power," *diacritics* 39:3 (2009), 35–53 © 2012 by The Johns Hopkins University Press.

I am also grateful to Alex Murray and Thanos Zartaloudis, Tom Frost, and Jenny Doussan (all great readers of Agamben) for invitations to speak at Birkbeck, Newcastle, and Goldsmiths, where I was able to present early versions of some of the arguments in this book.

Courtney Booker, Emilie Clark, David Copenhafer, Lytle Shaw, and Dana Stevens have been dear friends for many years. My personal and intellectual debt to them cannot be measured.

I offer my endless gratitude and love to my parents, Stephen Attell and Georgia Morrow, my sister, Carrie Attell, and my late grandparents, George and Theana Themelis. This book is just one small bit of what would have been impossible without them. Warmest thanks are due as well to Marlene Attell and David Morrow. Chapter 5 is dedicated to Houdini and Irma.

Finally, thanks of a different order are due to Sirietta Simoncini for all she has given to my work and to my life. More than any words can say. This book is for her and our daughter, Maria, with all my love.

ABBREVIATIONS

TEXTS BY AGAMBEN

CC   *The Coming Community*. Trans. Michael Hardt. Minneapolis: U of Minnesota P, 1993.
HS   *Homo Sacer: Sovereign Power and Bare Life*. Trans. Daniel Heller-Roazen. Stanford: Stanford UP, 1998.
IH   *Infancy and History*. Trans. Liz Heron. New York: Verso, 1993.
IP   *Idea of Prose*. Trans. Michael Sullivan and Sam Whitsitt. Albany: SUNY Press, 1995.
LD   *Language and Death: The Place of Negativity*. Trans. Karen E. Pinkus with Michael Hardt. Minneapolis: U of Minnesota P, 1991.
MWE   *Means without End*. Trans. Vincenzo Binetti and Cesare Casarino. Minneapolis: U of Minnesota P, 2000.
O   *The Open*. Trans. Kevin Attell. Stanford: Stanford UP, 2004.
P   *Potentialities*. Ed. and trans. Daniel Heller-Roazen. Stanford: Stanford UP, 1999.
PP   *La potenza del pensiero*. Vicenza: Neri Pozza, 2005.
Prof *Profanations*. Trans. Jeff Fort. New York: Zone, 2007.
RA   *Remnants of Auschwitz*. Trans. Daniel Heller-Roazen. New York: Zone, 2002.
S   *Stanzas*. Trans. Ronald L. Martinez. Minneapolis: U of Minnesota P, 1993.
SE   *State of Exception*. Trans. Kevin Attell. Chicago: U of Chicago P, 2005.

TTR *The Time That Remains.* Trans. Patricia Dailey. Stanford: Stanford UP, 2005.
WM "The Work of Man." Trans. Kevin Attell. *Giorgio Agamben: Sovereignty and Life.* Ed. Matthew Calarco and Steven DeCaroli. Stanford: Stanford UP, 2007.

TEXTS BY DERRIDA

Animal *The Animal That Therefore I Am.* Ed. Marie-Louise Mallet. Trans. David Wills. New York: Fordham UP, 2008.
Aporias *Aporias.* Trans. Thomas Dutoit. Stanford: Stanford UP, 1993.
BS *The Beast and the Sovereign, Vol. 1.* Ed. Michel Lisse et al. Trans. Geoffrey Bennington. Chicago: U of Chicago P, 2009.
BtL "Before the Law." Trans. Avital Ronell. *Acts of Literature.* Ed. Derek Attridge. New York: Routledge, 1992.
FL "Force of Law: The 'Mystical Foundations of Authority.'" Trans. Mary Quaintance. *Acts of Religion.* Ed. Gil Anidjar. New York: Routledge, 2002.
G *Of Grammatology.* Trans. Gayatri Chakravorty Spivak. Corrected ed. Baltimore: Johns Hopkins UP, 1997.
IOG *Edmund Husserl's "Origin of Geometry": An Introduction.* Trans. John P. Leavey Jr. Lincoln: U of Nebraska P, 1978.
K "Khōra." Trans. Ian McLeod. *On the Name.* Ed. Thomas Dutoit. Stanford: Stanford UP, 1995.
M *Margins of Philosophy.* Trans. Alan Bass. Chicago: U of Chicago P, 1982.
OS *Of Spirit: Heidegger and the Question.* Trans. Geoffrey Bennington and Rachel Bowlby. Chicago: U of Chicago P, 1989.
Pos *Positions.* Trans. Alan Bass. Chicago: U of Chicago P, 1981.
Rogues *Rogues: Two Essays on Reason.* Trans. Pascale-Anne Brault and Michael Naas. Stanford: Stanford UP, 2005.
SM *Specters of Marx.* Trans. Peggy Kamuf. New York: Routledge, 1994.
SP *Speech and Phenomena.* Trans. David B. Allison and Newton Garver. Evanston: Northwestern UP, 1973.
WD *Writing and Difference.* Trans. Alan Bass. Chicago: U of Chicago P, 1978.

GIORGIO AGAMBEN

INTRODUCTION
Agamben and Derrida: An Esoteric Dossier

In a letter to his wife dated September 5, 1966, Martin Heidegger wrote that upon arriving at the Provençal village of Le Thor, where he was to give an informal seminar on Heraclitus, he was greeted by the young poet Dominique Fourcade and "a highly talented young Italian from Rome" (*ein junger hochbegabter Italiener aus Rom*).[1] That young Italian was, of course, a twenty-four-year-old Giorgio Agamben, who had had, through a series of lucky connections, the good fortune to be invited to join the small seminar at the home of the poet René Char. Agamben's attendance at Heidegger's seminars in Le Thor in 1966 and 1968, and the significant influence this experience had on his early philosophical vocation, is by now a well-known story.[2] In many ways it marks the auspicious beginning of the long intellectual itinerary that would take Agamben repeatedly back through the ways and byways of Heidegger's thought—a body of work that, by any account, was and remains one of Agamben's major philosophical touchstones.

Though there is far less documentation to show it, the 1966 and 1968 seminars also mark another starting point in Agamben's intellectual itinerary, one that would also prove to be decisive through decades of thought. This is because 1966 and 1968 define the time in which Agamben begins to formulate a critical philosophical position with regard to the work of Jacques Derrida. In September 1968—that is to say, around the time of the second Le Thor seminar, and one year after the first Derridean annus mirabilis of 1967—Agamben published an article titled "L'albero del linguaggio" (The tree of language), which contains his first public engagement with Derrida. In this piece, which surveys several trends in contemporary linguistics—especially those associated with Jakobson and Chomsky—he notes how in recent years "linguistics has been led to renounce many of the postulates established by Saussure and to develop a semi-mathematical method that ... seems no longer to have much in common with that of traditional linguistics."[3] And yet, he writes, despite such a withdrawal from certain Saussurian claims,

> one postulate has remained unquestioned: the definition of language [*linguaggio*] as a system of signs, indissoluble unities of signified and signifier. Although there has been no lack of radical critiques on the part of philosophers, and there has even been recent talk of a "historical *closure*" of the "age of the sign," the dogma of the sign has remained intact. In this sense, it can be said that contemporary linguistics remains entirely faithful to the Saussurian semiological project.[4]

The reference in this passage is to Derrida's *Of Grammatology*, and within it lies the nucleus of a critique that Agamben will never fundamentally retract—that Derrida thinks his way to the outer limit of Saussurian semiology, but remains enclosed within a semiological understanding of language. While this critique, as we will see in the following chapter, reaches its full formulation in his 1977 book *Stanzas*, it is clear that, a decade earlier, Agamben was already consciously developing a post-Heideggerian thought somewhat at odds with deconstruction. Indeed, in this early essay Agamben continues his discussion of language in an overtly Heideggerian vein. Alongside the mathematical and semiological linguistic models, he writes,

> another one presents itself, one that, announced at the dawn of Greek thought, has remained so to speak in reserve through the history of the western reflection on language. According to the path that this possibility opens for thought, language is *logos*. *Logos*, however, does not mean simply "reason, calculation," but designates rather, according to its etymology, the act of gathering, of maintaining and carrying something before the gaze so that it appears as that which it is.[5]

Thus begin to emerge the outlines of an engagement with Derrida's thought that will continue to develop and deepen over the course of the following decades, sometimes overtly and pointedly, sometimes much more obliquely and, as it were, esoterically.

The title of this introduction is taken from a phrase in the fourth chapter of Agamben's *State of Exception*, "Gigantomachy Concerning a Void." The "esoteric dossier" to which Agamben refers in that work is the decades-long though frequently elliptical exchange (which he describes as a sort of obscure chess match) between Walter Benjamin and Carl Schmitt concerning a set of key concepts including sovereignty, law, and violence (*Gewalt*). Agamben's reading of the Benjamin-Schmitt debate will be discussed in due course in the following pages, but I adopt this phrase here as a fortuitous description of this other philosophical gigantomachy between Agamben and Derrida, this other obscure chess match, whose moves have been only partially recorded, and whose origins can, for more than convenience's sake, be traced back to that southern French Heideggerian milieu.[6]

While Agamben has always been in a manifest dialogue with a number of key twentieth-century thinkers—Heidegger, of course, but also Benjamin, Benveniste, Warburg, Arendt, Debord, and more recently, Schmitt and Foucault—his critical and at times polemical engagement with Derrida has often been conducted in passing comments or just below the surface of his texts. And yet, beginning in the late 1960s and continuing to his most recent texts, Agamben has consistently measured his thought against Derrida's. This book closely examines that often implicit engagement and demonstrates not only the extent to which Derrida must be considered Agamben's primary contemporary interlocutor but also the ways in which Agamben's critical engagement with deconstruction can indeed be identified as the context out of which emerge almost all of his key concepts—infancy, Voice, potentiality, sovereignty, messianism.[7] The aim of this book therefore is not to polemicize with deconstruction—though the analysis will trace a number of Agambenian polemics—but to show the extent and the significance of Agamben's debate with deconstruction (an engagement that, as the later chapters will demonstrate, becomes somewhat mutual as Derrida begins to acknowledge and respond to Agamben's positions in the 1990s).[8] Implicit in the argument of this book, then, is the belief that Agamben views deconstruction as perhaps the most significant body of philosophical thought in the postwar period, the work against which he must continuously measure his own. A corollary to this claim is that any understanding of Agamben's thought that does not take this context into account remains incomplete.

The methodology of this book can be described as twofold. On the one hand, Agamben's work is punctuated with references to Derrida and deconstruction. The following pages take these explicit engagements under consideration and closely evaluate their claims. But the book also shows, by excavating a number of much more implicit and oblique engagements, many of which have passed with little or no notice in the critical literature, that the critique of deconstruction runs like a sort of unconscious beneath the limpid prose of Agamben's entire oeuvre. This idea informs the second methodological strategy of the book, namely, the comparative analysis of Agamben's and Derrida's contesting readings of individual texts, beginning with their early pieces on Saussure and moving through readings of texts by Benveniste, Heidegger, Husserl, Plato, Aristotle, Benjamin, Schmitt, and others. Both Agamben and Derrida argue philosophically through readings of texts, and this book shows how these texts time and time again become the contested ground in the work of these master thinkers.

The book is divided into two roughly chronological parts. The first part, titled "First Principles," examines the development of some of Agamben's key concepts—infancy, Voice, potentiality—from the 1970s to approximately 1990 and traces the way these concepts consistently draw on and respond to specific texts by Derrida. The second part, titled "Strategy without Finality or Means without End," traces what has been described as the political turn in Agamben's and Derrida's thinking from about 1990 onward, beginning with their crucial investigations of legal force or violence and moving through their parallel treatments of the human-animal relation and finally messianism and the politics to come.

Though this book will often be sympathetic to Agamben's side on a given issue, its intention is not to show that Agamben always gets the upper hand. In fact, a more important aim of this study is to show how out of such similar terrain two very compelling philosophical systems—and I do think we can call even deconstruction a system, in the sense of a set of recognizable theses and procedures—arise.[9] Indeed, one implicit position of this book is that both Derrida and Agamben have "a philosophy." Even though they are both usually referred to as philosophers, this proposition is not universally accepted. Many commentators have instead suggested that they are each unsystematic and tactical thinkers and that their work does not, as a whole, put forward a universal philosophical "system." In contrast to this view, one of the secondary goals of the present study is to affirm that they do—or at least that they propose and consistently maintain certain central theoretical positions.[10] Clearly identifying these positions is crucial for understanding the importance of deconstruction for Agamben.

In each of their varied oeuvres, Agamben and Derrida address questions of art, religion, politics, history, literature, and so forth, and they have each provided the impetus for considerable bodies of work in a number of disciplines not properly philosophical. Perhaps the most striking, though by no means unique, example of this is the way Derrida's thought—preeminently via the work of Paul de Man—gave rise to Anglo-American deconstructive literary criticism, to great results. Agamben, whose influence on literary studies is perhaps still at an early stage, has likewise had considerable influence in recent years across a range of disciplines in the theoretical humanities.[11] Given their wide spheres of influence, and the likelihood that readers of this book will be working in one or several of those fields, an initial caveat may be in order here. Though the extension of deconstructive and Agambenian thought into such a broad range of debates and disciplines is of the highest interest and importance, this book tends not to venture very far into those spaces. It does not, for example, attempt to do justice to Derrida's impact on literary or legal scholarship, or to Agamben's influence upon bioethical debates or political theory after the so-called "war on terrorism." Rather, its focus remains trained rather tightly on the, so to speak, internal mechanics of Agamben's and Derrida's texts as they relate to one another. As noted above, both thinkers philosophize through readings of texts, and the following pages seek to rigorously and patiently track them through those readings. In this sense, one might say that this book attempts to reproduce—albeit at considerably lower wattage—the method of Agamben's and Derrida's texts themselves. And though the question at hand—the relation of Agamben's work to Derrida's—is a rather specific one, the resulting itinerary traces a line so close to the center of nearly every period and every key concept of Agamben's oeuvre that what emerges, I hope, is a vivid and full portrait of Agamben's thought (and indeed of Derrida's) from a hitherto underobserved vantage point.

Chapter 1, "Agamben and Derrida Read Saussure," focuses on the concluding section of Agamben's 1977 book *Stanzas*, where he launches his first sustained critique of deconstruction with an interpretation of Saussure that responds in close fashion to Derrida's famous reading in *Of Grammatology*. In response to this foundational text of deconstruction, Agamben offers a counterportrait of the Swiss linguist and a counterreading of his revolutionary work in the *Course in General Linguistics*. In viewing Saussure not as the founder of semiology but rather as a linguist who sought but failed to escape the double and differential logic of the sign, this interpretation not only suggests a compelling alternative to the way Saussure has been taken up within the structuralist and poststructuralist tradition, but also serves as the basis for the view of language (language considered as the potentiality for language) that will underlie Agamben's subsequent philosophical work to the present. This first chapter thus establishes how integral this early engagement with deconstruction will be to Agamben's own thought over the following decades, beginning with the theories of infancy and of the Voice that are the subjects of his next two books as well as the second chapter of this study.

In a preface to the French translation of his 1978 book *Infancy and History*, Agamben explains that his work from this period up to and including his 1982 book *Language and Death* might best be understood as a prologue, or parergon, to a work never written, to which he gives the title "The Human Voice." Chapter 2—which takes its title from Agamben's unwritten work—examines that parergon, which constitutes the first programmatic formulation of Agamben's critique of the Western metaphysical tradition. As is most fully explicated in *Language and Death*, Agamben views the fundamental—and largely unacknowledged—structure of Western philosophical thought to be that of negativity, the presupposition of a negative and unappropriable other to every positivity, a structure exemplified, as seen in the first chapter, in the divided nature of the linguistic sign (the most privileged metaphysical binary in Derrida's early work). In this diagnosis, Agamben's thesis meets with but runs precisely counter to Derrida's view that Western thought is a logocentric metaphysics of presence. For both thinkers, the negative structure of metaphysics renders immediacy and presence impossible, but when faced with this aporetic structure they adopt radically differing strategies. For Derrida, the deconstruction of the metaphysical dream of presence entails the affirmation of difference and deferral, in a word, *différance*.[12] For Agamben, the task of thought is instead to ask, as he puts it in a very early essay on Artaud, "how can an impasse be turned into an exit?"[13] After elucidating the dialogue between Agamben's texts and Derridean works such as the introduction to Husserl's *Origin of Geometry* and *Speech and Phenomena*, the chapter shows how Agamben turns to the concept of infancy as a possible "exit" from the aporetic logic of metaphysical semiology. For Agamben, the splitting of the sign is not simply a given, but must be seen as a result or condition of the fact that the human enters the world without language and must acquire it, that the human voice is "improper" to the human. Agamben's theory of this improper human "Voice" (with a capital "V") and of the infantile privation of language, are the groundwork for the development of what can legitimately be called his signal concept, potentiality.

Chapter 3, "*Potenza* and *Différance*," examines Agamben's theory of potentiality in relation to Derrida's central concepts of arche-writing and *différance*. After the more polemical engagements in the works discussed in the two previous chapters, Agamben's rhetorical strategy with regard to deconstruction changes in the later 1980s, the period in which he was refining his theory of potentiality. Following an extended discussion of Agamben's idiosyncratic adoption of this Aristotelian concept (which has often been imperfectly understood), the chapter goes on to examine how in his single essay explicitly devoted entirely to Derrida's thought, "*Pardes*: The Writing of Potentiality" (1990), Agamben stages what appears to be a rapprochement with Derrida, suggesting, from the moment of its title, that their central concepts are at least akin to one another. It is, however, an ambivalent or rivalrous kinship, a tenuous convergence that breaks open once again into clearer disagreement—now in political as well as philosophical terms—in the series of books for which Agamben initially gained renown in the English-speaking world.

Indeed, Agamben's best-known work is the ongoing *Homo Sacer* series, begun in 1995 with *Homo Sacer: Sovereign Power and Bare Life*. Though its concerns are obliquely anticipated by the aphoristic *The Coming Community* (1990), this volume firmly marks the arrival of Agamben's political thought. Chapter 4, "Sovereignty, Law, and Violence," opens the second half of the book with a consideration of the relation between Agamben's major political and ethical concepts and the ethico-political turn deconstruction took in roughly the same years. Foremost among these concepts, of course, are sovereignty and bare life, the twinned figures in what Agamben was among the first to concertedly investigate under the term "biopolitics." Agamben (drawing primarily on Carl Schmitt and Walter Benjamin) identifies the core of sovereignty and the foundation of the law as the power to decide on the "exception," the logic of which he elaborates as a nebulous and paradoxical inclusive-exclusion or "ban-structure" that establishes the law's power over life precisely by virtue of its self-suspension. This chapter shows how Agamben's analysis of the logic of sovereignty is a coherent modulation of his earlier analysis of the way potentiality passes into act, and places his theory in relation to Derrida's roughly contemporaneous readings of sovereignty, law, and violence in the thought of Schmitt and Benjamin. As has been noted in recent years by a number of commentators, Derrida and Agamben lay out divergent conceptions of politics and ethics in these later texts. It is, however, only through an understanding of the way Agamben's biopolitical thesis is based on the first principles of his earlier thought, examined in the first half of this book, that the true relation between Agamben and Derrida as political thinkers can be understood and evaluated.

The title of chapter 5, "Ticks and Cats," refers to the two figures that might be described as the secret protagonists of Agamben's and Derrida's books on the human-animal relation, *The Open* (2002) and *The Animal That Therefore I Am* (1999/2004). Adopting similar strategies of tracing the ways philosophical and scientific discourses have strategically separated the human from the animal, Agamben and Derrida both focus their interrogation on that ambiguous space that divides the two, and thus put into question the most fundamental gesture of humanism and anthropocentrism. But their convergence on this intervallic space reveals, as this chapter shows, the divergent paths they chart through this uncertain terrain. For Derrida, the question of the animal is one of responsibility and alterity, or more precisely a question of deconstructing the complacency of human self-definition based on the animal's supposed inability to answer, to recognize, to respond to the other in any way but a mechanistic reaction. Agamben's attention too falls on how, in contrast to the freedom of human "openness" to the World (in the Heideggerian terminology he adopts), the animal's relation to the stimuli of its environment is consistently figured as fixed and determined, thus reaffirming the divisive operation of the "anthropological machine of humanism." In both cases, but in fundamentally different terms that this chapter elucidates, the distinction between human and animal gives way under pressure put on that dividing line—a breaching obliquely represented by the secret protagonist who dwells on that border: the tick in a laboratory in Weimar-era Rostock who, Agamben tells us, was kept isolated from all stimuli in a state of suspended animation for eighteen years; the cat, Derrida's cat, whose disturbing and intimate gaze prompts him to muse: "and say the animal responded?"

The sixth and final chapter of the book is titled "A Matter of Time." In his 1978 essay "Time and History," Agamben writes: "The original task of a genuine revolution . . . is never merely to 'change the world,' but also—and above all—to change time" (*IH* 91). Thus more than a decade before what is considered the political turn in his thought, Agamben lays out the basis of the politically inflected messianism that he will most fully develop in his reading of the Pauline letters in *The Time That Remains* (2000). This chapter examines Agamben's concept of messianic time—a nonprogressive time that exists within linear time, a *kairos* within *khronos*, which Paul announces as the meaning of the messianic event. Agamben shares and contests this temporal terrain with Derrida, who most fully develops his key late concept of "messianicity" in *Specters of Marx* (1993). For Derrida, the time of messianicity is a time that is, in Hamlet's words, "out of joint," and thus is an experience of the nonpresence of the present, an experience of irreducible alterity and of *différance*. For Agamben, in explicit contrast to Derrida's valorization of the *à venir* of messianicity, "[t]he Messiah will only come when he is no longer necessary, he will only come after his arrival, he will come not on the last day, but on the very last day" (*P* 174), meaning that rather than holding the chronological and eschatological notions of time in abeyance or deferral, *khronos* must be decisively halted and neutralized, must arrive at the last day, before kairological messianic time can be experienced.

The analysis of the political valences of Agamben's and Derrida's work in the second half of the book ends with a coda considering a key term that from very early on has lain at the center of their work but has carried two distinct meanings. That term is "play." For Derrida, from the 1966 essay "Structure, Sign, and Play in the Discourse of the Human Sciences," play is the undecidable and unclosable slippage in every structure, which in the political-ethical sphere necessitates an endless, promissory openness to the other, unconditional hospitality, and "strategy without finality." For Agamben, beginning with the 1978 essay "In Playland," the experience of play—in the sense of a child absorbed in play—is an index or a prefiguration of what he calls a "truly political action," a praxis that has liberated itself from the metaphysical powers of law and sovereignty, a praxis which in its immediacy becomes a "means without end."

PART ONE

First Principles

1

AGAMBEN AND DERRIDA READ SAUSSURE

> Un vieux sphinx ignoré du monde insoucieux, Oublié sur la carte...
> —CHARLES BAUDELAIRE, "SPLEEN II"

OVERTURE: "BEFORE THE LAW"

Perhaps the best-known instance of Agamben's debate with Derrida comes, not surprisingly, from what is surely his best-known and most frequently cited book, *Homo Sacer: Sovereign Power and Bare Life*. While oblique and overt references to deconstruction are scattered throughout that work—and indeed, as we will examine in some detail in chapter 4 below, the book's central concept of the "ban-structure" of sovereignty is conceived in response to deconstruction—it is in the chapter on Franz Kafka's parable "Before the Law" that Agamben explicitly challenges Derrida's reading of Kafka's iconic text, and with it a number of fundamental tenets of deconstructive thought. The programmatic nature of both Agamben's and Derrida's readings of the Kafka text, in which each thinker plays in abbreviated and distilled form some of the central motifs of his work, makes this episode a fitting overture to the following pages' effort to trace the intricate and intertwining lines of their theoretical itineraries.

As is well known, Kafka's "Before the Law" tells the story of a "man from the country" who arrives one day at the gate of the law, would like to gain admittance and enter, but is prevented from doing so by an enigmatic doorkeeper. The man is, however, never physically barred by the doorkeeper, but rather told by him that though there is nothing preventing him from entering, he nevertheless cannot enter at the moment—a situation that proves to extend for days and years. The man waits before the door for what appears to be his entire lifetime, never succeeding in gaining access from the doorkeeper. In the end, as the man's eyes grow weak and the world begins to darken, the doorman tells him that this open gate was made for him alone, that no one else could ever enter it, and he moves to shut it.

The paradox of the tale, at least the one that interests us here, lies in the law's simultaneous openness and inaccessibility. The law both holds the man in its power and excludes him from its full presence, and it never takes the form of any specific command or statute beyond the pure force to hold the man fascinated in its power, to hold the man forever "before the law": an empty and absolute law with no specific laws, which demands submission before it but commands nothing, a law that is "in force without significance" (*HS* 51). As the priest who tells K this parable in *The Trial* says, "the court wants nothing from you. It receives you when you come and dismisses you when you go."[1]

In his essay on Kafka's parable, Derrida offers a reading of the paradoxical figure of the law that is in force without significance as a figure of *différance*, a juridical threshold that is as intangible as it is potent:

> The present prohibition of the law is not a prohibition in the sense of an imperative constraint; it is a *différance*. For after having said to [the countryman] "later," the doorkeeper specifies: "If you are so drawn to it, just try to go in despite my veto." Earlier he had said merely "not at the moment." He then simply steps aside and lets the man stoop to look inside through the door, which always remains open, marking a limit without itself posing an obstacle or barrier. It is a mark, but it is nothing firm, opaque or uncrossable. (*BtL* 202–3)

The gate is perpetually open, and yet never to be entered or crossed. This is not only because the man never does cross it, but also because, as the doorkeeper informs him, behind this door there is another and then another, each with a doorkeeper more frightening than the last—doorkeepers whom the man, in fact, never actually sees.

In a gesture that we will see in many modulations in the following pages, Derrida identifies this obscure threshold with *différance*, and what is more, with a *différance* that not only is impassable, but whose play of deferral and nullification is the foundational (non)source and (non)origin of the law. The countryman's entrance into the law is not directly prevented but endlessly deferred by the enigmatic doorkeeper, whose station, he tells the man, is simply the first of an evidently endless series of such deferring thresholds. What, then, is this place before the law where the countryman spends the rest of his life waiting patiently? It is, on Derrida's reading, the point, the place, the *topos*, at which the law, in holding the man purely in its power yet leaving him free, has its originary event (though, for Derrida, what is figured here is precisely neither a topological place nor an originary event).

> Guardian after guardian. This differential topology [*topique différantielle*] adjourns, guardian after guardian, within the polarity of high and low, far and near (*fort/da*), now and later. The same topology without its own place, the same atopology [*atopique*], the same madness defers the law as the nothing that forbids itself and the neuter that annuls oppositions. The atopology annuls that which takes place, the event itself. This nullification gives birth to the law[.] (*BtL* 208–9)

What the man from the country comes up against, then, is the structure—or, in Rodolphe Gasché's term, infrastructure—of *différance* itself, which is the unsurpassable limit that blocks or breaks up the path (*poros*) that leads to the (illusory) presence of the law and to its originary, establishing event.[2] The threshold before the law is a line not to be crossed; it is an impasse both impassable and impassive because it is a line that marks nothing but its own absence.

Agamben see things differently. For him, what Derrida is able to discern in the law that remains in force but prescribes nothing is not simply, or not only, an exposed *différance*, but the fundamental structure of sovereignty and sovereign exception that *Homo Sacer* attempts not only to uncover, but, more importantly, to undo. For Agamben, Derrida reads the parable in terms that bring to light the logic of law and sovereignty (and indeed define its paradox as the very logic of *différance*), but cannot or will not go beyond it. "According to the schema of the sovereign exception," Agamben writes, "law applies to [the man from the country] in no longer applying, and holds him in its ban in abandoning him outside itself. The open door destined only for him includes him in excluding him and excludes him in including him. And this is precisely the summit and the root of every law" (*HS* 50). The ban, the inclusive exclusion, the "relation of exception" (*HS* 18), Agamben argues, is the fundamental structure of law and sovereignty, and while Agamben and Derrida might agree on this *description* of the ban-structure (which, indeed, Agamben adopts from Jean-Luc Nancy, and which I will discuss in greater detail in chapter 4 below), what separates their readings of the parable is the nature or status they assign to that structure.

What is the significance of that impasse of the structure of sovereignty that includes in excluding and excludes in including, the law that is "in force without significance"? For Derrida, the impassability of this threshold indicates precisely the insuperability of *différance*:

> Their [i.e., the doorkeepers'] potency is *différance*, an interminable *différance*, since it lasts for days and "years," indeed, up to the end of (the) man. *Différance* till death, and for death, without end because ended. As the doorkeeper represents it, the discourse of the law does not say "no" but "not yet," indefinitely. . . . What is deferred forever till death is entry into the law itself, which is nothing other than that which dictates the delay. (*BtL*, 204–5)

The important comment to make here, for the purposes of this opening discussion, is that for Derrida, the image of the door of the law, which is open and impassable, which commands but "wants nothing," is the very figure of the originless displacement, the *différance*, that (un)grounds the structure of the law. Or, to say this another way, the inaccessibility of the law is the final juridical aporia which Derrida interprets as a figure for the *euporia* of *différance*: for the man (and for man) there is "no itinerary, no method, no path to accede to the law, to what would happen there, to the *topos* of its occurrence" (*BtL* 196). The entry to the law never happens, and the man from the country never sets foot in the place (*topos*) where the law is grounded, because there is no such place. There is only the *différance* that holds the man from the country (and the doorkeeper) always before the law, until the door is finally shut as the man approaches death.

Derrida's interpretation of the significance of this final event—the closing of the door—is precisely the point Agamben challenges in his counter-reading of the parable. For Derrida, the door of the law remains open and impassable "forever till death" because of its "differantial topology" or "atopology," and any desire to step beyond that threshold into the presence of the law amounts to a metaphysical dream of presence itself. But for Agamben, "not want[ing] to enter into the door of the Law *but [not permitting] it to be closed either*" is precisely the limitation of deconstruction, which, in not permitting the closing of the door, will not permit itself to imagine an undoing of the sovereign ban-structure at the root of all law and thus cannot read anything but death in the figure of the closing door (*HS* 54; my italics). Agamben, then, agrees with Derrida that the tale brings to light the "differantial topology" of sovereignty, but then sharply distinguishes himself from the deconstructive reading by suggesting that this structure is not the ultimate limit of thought, but precisely the obscure threshold whose abolition Kafka's tale gestures toward: "The prestige of deconstruction in our time lies precisely in its having conceived of the entire text of tradition as being in force without significance, a being in force whose strength lies essentially in its undecidability and in having shown that such a being in force is, like the door of the Law in Kafka's parable, absolutely impassable. But it is precisely concerning the sense of this being in force (and of the state of exception that it inaugurates) that our position distinguishes itself from that of deconstruction" (*HS* 54). What distinguishes their readings, then, is the way they understand the countryman's ultimate fate as he stands before the law.

What, then, according to Agamben, is the significance of the parable's cryptic ending? For him, too, the aporia becomes *euporia* at the end of the tale, but it is a wholly different one—another way, where "the two terms distinguished and kept united by the relation of ban [i.e., the man and the law, bare life and sovereignty] abolish each other and enter into a new dimension" (*HS* 55). In Agamben's reading, the countryman's waiting for days and years is neither failure nor endless deferral; rather, it is precisely a successful strategy that leads not to the recognition and affirmation of the empty yet forceful ban-structure of sovereignty and the law, but, in the tale's final image of the gatekeeper moving to shut the door, to the dissolution of the sovereign ban itself. "If it is true the door's very openness constituted ... the invisible power and specific 'force' of the Law," he writes, "then we can imagine that all the behavior of the man from the country is nothing other than a complicated and patient strategy to have the door closed in order to interrupt the Law's being in force" (*HS* 55).[3] And to reaffirm this point against his primary interlocutor:

> The final sense of the legend is thus not, as Derrida writes, that of an "event that succeeds in not happening" (or that happens in not happening: "an event that happens not to happen," *un événement qui arrive à ne pas arriver*), but rather precisely the opposite: the story tells how

something has really happened in seeming not to happen, and the messianic aporias of the man from the country express exactly the difficulties that our age must confront in attempting to master [*venire a capo*] the sovereign ban. (*HS* 57)[4]

As we will see over the course of this and the following chapters, Agamben's influential analysis of the logic of sovereignty and law has roots that lie in his earlier thought concerning language. This philosophical-linguistic background is indicated clearly enough here, though, for there is in both Derrida's and Agamben's readings of "Before the Law" a close analogy drawn between the status of law, or its conditions of possibility, and the status of the literary or linguistic. As Derrida asks in the course of his reading, "what if the law, without being itself transfixed by literature, shared the conditions of its possibility with the literary object?" (*BtL* 191). For Derrida, the man from the country's error, so to speak (for the law's inaccessibility "puzzles" him), is that he wants to enter the *topos* of the law, wants to touch it, and does not understand that the law is not a substantial thing to whose presence one might gain full access; instead, the law is (or functions like) a text to be read (*BtL* 196). "Perhaps man is the man from the country as long as he cannot read; or, if knowing how to read, he is still bound up in unreadability within that very thing which appears to yield itself to be read. He wants to see or touch the law, he wants to 'enter' it, because perhaps he does not know that the law is not to be seen or touched but *deciphered*" (*BtL* 197; my italics). The reading of the law in the tale (and of the law outside of the tale) is thus clearly folded into Derrida's thought on textuality, and as a text to be "deciphered" (a term that will assume greater importance toward the end of this chapter), the law is subject to the logic of the trace, to the play of *différance*, to reinscription, to the deconstructive unraveling to which Derrida subjects the entire text of Western metaphysics.

However, for Agamben, in volatilizing that ghostly limit, which is both impassable and open, the deconstructive reading of Kafka's parable, for all its patience, does not quite succeed in untying the law's tightly woven threads; rather, he suggests that deconstruction (like other earlier attempts to think the problem) "push[es] the aporia of sovereignty to the limit but still [does] not completely free [itself] from its ban. [It] show[s] that the dissolution of the ban, like the cutting of the Gordian knot, resembles less the solution of a logical or mathematical problem than the solution of an enigma" (*HS* 48). For Agamben, this entrapment in a logical problematic of which it cannot *venire a capo* is the basic limit that deconstruction runs up against, whether in its political or its linguistic version, and it is this knot that he proposes, from his earliest to his recent work, to cut through rather than untie. In order to make that cut, however, one must posit a dimension beyond the warp and woof of the texture of that textile; indeed, one must posit that there *is* an outside of the text.

SEMIOLOGY AND SAUSSURE

The figure of the "solution of an enigma" that appears here in *Homo Sacer* is, in fact, a clear echo from *Stanzas*, published eighteen years earlier, in 1977. Indeed, it is the central figure of that book's fourth and final section, titled "The Perverse Image: Semiology from the Point of View of the Sphinx," the full significance of which becomes clear only when it is read as a pointed response to the first part of Derrida's *Of Grammatology*, in particular to part 1, chapter 2, "Linguistics and Grammatology." Such a reading is, in fact, suggested by Agamben's text itself, for the footnotes to the last chapter contain two direct, though unelaborated, references to Derrida—one to *Of Grammatology* specifically and one to Derrida's general debt to Heidegger (to whose memory, moreover, *Stanzas* is dedicated). Yet, though these are only very brief footnotes, they indicate far more than a local disagreement to be mentioned only in the small print; rather, on closer consideration of the distance that Agamben takes from Derrida in these notes, one finds that this entire final section of *Stanzas* is organized so as to parallel and challenge many of the claims and strategies set forth in *Of Grammatology*. Like the first part of *Of Grammatology*, this final section of *Stanzas* traces a history of Western metaphysics back to the originary fracturing of presence that makes signification possible. And like Derrida in "Linguistics and Grammatology," Agamben turns here to a consideration of Saussurian linguistics as the culminating point of that long itinerary, where the antinomies of signification reach their extremes and, as Agamben says, "[come] to light in the most blinding way" (*S* 154). Moreover, as noted in the introduction, this section of *Stanzas* is a coherent and direct elaboration of the brief reading of Saussurian semiology, and of Derrida's engagement with it, that Agamben had presented nearly a decade earlier in the 1968 essay "L'albero del linguaggio." That is to say, *Stanzas* contains the full expression of a critique of deconstruction that dates at least as far back as the year following Derrida's annus mirabilis of 1967.[5] We will get to the significance of the riddling title of this section of *Stanzas* in a moment, but we must first look at the critique of Derrida contained in its closing pages.

It is worth mentioning that in focusing the first chapter of this book on these contesting readings of Saussure, I am following the chronology of Agamben's engagement with Derrida more closely than that of Derrida's own early itinerary. This point is not trivial, for even though Derrida's reading of Saussure in *Of Grammatology* (as well as a few other key texts of the period) is even today probably his best-known work, it occupies a rather specific position in the development of deconstruction. Specifically, it comes after more than a decade of intense work on Husserl.[6] This work will be discussed in relation to Agamben's texts *Infancy and History* (1978) and *Language and Death* (1982) in the next chapter—again following the chronology of Agamben's texts more closely than that of Derrida's—but in embarking here on a discussion of Saussure and semiology a few points should be noted.

Surely one of the reasons that Derrida's reading of Saussure was and remains among his most influential is that Saussurian general linguistics became the "pilot science" for structuralist thought in the post–World War II period, especially in France. And it is no accident that Derrida's extended reading of Saussure in *Of Grammatology* lies side by side with a reading of Claude Lévi-Strauss's work in structural anthropology. Thus *Of Grammatology* could appear to many as primarily an intervention in structuralism, which, of course, it partly was.[7] It is also the case, at least in the Anglo-American context, that Derrida's reading of Saussurian linguistics provided a conceptual and terminological vocabulary for what came to be known as deconstructive literary criticism. The tremendous impetus that Derrida's thought has lent to literary studies need not be more than acknowledged here, but given that, at least in its earliest versions, such work draws above all on Derrida's identification of an irreducible undecidability and instability within the structure of texts, that is to say, on Derrida's emphasis upon the impossibilities rather than possibilities of stable meaning that inhere in sign systems, Rodolphe Gasché could polemically write in 1979 that "deconstructive criticism seldom appears to be more than a very sophisticated form of structural analysis. It only differs from structural analysis in that the diacritical principle of meaning, that is to say, its dependence on differentially determined opposites, on the correspondence and reciprocity of coupled terms, is applied in a negative fashion."[8] For Gasché, early deconstructive criticism failed to grasp Derrida's most radical intervention in the philosophical tradition—namely, the process of *reinscription*, which I will discuss in a moment—and thus turned deconstruction into a sort of sophisticated negative version of New Critical close reading, an understanding of Derrida that Gasché's work of late 1970s and 1980s did much to challenge in the Anglo-American context.[9]

Be that as it may, all this is simply to note that from the beginning of his engagement with Derrida, neither of these frames is the primary one through which Agamben views deconstruction, even though it is to the portion of *Of Grammatology* dealing with Saussure that he first directs his attention. Certainly in 1968, Anglo-American deconstructive criticism would not be the most pertinent frame for the young Italian philosopher; but even the structuralist (or poststructuralist) milieu appears not to have decisively determined his interpretation of Derrida's work. Rather, it is within the context of Husserlian phenomenology and, above all, Heideggerian fundamental ontology that Agamben reads Derrida's engagement with Saussure.

Rather than summarize the salient points of Derrida's reading of Saussure—which are well known and in any case will come out in the exposition to follow—I will begin by quoting Agamben's own characterization of the grammatological project, which will focus the discussion on the elements central to his response and give an initial indication of how the early Agamben understands Derrida's early texts:

> According to [grammatology], metaphysics is founded on the privileged status of the signified, understood as the fullness of presence, with respect to the signifier, which is an external trace.... The specific character of the grammatological project is expressed, however, in the affirmation according to which the originary experience is always already trace and writing, the signified always already in the position of the signifier. The illusion of a full and originary presence is the illusion of metaphysics, which is embodied in the double structure of the sign. The closure of metaphysics, and of the semiotics in solidarity with it, implies the awareness that there is no possible origin beyond the signifier and the trace: the origin is *architrace*, which in the absence of an

origin establishes the very possibility of appearance and signification. (*S* 155–56)

Deconstruction in a nutshell, 1977. Yet, for Agamben, in undermining the illusion of the full presence of the signified by positing the originary arche-trace, deconstruction, while it may, in his words, "effect a salutary critique," simply exposes and radicalizes the problems inherent in the differential logic of the sign and of metaphysics, but has not "really succeeded in accomplishing that 'step-backward-beyond' metaphysics" (*S* 156). As closely as deconstruction pushes up against the limits of the logic of signification, it remains caught within it, resulting in what Agamben in a much more recent text, *The Time That Remains* (2000), describes as "concepts (or better yet, . . . non-concepts, or even as Derrida prefers to call them, . . . 'undecidables') [that] call into question the primacy of presence and signification for the philosophical tradition, yet . . . do not truly call into question signification in general" (*TTR* 103)—a critique of deconstruction that is entirely consistent with the one we are reading in *Stanzas*, written nearly twenty-five years earlier, and indeed with that sketched in "L'albero del linguaggio" a decade before that.

The "step-backward-beyond" metaphysics evokes an image from Heidegger's "Letter on 'Humanism,'" and the reference certainly indicates Agamben's understanding of his own project and his own critique of deconstruction as being largely a Heideggerian one (as is also suggested by the dedication of the book). This allusion, however, is perhaps even more precise than that, for Agamben's critique of Derrida here is very similar to Heidegger's critique of Sartre in the "Letter on 'Humanism,'" where he claims that Sartrean existentialism has simply reversed the hierarchy of *essentia* and *existentia* and has not, therefore, succeeded in escaping the logic of metaphysics. In a phrase that would not be out of place in Agamben's text, Heidegger writes that "the reversal of a metaphysical statement remains a metaphysical statement."[10] And in a phrase that *is* found in Agamben's text, we read: "The metaphysics of writing and of the signifier is but the reverse face of the metaphysics of the signified and the voice, and not, surely, its transcendence" (*S* 156). This, in fact, is the crux of Agamben's argument: that Derrida reverses the polarity but nevertheless remains entirely within the terms of "metaphysics, and of the semiotics in solidarity with it." Is he right?

Derrida is, of course, very sensitive to the pitfall of simply repeating such a reversal of hierarchical metaphysical terms (even if those terms are now signified and signifier, voice and writing, rather than *essentia* and *existentia*). His terminology, however, especially the terminology he adopts from Saussure, can give the impression that his ultimate intention is to valorize writing/the graphic signifier over the voice/the phonic signifier, since a crucial part of his strategy *is* to demonstrate that the former do not lend themselves to the illusion of presence-to-meaning that the latter do. Indeed, this resistance to the illusion of presence is what, in his reading of the *Course*, leads Derrida to discover the operation of writing within Saussure's every appeal to the primacy of the phonic sign, thus undermining all claims he makes for the exclusion of writing as derivative and inferior to speech (a "sign of a sign"). To be sure, a good deal of the close argumentation of this section of *Of Grammatology* is devoted to showing not only that (1) in Saussure's conception of *langue* as a system of arbitrary differential marks, the very nature of the sign must necessarily entail the materiality, repeatability, and externality associated with writing, but also that (2) Saussure's vehement insistence on dismissing writing as derivative, as a sign of a sign, reveals the deep phonocentric bias that he inherits from the Western tradition.

The two go hand in hand, since the spoken word—and above all, the *silently spoken* word of our inner monologue—can only give the illusion of unmediated and uncontaminated presence-to-meaning by virtue of its seeming ephemerality and immateriality, its evident ability to "erase itself or to become transparent, in order to allow the concept to present itself as what it is, referring to nothing other than its presence" (*Pos* 22). Writing, by contrast, insists on its external and material nature as a sign of a sign, and thus does not lend itself to any such illusions.[11] In this part of the argument, Derrida works to show that contrary to Saussure's basic phonocentric presupposition, the logic of writing encompasses the sphere of speech, and that against his own wishes, Saussure

> opens the field of a general grammatology. Which would not only no longer be excluded from general linguistics, but would dominate it and contain it within its field. Then one realizes that what was chased off limits, the wandering outcast of linguistics, has indeed never ceased to haunt language as its primary and most intimate possibility. Then

something which was never spoken and which is nothing other than writing itself as the origin of language writes itself within Saussure's discourse. (G 43–44)

Thus the hierarchy of writing and speech is reversed, with the derivative operation of writing coming to define "the entire field of linguistic signs" (G 44). Writing before speech, supplement before the supplemented, the "sign of a sign" as the original sign.

And yet, as important as this analysis is, and as influential as it has been, the generalization of writing, if left at this stage of the analysis, would amount to little more than the reversal of a metaphysical statement (speech before writing) that, albeit in a negative form, would nevertheless remain a metaphysical statement (writing before speech). If writing is simply what the tradition conceives as the negative opposite or derivative supplement to the positive and original vocal sign, then the field of a general grammatology would still maintain and depend on its constitutive relation to its now subordinated positive counterpart and therefore be every bit as caught up in the metaphysical logic we had hoped to exceed. It would seem that writing alone cannot lead us out of this impasse, and so Derrida appears to be faced with a conundrum.

While much of Derrida's thoroughgoing reading of Saussure is devoted to arriving at this point where the logic of writing (a "general grammatology") is shown to encompass the entire semiological field, it is only the first phase of his project. The reversal of hierarchy between speech and writing is the necessary stage-setting for what in truth is deconstruction's most distinctive and significant methodological gesture, namely, the reinscription of the reversed term into the discourse under scrutiny. As Gasché explains, "Two movements are thus characteristic of deconstruction: a *reversal* of the traditional hierarchy between conceptual oppositions (expression/indication, presence/sign) and a *reinscription* of the newly privileged term."[12] And with regard to the necessity and aims of this conceptual rerouting, Derrida notes: "Doubtless it is more necessary, from within semiology, to transform concepts, to displace them, to turn them against their presuppositions, to reinscribe them in other chains, and little by little to modify the terrain of our work and thereby produce new configurations; I do not believe in decisive ruptures, in an unequivocal 'epistemological break,' as it is called today" (*Pos* 24). Since no decisive rupture is possible, no break that would open out onto a space beyond that circumscribed by the metaphysical structures (for example, semiology) that we have inherited from the tradition, Derrida seeks to shake—or *solicit*, in his distinctive usage—metaphysical discourse from the inside by strategically transforming, displacing, and reinscribing its concepts.[13]

One way to conceive of deconstructive reinscription—say, of the term "writing"—is to imagine the term being turned into a sort of catachresis, whereby it retains its common, metaphysical, "vulgar" sense, but is fundamentally used to name something for which there is (and can be) no proper term, save, perhaps, a Derridean neologism. Indeed, the anteriority of "writing" to even the Saussurian distinction between speech and writing, the discovery of writing's necessary operations within the logic of signification at its most irreducible level, leads Derrida to propose the "new concept" (G 56) of "writing" or "arche-writing," which he

> continue[s] to call writing only because it essentially communicates with the vulgar concept of writing. The latter could not have imposed itself historically except by the dissimulation of the arche-writing, by the desire for a speech displacing its other and its double and working to reduce its difference. If I persist in calling that difference writing, it is because, within the work of historical repression, writing was, by its situation, destined to signify the most formidable difference. It threatened the desire for the living speech from the closest proximity, it *breached* living speech from within and from the very beginning. (G 56–57)

What the new concept of arche-writing seeks to describe catachrestically is not the simple reversal of the hierarchy between writing and speech, or negativity and positivity, or absence and presence, but rather something that makes the polar system of these opposed terms possible (as well as uncloseable). It is still called writing, but Derrida asserts that this is only because it has something in common with writing in the traditional sense, primarily the characteristics of exteriority and negativity, but it is no longer constitutively attached to its positive counterpart. It seeks to indicate a sort of hypernegativity and hyperexteriority that our metaphysical vocabulary cannot properly name. As Gasché explains, a term that has been deconstructed and redeployed in this way, "as a result of a reinscription of the negative image of absolute exteriority and Otherness . . . is no longer identical with the inferior term of the initial dyad. . . . Although it uses the same name as its negative image, the deconstructed term will never have been given in the conceptual opposition it deconstructs."[14] As a deconstructed term (indeed, as one of the most privileged of Derrida's deconstructed terms), arche-writing names something that is not identical with the (negative) term of writing but is nevertheless only manifest in that negative term, which in turn is only phenomenally sensible within the conceptual opposition of which it forms an indispensable pole. It provisionally names that which makes names possible but which itself withdraws from the sphere of names and conceptuality: "Arche-writing, at first the possibility of the spoken word, then of the *"graphie"* in the narrow sense [i.e., the written sign in the vulgar sense], the birthplace of 'usurpation,' denounced from Plato to Saussure, this trace is the opening of the first exteriority in general" (G 70).

It is by way of reinscription that Derrida seeks to shake the texts of metaphysics—in the present case, Saussure's text—from the inside. As a matter of reading strategy, Derrida does not come to the text of *Course* from an Archimedean point outside of its own vocabulary and conceptual repertoire. Instead, the breaching of the text's metaphysical logic is worked from within its own textual field, within the play of its opposing polarities, which in an essential way are inescapable. As Derrida writes in a key passage: "The movements of deconstruction do not destroy structures from the outside. They are not possible and effective, nor can they take accurate aim, except by inhabiting those structures. Inhabiting them *in a certain way*, because one always inhabits, and all the more when one does not expect it" (G 24). This restless reinhabitation is what is played out in Derrida's elaborate, playful, punning, disruptive readings of texts, perhaps most spectacularly in those written after 1967, into a number of which we will venture in the following pages.

Now, Agamben does not actually present a critique of the strategy of reinscription in *Stanzas*, but rather, as we have seen, characterizes Derrida's "metaphysics of writing and of the signifier" as a reversal and reaffirmation of the long-standing metaphysical impasse of semiology, albeit one that brightly illuminates that impasse. Again, is he right? While the case might well be made that Agamben has neglected or simply not grasped this second gesture of Derrida's project as it is performed in his reading of the *Course*, the more important point to make about his argument is that his evident indifference to deconstructive reinscription and the "certain way" in which deconstructive strategy inhabits texts is due to the fact that, on his own reading of Saussure, which the following pages will show is precisely a *counterreading* to Derrida's, the strategy of reinscription could only appear as the necessary response to an unnecessary aporia. That is to say, for Agamben the impasse of Saussurian semiology as presented in the text of the *Course in General Linguistics* need not lead only to the strategic redirection and reinscription of deconstructed terms such as arche-writing and the arche-trace. Rather, in *Stanzas*, Agamben suggests that Derrida (along with nearly the entire post-Saussurian tradition) misses an important opening, an alternative questioning of "signification in general" that had been glimpsed by Saussure, but one that is not quite legible in the published text of the *Course*. Indeed, what if hidden in the text of the *Course* there were indications of another path into (and beyond) the mysteries of the linguistic sign, though one that Saussure did not or could not ultimately take? What if, as Agamben suggests, the *Course* were not a "series of positive results" but "in reality the final reef against which Saussure had shipwrecked"? (S 152). In following out this possibility, Agamben seeks to call into question both Derrida's reading of Saussure and the radicality of the deconstructive project, suggesting that rather than being an exemplary and committed exponent of the coherent logic of the linguistic sign, Saussure had instead peered for a moment over the walls of metaphysical semiology but was ultimately unable to scale them—and that he had remained something of a broken man because of it. "Saussure," Agamben writes, "represents in fact the precious instance of a philologist who, caught in the net of language, felt, as Nietzsche did, the insufficiency of philology, and who had to become a philosopher or succumb. Saussure did not abandon linguistic study as Nietzsche had done, but clos[ed] himself for thirty years in a silence that appeared inexplicable to many" (S 152).

This rather melancholy portrait of the linguist is very much at odds with the one we find in *Of Grammatology*, where Derrrida casts Saussure as a vehement defender against the heresy of the written sign. We recall here his comments on the righteous and moralizing tone of Saussure's denigration and exclusion of writing:

> The contamination by writing, the fact or the threat of it, are denounced in the accents of the moralist or preacher by the linguist from Geneva. The tone counts; it is as if, at the moment when the modern science of

the logos would come into its autonomy and its scientificity, it became necessary again to attack a heresy.... Thus incensed, Saussure's vehement argumentation aims at more than a theoretical error, more than a moral fault: at a sort of stain and primarily at a sin. (G 34)

But while Derrida looks for (and indeed finds) this pulpit-pounding sermon in the published text of the *Course*, Agamben, in an effort to paint what I am suggesting is a counterportrait of Saussure, looks into the fissures and cracks of that reconstructed text to discover a linguist who is anything but a defender of the semiological faith. Against Derrida's use of the published text, Agamben reads not the *Course* itself, but the unwritten work whose absence the *Course* marks. And here again a glance at the footnotes can indicate the terrain of the debate. In note 38 to "Linguistics and Grammatology," Derrida acknowledges the possibility that the *Course* may not actually be representative of Saussure's thought and intentions:

[I]t is not impossible that the literality of the *Course*, to which we have indeed had to refer, should one day appear very suspect in the light of unpublished material now being prepared for publication.... What I could read—and equally what I could not read—under the title of *A Course in General Linguistics* seemed important to the point of excluding all hidden and "true" intentions of Ferdinand de Saussure. If one were to discover that this text hid another text—and there will never be anything but texts—and hid it in a determined sense, the reading that I have just proposed would not be invalidated, at least for that particular reason. Quite the contrary. (G 329n38)

Without lingering excessively on the issue, it is nevertheless worth noting how in this passage Derrida presents an odd defense of his reading against the possibility of new information or a different version of this text, whatever that new information or version might be. Whatever this hidden or undiscovered text might contain—that is, whatever the text might say—is ultimately a matter of indifference, since it could not invalidate the reading offered above; "quite the contrary," it could only further confirm it.

On one hand, Derrida's justification for this claim is based on the vast influence of the published text on twentieth-century (structuralist) thought, which is itself held up to scrutiny in Derrida's reading of the *Course*. To be sure, the influence of the *Course* on subsequent structuralist thought is a matter of historical fact; the *Course* has already initiated and determined the shape of this epoch-making discourse, and so the possible discovery of "another" Saussure would not invalidate the reading of the *Course* as the source text of structuralism. But on the other hand, there is also in this passage the distinct suggestion that such a hidden and "true" text—*insofar as it is a text* and "there will never be anything but texts"—would inevitably yield the same reading as the published *Course* alone.

While the unpublished material to which Derrida is referring in this note appears to be the work on anagrams that Jean Starobinski published in excerpts from 1964 to 1970, Agamben investigates the possibility, which Derrida acknowledges, that the *Course* itself is not what it seems, and turns this possibility into the critique that Derrida seeks here to address in advance.[15] And he does so by examining Saussure's notes, drafts, and letters, taking care to state that, far from being unavailable, "the documents of [Saussure's] crisis were long ago published by Benveniste and then reiterated in a memorable article by him" (S 153). The pieces are from 1954 and 1963 respectively, and it is not difficult to hear in this phrase Agamben polemically suggesting that these texts have long been there for Derrida to have read.

And Derrida surely did read at least the 1963 piece, "Saussure after Half a Century," which was reprinted as chapter 3 of *Problems in General Linguistics*, a book which Derrida examines in detail in his 1971 essay "The Supplement of Copula," though in that piece he does not refer to this particular chapter.[16] I will discuss Derrida's essay on Benveniste, and his focus on certain texts by Benveniste, in the next chapter, but suffice it here to say that though Derrida is indeed aware of the publication history of Saussure's lectures, his reading of the reconstructed *Course*—as both a privileged example of Western logocentrism and one of the master-texts of structuralism—includes, explicitly, virtually no investigation of this "hidden text."[17]

This is also the case in Derrida's 1968 essay "Différance," where Saussure's *Course* provides, once again, the linguistic coordinates for Derrida's elaboration of his signal (non)concept of *différance*. In a discussion of the "principle of difference" as the "condition of signification," Derrida cites this key passage from Saussure:

> The conceptual side of value is made up solely of relations and differences with respect to the other terms of language, and the same can

be said of its material side.... Everything that has been said up to this point boils down to this: in language there are only differences. Even more important: a difference generally implies positive terms between which the difference is set up; but in language there are only differences *without positive terms*. Whether we take the signified or the signifier, language has neither ideas nor sounds that existed before the linguistic system, but only conceptual and phonic differences that have issued from the system. The idea or phonic substance that a sign contains is of less importance than the other signs that surround it.[18]

From this passage Derrida draws several important conclusions. The first is that "the signified concept is never present in and of itself," since it is "inscribed in a chain or in a system within which it refers to the other, to other concepts, by means of the systematic play of differences"—namely, the play of *différance* (M 11). But even more importantly for our discussion, Derrida also concludes that this *différance* will itself

> be the playing movement that "produces"—by means of something that is not simply an activity—these differences, these effects of difference. This does not mean that the *différance* that produces differences is somehow before them, in a simple and unmodified—in-different—present. *Différance* is the non-full, non-simple, structured and differentiating origin of differences. Thus, the name "origin" no longer suits it. (M 11)

In a logical gesture that is repeated frequently in his argumentation, Derrida here absolutizes, by means of a sort of semiological *epokhē*, the Saussurian differential structure in order then to reinscribe the deconstructed negative term of that structure (be it arche-writing or arche-trace) into the text.[19] In its solicitation of the text, the reinscribed term exerts a destabilizing force from within the structure that it inhabits and thus, through its effects more than anything it lexically represents, catachrestically shows the workings of irreducible *différance*, which, though not anything that we might recognize as a positive origin, is nonetheless the original "producer" of differences and signification.

Now, it must be noted that, though Derrida explicitly grants some sort of privilege to the Saussurian problematic, it cannot be claimed that deconstruction is founded solely on Saussurian linguistics, and therefore a critique of his reading of the *Course* (or of the *Course* that he reads) must not be presented as a critique of the logic of deconstruction in toto. Another way of putting this would be to say that Derrida does not derive his deconstructive position from semiology but rather reads Saussurian semiology as a prime example of the logocentrism that he uncovers in numerous texts throughout the Western tradition. And as noted above, Derrida's reading of the *Course* indeed draws its fundamental impetus from his earlier work on Husserl, which I will discuss in the next chapter. However, it should be equally noted that in passages such as the one just cited from "Différance," it does appear that Derrida employs Saussurian logic to make and support a positive, and not merely local, claim about the (non)origin (the "production") of this (non) original *différance*. The line between a deconstruction of Saussure's text and the development of a general concept of *différance* based on the claims made by that text is indeed subtle at this point. However, it should not be controversial to say that in these sections of *Of Grammatology* and the essay "Différance," Derrida, working within and working at the limits of Saussurian vocabulary, reveals the aporetic impasses that undermine any eventual phonocentric recourse to the presence of either the spoken word or the signified as these terms are developed in Saussure's text. And his point is to show that, since Saussure (even though he also "opens the field of a general grammatology" [G 43]) does have recourse to that presence, indeed does so in a strident, "incensed" manner, his thinking is (either willfully or unconsciously) blind to what his own argument cannot help but reveal under the pressure of deconstructive reading—namely, that the spoken and the written, and the signifier and the signified, are equally caught up in an irreducible, undecidable play of their reciprocal difference. Leaving aside, then, any questions concerning the specific nature of the centrality of Saussure to Derrida's thought in general, what these few examples (and indeed the focus on Saussure in this opening chapter) are intended to show is not deconstruction's exclusive foundation in Saussurian linguistics, but (1) the specific terrain of this particular debate between Agamben and Derrida, which takes place in that field; and (2) how Derrida's use of Saussure is based specifically on a reading (and on a particular characterization of the tone) of the published text of the *Course*.

In a gesture, however, that runs in a rather different direction from Derrida's, Agamben does not focus on the published text of the *Course* so much as return to Saussure's unpublished notes and letters, pointing out how in these obscure texts, in what can only be read as a tone of exasperation if not desperation, Saussure calls into doubt the validity of the entire science of linguistics and speaks of one day writing a book "in which I shall, without enthusiasm or passion, explain why there is not a single term used in linguistics to which I grant any meaning whatsoever" (S 153).[20] Agamben also reminds us (as do the editors of the *Course*) that Saussure had explicitly ruled out the possibility of publishing the lectures at all, that he had destroyed his daily lecture notes, that he evidently improvised much of his lectures, and that his notes that do survive bear an uneven resemblance to those taken by the students of the *Course*. "As for a book on the subject," Saussure had said, "one cannot dream of it; it must be the definitive thought of its author" (S 157n2).[21]

What is it, then, that Agamben sees as, in Derrida's words, Saussure's "hidden and 'true' intentions"? The answer is not only relevant for our understanding of Saussure's thought but, more to the point of the present discussion, also provides a preliminary indication of the fundamental difference between Derrida's and Agamben's positions concerning language—and this difference has to do with understanding the meaning of the originary displacement between the signifier and signified, with the nature of the original noncoincidence that inheres in the sign, with the question of the bar or barrier between signifier and signified that itself resists signification: the obscure space or interval between these two terms, which Derrida represents as the space—or spacing—of *différance*.[22]

Unlike Derrida's argument, what Agamben's reading of the paradoxical disunity and internal division of the sign focuses on is not the dynamic interplay and traditional hierarchical relation between the two polar terms, but "the meaning of this bar or barrier [that] is constantly left in shadow [in the Western metaphysical tradition], thus hiding the abyss opened between signifier and signified" (S 137). What Agamben believes Derrida glimpses but fails adequately to interrogate is the nature of this abyss and the nature of that paradoxically separating-and-conjoining nexus point of the bar (/); that is, he does not fully inquire into the possibility and presupposition underneath (or in the middle of) the differential structure itself, which, on his reading, is precisely the question that drove Saussure to reclusion and near-silence. In an 1894 letter to Antoine Meillet that Agamben cites, Saussure writes:

> The truly ultimate law of language, at least so far as we dare to speak of it, is that there is never anything that can reside in a *single*

term. ... [Linguistic symbols] are without value except through their reciprocal difference. ... [No term has value] except by means of this same plexus of eternally negative differences. *It is astonishing. But where in truth would the possibility of the contrary lie? Where would be for a single instant the point of positive irradiation in all of language*, once granted that there is no vocal image that responds more than any other to what it must say? (qtd. in S 153–54; second italics mine)

Again, the troubling doubts expressed in this letter—doubts about the "possibility of the contrary" and the "point of positive irradiation"—are dissimulated, or at least muted, in the reconstructed published text of the *Course*, even though, as Agamben points out, in Engler's critical edition variant readings of the moment at which Saussure appears to assert the positivity of the sign suggest that he was, in fact, more equivocal on this point.[23] And indeed, this passage from Saussure's correspondence, when read in conjunction with the confident tones of the passage from the *Course* cited above, to which Derrida gives great weight in his explication of *différance*, seems to be, if not a refutation of the *Course*'s claims, at least a private expression of doubt, or even a confession of a guilty conscience.

On one level, in citing these letters and variant readings, Agamben seeks to counter Derrida's characterization of Saussure as an "incensed" semiological "moralist or preacher ... attack[ing] a heresy" (G 34), a move that in fact has quite serious implications, for it is central to Derrida's overall project in *Of Grammatology* that Saussure be seen as a vehement disparager and enemy of the written sign. Saussure's work is presented in that book as one of the many examples (indeed a "privileged" one, in Derrida's own account [see G 29, 329n38]) of the unacknowledged phonocentrism and logocentrism—"the debasement of writing, and its repression outside 'full' speech" (G 3)—that have characterized Western thought from antiquity. There is, then, a good deal at stake in Derrida's characterization of Saussure's moralizing fury.[24]

On another and more important level, however, this picture of Saussure's quandary provides Agamben with an alternative perspective on what the paradoxical duality of the sign reveals, which he suggests has been all but forgotten:

In modern semiology, the forgetting of the original fracture of presence is manifested precisely in what ought to betray it, that is, in the bar (/)

of the graphic S/s.... Every semiology that fails to ask why the barrier that establishes the possibility of signifying should itself be resistant to signification, falsifies, with that omission, its own most authentic intention.... The question that remains unasked is the only one that deserved to be formulated: why is presence deferred and fragmented such that something like "signification" even becomes possible? (S 137)

The deepest paradox of language resides, for Agamben, not in the mutual attraction and repulsion of signifier and signified (or sign and sign) across the generative space or spacing of their difference (or of *différance*), that is to say, not in the irreducible play of the terms in the structure that semiology writes as "S/s," but rather in what is pointed to, what is presupposed, in that bar or barrier between "S" and "s" itself.

What does this diagonal line separating signifier and signified signify? What does it mean? Because that separating-conjoining bar resists signification, the answer to this question is a difficult one to formulate, since it can pertain to neither the sphere of the signifier nor that of the signified. The sphere to which one must have recourse in order to investigate the meaning of this bar—wherein neither *signans* nor *signatum* is the valorized domain of originary presence—is one that exceeds or precedes those that represent either side of the fracture that inheres in the linguistic sign. How to conceive, then, of this sphere? What can precede significance and the mechanics of linguistic meaning? What is presupposed by the logic of the sign, which has, but is unable to see, at its center this abyssal void or bar?

While Derrida might answer "*différance*" (or one of its near-synonyms, "trace," "reserve," "writing" [G 93]), and might pursue that *différance* through the reinscription of the deconstructed metaphysical terms of semiology, Agamben's answer is: the signifying event itself, "the pure fact that one speaks, that language exists" (*IH* 5).[25] For Agamben, what is indicated by that barrier that resists signification (which is neither a word nor a concept) is the presupposition of the fact of language and signification taking place—in Saussure's words, "the possibility of the contrary," "the point of positive irradiation in all of language," the generative act that, as it were, stitches together the textual weave of negative differences. It is a possibility, point, and act that, according to Agamben, Saussure was unable to think through, and one that the semiological problematic of the *Course* in no way represents an account of (though perhaps Saussure had something like it in mind when he promised the students of the 1910–11 course a future course on the "linguistics of speaking").[26] But by returning to the prehistory of the *Course* and discovering there (and attempting to follow) not the path that led to the logic of what came to be known as Saussurian semiology and the structuralism for which it was the pilot science, but rather the obscure route that Saussure was unable to see his way fully into, Agamben proposes an alternative thinking on the paradoxical nature of signification, an alternative whose mythical emblem is the Sphinx.

SEMIOLOGY AND THE SPHINX

As noted previously, the title of the final section of *Stanzas* is "The Perverse Image: Semiology from the Point of View of the Sphinx." And it is precisely the failure—the forgetting—to view the enigma of language "from the point of view of the Sphinx," and the consistent tendency to view it from the point of view of Oedipus, that defines, for Agamben, the Western reflection on the sign—including, most pointedly here, Derrida's. As the remaining pages of this chapter will show, on Agamben's account, the true, archaic meaning of the riddle of the Sphinx is one that has (like the meaning of the barrier between "S" and "s") remained hidden by a tradition that finds its emblematic figure in Oedipus, the code breaker.

In a surprising reading of the myth, Agamben suggests that Oedipus's great sin is "not so much incest as it is hubris toward the power of the symbolic in general" (S 138), the belief that he can decipher and restore the unity of the Sphinx's enigmatic speech in the solution of a riddle. According to Agamben, readings and renderings of the myth that have focused on—and valorized—Oedipus's solution of the riddle (and consequent salvation of the city) misunderstand the original sense of the Sphinx's enigma because they "[belong] to a subsequent age that no longer understood what the enigma brought to language, that no longer had any knowledge of enigmas except in the degraded forms of the riddle and the guessing game" (S 138). Such readings see in Oedipus's relatively simple answer—the vanquishing of the monster and liquidation of the enigma—the civilizing gesture par excellence: the restoration to health of the city, the reestablishment of order, and so on. Whatever flaw causes these triumphs ultimately to come to tragic ends is, Agamben suggests, always sought in the hubris toward the oracles and the sin of incest, but not in the episode of the Sphinx. Thus, the episode is pushed into the background and its original significance lost.[27] Agamben, however, proposes to return it to the center of the stage and to restore the true meaning of the Sphinx's enigma.

Agamben argues that the canonical reading of the myth depends on an understanding of the Sphinx's language as a matter of coding and deciphering, of hiding the proper (the signified) with the improper (the signifier).[28] That is, it sees the task of Oedipus as the bringing to light of the true signified that is hidden beneath the enigmatic signifier—the riddle—of the Sphinx's speech, a problematic that closely reproduces the structure of Saussurian semiology, not to mention the metaphysics of presence. However, in what can be read as an early programmatic statement of his own project, Agamben writes: "What the Sphinx proposed was not simply something whose signified is hidden and veiled under an 'enigmatic' signifier, but a mode of speech [*un dire*] in which the original fracture of presence was alluded to in the paradox of a word that approaches its object while keeping it indefinitely at a distance. The *ainos* (story, fable) of the *ainigma* is not only obscurity, but a more original mode of speaking [*un modo più originale del dire*]" (S 138).[29] This, despite initial appearances, is not a statement of affinity with the deconstructive notion of *différance* but rather something like an effort to step backward beyond it. For while there is, in Agamben's reading, an irreducible disjuncture within the paradox of the enigma, what the paradox itself points to is not its own decipherment (or the infinite deferral of it) but to the original mode of speech whose "referent" is the fracturing, the taking place of language itself—a speaking (*un dire*) whose "referent" is itself. This original mode of speaking is not founded on the presence or representation of the signified at all, and believing that it is, which is tantamount to dismissing this original fracture of presence, is precisely what Agamben believes to be Oedipus's—and the Western metaphysical tradition's—error.

In proposing to approach the enigma of language from the point of view of the Sphinx—in seeking the language of a different monster, and a different monstrosity—Agamben obliquely casts Derrida as the unwitting heir of Oedipus, the decoder of the riddle, or better, the one who assumes that the enigma of language has fundamentally to do with deciphering the riddle of the sign (even if this turns out to be inherently impossible).[30] As natural as this model of the enigma and of language may seem, Agamben suggests that there is, nevertheless, "nothing in principle [that] requires the consideration of 'signifying' as an 'expression' or an 'eclipse'" (S 137), absolutely limiting us to the semiological-metaphysical view of language. Instead, he writes:

> Every interpretation of signifying as the relation of manifestation or expression (or, inversely, of coding and eclipse) between a signifier and a signified . . . places itself necessarily under the sign of Oedipus: under the sign of the Sphinx must be placed every theory of the symbol that, refusing the model of Oedipus, focuses its attention above all on the barrier between signifier and signified that constitutes the original problem of signification. (S 138–39)

What is important to note here is Agamben's suggestion that the barrier is not unsurpassable and not unthinkable; it is not the absolute aporia that is itself redirected into *euporia*, but rather indicates the way toward *euporia*. "The algorithm S/s must therefore reduce itself to simply the barrier (/) but in this barrier we should not see merely the trace of a difference, but the topological game of putting things together and articulating (*sunapseis*), whose model we have attempted to delineate in the apotropaic *ainos* of the Sphinx" (S 156). For Agamben, the disjuncture between "S" and "s" is not itself the nonoriginary origin, or "producer," of signification, but the index of that originary "topological" problem of signification, which remains to be thought—and thought precisely on terrain other than that of the semiotic logic of the signifier and the trace.

In *Of Grammatology*, Derrida writes: "*The trace is in fact the absolute origin of sense in general. Which amounts to saying once again that there is no absolute origin of sense in general. The trace is the différance* which opens appearance and signification" (G 65). But for Agamben, in viewing *différance* as the unsurpassable limit and (non)origin of signification, and thus foreclosing the possibility of neutralizing or circumventing the metaphysics that is founded on this logic, Derrida is confined to the Oedipal understanding of the enigma, an understanding of language fundamentally as code. Thus, in response to Derrida's deconstruction of the metaphysical logic of the sign, Agamben claims that "To isolate the notion of the sign, understood as a positive unity of *signans* and *signatum*, from the original and problematic Saussurian position on the linguistic fact as a 'plexus of eternally negative differences' is to push the science of signs back into metaphysics" (S 155).

It may, however, appear that Agamben is here simply proposing a version of the originary presence and logocentric plenitude that Derrida tirelessly demystifies and dismantles. Yet he avoids making any such appeals to presence, at least not, to take the terms of this debate, the presence associated with the plenitude of either the vocal sign or the signified. Nevertheless, Agamben *is* in a certain sense logocentric, though not in quite the way Derrida intends in *Of Grammatology*, for he has a different view of what the *logos* is: not the (illusory) fully present word, before its supplementation by writing and the trace, but rather what is "alluded to" by the paradoxical splitting itself, the barrier that permits and resists signification, which, in *Stanzas*, he will also call the human.[31] "The originary nucleus of signification," he writes, "is neither in the signifier nor in the signified, neither in writing nor in the voice, but in the fold of the presence on which they are established; the *logos* . . . is this fold that gathers and divides all things in the 'putting together' of presence. And the human is precisely this fracture of presence" (S 156).[32]

As Derrida in *Of Grammatology* attempts to "designate the crevice through which the yet unnamable glimmer beyond the closure of metaphysics can be glimpsed" (*G* 14), so, too, in *Stanzas* Agamben's analysis offers only a "glimpse" of what "a semiology freed from the mark of Oedipus and faithful to the Saussurian paradox would finally bring to the 'barrier resistant to signification'" (S 139); it is an argument that "attempts to point toward the originary apotropaic stage of language in the heart of the fracture of presence" (S 139), the experience of which "we cannot but approach" yet that "must, for the moment, remain at a distance" (S 157). In his 1989 preface to *Infancy and History* (1978), to which we will turn shortly, Agamben states that "[i]n both [his] written and unwritten books, [he has] stubbornly pursued only one train of thought: what is the meaning of 'there is language'; what is the meaning of 'I speak'?" (*IH* 5). And this set of questions characterizes his work up to and including more recent work such as *Profanations* (2005), in which he describes the intention of Paul's messianic *pistis* as an attempt to bring about a "new experience of the word" (*Prof* 88).

As we will see in the following pages, this new *experimentum linguae* entails thinking that which gives rise to the aporetic structure of significance, that which happens in the space of the stanza, or in the "nowhere" of the Sphinx, which in Agamben's words, we must map as a "topology of the unreal" and which we must accustom ourselves to think of "not as something spatial, but as something more original than space. Perhaps, following Plato's suggestion, we should think of it as a pure difference, yet one given the power [*potere*] to act such that 'what is not, will in a certain sense be; and what is, will in a certain sense not be'" (S xviii). Here, once again, where Agamben's thought appears at first glance to be very near to Derrida's, on closer examination it shows its decisive distance from it, for in that difference that is more original than space or spacing, before the aporias of Oedipal semiology and the metaphysics of presence, before the signifier and the trace, there is not simply *différance* but that which can both be and not be, which will later be elaborated as one of Agamben's signal concepts: potentiality. For Agamben, as we will see in chapter 3, it is only in thinking potentiality—and particularly the potentiality of language—as that which invisibly articulates and puts together presence, that "the step-backward-beyond metaphysics . . . becomes really possible" (S 157).

Here comes into view the central idea that will, in various guises, guide all of Agamben's engagements with Derrida. For Agamben, Derrida's thought exposes but stops short of overcoming that crisis of Oedipal semiology, and thus remains within but is unable to think its way to the bottom of the Sphinx's enigma, the question of "signification in general," the meaning of "there is language," the meaning of "I speak." As he writes in the 1968 essay "L'albero del linguaggio: "[In] the history of linguistics, one postulate has remained unquestioned: the definition of language [*linguaggio*] as a system of signs, indissoluble unities of signified and signifier. Although there has been no lack of radical critiques on the part of philosophers, and there has even been recent talk of a 'historical *closure*' of the 'age of the sign,' the dogma of the sign has remained intact."[33] The meaning of the *logos*, then, is the chess piece that Agamben begins to move against Derrida here and will continue to move for the next three-and-a-half decades, starting again with the investigation of the concepts of "infancy" and "Voice" in the books he would publish in the years immediately after *Stanzas* and to which we will turn in the next chapter.

2

"THE HUMAN VOICE"

> The voice was the first, Furriskey was saying. The human voice. The voice was Number One. Anything that came after was only an imitation of the voice. Follow, Mr. Shanahan?
>
> —FLANN O'BRIEN, *AT SWIM-TWO-BIRDS*

In his 1989 introduction to the French edition of *Infancy and History*, Agamben describes his work from 1977 to 1982 (the year of *Language and Death*) as constituting a single, and in large part unrealized project, to which he gives the title "The Human Voice":

> [B]etween *Infancy and History* (1977) and *Language and Death* (1982), many pages have been written which attest the project of a work that remains stubbornly unwritten. The title of this work is *La voce umana* (The Human Voice) or, as otherwise noted, *Etica, ovvero della voce* (Ethics, an essay on the voice). One of these pages contains this *incipit*:
>
>> Is there a human voice, a voice that is the voice of man as the chirp is the voice of the cricket or the bray is the voice of the donkey? And, if it exists, is this voice language? What is the relationship between voice and language, between *phōnē* and *logos*? And if such a thing as a human voice does not exist, in what sense can man still be defined as the living being which has language? The questions thus formulated mark off a philosophical interrogation. In the tradition of the ancients, the question of the voice was a cardinal philosophical question. *De vocis nemo magis quam philosophi tractant* [In treating (the question

of) the voice, no one is better than the philosophers], we read in Servius, and for the Stoics, who gave the decisive impulse to Western thinking on language, the voice was the *arkhē* of the dialectic. Yet philosophy has hardly ever posed the question of the voice as an issue ... (*IH* 3–4)[1]

Thus Agamben sets out the coordinates of the five-year period of work for which this brief but crucial text serves as a belated introduction. As we will see, the voice, this concept that according to Agamben has so rarely been posed as an issue, emerges as something like the supreme term in Agamben's thought of this period, and thus the paradoxical neglect of the notion in the philosophical tradition is meant to be taken as a striking oversight. What might, however, strike the contemporary reader as an even greater provocation in this claim is the implicit liquidation or dismissal of the critique of logocentrism—and more pointedly *phono*centrism—that Derrida had launched most spectacularly in the annus mirabilis of 1967 (which, of course, included the publication of his extended essay on Husserl, *Speech and Phenomena*, whose original French title, *La Voix et le phénomène*, indeed puts the "question of the voice" on the book's cover).[2] While *Stanzas* pointedly engages Derrida's reading of Saussure, "The Human Voice" thus presents itself as a counterpoint to Derrida's critique of phono-logocentrism in Husserl.

Derrida's first substantial publication on Husserl, however, was the long introduction to his translation of Husserl's *Origin of Geometry* in 1962, and it is worth reviewing certain pertinent elements of its argument before turning to *Speech and Phenomena*, which Derrida once suggested could be read as the earlier piece's "other side (recto or verso, as you wish)" (*Pos* 5). As Derrida notes, in this earlier commentary "the problematic of writing was already in place as such, bound to the irreducible structure of 'deferral' in its relationship to consciousness, presence, science, history and the history of science, the disappearance or delay of the origin, etc." (*Pos* 5). Indeed, in the close reading of Husserl's texts he pursues here, Derrida meticulously traces the ways in which, in his attempts to isolate and describe a pure and transcendental consciousness, Husserl cannot escape—or even quite acknowledge—the irreducible contaminating effects of writing and difference.

THE INTRODUCTION TO *ORIGIN OF GEOMETRY*

Perhaps the central question with which Husserl grapples in the *Origin* is how ideal objectivities (geometric objects, and more generally mathematical and scientific objects) can be both "inventions" of individual geometers and at the same time transcendental and surpatemporal idealities accessible to many subjects. "[H]ow does geometrical ideality (just like that of all sciences) proceed," asks Husserl, "from its primary intrapersonal origin, where it is a formation produced within the conscious space of the first inventor's soul, to its ideal Objectivity?" (*IOG* 76, 161; *IH* 45). The answer he gives—as noted by both Derrida and Agamben—is: "[It occurs] by means of language, through which it receives, so to speak, its linguistic flesh" (*IOG* 76, 161; *IH* 45). On the one hand, geometric knowledge is a historical achievement, the product of individual thinkers who have worked out the principles and theorems of geometry and mathematics. But on the other hand, the transmission and perdurance of these principles, that is, what makes them more than a mute, private, and fleeting intuition on the part of, say, a semi-historical Thales, depends on their exteriorization and incarnation in the flesh of language. Geometric truth is an objective truth, and yet at its origin it relies on a public language for its constitution. As Derrida rather straightforwardly writes:

> [T]he Objectivity of this truth could *not* be constituted *without* the *pure possibility* of an inquiry into a pure language in general. Without this pure and essential possibility, the geometrical formation would remain ineffable and solitary. Then it would be *absolutely bound to the psychological life of a factual individual*, to that of a factual community, indeed to a particular moment of that life. . . . The paradox is that, without the apparent fall back into language and thereby into history, a fall which would alienate the ideal purity of sense, sense would remain an empirical formation imprisoned as fact in a psychological subjectivity—*in the inventor's head*. Historical incarnation sets free the transcendental, instead of binding it. This last notion, the transcendental, must then be rethought. (*IOG* 77)

Historical incarnation sets the transcendental free of the empirical and factual because it is the extrapersonal materiality of a language (say, Greek)—wherein geometric truths find their incarnation—that guarantees these truths' transcendence over the merely individual and psychologistic. This, however, is not to say that a prelinguistic and transcendental truth simply finds its expression in language, but rather that such truths must exist in a constitutive relation to language if they are to be conceived as suprapersonal, supratemporal, and ideal in the first place. This conflation of transcendence and linguistic incarnation leads Derrida to his argument concerning writing's priority over and contamination of the transcendental field.

"To *constitute* an ideal object," he writes, "is to put it at the permanent disposition of a pure gaze.... [and this entails] the production of a *common* object, i.e. of an *object* whose original owner is thus dispossessed" (*IOG* 78). A common and perduring object, even an intellectual object such as a geometric idea, must be extricable from its originator and owner if it is to be anything other than a purely subjective possession—that is, if it is to be constituted as an ideal object at all; such is the condition of possibility for an object to be appropriable and accessible to the community and available for historical transmission through the tradition. How, then, does Husserl account for the constitution and communalization of such idealities? Derrida claims that when describing this expropriating-appropriating dynamic, Husserl is consistent in his appeal to language's power to "document" and to give "*spiritual corporeality*" to ideal objects insofar as it has the function of "*stating*" them and "*communicating [them] to others*" (*IOG* 78–79). This is to say that for Husserl the production of a "common object" is synonymous with that object's exteriorization and verbal incarnation in the speaker's act of communicating a statement concerning that object to another member of the linguistic community.

But how, then, must we conceive of language if it is to be the repository of such "statements" that can maintain their consistency and identity as common object even in the absence of the original speaker from whom they have been "dispossessed"? What kind of language would be capable of the historical repetition and transmission of these objective truths down through a tradition independently of the presence of the factual and individual speakers who, so to speak, invented and first communicated them? In clear anticipation of the grammatological argument that Derrida would fully develop in the years immediately following the introduction, the answer he gives is: a language that withstands the disappearance of speakers, a language that perdures in the manner of a physical object—in short, a material, graphic language: writing.

> The possibility of *writing* will assure the absolute traditionalization of the object, its absolute ideal Objectivity—i.e., the purity of its relation to a universal transcendental subjectivity. Writing will do this by emancipating sense from its *actually present* evidence for a real subject and from its present circulation within a determined community.... Without the ultimate objectification that writing permits, all language would as yet remain captive of the de facto and actual intentionality of a speaking subject or community of speaking subjects. By absolutely virtualizing dialogue, writing creates a kind of autonomous transcendental field from which every present subject can be absent. (*IOG* 87–88)

This insight, however, concerns not only, and perhaps not even primarily, the *afterlife* of invented or discovered truths that are passed down through the tradition, but also the very constitution of the objective transcendental truth of such idealities in the first place. For as Derrida argues, once writing is identified as the mechanism by which objective sense can (and must) be separated from empirical, factual speakers, "[t]he possibility or necessity of being incarnated in a graphic sign is no longer simply extrinsic and factual in comparison with ideal Objectivity: it is the *sine qua non* condition of Objectivity's internal completion.... Paradoxically the possibility of being written [*possibilité graphique*] permits the ultimate freeing of ideality" (*IOG* 89–90). The linguistic inscription—language *as* inscription—is not simply a recording instrument that preserves an expression of ideal truths for the tradition, but is rather the mechanism by which ideality itself can be "deposited" and "produced" at all (see *SP* 25).

While writing thus proves to be the condition of possibility for the transcendental field, the primacy of the written sign also inscribes the death—or at least the absence—of the speaker and the spoken to into the very consistency of discourse. Insofar as the written sign exists and signifies in the absence of the original parties to a verbal dialogue, indeed insofar as this is more or less the essential fact about the written sign, the possibility of the speaker's and addressee's disappearance and death is thus an essential structural element of writing. The implications of Derrida's claim that "writing creates a kind of autonomous transcendental field from which every present subject can be absent" are more fully developed in the 1971 lecture "Signature Event Context," where he discusses the "iterability" of written communication:

> It must be repeatable—iterable—in the absolute absence of the addressee or of the empirically determinable set of addressees.... A writing that was not structurally legible—iterable—beyond the death of the addressee would not be writing.... All writing, therefore, in order to be what it is, must be able to function in the radical absence of every empirically determined addressee in general. And this absence is not a continuous modification of presence; it is a break in presence, "death," or the possibility of the "death" of the addressee, inscribed in the structure of the mark. (*M* 315–16)

And furthermore, "[w]hat holds for the addressee holds also, for the same reasons, for the sender or the producer" (*M* 316). The constitution of the transcendental field (and "common" ideal objectivities) is predicated on the iterability of written communication, which in turn is also the insinuation of the necessary possibility of death into every speaking subject qua speaking subject.

The implications of this argument are many, but I wish to emphasize that the nascent notion of arche-writing comes to ground a deconstructive attack on one of the central tenets of Husserl's phenomenology, the "Living Present."[3] While Husserl searches for a transcendental ground or locus on which an absolute present—living or otherwise—could come to rest, Derrida shows how such a ground is always upset and displaced by the topological disturbance of difference/*différance*:

> The impossibility of resting in the simple maintenance [nowness] of a Living Present, the sole and absolutely absolute origin of the De Facto *and* the De Jure, of Being *and* Sense, but always other in its self-identity; the inability to live enclosed in the innocent undividedness [*indivision*] of the primordial Absolute, because the Absolute is *present* only in being *deferred-delayed* [différant] without respite, this impotence and this impossibility are given in a primordial and pure consciousness of Difference." (*IOG* 153)

Or to put this even more forcefully: "The primordial Difference of the absolute Origin ... is perhaps what has always been said under the concept of '*transcendental*,' through the enigmatic history of its displacements. Difference would be transcendental" (*IOG* 153). Thus the introduction to *Origin of Geometry* anticipates much of the argumentation of the texts from the annus mirabilis and after.[4]

While the introduction to *Origin of Geometry* traces (1) the way writing—language *as* writing—is the condition of possibility for the constitution of the transcendental field, and (2) the way writing introduces death and absence into the Living Present, Derrida is nevertheless only obliquely concerned there with the question of phonocentrism in Husserl's thought, something that he in fact confronts with full force a few years later in *Speech and Phenomena*. It is perhaps this latter text's status as an exemplary reading of phonocentrism in "the history of metaphysics, and metaphysics in its most modern, critical, and vigilant form [i.e., Husserl's transcendental phenomenology]" that leads Derrida to affirm that it "is perhaps the essay that [he] like[s] the most" (*Pos* 4–5). However that may be, as a sort of complement to the introduction—one that fills out the repertoire of deconstructive motifs within a reading of Husserl's texts—*Speech and Phenomena* concentrates on the internal, "differant" displacement that writing introduces in the *voice*.

SPEECH AND PHENOMENA

Toward the end of *Speech and Phenomena*, Derrida turns to the topic of the voice as the culmination of a series of modulations of the way the phenomenological purity of "lived experience" (which Husserl consistently seeks to locate and stabilize) is contaminated by the irreducible displacement of *différance*. The voice—the "vocal medium"—is the last bulwark Husserl sets up against the half-realized and half-disavowed aporias and quandaries that undermine his phenomenological "principle of principles," which Derrida glosses as "the original self-giving evidence, the *present* or *presence* of sense to a full and primordial intuition" (*SP* 5).[5] The ruin of this first principle is devastating not only for Husserl's phenomenology but also for the whole of Western metaphysics, of which Husserl's thought here serves as a privileged representative. For what the deconstruction of the phenomenological "principle of principles" undoes, Derrida writes, is "the certainty, itself ideal and absolute, that the universal form of all experience (*Erlebnis*), and therefore of all life, has always been and will always be the *present*";

and along with this certainly goes the conviction that "[t]he present alone is and ever will be . . . [and that] [b]eing is presence or the modification of presence" (*SP* 53). As Derrida shows, the appeal to the *voice* is Husserl's last defense against the contamination of the present by nonpresence, of being by nonbeing. To see this, however, we must first briefly retrace his analyses of one crucial problem in Husserl's thought that the recourse to the voice is aimed at mastering and reabsorbing into the present/presence of phenomenological experience.

This is the problem of signification, which Derrida examines primarily in chapters 1–4 of *Speech and Phenomena*.[6] As he had in the introduction to *Origin of Geometry*, Derrida notes that Husserl appears unwilling or unable to confront language directly as a fundamental problem: he "had to postpone, from one end of his itinerary to the other, all explicit meditation on the essence of language *in general*" (*SP* 7). It is important to specify here what Derrida means by "the essence of language in general" or "signification and language in general" (*SP* 3): what he intends by this is signification as *semiology*, "the *structure of the sign in general*" (*SP* 23).

The nature of the sign in general, he suggests, fundamentally eludes Husserl, but this is by no means to say that the question of signs is not a concern for him. Indeed, Husserl famously makes a distinction between two kinds of sign (*Zeichen*): "expression" (*Ausdruck*) and "indication" (*Anzeichen*). To put Husserl's argument roughly, *expression* corresponds to linguistic signs proper, to the elements of linguistic communication (sentences, words, phonemes), while *indication* corresponds to any significant mark or gesture (such as the canals of Mars, which might indicate intelligent life, or a chalk mark on a door of a house, indicating that it is to be robbed). While both expressions and indicative signs signify, the nature or content of what they signify differs. As a "purely linguistic sign" (*SP* 18), an expression is the bearer of *Bedeutung* (meaning) or *Sinn* (sense). There is no such thing as an expression without a corresponding meaning; indeed, this is more or less the definition of the linguistic sign—it "always supposes the ideality of a *Bedeutung*" (*SP* 18), which can be approximately translated into the Saussurian "concept" or "signified." Indicative signs, on the other hand, are signs that have no "meaning" in the sense of an ideal *Bedeutung*.[7] As meaningless (*bedeutungslos*) signs, indications do not function according to the semiotic logic of signifier and signified. Instead, there is a much more empirical and "analogical" relation between the indicative sign and its signification.

As Derrida explains (see *SP* 27ff.), rather than corresponding to a meaning, the indicative sign instead works by "motivating" the thinking mind to pass from one existing phenomenon to another—say, from the existing chalk mark on the door to the existing house to be robbed, or to a future or virtually existing phenomenon, such as the robbery itself—without the latter ever really becoming something so abstract, ideal, and conceptual as the "meaning' of the mark. In contrast to what is "supposed" by the expressive sign, there is no "ideality of a *Bedeutung*" involved in indication, but simply a mental passage from one empirical thing to another. While this, Husserl acknowledges, is certainly a mode of signification, its operation is different from (and for him ultimately incommensurable with) that of expression.

It is the latter mode of the sign—expression—with which Husserl is ultimately concerned, and the primary goal of his drawing this distinction between indication and expression in the first place is to separate out and exclude indication ("as an extrinsic and empirical phenomenon" [*SP* 27]) from the proper signifying function of expression. As Derrida explains, "His logical and epistemological concern here is to secure the originality of expression as 'meaning' and as relation to an ideal object" (*SP* 27). Indication is to be reduced in order to approach expression in its purity. But why is expression so valorized by Husserl? What is the logic of expression and why does it enable a relation to an ideal object?

Just as the analogic or associative structure of indication guarantees the infra-worldliness of its (not properly linguistic) signifying function, the ideality of the object in expression—which entails "sign[s] charged with meaning" (*SP* 32)—is guaranteed by its topological structure. Again the analogy with Saussure's account of the sign is useful, insofar as the sign is essentially defined as the combination of a material signifier (whether audible or graphic) and an immaterial concept or signified. Saussure is, in truth, less concerned with the ideality of the conceptual side of the sign (and indeed has an account of signified's historical mutability), but in strictly structural terms, mapping the Saussurian account of the sign onto Husserl's similar account of the expressive sign enables us to see more clearly its transcendentalizing effect.[8] Expression, as Derrida explains, is always a matter of exteriorization, which "imparts to a certain outside a sense which is first found in a certain inside" (*SP* 32). Having reduced the indicative level of signification on the grounds both that it is wholly contained in the empirical and worldly and that it can function without any intending subject that wants to communicate a particular meaning (e.g., the canals of Mars), Husserl goes on to conceive both the outside and inside involved in expression to be transcendental idealities, the "outside" of the ideal object (*Bedeutung*) and the "inside" of transcendental consciousness. In this sense, one could say that expression provides the medium for the entire project of transcendental phenomenology. This wholesale transcendentalization and dematerialization is, on Derrida's reading, the upshot of the distinction between indication and expression, for if indication is part and parcel of the empirical, then "[t]he whole stratum of empirical effectiveness, that is, the factual totality of speech, thus belongs to indication" (*SP* 34), and as such indication must be set aside in the *epokhē*. More important than the exteriorizing/interiorizing structure of expression is the fact that, unlike indication, which is a matter of associative or analogical relations between worldly phenomena, expression need not be rooted and need not be uttered in the empirical world—indeed, in the last analysis, it must not.

Derrida rejects Husserl's attempt to smelt expression from indication, arguing instead that "*All speech inasmuch as it is engaged in communication and manifests lived experience operates as indication*" (37–38). The binary distinction, so crucial for Husserl, between indication and expression is thus dealt a grave blow in Derrida's first offensive, and the details of Derrida's deconstruction of the indication-expression opposition would certainly merit a full examination.[9] For the purposes of the present discussion, however, it will be more helpful to follow Derrida's subsequent critique of the way Husserl ultimately appeals to the figure of the *voice* as a way of resolving the quandaries of "solitary mental life" and the silent monologue that animates the lived experience of the phenomenological subject. The structure of this dematerialized expression leads Husserl, even though he "believes in the existence of a pre-expressive and prelinguistic stratum of sense, which the reduction must sometimes disclose by excluding the stratum of language" (*SP* 31), to conceive of the soliloquy involved in solitary mental life as an unbroken monologue spoken by a purely silent voice, the "phenomenological voice" in which Derrida identifies Husserl's ultimate phonocentrism.

In an argument that recalls the problem of the constitution of geometric idealities discussed above, Husserl arrives at the notion of a phenomenological voice by way of the problematic relation between the transcendental subject and the ideal object devoid of all worldly or empirical attributes. In solitary mental life, sense must be both inherent to the ideal object and present to the subject without making any detour through the empirical (or through indication). And yet, since there is still a *relation* between two nonidentical terms, however abstracted and unworldly these two may now be, that is to say, "[s]ince sense is determined on the basis of a relation with an object, the element of expression consequently must protect, respect, and restore the *presence* of sense, *both as the object's being before us*, open to view, and *as a proximity to self in interiority*" (SP 75). But how can expression be conceived in such a way as to preserve both modes of presence/proximity while at the same time fulfilling the signifying function? Indeed, insofar as the logic of the sign always entails an interior and an exterior, or an ideal meaning and an empirical signifier, how can transcendental sense be purified of all the contingency and empiricity of the worldly (and by extension indicative) mark? There is, Derrida argues, an "unfailing complicity . . . between idealization and speech [*voix*]" (SP 75). This is because the mode of expression that is able to exteriorize meaning into an immaterial signifier "freed from all mundane spatiality" (SP 75), and thus not exteriorize itself into the world at all, is that of the silent interior monologue of the paradoxically mute phenomenological voice—"the voice," as Derrida puts it, "that keeps silence" (SP 70).

Ideal objects are theoretically free and independent of their empirical manifestations; their sense is a supratemporal ideality. But, if such idealities are to be available and accessible to thought, if they are to constitute the object of any experience, then they must be susceptible to the sense-bearing structure of expression. This leads Husserl to imagine an expressive "medium which both preserves the *presence of the object* before intuition and *self-presence*, the absolute proximity of the [intending] acts to themselves" (SP 76). In short, Husserl must imagine both an immediate and immutable relation between signifier and signified and an absolute intimacy between that unified sign and the intending mind. From these theoretical exigencies, Derrida argues, comes the "strange prerogative of the vocal medium" (SP 70) in Husserl's argument.

> The ideality of the object, which is only its being-for a nonempirical consciousness, can only be expressed in an element whose phenomenality does not have worldly form. *The name of this element is the voice.*

> Phonic signs ("acoustical images" in Saussure's sense, or the phenomenological voice) are heard [*entendues* = "heard" plus "understood"] by the subject who proffers them in the absolute proximity of their present. (*SP* 76)

Unlike the not-properly-linguistic indicative sign and unlike the graphic linguistic signifier, which is exteriorized in an insistently material, visible, and empirical body, the phonic signifier is heard/understood in a way that appears far more intimate and immediate. The medium of expression that exists in the sphere of transcendental experience must be a vocal one, permitting the subject that hears/understands itself speaking to remain in an unbroken continuity with itself (while the subject that "sees" itself exteriorized in the material and worldly graphic sign has necessarily passed through the detour of empirical phenomenalization). In short, the ephemeral and immediate voice appears to bind the subject immediately to the ideal meaning or *Bedeutung* of speech; it not only gives the illusion of a proximity between the transcendental subject and the ideal object, it serves as the guarantor of the presence or "absolute proximity" of the subject to itself.

Thus this ultimate recourse to the voice as the medium of transcendental sense achieves two metaphysical assurances: (1) In the internal monologue "the phenomenenological 'body' of the signifier seems to fade away at the very moment it is produced. . . . This effacement of the sensible body and its exteriority is *for consciousness* the very form of the immediate presence of the signified" (*SP* 77); and (2) the transcendental subject that hears/understands itself speaking internally is present to itself in the security of having bypassed the contingencies, dangers, and contaminations of the empirical world. The voice of the interior monologue is a sort of silent dialogue with the self in absolute proximity to itself, a division with no division, a difference with no difference, a distance with no distance. The voice "can *show* the ideal object or ideal *Bedeutung* connected to it without venturing outside ideality, outside the interiority of self-present life" (*SP* 78). The voice is not only the signifying medium that remains faithful to ideality and the transcendental subject, it is the unitary and universal medium that encompasses and encloses them both within its sphere.

If Western metaphysical phono-logocentrism is, as Derrida has tirelessly argued, motivated by the dream of achieving a pure presence to meaning, an experience of the transcendental signified, then Husserl's argument is a perfect example. But as is suggested by the paradoxical formulations of "difference with no difference" and "division with no division," such an attempt at metaphysical closure in the *phōnē* is not without its breaches. Like the writings of all of the thinkers on whom Derrida has focused his deconstructive lens, Husserl's texts unravel themselves around precisely this node. For even though Husserl has appealed to the immateriality and evident immediacy of the vocal medium—the spatial and temporal inseparability of the vocal sign from its *Bedeutung*—and has imagined a sort of dialogue within the self that occurs without the passage through the empirical world (which has been bracketed off in the reduction), there is nonetheless an irreducible movement of auto-affection. For Derrida, this opens the entire system up to the contaminations of temporality, spatiality, and difference.[10]

Take, for example, the question of the primacy and constitution of the subject of "lived experience." While Husserl presupposes the transcendental subject as primary and antecedent in its relation with transcendental sense or signification, Derrida counters: "As soon as it is admitted that auto-affection is the condition for self-presence, no pure transcendental reduction is possible.... Auto-affection is not a modality of experience that characterizes a being that would already be itself (*autos*). It produces sameness as self-relation within self-difference; it produces sameness as the nonidentical" (*SP* 82). And if this is the case, the unity and purity of the spatial and temporal presence of the "living now" (*SP* 85), which the vocal medium would sanction and guarantee, succumbs to the temporal and spatial play of *différance*, the trace, and writing.

> The living present springs forth out of its nonidentity with itself and from the possibility of a retentional trace. It is always already a trace. This trace cannot be thought out on the basis of a simple present whose life would be within itself; the self of the living present is primordially a trace. The trace is not an attribute; we cannot say that the self of the living present "primordially is" it. Being-primordial must be thought on the basis of the trace, and not the reverse. This protowriting is at work at the origin of sense. Sense, being temporal in nature, as Husserl recognized [without being able to square it with his phonocentrism], is never simply present; it is always already engaged in the "movement" of the trace, that is in the order of "signification." (*SP* 85)

The complicity between the voice and presence—or rather, between the illusory immediacy of the voice and the presence that it falsely guarantees—becomes the core of the metaphysical system underlying Husserl's analysis. The voice serves to stabilize and ground the presence-to-self of the subject and the ideality of the meaning that serves as the content of the subject's lived experience. But all of this, in exemplary phono-logocentric fashion, is predicated on a repression and blindness to the anterior and irreducible contamination of *différance* that lies at the (non)origin of all of these idealities. Through Husserl, Derrida powerfully argues that there "is" neither subject nor object of lived experience—and certainly no transcendental vocal medium uniting them—that escapes the primordial inscription of the trace and the displacing play of *différance*.

INFANCY AND HISTORY

Let us return now to Agamben's introduction to *Infancy and History*. Given Derrida's powerful analyses and the profound influence they had already had on continental thought in the 1960s and 1970s, it is clearly provocative to suggest that "philosophy has hardly ever posed the question of the voice as an issue." However one views the merits of that claim as such, it does offer us a particular way to approach the essay that gives the volume its title, namely, as a pointed response to Derrida's critique of Husserl's phonocentrism. Such a reading of "Infancy and History" will in turn lead us to Agamben's analysis of the "Voice" in *Language and Death*.

In point of fact, Husserl is a thinker to whom Agamben has devoted relatively little direct attention in print. Nevertheless, like Derrida, in "Infancy and History" Agamben identifies in Husserl's thought an ultimate and problematic recourse to an irreducible *voicing* of primordial experience or *Erlebnis* ("lived experience"). In attempting to formulate the starting point for a radical "descriptive theory of consciousness," Husserl writes in a passage that Agamben cites: "Its beginning is the pure—and, so to speak, still dumb—psychological experience, which now must be made to utter its own sense with no adulteration. The truly first utterance, however, is the Cartesian utterance of the *ego cogito*" (qtd. in *IH* 37).[11] Now, on the one hand, psychological experience has been pared down to a prelinguistic (dumb) state, but on the other, this experience can only be undergone through a primordial utterance: "I think." As Agamben writes, in a condensed argument that strongly recalls Derrida's analysis, "With this concept of *mute* experience ... Husserl had got closest to the idea of a pure experience—that is, something anterior both to subjectivity and to an alleged psychological reality. It is strange that he then should have identified it with its 'expression' in the *ego cogito*, thus from *mute* to *voiced*" (*IH* 37).

Yet unlike Derrida, Agamben continues to be invested in this concept of mute experience that Husserl cannot quite get to the bottom of. In the Derridean and Agambenian analyses, then, we arrive once again at a threshold or impasse, yet this impasse leads Agamben not to an extended reading of the irreducible phonocentric presuppositions that will ultimately cause Husserl's text to undo itself, but rather to the question that, as we saw in the fragment cited at the opening of this chapter, will animate the final section of "Infancy and History," and indeed all of his work on "the human voice" to follow. He asks: "does a mute experience exist, does an *in-fancy* of experience exist? And, if it does, what is its relationship to language?" (*IH* 37).

Agamben pursues this question in the final section of "Infancy and History," which begins by shifting the discussion (perhaps a little brusquely) from a Husserlian horizon to one whose terms are drawn primarily from Émile Benveniste, and in particular from his work concerning the theory of enunciation, which in turn will provide the coordinates for Agamben's own concept of infancy (and later, as we will see, Voice). For Agamben, Kant's and Husserl's investigations of the transcendental subject, and of any possible experience of this subject, fundamentally err in that they have inadequately understood the true relation of priority between subjectivity and language. While Agamben notes J. G. Hamann's earlier critique of the Kantian transcendental subject, it is Benveniste who, in "confirming Hamann's intuition of the necessity for a metacritique of the transcendental subject" (*IH* 45), provides the terms by which Agamben definitively shifts the debate from Husserlian phenomenology to the linguistics of enunciation.[12]

At base, Agamben argues that Husserl is destined to fail in his search for a pure *Erlebnis* because he more or less assumes a subjectivity that preexists language, a transcendental "I" that would be the subject of this mute experience. Thus Husserl (like Kant before him) is "prevented ... from discerning the original place of transcendental subjectivity *within* language, and therefore from clearly tracing the boundaries separating the transcendental and the linguistic" (*IH* 44; my italics). And this failing can be most clearly seen in the way Husserl had "completely failed to grasp" the specific meaning and nature of the first-person pronoun, believing simply that

> [i]n solitary discourse, the meaning [*Bedeutung*] of *I* has its essential realization in the immediate representation of our own personality, and that is also where the meaning of this word resides in the discourse of communication. Each interlocutor has his own representation of the I (and therefore his individual concept of the *I*); thus what is signified by this word changes with each individual. (*1st Investigation* § 26, qtd. in *IH* 46)

In acknowledging the unstable nature of the pronoun, Husserl has, to be sure, come close to describing the site where subjectivity and discourse co-originate. But he nevertheless implicitly takes such things as "personality," "interlocutors," and "individuals" as substantial (albeit amorphous) entities preexisting the invocation of the "I" in discourse. As with the previously noted "mute experience" that is nevertheless "voiced," Husserl falls into an unresolved paradox wherein the transcendental subject is always imbedded in and dependent on language.

In Agamben's critique, Husserl's failure to understand the "I" is not merely one example among others of the impossibility of isolating a prelinguistic transcendental subjectivity. Rather, the first-person pronoun—as analyzed above all by Benveniste in his work of the 1950s and 1960s—turns out precisely to be the key to the door that for Agamben will lead past the paradoxes of subjectivity and phenomenological experience.[13] Indeed for Agamben, Benvensite's work, especially the essays "The Nature of the Pronoun" and "Subjectivity in Language," provides the lens to clearly see how "Subjectivity is nothing other than the speaker's capacity to posit him or herself as an *ego*, and cannot in any way be defined through some wordless sense of being oneself, nor by a deferral to some ineffable psychic experience of the *ego*, but only through a linguistic I transcending any possible experience" (*IH* 45).

Benveniste himself, in fact, presents his analysis of personal pronouns, which is in many respects similar to Roman Jakobson's analysis of shifters, as a direct critique of phenomenological and psychological accounts of subjectivity. In "Subjectivity in Language," for example, he writes:

> It is in and through language that man constitutes himself as a *subject*, because language alone establishes the concept of "ego" in

reality.... Now we hold that "subjectivity," whether it is placed in phenomenology or in psychology, as one may wish, is only the emergence in the being of a fundamental property of language. "Ego" is he who *says* "ego." That is where we see the foundation of "subjectivity," which is determined by the linguistic status of "person."[14]

The origin of the subject, then, is the instance of utterance, whose index or operator is the pronoun "I." In following Benveniste's thought here, Agamben circumvents the Husserlian problematic of the transcendental subject of *Erlebnis* and moves the first-philosophical debate into the realm of the theory of enunciation, or the instance of discourse, which is a sort of baseline ontological or ontogenetic event. "[T]he transcendental sphere as subjectivity, as an 'I think,' is in fact founded on an *exchange* between the transcendental and the linguistic. *The transcendental subject is nothing other than the 'enunciator'*" (*IH* 46–47; first italics mine).

This linguistic event, enunciation, does not rest solely on language as *langue*, but rather on the passage from *langue* to discourse, or, in Benveniste's terms, from the semiotic to the semantic. And this event hinges on the operation of this now rather ambiguously defined individual—the enunciator—who in uttering "I" refers to and effects its own speaking self. This requires us to rethink the nature of the speaking subject, insofar as it has been traditionally conceived of either as a psychological subjectivity or as the being that "has" language at its disposal. Rather, the subject appears here as a sort of precipitate of the operation of language and of its split topological structure, arising only in the passage—or "exchange"—between one linguistic sphere and another in the event of enunciation. As Agamben writes, "each speaking individual is the site of this difference" (*IH* 51). While Benveniste's analysis of enunciation and of the role of shifters and indicative pronouns thus fundamentally informs Agamben's conception of language's ontological and ontogenetic function, as the following pages will continue to argue, one element that he adds to Benveniste's thought here—and one that serves as the centerpiece of his thought in this period of work—is that of *infancy*.

For Agamben, the split between language and discourse is a residue or result of the fact of infancy. It must, however, be emphasized that Agamben is interested in infancy more as a structural fact than as a chronological one; it is the paradoxical or circular set of relations among enunciation, infancy, *langue*, and *parole* in every act of speech that provides the clue to what Agamben will identify as the most basic problem in thinking about primary experience. Infancy, he writes, "cannot merely be something which chronologically precedes language [*linguaggio*] and which, at a certain point, ceases to exist in order to spill into speech. It is not a paradise which, at a certain moment, we leave for ever in order to speak; rather, it coexists in its origins with language [*linguaggio*]—indeed, is itself constituted through the appropriation of it by language [*linguaggio*] in each instance to produce the individual as subject" (*IH* 48) The split nature of human language, the structure that distinguishes human language from animal vocalizations and communication, arises out of the primordial expropriation of experience that is the origin of the speaking human subject, which in turn is also the origin of human language itself: "language [*linguaggio*] in its double reality of *langue* and *parole*" (*IH* 48). As Agamben writes, "It is not language [*lingua*] in general that marks out the human from other living beings—according to the Western metaphysical tradition that sees man as a *zōon logon ekhon* (an animal endowed with speech)—but the split between language [*lingua*] and speech, between semiotic and semantic (in Benveniste's sense), between sign system and discourse" (*IH* 51–52).

The human in a rigorous sense is actually the living being that does *not* have language, or at least is not born into language. We come gradually into one—say, English—and we must slowly learn to use it and put it into discourse; that is to say, we do have an actual, chronological, biographical period of infancy. For Agamben, this fact reveals the defining structure of human language, namely, that it is split into two incommensurable but mutually dependent spheres. Infancy, he writes, "sets up in language that split between *language* [*lingua*] and *discourse* which exclusively and fundamentally characterizes human language [*linguaggio*]. For the fact that there is a difference between language (*langue*) and speech (*parole*), and that it is possible to pass from one to the other, and that each speaking individual is the site of this difference and this passage, is . . . the central phenomenon of human language" (*IH* 51). And anticipating a much later text—*The Open*, which I discuss in chapter 5—he continues: "Animals do not enter language, they are already inside it. Man, instead, by having an infancy, by preceding speech, splits this single language [*lingua*] and, in order to speak, has to constitute himself as the subject of language—he has to say *I*" (*IH* 52).

As noted above, Agamben identifies the central question of *Infancy and History* as follows: "[I]s there such a thing as human in-fancy? How can in-fancy be humanly possible? And if it is possible, where is it sited?" (*IH* 47). His answer turns out to be that not only is an infancy of experience possible, but it is a condition of possibility for experience: "*The individual as not already speaking, as having been and still being an infant—this is experience*" (*IH* 50). And this experience occurs at the disjunction between the semantic and the semiotic, in a space "located in the correspondence-difference (in the *khōra*, as Plato would have said) between the two regions, in a 'site' which can perhaps be described only in its topology and which coincides with that historico-transcendental region . . . which we have defined above as infancy" (*IH* 58). To return to the Husserlian question with which Agamben's analysis began, experience is not subjective, or rather it is not subjective in the sense of some prelinguistic *Erlebnis* that the more or less psychological and transcendental subject has or undergoes. But experience is nevertheless not unrelated to the subject and to subjectivity. Indeed, what Agamben argues is that experience is *eminently* subjective in a very particular way. It is precisely the taking place of subjectivity in the event of saying "I," which in turn is a taking place—or *taking one's place*—in the linguistic field; and this taking one's place is the moment of passage between language's split poles of *langue* and *parole*, the moment of enunciation.

That Agamben's 1977 text is a response to Derrida's well-known reading in *Speech and Phenomena* is relatively evident from the discussion—as brief and elliptical as it may be—of the status of the voice in Husserl. The impasse that language and the voice create in Husserl's analysis of transcendental subjective experience is indeed a central observation for both the Derridean and Agambenian readings. And yet Agamben very pointedly does not follow Derrida's lead in deconstructing the Husserlian text; rather, he finds that Benveniste and the concept of infancy offer a way around the Husserlian impasse. Infancy necessitates saying "I," taking the subject position. As we will see in a moment, this will lead Agamben to the analysis of the Voice in *Language and Death* and a further movement away from the critique of phonocentrism as exemplified in *Speech and Phenomena*. But first an excursus.

EXCURSUS: AGAMBEN AND DERRIDA READ BENVENISTE

None of the preceding discussion, of course, is to suggest that Derrida is not also an intensely thorough reader of Benveniste, but he is a particularly focused one. An examination of an essay in which Derrida explicitly takes up Benveniste's work shows how his eye is attracted in a grammatological direction when presented with the very same problematic that Agamben has indicated in the texts of and about Saussure discussed in chapter 1 and in the Husserlian texts read in *Speech and Phenomena* and the introduction to the *Origin of Geometry*. In his essay on Benveniste, "The Supplement of Copula: Philosophy before Linguistics" (1971), Derrida begins with a brief statement concerning the problem of philosophy's confinement within the structures and strictures of language. How, the question runs, can philosophy hope to attain to truth when it is enslaved within the bonds of a given language, which is an arbitrary system of signs and which has over time developed certain fixed logical, lexical, and rhetorical possibilities (and impossibilities) within it? How can philosophy escape such historical contingency when it "always reappropriates for itself the discourse that de-limits it"? (*M* 177). What would a true philosophical language look like? What could constitute a language of truth?

In these opening pages of the essay, Derrida cites two passages, one from Nietzsche and one from Heidegger, in which this very problem is presented. First Nietzsche:

> Logic is only slavery within the bonds of language (*die Sklaverei in den Banden der Sprache*). Language, however, has within it an illogical element, metaphor. Its primary force operates (*bewirkt*) an identification of the nonidentical (*Gleichsetzen des Ungleichen*); it is therefore an operation of the imagination (*Wirkung der Phantasie*). The existence of concepts, forms, etc. rests thereupon. (qtd. in *M* 178)

The second passage comes from Heidegger's "Letter on 'Humanism,'" and it, too, names precisely the central question of that text.

> Metaphysics, which very early on in the form of Occidental "logic" and "grammar" seized control of the interpretation of language. We today can only begin to descry what is concealed in that occurrence.

> The liberation of language from grammar into a more original essential framework is reserved for thought and poetic creation.[15]

After citing these two philosophical passages in his preamble, however, Derrida abruptly shifts the focus of his discussion, naming the foregoing problematic as a sea voyage he will not actually undertake here: "Rather than follow this immense problematic onto the high seas, so to speak, perhaps it would be better, given the demands and limits of this essay, to take our point of departure from the propositions of a modern linguist" (*M* 179), namely, Benveniste's propositions in "Categories of Thought and Language." It is clear enough, then, that Derrida's reading of Benveniste is intended as an answer to, or example of, the problems outlined by Nietzsche and Heidegger in the preamble, not only because the philosophers provide the essay's opening gestures, but because Derrida's analysis forcefully returns to Heidegger in closing. Indeed, Derrida's essay is, in an oblique way, ultimately about Heidegger, and his reading of Benveniste therefore illuminates the way Derrida either addresses or liquidates a problematic that is so central, as we will see, to Agamben's thought. And so, while the debate here centers on Benveniste (and, by extension, Saussure), perhaps the higher stakes are those of the Heideggerian inheritance. How then, does Benveniste's essay on "Categories of Thought and Language" develop, and how is it linked to Heidegger?

Benveniste's well-known claim in this essay is that Greek philosophical thought (specifically Aristotle's) is determined in a fundamental way by the resources and limits of the particular language in which it is articulated. Through an analysis of the various grammatical and syntactical functions of Greek parts of speech, Benveniste shows that, rather than being essential categories or modalities of thought, Aristotle's categories are in fact categories of language that are then projected onto the plane of the extralinguistic. On first glance it might seem as if Derrida would be in sympathy with the claim that Greek philosophical thought is determined by its grammar.[16] Yet the piece turns out to be a strong critique of Benveniste. Why? Over the course of this essay, Derrida identifies many points where he finds Benveniste's argument to be reductive, selective, derivative, careless, "rhapsodic," or wrong, but his ultimate objection is that Benveniste is not radical enough in his analysis, that he stops short of interrogating the final, or first, presupposition of the argument concerning the categories of thought and language. He leaves the category (or supercategory) of being intact.

Benveniste's essay, in fact, appears precisely *not* to leave the category or notion of being intact, for he states that, just as the functions of the parts of speech determine the functions of the various categories, it is only because the verb "to be" functions in such ways grammatically, syntactically, and morphologically (for example, it can easily become a nominal with the addition of the article) that "the whole Greek metaphysics of 'being' was able to come into existence and develop."[17] For Benveniste, on Derrida's reading, this all suggests that Greek ontology is simply a derivative problematic arising out of the grammatical forms of the Greek language, which then get "transposed" into philosophical thought.

Derrida, however, finds Benveniste's critique of Greek ontology wanting because it unwittingly depends on the transcategoriality of being in order to make the argument about the projection of categories of language onto categories of thought in the first place. Unlike every other category, "being" is both present and absent in every language. It is present because even in those languages where the verb "to be" is not so stably unified as it is in Greek, its function appears to be present but divided among other verbs. Benveniste is equivocal on this point, and Derrida takes him to task for contradicting, or at least not fully supporting, his claim that there are languages in which the function of "to be" is absent. However, it *is* also absent in every language, not because, as Benveniste would have it, there are languages that do not make use of its function, but because, as Derrida writes, "'to be,' at least as the copula, does 'not actually signify anything,' because it unfolds its extension to infinity.... [I]t is no longer linked to the determined form of a word, or rather of a name (a name in the Aristotelian sense, which includes nouns and verbs), that is, to the unity of a *phōnē sēmantikē* armed with a content of meaning" (*M* 196). "Being," as a predicate, is both meaningless and necessarily inherent in every predicate. That is to say, "to be" occupies an odd position within the syntactic and grammatical system, a position that at once always escapes the immanent and self-contained set of signifiers (and their signifieds) but is always there to guarantee the play of correspondences between those signifiers and signifieds.

This leads us to what is, for our purposes, a more important objection by Derrida, which is that Benveniste approaches "to be" as if it were simply a word like any other. And yet the uninterrogated containment of the verb "to be" within a supposedly closed and self-immanent language system (which Benveniste examines, Derrida suggests, as a philologist rather than a philosopher) is ruptured by the way "being" is precisely the thing that allows the very opening of language onto the nonlinguistic. Being does "not actually signify anything" at a categorical or nominative level; it does not refer to any specific thing; it is not a predicate. And yet, as Benveniste notes with evident puzzlement, "without being a predicate itself, 'being' is the condition of all predicates."[18] There is an ontical ground assumed in every predication, and this ground manifests itself in the semiotic system in this paradoxical contentlessness and necessity of the copula. To put this another way, "being" is a pivot, an enigmatic threshold and link between the semiotic and the semantic.

The transcategorical and transcendental nature of "being" is what rhetorically enables the differentiation between the linguistic and nonlinguistic in both Aristotle and Benveniste (and Derrida suggests that Aristotle was far more cognizant of this fact than is Benveniste). In order to claim that thought and language are separate and that one determines the other, that is, in order to describe any sort of transition—whether by "projection," "transposition," or "transcription" (see *M* 189)—between the categories of thought and those of language, one must have recourse to the supracategorical ground across which these transitions happen. "Without the transcategoriality of 'to be,' which 'envelops everything,' the transition between categories of language and categories of thought would not have been possible, either in one sense or the other, for Aristotle or for Benveniste" (*M* 197). Thus Derrida's fundamental objection to Benveniste's argument is that he has not sufficiently questioned this primary presupposition that enables the very question about any relations between thought and language to be asked, and that however deftly Benveniste might analyze the syntax and morphology of the verb "to be," he has not sufficiently understood the way "being" provides the very ground of the problematic.

Derrida seeks to show in this essay (whose subtitle is "Philosophy before Linguistics") that the linguist has not interrogated the much more basic "philosophical" question, an intention strongly signaled by his preamble, in which he quotes both Nietzsche and Heidegger on the question of the barriers language raises for philosophizing. One point Derrida is making here is that, in confrontation with the linguist, the philosophers have won the day, that "[p]hilosophy is not only *before* linguistics as one might find oneself *facing* a new science, a new way of seeing or a new object; it is also *before* linguistics, preceding linguistics by virtue of all the concepts philosophy still provides it, for better or for worse" (*M* 188). While it is superfluous to note that Derrida takes Heideggerian ontology to task elsewhere, here his argument is actually to show that Benveniste's analysis falls short of that of Heidegger, with whom he begins and ends the essay.

But it is interesting to note that if this is ultimately an essay about philosophy's primacy over linguistics, each time we do take a step into the Heideggerian "high seas," Derrida redirects the argument toward the grammatical or grammatological. And to be precise, he directs the argument to a particular selection of texts by Benveniste (which he, of course, reads in a particular way). We saw a moment ago how after the philosophical preamble Derrida chooses to "take [his] point of departure from the propositions of a modern linguist" (*M* 179), that is, from Benveniste's "Categories of Thought and Language." A similar thing occurs later in the essay, where Derrida reintroduces Heidegger into the argument for a second time.

In a discussion of the Ewe language, which Benveniste chooses as an example of a language that lacks the verb "to be" (though Derrida points out that its function, more precisely, is actually "divided among several verbs" and thus not exactly *absent*), Benveniste considers what the consequences of such a lack—or at least lexical diffusion—would be for a hypothetical philosopher from Togo. Could one do metaphysics in a language that did not make use of the verb "to be"? The point of this question is not to suggest, in vulgarly ethnocentric fashion, that this non-European language and those who speak it are "*deprived* of the surpassing mission of philosophy and metaphysics" (*M* 199), but rather to hold the nature of Western metaphysics up to even greater scrutiny. For in positing such a lack in a given language, Benveniste's central hypothesis of cross-categorical determination is further complicated. Derrida asks: "Is such an absence possible and how is it to be interpreted? This is not the absence of a word from a lexicon; in the first place because the function 'to be' is conveyed by several words in the Indo-European languages. No more is it the absence of a determined semantic content, of a simple signified, since 'to be' signifies nothing determinable; thus it is even less the absence of a thing that could be referred to" (*M* 199).

At this point, Derrida notes that Heidegger had also asked this very question, and had pronounced the impossibility of such a lack within a language, but this impossibility has little to do with a given language's lexicon. He cites Heidegger's "On the Grammar and Etymology of the Word 'Being'":

> Let us suppose that this indeterminate meaning of Being does not exist and that we also do not understand what this meaning means. What then? Would there merely be a noun and a verb less in our language? No. *There would be no language at all.* No being *as such* would disclose itself in words, it would no longer be possible to invoke it and speak about it in words. For to speak of a being as such includes: to understand it in advance as a being, that is, to understand its Being. Assuming that we did not understand Being at all, assuming that the word "Being" did not even have its vaporous meaning, there would not be a single word.[19]

Now, what does Heidegger mean when he says that without "Being" there would be no language at all? Certainly not that languages that do not dispose of the verb "to be" are not languages. Clearly it is not the presence (or absence) of the unified word or concept "to be" that Heidegger considers as the condition of possibility (or impossibility) of language, "but an entirely other possibility which remains to be defined" (*M* 199). At this point, Derrida closes the Heideggerian parenthesis and returns to Benveniste: "In order to approach this possibility—and as we cannot systematically examine all of Heidegger's text here—let us come back to Benveniste. But this time let us consider another essay than the one we have been concerned with until now: 'The Linguistic Function of "To Be" and To Have"'" (*M* 200).

Here once again Derrida focuses on a text by Benveniste where the problem of the transcategorical and transcendental nature of "being," the problem of the ontological grounding or production of language, is sought in the grammar of the verb "to be," and with unsurprisingly unsatisfactory results. Not only does Benveniste appear to throw up his hands in the face of the problem ("The data seems to elude analysis, and the whole problem is still so poorly worked out that one finds no firm ground to stand on"), but the confusions of his analysis lead Benveniste, according to Derrida, to tellingly contradict his earlier claim that there are languages that lack the verb "to be."[20] For as Derrida writes, "Benveniste demonstrates the universality of the grammatical function of the copula with an abundance of examples. This function is found in every language that does not possess the verb 'to be' in its lexical presence" (*M* 201). This function can be observed not only in the several distinct verbs that taken together serve as "to be" in Ewe, but also, and more crucially, in certain Indo-European syntactic structures that do not make use of the copula or any other verb at all (such as the "nominal sentence"). In all cases, the function of this absent verb is always carried out by other means, by a lexical or grammatical or aural supplement—even by a silent punctuation mark or by a temporal pause between the "coupled" terms of the nominal sentence. That is to say, the presence of the absent word (and it is not just any word) is marked in written or spoken language by a nonlexical supplementary mark or indeed by an absence itself, a pause or gap in speech. But if the function of the copula is operative equally in both the word and the nonlexical supplement to the word's absence, what then is this word and the signified to which it refers, and how can we even begin to approach its meaning when our starting point is the lexeme and the lexicon of a given language (say, Greek)? It is in the face of this unresolved oscillation between lexico-grammatical absence and presence, Derrida suggests, that Benveniste must ultimately throw up his hands.

The contradictions and impasses of Benveniste's linguistic analysis of the copula, which Derrida rigorously uncovers and accumulates, show how it is impossible for him sufficiently to answer—or indeed sufficiently to ask—the question concerning the relation between being and language. And the structure underlying and articulating those two poles collapses upon itself when its unexamined presupposition is revealed to be (though in this piece never so named) the supplementary play of *différance*, a word—if it is a word—"that would surely not be for philosophy or linguistics as such to say" (*M* 205).

Having earlier reviewed Agamben's reading of what he believes to be Saussure's true, though more obscure, problematic (for which he draws heavily on Benveniste's texts), we are familiar with his argument that the deconstructive or grammatological project is based on a misunderstanding (or limited understanding) of the nature of language's originary fracture and a refusal to acknowledge that thought has ever been able, try as it might, to glimpse beyond the limit of *différance*. With this in mind, we might suggest that when Derrida twice shifts from Heidegger to Benveniste in "The Supplement of Copula," he does not direct the argument toward that aspect of Benveniste's thought that would perhaps best address the "philosophical" questions that "linguistics" fails to solve, and that indeed would provide some of the terms for Agamben's critique of deconstruction. By directing us straight into the grammatical, and by closing the doors to that cage of language (or, perhaps better, by kicking away the ladder leading up to it), Derrida limits and excludes the questions Benveniste considers in his analysis of the "enunciative function." Derrida's reading of Benveniste leads us to ask the grammatological question and not the question of enunciation, but a very different reading of Benveniste might have resulted had Derrida redirected us not to "Categories of Thought and Language" and "The Linguistic Functions of 'To Be' and 'To Have'" but to the articles where Benveniste develops what Agamben believes to be perhaps his "most felicitous creation" (*RA* 137). This, in any case, is the direction Agamben leads us.[21]

Perhaps the best way into Agamben's counterreading of Benveniste here would be to jump ahead a few decades. In the final chapter of *Remnants of Auschwitz* (1999), Agamben appears to include not only an oblique critique of Derrida's avoidance of Benveniste's (and for that matter Foucault's) idea of the enunciative function, but also an implicit reply to Derrida's argument regarding Benveniste's reading of the word/concept "being" in "The Supplement of Copula." In fact, Agamben seems precisely to redeploy Derrida's own argumentation concerning the transcategorialty of being, turning it against Derrida in Benveniste's favor. Here, however, rather than "being," the problematic transcategorical is the linguistic deictic or shifter.

Benveniste's article "L'appareil formel de l'énonciation" appeared in the March 1970 issue of *Langages*, eight months before Derrida's "The Supplement of Copula" appeared in the very same journal. In *Remnants*, however, Agamben refers us not to this esssay but to the 1969 article "Sémiologie de la langue" and Benveniste's effort there to outline a "research program that moves beyond Saussurian linguistics" (*RA* 137). Though Benveniste did not succeed in fully developing this project in his lifetime, certain of its contours are nevertheless visible in what Benveniste did leave behind. "It is not surprising," Agamben writes,

> that the basis for this program lies in the theory of enunciation, which may well constitute Benveniste's most felicitous creation. The overcoming of Saussurian linguistics, he argues, is to be accomplished in two ways: the first, which is perfectly comprehensible, is by a semantics of

discourse distinct from the theory of signification founded on the paradigm of the sign; the second, which interests us here, consists instead "in the translinguistic analysis of texts and works through the elaboration of a metasemantics that will be constructed on the basis of a semantics of enunciation." (*RA* 137)[22]

The difficulties involved in developing, or even conceiving of, a semantics of enunciation arise out of enunciation's obscure position outside of, and indeed logically prior to, both the semiotic and semantic. If the abstract, structural resources of a given *langue* are actualized in every act of *parole*, it is the enunciative function that names this activity that effects the transition or actualization. But understanding the *meaning* of such a linguistic event (that is, the event of language itself), developing a "semantics" of it, is a paradoxical and difficult task. For how can we speak of meaning before the signifying structure and logic of the sign? Like infancy, to which it is intimately related, the enunciative function appears to elude all linguistic categories and acts, while at the same time inhering in them as their condition of possibility.

As elusive as it is, however, the enunciative function nevertheless has its lexical index: the shifter. The shifter is self-referential, but not in a grammatical or syntactical sense. Rather, the self-referentiality of the shifter escapes (while also remaining within) the formal, semiotic sphere and refers to the concrete act of discourse that produces the semiotic text. For Agamben (and, according to Agamben, for Benveniste also), *the shifter—rather than the verb "to be"—is the transcategorical ontological operator that effects the link between the linguistic and the extralinguistic.* If this is true, then Derrida's critique of Benveniste, while it may be accurate with regard to the texts he examines, is actually misplaced, for the fundamental problematic truly comes to light and is truly addressed in Benveniste's thinking on enunciation and shifters. Agamben writes:

> It is certainly possible to define something like a meaning of the shifters "I," "you," "now," "here," . . . ; but this meaning is completely foreign to the lexical meaning of other linguistic signs. "I" is neither a notion nor a substance, and enunciation concerns not what is said in discourse but the pure fact that it is said, the event of language as such, which is by definition ephemeral. Like the philosophers' concept of Being, enunciation is what is most unique and concrete, since it refers to the absolutely

singular and unrepeatable event of discourse in act; but at the same time, it is what is most vacuous and generic, since it is always repeated without its ever being possible to assign it any lexical reality. (*RA* 138)

What is of interest to Agamben here is that the shifter problematizes—or brings into stark relief (which may be the same thing)—the differential system of the semiotic much as, for Derrida, the concept of "being" problematizes the categorical analysis of Benveniste's text. Insofar as "being" is both inside and outside the categorical, and insofar as it is both unique and vacuous in every text, it denies the closure of the semiotic structure and opens it onto the extralinguistic. This, as Derrida shows, raises serious problems for the two texts by Benveniste that he discusses in "The Supplement of Copula." But here, Agamben suggests that a more adequate or pertinent consideration of precisely this problem can be found in *another* of Benveniste's analyses, and though it is not clear that he has that particular moment of Derrida's "Supplement of Copula" in mind specifically, his argument nevertheless permits itself to be read as a direct reply to that text.

This is to say that, for Agamben, the questioning of transcategoriality and of being's relation to language truly takes place in Benveniste's work, not in his discussion of the grammar of the word "being" in Greek or the nominal sentence, but in his analysis of the enunciative function and the metasemantics of enunciation, the "linguistics of speaking," which he—like Saussure—did not live to develop. This is the project that Agamben explicitly takes up at this point in *Remnants*, but it is one that he had been developing for quite some time. For that "metasemantics founded on the semantics of enunciation" which Benveniste "glimpse[d] before falling into aphasia" (*RA* 138) is what Agamben, more than twenty years before his analysis of testimony, called "semiology from the point of view of the Sphinx," and which he further investigates in "The Human Voice," to which this chapter will now return.

LANGUAGE AND DEATH

In "Infancy and History," Agamben's concern is to establish the subject as a precipitate of a linguistic operation. The result is that in Agamben's thought, primary to any subjectivity, what we have as a more primordial or anterior state of the human is what we might call the "speaking being." As such, the human is defined by a particular activity, speech. Is this not, then, a pure and simple phonocentrism? Surely the argument can and will be made. But it is important to recall that even in "Infancy and History," the most crucial state of this speaking being is, in fact, not the act of speech, but rather the infancy that precedes and persists within speech, making speech anything but a pure and immediate self-presence. Let us recall Agamben's guiding questions: (1) is infancy possible? and (2) is there a human voice? Though obviously related, these are two distinct inquiries. The preceding pages sought to trace the argument that leads Agamben to claim that infancy is not only possible, but is the very condition of possibility for a human speaker to emerge. Now we must look at what is implied in the notion of a speaking being. With what or by means of what does a being speak? The answer is "the Voice," the central issue in *Language and Death: The Place of Negativity*.

The thesis of *Language and Death* exemplifies the fundamental difference between Agamben's and Derrida's most basic first-philosophical positions, for while Derrida's work is a critique of what he calls the metaphysics of presence—at base a search for (and implicit granting of) the unity and irreducibility of presence (whether that be in the form of the voice, the signified, being, etc.)—with *Language and Death*, Agamben formulates most clearly his own critique of the metaphysical tradition, namely, that it is based on negativity. On the one hand, then, a metaphysics of presence; on the other, a metaphysics of negativity. Put in these terms (which the following pages will attempt to justify), one would be hard put to imagine more differing positions. Contra Derrida's idea of phonocentrism as a dream of presence, Agamben argues that the Voice is precisely the foundational negativity of ontology.

The inquiry of *Language and Death* takes its cue from a comment made by Heidegger in "The Nature of Language": "The essential relation between death and language flashes up before us, but remains still unthought" (qtd. in *LD* xi). Agamben identifies death and language here as the two primary categories by which the human has always been distinguished from non-human beings in the Western tradition; more precisely, Agamben identifies death and language as the two essential "faculties" that make the human human. Throughout the Western tradition, he notes, "humans appear as both *mortal* and *speaking*" (*LD* xii), but as Heidegger has suggested, the relation between these two constitutive characteristics of the human has not been thought through to its base. As the book's investigation will show, thinking these two together entails locating the human in a very particular topological "place," which, as the work's subtitle indicates, is that of negativity. Agamben writes: "Both the 'faculty' for language and the 'faculty' for death, inasmuch as they open for humanity the most proper dwelling place, reveal and disclose this same dwelling place as always already permeated by and founded in negativity. Inasmuch as he is *speaking* and *mortal*, man is, in Hegel's words, the negative being who 'is that which he is not and not that which he is' or, according to Heidegger, the 'placeholder (*Platzhalter*) of nothingness'" (LD xii). To refer back to the discussion above, this place of negativity is the very "site" of infancy; in the following pages, we will see that it is also the place of the "Voice"; and to anticipate a discussion in the next chapter, this place is also the "site" of potentiality.

It is, moreover, worth emphasizing here that in his introductory framing of *Language and Death* as a critique of the metaphysics of negativity, Agamben pointedly asserts that the "nihilism" at which that tradition has arrived (and to which it was destined to arrive) is one "beyond which contemporary thought and praxis (or 'politics') have not yet ventured. On the contrary, that which thought attempts to categorize as the mystical, or the Groundless, of the *gramma*, is simply a repetition of the fundamental notion of ontotheology" (xiii). This diagnosis of the ailment afflicting both the long tradition of Western thought and the most recent philosophical reflection—most pointedly Derrida's—determines the framing and direction of the book's investigation, and alerts us to the great pitfall that Agamben seeks to avoid. "Above all," he writes, "it [is] important that the structure of this negative foundation . . . should not simply be replicated in our reflections, but that finally, an attempt might be made to *understand* it" (xiii).

Agamben's discussion of shifters (especially the first-person pronoun) in *Remnants* is a continuation of the argument in *Langauge and Death*, and in particular that of the chapter titled "Third Day," in which the structure of the linguistic shifter is shown to be precisely that of transcendence itself.[23] Tracing the issue through ancient, medieval, and modern linguistics up through Benveniste and Jakobson, Agamben provides in this chapter an account of the peculiar status and function of demonstrative pronouns (deictics, shifters), namely, that they are "'empty signs,' which become 'full' as soon as the speaker assumes them in an instance of discourse. Their scope is to enact 'the conversion of language into discourse' and to permit the passage from *langue* to *parole*" (*LD* 24). As noted above, in enacting this conversion—that is, in becoming significant only by virtue of the enunciation that they enable to be enacted, and to which they refer—these demonstratives do not "simply demonstrate an unnamed object, but above all the very instance of discourse, its taking place" (*LD* 25). While the implications of this dynamic are many (and some have already been noted), the self-referentiality of the "indicator of utterance" shows more than simply the passage from *langue* to *parole* as conceived in strictly Saussurian linguistic terms. Indeed, in this chapter's brief but dense tour through two millennia of reflection on signification, Agamben seeks to demonstrate how throughout those centuries of thought this pronominal self-reference has been conceived in ontological terms of the highest importance. The structural linguistic frame can identify the dimension of the utterance as that in which discourse is enacted, but, Agamben argues, "throughout the history of Western philosophy, this dimension has been called *being, ousia*" (*LD* 25). That is to say, more than just the category in which language refers to itself, the pronominal *demonstratio* is the supercategorical and transcendental dimension that opens up the space for the taking place of being. Agamben writes:

> That which is always already demonstrated in every act of speaking..., that which is always already indicated in speech without being named, is, for philosophy, being. The dimension of meaning of the word "being," whose eternal quest and eternal loss... constitute the history of metaphysics, coincides with the taking place of language.... Only because language permits a reference to its own instance through *shifters*, something like being and the world are open to speculation. The transcendence of being and of the world—which medieval logic grasped under the rubric of the *transcendentia* and which Heidegger identifies as the fundamental structure of being-in-the-world—is the transcendence of the event of language with respect to that which, in this event, is said and signified; and the shifters, which indicate the pure *instance* of discourse, constitute... the originary linguistic structure of transcendence. (*LD* 25–26)

The reference here to Heidegger, and specifically the identification of being-in-the-world with the linguistic structure of transcendence, directs our attention to what, for the purposes of the present discussion, is the central figure and most contested philosophical legacy in Agamben's and Derrida's divergent arguments concerning the end or closure of metaphysics.

The centerpiece—and, it might be said, the protagonist—of Heidegger's fundamental ontology is, of course, Dasein. And according to the reading Agamben proposes in this book, there is much more than a mere analogy to be discerned in the similarity between the way the linguistic shifter achieves a content—becomes "full"—only in the moment of discourse and the way Dasein is constitutively structured by its potentiality-for-being (*Seinkönnen*). Indeed, for Agamben, the key to understanding the existential structure of Dasein (and, as we will see, the relation between the "faculties" of language and death) lies precisely in the shifter imbedded in the term "Dasein" itself: "Da," "there." In a move that is perfectly analogous to the one he makes in reading Benveniste's enunciative function against Derrida's reading of the copula, Agamben argues that it is the shifter and not the verb "to be" within the compound word "Dasein" that proves to be the ontological operator on which everything depends.

While Heidegger's term "Dasein" is usually glossed in English as "being-there" (and in Italian as "*esserci*"), Agamben persuasively argues that a more precise reading would be "being-the-*Da*," "being-the-*there*." The implications of this translation or interpretation of the term are significant, and Agamben notes that Heidegger himself took pains to explain the meaning of Dasein in precisely this way. First, in section 28 of *Being and Time*:

> The entity which is essentially constituted by Being-in-the-world *is* itself in every case its "there" [*Da*]. According to the familiar signification of the word, the "there" points to a "here" and a "yonder." . . . "Here" and "yonder" are possible only in a "there"—that is to say, only if there is an entity which has made a disclosure of spatiality as the Being of the "there."[24]

And again in a 1945 letter to Jean Beaufret:

> *Da-sein* is a key word in my thought [*ein Schlüssel Wort meines Denkens*] and because of this, it has also given rise to many grave misunderstandings. For me *Da-sein* does not so much signify here I am, so much as, if I may express myself in what is perhaps impossible French, *être-le-là*. And *le-là* is precisely *Alētheia*: unveiling-disclosure. (qtd. in *LD* 4)

72 *First Principles*

Dasein is not an entity that is "there" in the sense of an entity with extension at a particular location in space; it is the "there" itself, the empty "placeholder of nothingness (*Platzhalter des Nichts*)" (qtd. in *LD* 5) that, like the shifter, becomes "full" only in its ontological disclosure of spatiality. Understanding Dasein in this way ultimately enables Agamben to establish a correlation between the ontological difference and the transcendental structure of deixis. As he writes, "The opening of the *ontological* dimension (being, the world) corresponds to the pure taking place of language as an originary event, while the *ontic* dimension (entities, things) corresponds to that which, in this opening, is said and signified" (*LD* 26). But it also, and more importantly, reveals the way Heidegger, though he "questions the efficacy of the categories within which, throughout the history of Western philosophy, logic and ontology have attempted to think the problem of the ontological origin (*ontologische Ursprung*) of negativity" (*LD* 3), nevertheless succumbs to an ultimate appeal to the *voice* as a negative ground of being. And it is from this basis that Agamben will develop the alternative critique of "phonocentrism" that, in the present context, is the argument that most concerns us.

Dasein's outer limit, of course, is death. As is well known, Dasein's structure as potentiality-for-being means that it cannot experience itself as a totality except in the experience of death, which is each Dasein's individual and ultimate limit and boundary. This is the anticipatory structure that leads Heidegger to define Dasein as "Being-toward-death." But death, which thus defines Dasein's outer boundary and its totality, is a purely negative limit, one which can neither be experienced as such by Dasein, since it entails Dasein's disappearance, nor be conceived as concrete possibility to be actualized by Dasein, since such an actualization would be precisely the impossibility of all of Dasein's possibilities. Thus the space opened up by Dasein—that is, the spatiality opened by Dasein's being-the-"there"—is one that is shot through with negativity. As Agamben notes, "Only in the purely negative register of this being-for-death, when it experiences the most radical impossibility, can Dasein reach its ownmost proper dwelling place and comprehend itself as a totality," and this in turn means that "Dasein's experience of its ownmost authentic possibility coincides with its experience of the most extreme negativity" (*LD* 1–2). Deixis (the opening) and death (the closing) converge on—or better, define the contours of—the same negative space.

But what does this have to do with the voice? As we will see in a moment, Agamben will go on from this analysis to uncover the negativity underlying Heidegger's appeal to the "voice of conscience" as that which calls Dasein to its ontological disclosure, but the crux of the broader argument in *Language and Death*, and the basis of Agamben's critique of Derrida in that book, is not simply that Heidegger (or Hegel) cannot avoid the negativity of deictic indication, but that (1) the Western philosophical tradition has *always* appealed overtly to the voice for its ontological grounding and that (2) this grounding in the voice is a negative one; that is to say, the voice is and always has been the *negative* ground of ontology. In this argument, Agamben's simultaneous proximity to and ultimate distance from Derrida come to light in a particularly stark way—and in precisely the same terms that make up the central vocabulary of Derrida's early work: voice, trace, *gramma*.

In the chapter titled "The Fourth Day," Agamben focuses more tightly on the question of what it means to indicate the instance of discourse and how this indication comes about. The two key theorists on whom he draws, Benveniste and Jakobson, both emphasize the way the indication of utterance entails the presence of the speaker of that utterance; in Benveniste's case, it is the "contemporaneity" of the discourse and the person, while Jakobson speaks of an "existential relation" between the pronoun "I" and the I who utters it (see *LD* 31–32). The conclusion he draws from this, in what up to this point would be a perfectly canonical Derridean trajectory, is that "*The utterance and the instance of discourse are only identifiable as such though the voice that speaks them.* . . . [H]e who utters, the speaker, is above all a voice. The problem of *deixis* is the problem of the voice and its relation to language." (*LD* 32). It is, however, at this point that Agamben's analysis will diverge sharply from a Derridean reading, for this peculiar status of the voice—that is, "the necessary presupposition of the voice in every instance of discourse" (*LD* 32)—is, Agamben suggests, of critical if underappreciated concern for philosophy and linguistics from at least late antiquity. Citing a series of texts by Augustine, Gaunlio, Roscelin, John of Salisbury, and Anselm in which the relation between the purely phonic, physical element of the voice is identified as the distinct but inseparable material support for the semantic or signifying level of speech, Agamben excavates a sort of history of inquiry into the ambiguous status of the voice as medium for signification. But even more importantly than this, in identifying a specifically linguistic, meaning-bearing *phōnē* that is on the one hand a physical, animal voice (since animals vocalize as well as humans, and humans are, after all, animals) and on the other hand, not merely that animal voice (since it is also the support for—or presupposition of—signification), Agamben sets the terms for his analysis of the voice as the place of negativity on which Western ontology has unfolded.

Occupying a sort of intermediate position in the topology of signification between meaningless animal vocalizations and meaningful speech, the voice is the site of a double removal or double negativity. Of course the voice *is* the physical movement of air through the vocal cords, throat, and mouth—"the mere sonorous flux emitted by the phonic apparatus" (*LD* 35)—but in this sense it is no different from animal sounds. In order for the voice to give rise to signification, the animal *phōnē* must be both presupposed and removed so that it may move into that space—the space of indication—where it can refer to the instance of discourse. As Agamben puts it, "The voice, the animal *phōnē*, is indeed presupposed by the shifters, but as that which must necessarily be removed in order for meaningful discourse to take place" (*LD* 35). Hence, a first negation of the voice, which leads to a second "Voice"—which Agamben at this point capitalizes in order to distinguish it from the first, removed animal voice—that is the disclosive and ontogenetic Voice of human speech. He writes, in an italicized passage: "*The taking place of language between the removal of the voice and the event of meaning is the other Voice . . . that, in the metaphysical tradition, constitutes the originary articulation (the* arthron*) of human language*" (*LD* 35).

For Agamben, then, such a Voice, which straddles the space of the animal *phōnē* and human language, is the site of a double negativity; it has "the status of a *no-longer* (voice) and of a *not-yet* (meaning)" and thus "necessarily constitutes a negative dimension" (*LD* 35). And this negative dimension turns out to be the negative ontological *ground*, "in the sense that it goes *to the ground* and disappears in order for being and language to take place" (*LD* 35). Voice is the (in itself meaningless) linguistic operator that gives rise to meaningful speech, the vocal medium that effaces itself in the act of opening the linguistic space for meaning to occur. Noting the similarity between this dynamic and Heidegger's analysis of the ontological difference between being and beings, Catherine Mills has suggested that the capitalization of "Voice" as the term for this supreme ontological shifter in distinction to the lowercase "voice" that is the animal *phōnē* can be seen as a close analogy of the Heideggerian distinction between ontological "Being" and ontic "being."[25] The point is a good one, for what characterizes Being is precisely its withdrawal-in-the-act-of-giving-beings, just as the Voice is concealed within every act of meaningful speech to which it gives rise.

In a closely argued analysis that can only be briefly recalled here, Agamben devotes a chapter of *Language and Death* to uncovering a "philosophy of the Voice" (*LD* 54) in Heidegger's thought. In one sense, it would be difficult to ascribe to Heidegger any recourse to the animal voice, since he emphatically seeks to think Dasein in terms that exclude the animal or the living being. For Heidegger, Dasein is not (as the human is for much of the Western tradition) a "living being that has language" but is, rather, separated by an abyss from the mere *Lebewesen* (see *LD* 55). Dasein—and the language of Dasein—are not to be seen as modifications of or capacities added to the animal and its voice. And yet, on Agamben's reading, the voice—or *Stimme*—makes a surreptitious and crucial return in Heidegger's thought in the form of the closely related term *Stimmung* (mood, attunement), one of the key terms in Heidegger's analysis of Dasein in *Being and Time*.

We have seen above how the key characteristic of Dasein is that it is its "there." But Dasein's sense of its own topological displacement into the "there" is not a matter of any determinate knowledge or rational deduction. Instead, in Heidegger's terminology, Dasein is aware of its status as the *Da* by virtue of its fundamental *Stimmung*. As Heidegger writes: "As being, Dasein is something that has been thrown; it has been brought into its 'there,' but *not* of its own accord. . . . Although it has *not* laid that foundation *itself*, it reposes in the weight of it, which has been made manifest to it as a burden of Dasein's mood (*Stimmung*)."[26] Dasein's *Stimmung* (preeminently anxiety) reveals that Dasein is displaced or thrown into the there by something other than its own will, and thus what reverberates in this mood is the echo of something that is emphatically not Dasein's own. Agamben argues that what is implied in this expropriation of the *Da*—conceived, again, along the lines of the deictic utterance—is that for Heidegger, the Voice that speaks this disclosive shifter is not retraceable or reducible to any animal or physical voice (and to the sort of brute presence-to-itself that this would imply). The language of Dasein is not "proper" to Dasein as a living being. Dasein's *Stimmung* is not *Stimme*, but rather precisely "the experience that language is not the *Stimme* of man, and so the disclosure of the world that it puts into effect is inseparable from negativity" (*LD* 56). This line of reasoning is perfectly in keeping with Heidegger's overt intention to think Dasein as separated from the animal and from the animal *phōnē*. As Agamben writes, for Heidegger, "Dasein, Being-the-*Da*, signifies: to maintain oneself in the *Stimmung*, in this nothingness that is more originary that any *Stimme*" (*LD* 57). But it is at this point that Agamben proceeds to uncover what we could legitimately call a phonocentrism underlying and undermining Heidegger's argumentation.

Having excluded *Stimme* from the structure of Dasein, Heidegger nevertheless in paragraphs 54–62 assigns a crucial function to what he calls the "call" of a "voice of conscience (*Stimme des Gewissens*)," which, on Agamben's reading, reproduces the logic of the doubly displaced Voice as Agamben has identified it. The function of this call of conscience in these pages of *Being and Time* is to seat Dasein most firmly in its disclosive space, to separate Dasein from the idle talk of the "they" (*das Man*), and lead Dasein to a resolute and authentic comprehension of its structure as potentiality-for-being and being-toward-the-end, that is, its structure as being-the-*there*. The pertinent aspect of Agamben's reading of Heidegger's argument, however, can be seen immediately in the way he glosses the function of this *Stimme des Gewissens*; Agamben writes, "In paragraphs 54–62 of *Sein und Zeit*, in the disclosure of Dasein, the call (*Anruf*) of a Voice of conscience appears, and imposes a more originary comprehension (*ursprünglicher Fassen*) of this very disclosure, determined through the analysis of the *Stimmung*" (*LD* 58). In glossing Heidegger's "voice of conscience" as the "Voice of conscience," Agamben anticipates and encapsulates the upshot of his reading, namely, that the existential analytic of Dasein will reduce and ultimately ground itself on this Voice that lies halfway between two negativities—the removed animal voice and "not-yet" of meaningful speech: "The call," Heidegger writes, "dispenses with any kind of utterance. It does not put itself into words at all; yet it does not remain obscure and indefinite. *Conscience discourses solely and constantly in the mode of keeping silent.*"[27]

On the one hand, this silent call of conscience is what seats Dasein firmly—decidedly, resolutely—in its disclosive space because it is what enables Dasein to achieve an authentic relation to its own unique finitude and to ground itself in its own abyssal negativity. As Agamben puts it, "If guilt stemmed from the fact that Dasein was not brought into its *Da* of its own accord and was, thus, the foundation of negativity, then, through the comprehension of the Voice, Dasein, now decided, assumes the function of acting as the 'negative foundation of its own negativity'" (*LD* 59). On the other hand, however, and perhaps even more crucially, this empty Voice that plays such a decisive role in Dasein's ontological and existential structure in *Being and Time* becomes in Heidegger's later work something like a synonym for Being itself. Citing key passages from the 1929 essay "What Is Metaphysics?" and the "Postscript" that Heidegger added to it in 1943, Agamben argues that in this text the "recuperation of the theme of the Voice is completed" (*LD* 60), for example in this passage:

> Originary thinking [*das anfängliche Denken*] is the echo of being's favor [*Gunst des Seins*], of a favor in which a singular event is cleared and lets come to pass [*sich ereignen*]: that beings are. This echo is the human response [*die menschliche Antwort*] to the word [*Wort*] of the silent Voice of being. The response of thinking is the origin of the human word, which word first lets language arise as the sounding of the word into words.[28]

In this migration of the "Voice of conscience" to the "Voice of being," Agamben observes a latent and persistent appeal to precisely what Heidegger has sought, in separating Dasein from the *zōon logon ekhon*, to eliminate from his analysis of Dasein and its uniquely disclosive relation to a language that is not rooted in the animal voice but is nevertheless rooted in the doubly removed Voice. This, however, consigns Heidegger to the limits and aporias of the negative metaphysics whose outer borders his thought indeed touches but does not finally breach. "[I]f metaphysics," he writes, "is not simply that thought that thinks the experience of language on the basis of an (animal) voice, but rather, if it always already thinks this experience on the basis of the negative dimension of a Voice, then Heidegger's attempt to think a 'voice without sound' beyond the horizon of metaphysics falls back inside this horizon. . . . The thought of Being is the thought of the Voice" (*LD* 61).

A metaphysical phonocentrism, then: here Agamben arrives at an ultimate and problematic appeal to the voice—or rather, Voice—in Heidegger's fundamental ontology. And this Voice is, as the preceding pages have roughly sketched, a negativity on which Heidegger's thought ultimately (un)grounds itself. Though Agamben's mode of argumentation is starkly different from Derrida's, the end point at which he arrives is not so far afield from a Derridean critique of a phonocentric presupposition underlying Western philosophical thought, represented here by its culminating figure, Heidegger. Yet once again, the significance and the nature of that *phōnē* are fundamentally different in Agamben's account; indeed, Agamben's Voice could be described as the diametric opposite of the Derridean *phōnē*. Rather than presence—for example, the presence of the living voice—the Agambenian Voice is precisely *negativity*, the negativity that inheres in meaningful, human language, which in the Heideggerian account is precisely the disclosive dimension of Dasein. In *Language and Death*, Agamben thus offers a reading of the "philosophy of the voice" in Heidegger that can be read as a counterinterpretation to a Derridean reading, but there is also a direct critique of Derrida in the book, to which this chapter now turn in conclusion.

The Voice is not the animal *phōnē*, but rather what results from the removal of the animal voice in the taking place of meaningful language. As noted above, for Agamben this is "*the other Voice . . . that, in the metaphysical tradition, constitutes the originary articulation (the* arthron*) of human language*" (*LD* 35). Such an identification of the Voice as different from the animal *phōnē*, however, leads to a further question that in the third "Excursus" of *Language and Death* (*LD* 38–40) Agamben traces back at least as far as Aristotle's *De interpretatione*—a text that "for centuries, determined all reflection on language in the ancient world" (*P* 36)—namely, "What is in the [human] voice? What are *ta en tēi phōnēi?*" (*LD* 38). According to Agamben, the answer Aristotle gives is: the letter, writing. Agamben interrogates the peculiar status of the *gramma* as the distinctive element of the Voice in this excursus of *Language and Death* as well as in a closely related essay of 1984 titled "The Thing Itself" (which, as it happens, is dedicated to Jacques Derrida). In the reading of Aristotle offered in these two essays, Agamben both reaffirms the fundamental and original status of the *gramma* in the Western reflection on language and reveals the *gramma* as the constitutive element of that Voice that is the ground of the metaphysics of negativity being held up for scrutiny in *Language and Death*.

What, then, does Aristotle say about the *gramma* within the structure of signification? In the opening moments of *De interpretatione*, he writes:

What is in the voice [*ta en tēi phōnēi*] is the sign of affections in the soul [*en tēi psukhēi*]; what is written [*ta graphomena*] is the sign of what is in the voice. And just as letters are not the same for all men, so it is with voices. But that of which they are signs, that is, affections in the soul, are the same for all; and the things [*pragmata*] of which the affections are semblances [*homoiōmata*] are also the same for all men. (qtd. in *P* 36, *LD* 38)

In this schematization of signification we can see an interrelation among four distinct terms: things (*pragmata*), affections in the soul (*en tēi psukhēi*), the voice, and what is written (*ta graphomena, grammata*). Now, among the first three terms (or "interpreters"), there is a fairly clear relation of symbolic representation, in which the mental image "interprets" the thing and the voice "interprets" the mental image. The question, however, arises when we consider the status and function of the *grammata*, which is "the sign of what is in the voice." "Why," Agamben asks, "does Aristotle introduce this 'fourth interpreter,' which seems to exhaust the order of signification?" (*LD* 38). The reason Aristotle must introduce this fourth interpreter is precisely because the Voice is not the animal *phōnē*, that is, because the *phōnē* has been altered or translated—interpreted—into the circle of signification and thus cannot itself constitute an end point to the circle of signification. It is, Agamben writes, "necessary to introduce a fourth element to assure the interpretation of the voices themselves" (*LD* 38); or in other words, the voice needs to be interpreted in order to become Voice and not remain meaningless, inarticulate sound. This is why the *gramma*, rather than the voice, is "the final interpreter, beyond which no *hermēneia* is possible: the limit of all interpretation" (*P* 37). The *gramma* thus represents a sort of end point or ultimate limit to the process of signification in the Aristotelian schema. As such, Agamben argues, "the *gramma* is the ground that sustains the entire circle of signification" (*LD* 39).

But the difficulty that the *gramma* presents, and that the ancient grammarians and commentators on *De interpretatione* attempt to get to the bottom of, according to Agamben, is that *grammata* are both interpreters (that is, signs) of the voice and at the same time *elements* of the voice. "This is why ancient grammarians," he writes, "in analyzing *De interpretatione*, said that the letter, which is the sign of the voice, is also *stoikheion tēs phōnēs*, that is, its element. Insofar as it is the *element of that of which it is a sign*, it has the privileged status of being an *index sui*, self-demonstration" (*P* 37). The paradoxical dual status of the *gramma* in the voice—that it is both a physical "quantum of the signifying voice" (*LD* 39) and a sign of itself, that it is precisely the sign of its own removal in the translation of voice to Voice—means, for Agamben, that the *gramma* is negativity, "pure temporality" (*LD* 39), "the form of presupposition itself and nothing else" (*P* 37). Like the Aristotelian "*protē ousia*, of which it constitutes the linguistic cipher, it shows itself, but only insofar as it *was* in the voice, that is, insofar as it always already belongs to the past" (*P* 37). The removal of the animal voice in the process of becoming Voice entails the articulation of the Voice by *grammata*. And this in turn entails that "what is in the [human] voice" is the pure negativity of the *gramma*'s self-affection. The Voice is thus defined by its "grammatical" negativity, and this, on Agamben's reading, is the negative ground on which Western metaphysics rests:

> This means that, from the beginning, Western reflections on language locate the *gramma* and not the voice in the originary place, In fact, as a sign the *gramma* presupposes both the voice and its removal, but as an element, it has the structure of a purely negative self-affection, of a trace of itself. Philosophy responds to the question, "What is in the voice?" as follows: Nothing is in the voice, the voice is the place of the negative, it is Voice. (*LD* 39)

This passage provides a succinct statement of what we might legitimately call the Agambenian critique of Western metaphysical phonocentrism; but it is fundamentally divergent from the better-known Derridean critique of metaphysical phonocentrism in that it identifies the Voice as the site of a metaphysical negativity rather than as presence. That this reading of Aristotle's fourth interpreter is engaged in a debate with Derridean grammatology is made explicit in a sharply polemical paragraph that merits quotation at length:

> From this point of view it is possible to measure the acuteness of Derrida's critique of the metaphysical tradition and also the distance that remains to be covered. Although we must certainly honor Derrida as the thinker who has identified with the greatest rigor . . . the original status of the *gramma* and of meaning in our culture, it is also true that he believed he had opened a way to surpassing metaphysics, while in truth he merely brought the fundamental problem of metaphysics to light. For metaphysics is not simply the primacy of the voice over the

gramma. If metaphysics is that reflection that places the voice as origin, it is also true that this voice is, from the beginning, conceived as removed, as Voice. To identify the horizon of metaphysics simply in that supremacy of the *phōnē* and then to believe in one's power to overcome this horizon through the *gramma*, is to conceive of metaphysics without its coexistent negativity. Metaphysics is always already grammatology and this is *fundamentology* in the sense that the *gramma* (or the Voice) functions as the negative ontological foundation. (*LD* 39)

In this passage, Agamben recasts the Derridean critique of phonocentrism by redefining the *phōnē* of metaphysics, arguing that the *gramma is* the Voice, because it is the voice's originary removal in *logos*. *Gramma* is the negativity in Voice, but Voice is not the immediate animal *phōnē* because that has always already been removed. This Voice thus emerges not as presence, but precisely as the original negative foundation of metaphysics. It is not the negative breach within the hegemonic metaphysics of presence, but rather the very ground of the hegemonic metaphysics of negativity.

This argument, it should be noted, is slightly different, or perhaps more evolved, from the one presented in the closing pages of *Stanzas*, which was discussed in the first chapter. There, following Heidegger's claim in the "Letter on Humanism" that Sartre has simply reversed the hierarchy of essence and existence and thus remained stuck in a metaphysical logic, Agamben had suggested that the reversal of hierarchy between voice and writing simply reproduces the aporias of semiological/metaphysical logic. Here, however, while certainly retaining this earlier critique, Agamben has now imbedded the *gramma* within the Voice as its negativity itself, collapsing the two as the original negative ground of Western thought. In a sense, the thought of the *gramma*, which in Agamben's words, Derrida has undertaken with the greatest rigor, is inseparable from the thought of the Voice, since they ultimately constitute the same thing—the negative ground of metaphysics.

The analysis of the *gramma* as the negativity of the Voice caps a period during which Agamben frames Derrida's thought almost exclusively though grammatological-semiological-linguistic categories. As the preceding pages have shown, the aporias produced by the metaphysics of negativity appear in this period primarily as the relations among—and more precisely, the space between—such paired terms as *langue* and *parole*, the semiologies of Oedipus and of the Sphinx, the *gramma* and the *phōnē*. The early 1980s, however, also mark the beginning of the period in which Agamben's center of focus changes (without, of course, ever losing sight of the path already traversed). In the belatedly added introduction to *Infancy and History*, titled "Experimentum linguae," Agamben writes of the incommensurable division between *langue* and *parole*, and of the site or space that separates them:

> The double articulation of language [*lingua*] and speech [*discorso*] seems, therefore, to constitute the specific structure of human language [*linguaggio*]. Only from this can be derived the true meaning of that opposition between *dunamis* and *energeia*, of potency [*potenza*] and act, which Aristotle's thought bequeathed to philosophy and Western science. Potency—or knowledge—is the specifically human faculty of connectedness as lack; and language [*linguaggio*], in its split between language [*lingua*] and speech [*discorso*], structurally contains this connectedness, is nothing other than this connectedness. (IH 7)

In the context of an introduction to 1978's *Infancy and History*, in which Aristotle's analysis of *dunamis* and *energeia* do not in fact play a central role, this link—indeed near-identification—between the structure of human language and that of *dunamis/energeia* can appear rather cryptic. In the context, however, of the work Agamben was undertaking at the time of the writing of this introduction (1988–89), this claim becomes much clearer. And so it is to the work of that period, and most particularly to Agamben's theory of potentiality, that the next chapter will turn.

3

POTENZA AND DIFFÉRANCE

> I recall now how he once said to me that one of the chief difficulties of writing consisted in thinking, with the tip of the pen, solely of the word to be written, whilst banishing from one's mind the reality of what one intends to describe.
>
> —W. G. SEBALD, *THE RINGS OF SATURN*

In one of the final, aphoristic chapters of his 1985 book *Idea of Prose*, Agamben tells a story about the great Buddhist philosopher Nagarjuna and his fraught relation to both his adversaries and his disciples. While the nomadic philosopher, author of *Stanzas of the Middle Way*, found the ritual of refuting the objections of the orthodox monks who charged him with nihilism to be tedious and depressing, Agamben tells us that

> [w]hat distressed him were the arguments of those logicians who didn't even come forward as adversaries, but rather claimed to profess the same doctrine as himself. The difference between their teaching and his own was so subtle that at times he himself was unable to grasp it. And yet one could not imagine anything farther from his own position. For it was in fact the same doctrine of emptiness but one constrained within the limits of representation. (*IP* 131)

Later on in this vignette, Agamben has Nagarjuna meditating on the fact that this "imperfect doctrine" of his false allies has even penetrated into the thought of his own disciples, causing them to fall into error. Agamben then has the philosopher speak these words to his pupil Candrakirti:

> Those who profess the truth as a doctrine, as a representation of the truth, treat the void as if it were a thing, they make a representation of

the emptiness of representation. But the awareness of the emptiness of representation is not, in its turn, a representation. . . . If the void doesn't remain a void, if you attribute being or non-being to it, this and only this is nihilism. . . . [I]f, at this point, you don't understand the nature of emptiness and you continue to make of it a representation, then you fall into the heresy of the grammarians and the nihilists: you're like a magician bitten by the serpent he didn't know how to take hold of. (*IP* 132–33, modified)

In this chapter I do not intend to examine the philosophy of Nagarjuna. Nor do I intend to examine the relation of Agamben's thought to that of the "second Buddha" (even though it appears—if only for the tone of this late chapter of *Idea of Prose*—that Agamben sees some affinity between his own thought and Nagarjuna's "middle way"). Rather, I begin this chapter with these passages in order to suggest that the parable they relate is fundamentally not about Nagarjuna and his contemporaries at all, but rather about the relation between Agamben himself and that school of thought to which he bears a similar relation of both intimate proximity and at the same time radical divergence, a school that is more than implicitly alluded to in that final mention of the grammarians.[1]

The occasional tendency to assimilate Agamben's thought with deconstruction seems to owe primarily to his texts of the 1980s and is understandable given the frequency with which Agamben himself in this period adopts a seemingly deconstructive vocabulary and appears even to align himself with Derrida.[2] But such similarity of lexicon and thematic concern—even when Agamben himself appears to be emphasizing it—does not necessarily reveal that there is an ultimate identification and congruence; rather, it can also indicate and define a particular terrain in *dispute*. This elusive convergence of affinity and dispute—so well described in Agamben's parable of Nagarjuna—becomes most pronounced in work of the period from which *Idea of Prose* comes, and in this chapter I will focus primarily on texts from this decade in which Agamben's relation to deconstruction is both highly pronounced and highly ambiguous. Indeed, after the "Human Voice" project discussed in the last chapter, the texts from "Language and History" (1983) and "The Thing Itself" (1984) to "*Pardes*" and *The Coming Community* (both 1990) frame a period in which Agamben's work proceeds through a gradual (though perhaps only apparent) closing of the distance from Derrida's thought and culminates with the full development of Agamben's signal concept: *potentiality*.

While Agamben discusses the interplay between the Aristotelian concepts of *dunamis* and *energeia*, potentiality and act, as early as his first book, *The Man without Content* (see chapter 7, "Privation Is Like a Face"), it is not until the 1980s that potentiality assumes such an explicitly central role in his work. When Agamben introduces the paired concepts of sovereign power and bare life in 1995's *Homo Sacer* (the book and concepts for which he is perhaps best known), the elaboration of the sovereign's biopolitical production of and dominion over the bare life of the *homo sacer* is explicitly articulated with his earlier analyses of potentiality and is indeed presented as a further development of that earlier theory. In chapter I.3 of *Homo Sacer* ("Potentiality and Law"), Agamben's argument concerning the sovereign suspension of the legal order in the state of exception is intimately entwined with his understanding of the ambiguous interplay between *dunamis* and *energeia*. In fact, for reasons that will become clear in this and the next chapter, one could say that "Potentiality and Law" can be seen as the most significant link between Agamben's earlier first-philosophical work and the more explicitly political thought from *Homo Sacer* on, which the second half of this book will take up. No less than the "paradigm of sovereignty [in] Western philosophy" (*HS* 46), Aristotle's doctrine of potentiality provides Agamben with the theoretical architecture of the biopolitical theory that has, perhaps more than any other single element of his wide-ranging work, placed him at the center of contemporary philosophical thought.

"*Experimentum linguae*"—the 1989 introduction to 1978's *Infancy and History*—is therefore that much more interesting, since it not only evokes and traces Agamben's itinerary from language to potentiality, but it affirms that these two inquiries are ultimately one and the same. Commentators have, of course, noted that the problematics of speaking and of potentiality are intimately related in Agamben's thought, but what has not been as noted is the extent to which Agamben develops his concept of potentiality in response to—and I would suggest as a counterconcept to—the central gestures (writing, the *gramma*, *différance*) of deconstruction.

DUNAMIS AND ENERGEIA

Agamben's argument concerning potentiality certainly has a largely, if often implicitly, Heideggerian provenance, but it most explicitly rests on a rather idiosyncratic reading of Aristotle's term *dunamis*. While Agamben turns to Aristotle at some point in nearly every one of his published books, his interpretation and appropriation of Aristotle's doctrine of potentiality is presented most concisely in his 1987 essay "On Potentiality" and, as just noted, chapter I.3 of *Homo Sacer* (which repeats parts of the earlier essay verbatim). In the course of their argumentation, both of these texts—as well as the 1993 essay "Bartleby, or On Contingency," to which this chapter will turn in closing—end up centering on one of the most interesting and problematic evocations of the term *dunamis* in the Aristotelian corpus—namely, a particularly baffling sentence that Agamben claims has been misunderstood by virtually the entire Western philosophical tradition. That sentence is *Metaphysics* 1047a 24–26 in book *Theta*: "*esti de dunaton touto hōi ean huparxēi hē energeia hou legetai ekhein tēn dunamin, outhen estai adunaton*," which Hugh Tredennick translates as, "A thing is capable of doing something if there is nothing impossible in its having the actuality of that of which it is said to have the potentiality."[3] The following pages will focus on this particular sentence not only because of its oddness and Agamben's idiosyncratic reading of it, but also because it turns out to be the very point on which Agamben constructs the most important aspect of his theory of potentiality—namely his account of the way potentiality passes (or does not pass) into act or *energeia*.

To begin, let us dwell for a moment on the insistently polemical way in which Agamben presents his own reading as a corrective to the way this crucial sentence has been misinterpreted by virtually all previous translators and commentators. For Agamben, this passage "constitutes, even in its drastic brevity, one of the most extraordinary testaments of [Aristotle's] philosophical genius; and yet it has fallen on deaf ears [*è rimasta senza ascolto*] in the philosophical tradition" (P 183; PP 283).[4] He continues: "Usually this sentence is interpreted as if Aristotle had wanted to say: 'What is possible is that with respect to which nothing is impossible,'" (P 183; PP 284), or in other words, "what is not impossible is possible" (HS 46). Taken as such, the statement is rather clear and seems true enough; in fact, it seems to be more than true: a truism, a tautology. And with regard to this canonical reading of the sentence, Agamben further notes (with obvious approval) that "Heidegger, in his course on Book *Theta* of the *Metaphysics*, had spoken ironically about the 'empty cleverness' of the interpreters who, with a certain 'poorly-disguised feeling of triumph' attribute such a tautology to Aristotle" (*PP* 284).[5]

Agamben, in fact, has good reason to claim that the "modern commentators" tend to read Aristotle as having uttered what appears to be a tautology here (*P* 183; *PP* 285), but it is perhaps unfair to say that he and Heidegger are alone in finding the passage, construed in this tautological way, to be an uncharacteristically banal definition of *dunamis* on Aristotle's part, or that all commentary on this sentence has the tone of having caught Aristotle out. For example, while it is true that Pierre Aubenque notes the "circularity" of this definition of the possible (*dunaton*), W. D. Ross writes: "Considered as a definition of *dunamis*, this statement is evidently circular and therefore worthless. But it does not claim to be a definition. It only amounts to saying that before you can pronounce anything to be possible, you should satisfy yourself that none of its consequences are impossible. It is a criterion for the determination of possibility in doubtful cases."[6] Giovanni Reale, however, rejects Ross's argument on the grounds that even in the move from definition to criterion, "the same difficulties remain, only shifted to a different level," and he suggests that the tautology in the definition is inevitable: "potentiality and act are concepts that cannot be resolved into other, more elementary and originary ones, being themselves originary; they therefore intuit each other immediately, and if they define each other the *idem per idem* cannot be avoided."[7] Their differences notwithstanding, however, in each of these cases the commentators more or less do agree on the "tautological" interpretation of the sentence and attempt to justify or explain its argumentative force, with results that the reader can accept or reject.[8]

Yet, though these readings may represent the most canonical line of interpretation of this passage, they do not constitute the only, and perhaps not even the most subtle, debate over its meaning. And indeed their similar translations do not offer the only way the sentence—and more to the point, the key terms *dunaton*, *dunamis*, and *adunaton*—have been glossed. Before turning to Agamben's own translation and interpretation, it may be helpful to further prepare for his reading by placing it in dialogue with several recent commentaries that, though still differing significantly from

Agamben's, are closer in intention and should throw additional light on the matter.

Dunamis is an ambiguous term in Aristotle. Indeed, he devotes a good deal of discussion to the numerous meanings and uses attached to the term, and thematizes the several types of ambiguity one must account for in any attempt to think clearly about potentiality. For example, in language that closely parallels that of his discussion of the multiple senses of the word "being" in book *Gamma* (1003a 32–34), early in book *Theta* he writes: "We have made it plain elsewhere [i.e., *Delta*, section 12] that 'potentiality' and 'can' have several senses [*legetai pollakhōs*]. All senses which are merely equivocal [*homōnumōs*] may be dismissed" (1046a 4–7).[9] While Aristotle may not always be consistent in maintaining the distinction between specific homonymous and nonhomonymous uses of the term, the point being made at this moment in book *Theta* is that there are two fundamental kinds of ambiguity in the term *dunamis/dunaton*. On the one hand, there is ambiguity due to accidental homonymy, mere ambiguity or equivocation, which Aristotle quickly dismisses as a result of employing loose analogies; and on the other, there is a multiplicity of senses that merit deeper inquiry: the legitimate ways in which *dunamis* is *legetai pollakhōs*.[10] Unlike merely homonymous uses of the term, then, some seemingly disparate senses of *dunamis* and its derivatives (e.g., "can," *dunasthai*) do have some essential relation to one another, for he writes: "But all potentialities that conform to the same type are starting points (*arkhai*), and are called potentialities in reference to one primary kind, which is a starting point of change in another thing or in the thing itself *qua* other" (1046a 8–11). It is here that the terrain of our question really comes into view.

For the purposes of the present discussion, we can limit the senses of the term *dunamis* to two: namely, possibility and capacity.[11] The former indicates something like pure logical possibility, what may possibly take place in the future, an event or state of affairs that is not logically impossible. This is the primary sense in which Tredennick and the "canonical" commentators interpret the terms *dunaton*, *dunamis*, and *adunaton* in the passage at 1047a 24–26, giving us variations of the coherent but banal reading "what is not logically impossible is possible." However, introducing the second sense of *dunamis*—capacity or capability—into the equation allows a distinctly different and perhaps more interesting reading of the passage.

Whereas Tredennick, Aubenque, Ross, and Reale all read this sentence as being fundamentally about the possible, possibility, and the impossible, Terence Irwin in his study *Aristotle's First Principles* argues that in this particular passage only *adunaton* refers to logical impossibility while *dunaton* and *dunamis* refer specifically to capacity. Irwin thus emphasizes the distinction between potentiality as a capability of a thing (as either an agent or patient) and the possibility (or impossibility) of a certain state of affairs. In fact, he takes the intention of 1047a 20–26 precisely to be "to explain the relation of potentiality to possibility" and he translates it thus: "Something is capable to which if there belongs the actuality of that of which it is said to have the potentiality, nothing impossible will be the case."[12] This is to say that something (or someone) is able to realize a potentiality or capability if external conditions do not prevent the exercise of that potentiality, i.e., make its actualization impossible. Or, in other words, I can exercise a capacity if nothing prevents me from doing so. If this is right, then Aristotle's sentence turns out to be making a rather important point not about possibility and impossibility, but about the nature of potentiality as such, for it means that while external conditions of possibility may determine whether I can exercise certain capacities, they do not determine the *existence* of these capacities. This, in turn, implies that potentialities persist even in the absence of the conditions in which they may be realized, or as Irwin writes: "If I am a builder, but I lose all my tools and cannot replace them for a week, then for a week it is impossible for me to build; but since I do not change, I do not lose my potentiality to build."[13] And as Irwin reminds us, the fundamental point of this whole section of the *Metaphysics* is to show (against the Megarian position) that potentialities persist even when they are not in act. Thus, on Irwin's reading the two distinct senses of *dunamis* in this passage are not only acknowledged but are exploited to make the case for the autonomous existence of potentialities as such.

Although, as we will see in a moment, Agamben reads *dunaton, dunamis,* and *adunaton* in this sentence as always referring to the potentiality or capability of a thing to be or to do, and never to purely logical possibility and impossibility, his and Irwin's interpretations share some important common ground. For like Irwin, Agamben argues that Aristotle's point here is not to provide criteria for modal possibility but precisely to establish the persistent *existence* of potentialities that are not—and may never be—actualized. For Irwin, in splitting the two senses of *dunamis*, Aristotle is attempting to show not only that possibility is not identical with potentiality, but also that it is neither necessary nor sufficient for it.[14] *Contra* the Megarian position, for Aristotle potentialities *exist*, regardless of whether the conditions for their actualization exist. Or as Agamben puts it: "There is a form, a presence of that which is not in act, and this privative presence is potentiality" (*PP* 277), and more fully in *Homo Sacer*, "[w]hat Aristotle undertakes to consider in Book *Theta* of the *Metaphysics* is ... not potentiality as a merely logical possibility but rather the effective modes of potentiality's existence" [*HS* 45].[15] And this latter consideration—that is, of the effective modes of potentiality's existence—goes right to the heart of Agamben's first-philosophical project: the affirmation of an existence of potentiality as such, of potentiality as *"the existence of non-Being,* the presence of an absence" (*P* 179).[16]

In *Homo Sacer*, Agamben asserts that there is a "constitutive ambiguity of the Aristotelian theory of *dunamis/energeia*," and "it is never clear, to a reader freed from the prejudices of tradition, whether book *Theta* of the *Metaphysics* in fact gives primacy to actuality or to potentiality" (*HS* 47). Whether or not this is indeed unclear in Aristotle, it nevertheless *is* clear that Agamben wants not only to call this hierarchy into question but also to tilt the balance distinctly toward potentiality. And indeed the aim of this remapping of the relation between *dunamis* and *energeia* seems to extend beyond a mere reequilibration of the two or even an inversion of the hierarchy, but also toward a thinking of potentiality wholly detached from actuality: a thinking of pure potentiality or potentiality as such. Actuality, Agamben suggests, must thus be reinscribed within the domain of potentiality, which *exists* no less than entities and essences, and indeed must be thought of as anterior and superordinate to realized beings and events. And in what is more or less a programmatic description of his own project (which we might thus call a fundamental "dunamology" or "potentiology"), Agamben here calls for "a new and coherent ontology of potentiality ... [one that will replace] the ontology founded on the primacy of actuality and its relation to potentiality" (*HS* 44) and will enable us to truly follow Aristotle's affirmation of the "autonomous existence of potentiality" (*HS* 45).

It is in Agamben's claim for the primacy of potentiality over actuality that the Heideggerian provenance of his argument can be seen most clearly, for it is the structure of Dasein as the being whose essence is potentiality-for-being (*Seinkönnen*), that is, Dasein's unique temporal structure, that provides the framework for thinking potentiality over actuality. As Heidegger writes, for example, in *Basic Problems of Phenomenology*:

> Fundamentally it must be noted that if we define temporality as the original constitution of the Dasein and thus as the origin of the possibility of the understanding of being, then Temporality as origin is necessarily richer and more pregnant than anything that may arise from it. This makes manifest a peculiar circumstance, which is relevant throughout the whole dimension of philosophy, namely, that within the ontological sphere the possible is higher than everything actual.[17]

This claim is rewritten in the following passage from *Being and Time*, where Heidegger, in terms that we can clearly recognize in Agamben's analysis, additionally affirms that potentiality on the existential level must be thought not only as distinct from logical possibility but as the utterly primordial disposition of Dasein:

> The Being-possible which Dasein is existentially in every case, is to be sharply distinguished both from empty logical possibility and from the contingency of something present-at-hand, so far as with the present-at-hand this or that can "come to pass." As a modal category of presence-at-hand, possibility signifies what is *not yet* actual and what is *not at any time* necessary. It characterizes the *merely* possible. Ontologically it is on a lower level than actuality and necessity. On the other hand, possibility as an *existentiale* is the most primordial and ultimate positive way in which Dasein is characterized ontologically.[18]

Viewed within the Aristotelian-Heideggerian-Agambenian framework sketched thus far, actuality must be reinscribed within the domain of potentiality, which *exists* no less than entities and essences, and indeed must be thought of as anterior and superordinate ("richer and more pregnant") to actualities.

But even having said this much about *dunamis* and *energeia*, it is only half of the story, and we still have not arrived at Agamben's reading of the passage from *Metaphysics*. In a sense, we have said what potentiality is not, but what *is* it?

DUNAMIS AND ADUNAMIA

Agamben's attempt to level or reequilibrate—and eventually dissociate—the paired terms *dunamis* and *energeia* is, however, not the most audacious interpretive or philological move in his reading. On a philological level, Agamben's most idiosyncratic interpretation of Aristotle's text is, in truth, not that of *dunamis* at all, but of *dunamis*'s other conjoined twin: *adunamia*. What is *adunamia* (from which is derived the adjective *adunaton*)? The majority of Aristotle's translators and commentators understand the alpha-privative as indicating the negation or opposite of *dunamis* (whether as possibility or as capacity) and thus read *adunamia* as meaning either impossibility or incapacity/impotence. Agamben, however, offers a very different reading: not impossibility or incapacity, but "potentiality not to," "capacity not to," or in his distinctive usage, "impotentiality" (*impotenza*).[19]

The potentiality not to (be or do) is, of course, absolutely essential to any potentiality. Indeed, you cannot have the latter without the former, since without the potentiality not to pass over into act, potentiality would always simply be or immediately lead to actuality; all potentialities would always be realized and the Megarians would be right. The two form an indissoluble pair and cannot be conceived independently of one another, or in Aristotle's words, "there is an impotentiality corresponding to each kind of potentiality" (1019b 20), and "every potentiality is impotentiality of the same and with respect to the same" (1046a 32; qtd. in *HS* 45). To every potentiality there corresponds a potentiality not to, a contrary possibility, which is to say that *adunamia* is the constitutive counterpart to *dunamis*, otherwise *dunamis* would simply be *energeia*: in a very rigorous sense, "all potentiality is impotentiality" (*P* 181; *PP* 280). This, for Agamben, is "the cardinal point on which [Aristotle's] entire theory of *dunamis* turns" (*HS* 45), and when he notes this relation, for example, in *The Coming Community* (among a number of other places), he emphatically tilts the scale on the side of impotentiality, writing that "Of the two modes in which, according to Aristotle, every potentiality is articulated, the decisive one here is that which the philosopher calls 'potentiality not to be' [*dunamis mē einai*] or also impotentiality [*adunamia*]" (*CC* 35, modified). It is crucial to note this intimacy of the bond between potentiality and potentiality-not-to (as well as the "decisiveness" of the latter) if we are to understand Agamben's reading of 1047a 24–26, in which he—and perhaps he alone—interprets *adunaton* precisely as this "potentiality not to" rather than "impossibility."

In his important introduction to *Potentialities*, Daniel Heller-Roazen succinctly glosses Agamben's argument concerning this section of the *Metaphysics*, and in doing so throws a helpful light on Agamben's reading of the passage. For Agamben, what is at stake in this sentence is neither a definition nor a criterion of *dunamis*, but a description of what occurs in the passage from potentiality to act. As Heller-Roazen writes:

> The potential not to be (or do), Agamben suggests, is not effaced in the passage into actuality; on the contrary, actuality is itself nothing other than the full realization of the potential not to be (or do), the point at which, as Aristotle writes, "there will be nothing impotential" [*outhen estai adunaton*]. Far from stating that "what is potential is what is not impotential," Aristotle's definition of potentiality therefore concerns the precise condition in which potentiality realizes itself. (P 17)[20]

But how exactly does Agamben interpret the sentence as a description of the passage from potentiality to act?

What complicates the issue here is that in showing impotentiality to be an essential and equal component of potentiality, Agamben has established that the passage to act cannot be seen simply as the inevitable end result of potentiality's irresistible tendency to realize itself. Being or doing is not founded on the inherent tension of potentiality toward being or doing, but also on a modification or alteration of the equally forceful potentiality not to be or do. In short, *energeia* is not the realization solely of potentiality-to, but a sort of precipitate, the result of a process that happens in the autonomous realm of *dunamis* and *adunamia*, which in itself is relatively indifferent to *energeia*. Since impotentiality is an integral component of (or, better, since it *is*) potentiality, then conceiving of the passage to act is not as simple as saying that *energeia* is a matter of potentiality realizing itself by overcoming the obstacle of *adunamia*, for *energeia* is also, as Heller-Roazen notes, "nothing other that the full realization of the potential not to be (or do)," which in turn must also be an element that in some way persists in that realization.

What we have in Agamben's reading of 1047a 24–26, then, is neither a definition nor a criterion but an account of *what happens* in the passage from potentiality/impotentiality to actuality. That this is the point of Agamben's reading is suggested by the fact that the section of "On Potentiality" in which the discussion of this passage is found is titled "The Act of Impotentiality." In the Italian version of the essay, however, this section bears the title "Nulla sarà di impotente" (There will be nothing impotential), which indeed is the last clause of 1047a 24–26 as Agamben translates it: "What is potential is that for which, if the act of which it is said to have the potential comes about, there will be nothing impotential." (*È potente ciò per il quale, se avviene l'atto di cui è detto avere la potenza, nulla sarà di impotente.*) (P 183; PP 284). Both of those titles—"The Act of Impotentiality" and "Nulla sarà di impotente"—are pertinent to this crucial argument, and we must now focus on each, beginning with the second: "There will be nothing impotential." It would not be an exaggeration to suggest that Agamben's entire argument hinges on his reading of this last phrase of Aristotle's opaque sentence. Unfortunately, however, though much of his argument can be pieced together from chapter I.3 of *Homo Sacer* as well as the Bartleby essay and a few other texts, Agamben's precise reading of Aristotle's key sentence is more or less illegible in the version of "On Potentiality" published in *Potentialities*.

"On Potentiality" was delivered as a lecture in Lisbon in 1987 and appeared in print for the first time in Heller-Roazen's English translation for the landmark 1999 collection *Potentialities*. It appeared more recently, however, in a substantially different form in the Italian analogue to *Potentialities*, titled *La potenza del pensiero* (where it in fact now bears the same title as the collection). Among the changes to the Italian version is the inclusion of a long passage that explains in considerable detail how we are to understand the phrase concerning the *adunaton*, and in turn Agamben's entire doctrine of impotentiality.

On the question of what Aristotle means by the negated *adunaton* in the final clause *outhen estai adunaton*, Agamben makes two central claims. The first, which we have already discussed, is that *adunaton* does not mean "impossible" but rather "potential not to (be or do)," and the second is that we must understand the negation of *adunaton* (*outhen estai*) in a "privative mode" rather than as a "modal" negation.[21] In a long passage not included in the English edition, he writes that, in contrast to the reading of *adunaton* as "impossible,"

The impotentiality of which it is said that in the moment of the act will be nothing cannot be anything but that *adunamia* which, according to

Potenza *and* Différance   95

Aristotle, belongs to every *dunamis*: the potentiality not to (be or do). The correct translation would thus be "What is potential is that for which, if the act of which it is said to have the potential comes about, nothing will be of the potential not to (be or do)." [*È potente ciò per il quale, se avviene l'atto di cui è detto avere la potenza, nulla sarà di potente non (essere o fare).*] But how are we then to understand "nothing will be of the potential not to (be or do)"? How can potentiality neutralize the impotentiality that co-belongs with it?

A passage from *De interpretatione* provides us with some precious indications. With regard to the negation of modal statements, Aristotle distinguishes and, at the same time, puts in relation the problems of potentiality and modal enunciation. While the negation of a modal statement must negate the mode and not the *dictum* (thus the negation of "it is possible for it to be" is "it is not possible for it to be" and the negation of "it is possible for it not to be" is "it is not possible for it not to be"), on the plane of potentiality things are different and negation and affirmation do not exclude one another. "Since that which is potential is not always in act," writes Aristotle, "even the negation belongs to it: indeed, one who is capable of walking can also not walk, and one who can see can not see" (21b 14–16). Thus, as we have seen, in book *Theta* and in *De anima*, the negation of potentiality (or better, its privation) always has the form: "can not" (and never "cannot"). "For this reason it seems that the expressions 'it is possible for it to be' and 'it is possible for it not to be' follow each other, since the same thing can and can not be. Statements of this type are therefore not contradictory. However, 'it is possible for it to be' and 'it is not possible for it to be' never go together" (21b 35–22a 2).

If we call the status of the negation of potentiality "privation," how should we understand in a privative mode the double negation contained in the phrase: "nothing will be of the potential not to (be or do)"? Insofar as it is not contradictory with respect to the potentiality to be, the potentiality not to be must not simply be annulled, but, turning itself on itself, it must assume the form of a potentiality not to not be. The privative negation of "potential not to be" is therefore "potential not to not be" (and not "not potential not to be").

What Aristotle then says is... *If a potentiality not to be originally belongs to every potentiality, one is truly capable [potente] only if, at the moment of the passage to the act, one neither simply annuls one's own potentiality not to, nor leaves it behind with respect to the act, but lets it pass wholly into it as such, that is, is able not to not pass to the act.* (PP 284–85; italics in original)[22]

It thus is clear why Agamben titles this section of the essay "Nulla sarà di impotente," the phrase on which everything hinges; for in this very unusual "privative" interpretation of the negated impotentiality in that final clause of the sentence, Agamben sees an account of what the passage to the act must entail when impotentiality is viewed as co-belonging to potentiality. Impotentiality is not simply annulled or left behind, but is itself also fulfilled, actualized in the act, which means that the act itself is a sort of "privative" self-suspension of the potentiality-not-to, the *impotenza* that in the act turns on itself and suspends itself in the form of a potential not to not be. For Agamben this is the meaning of the clause *outhen estai adunaton*, "there will be nothing impotential."

This is also why, as noted above, the title of this same section in the English version of the essay, "The Act of Impotentiality," is also entirely appropriate. If impotentiality is indeed the "decisive" sense of potentiality, then actuality or *energeia* must decisively be thought of as the fulfillment (the act) of impotentiality. At stake in Agamben's "impotential" reading of this passage is his broader critique of the primacy of actuality in the philosophical tradition, which we already saw an element of in his more or less Heideggerian affirmation of potentiality over actuality. This analysis of the passage of *impotentiality* into act, however, constitutes a second element of this reconceptualization and revaluation of actuality. As suggested at the end of this long passage, for Agamben, in *energeia*, it is not only potentiality but also and above all impotentiality that as such passes wholly over into the act, and if this is the case, then actuality must be seen not as the cancellation of impotentiality and the fulfillment of potentiality, but rather as the precipitate of the self-suspension of impotentiality, which produces the act in the far more obscure, but for Agamben absolutely fundamental, mode of privation or *sterēsis*. It produces the act not in the fashion of a positive ground or even a negative ground, but in a paradoxical structure of a privation that is not a negation.

The identification and description of this peculiar form of relation—which seems to be precisely a form of unrelation—is of utmost importance for Agamben's thought, and as we will see in the next chapter, in *Homo Sacer* this relation between a potentiality-not-to (be or do) and the reality or act that it privatively produces and includes will be given the name "relation of ban" or "relation of exception," and its logic will be elaborated in terms of the paradox of sovereignty, that is, the power that grounds the juridical order by virtue of its ability to suspend the law. One of the fundamental discoveries of *Homo Sacer* (via Schmitt) is that the structure of this potentiality-not-to that withholds itself while privatively giving being—which is also the "essential structure of the metaphysical tradition" (*HS* 8)—is none other than the structure of sovereignty, "the originary structure in which law refers to life and includes it in itself by suspending itself" (*HS* 28, translation modified), "the hidden foundation on which the entire political system rest[s]" (*HS* 9).[23]

It should, however, be acknowledged that unsympathetic readers will no doubt object that Agamben's reading of Aristotle is philologically and/or conceptually incorrect—or at least highly debatable. The question of whether or not his reading of Aristotle is correct *as a reading of Aristotle* will have to be left in suspension here. However, one fundamental and illuminating difference between Aristotle's and Agamben's uses of the concept of potentiality can be affirmed, and by way of this affirmation questions about the accuracy and force of Agamben's interpretation can at least be contextualized.

A consideration of the specific polemical context of the opening sections of book *Theta* of the *Metaphysics* suggests that Aristotle's basic reasons for investigating potentiality and actuality are in truth, and unsurprisingly, quite different from Agamben's. Aristotle develops his inquiry into potentiality in order to answer certain questions about matter and form, about primary substances and subjects. On most accounts (not Agamben's), Aristotle's end point is to valorize actuality over potentiality, as is strongly suggested in *Theta* 9, where he enumerates the various ways actuality precedes potentiality (because it defines the nature of the potentiality, because it chronologically precedes potentiality as a cause, and because it is the end for which each potentiality exists [see 1049b 12—1050a 14]). The reason Aristotle makes his defense of *dunamis*, however, is that he wants to counter the Megarian claim that there are only actualities and no unrealized potentialities (as well as the converse, Protagorean, view that there is at base only pure unformed matter in ceaseless flux). In order to account for the persistence and consistency of subjects through changes, Aristotle wants to be able to describe a potentiality for change that inheres in basically stable subjects. In Charlotte Witt's words: "Aristotle does not find the Megarian position ludicrous because it resembles his own in certain respects. Both Aristotle and the Megarians assign ontological priority to actuality in relation to *dunamis*. Yet, Aristotle *also* wants to maintain, against the Megarians, that powers exist even when they are not active or actualized."[24] If there is no persistent capacity for change in stable subjects (held together as forms)—if there is only changing matter but no enduring form—then there is in truth nothing but flux (or inversely, stasis). The analysis of potentiality as presented in book *Theta*, then, must be read in large part as a specific countermove against the Megarian position, and it stands to reason that the Aristotelian doctrine of hylomorphism as presented within his science of being as being arrives at the claim that actuality (form) is primary to potentiality (matter). Some of the details of that debate have been sketched above, and we must leave it at that—though there is, of course, much more to say about it.

Writing at the "end" rather than the beginning of the Western philosophical tradition, however, Agamben's appropriation and use of Aristotle's concept is determined by a particular and historically specific problematic: namely, the modern project of the critique (as opposed to the establishment) of metaphysics, the science of being as being. Thus, rather than the Megarians and Protagoreans, Agamben's most important interlocutors include not only Heidegger, as mentioned above, but also Derrida and his own distinctive unraveling of the "essential structure[s] of the metaphysical tradition."[25] What is at stake, then, in Agamben's reconceptualization of actuality in terms of potentiality/impotentiality is the status of the present and presence which contemporary philosophy has identified as the fundamental assumption and blind spot of the tradition that is christened with Aristotle's text. In *Homo Sacer*, Agamben says of the "constitutive ambiguity of the Aristotelian theory of *dunamis/energeia*" that "it is not [the result] of a certain indecisiveness or, worse, contradiction in the philosopher's thought but [arises] because potentiality and actuality are simply the two faces of the sovereign self-grounding of Being" (*HS* 47). This sovereign self-grounding is the "24 centuries"-long (*HS* 11) impasse that Agamben's thought seeks to break, for rather than thinking the meaning of being or even the passage from potentiality to actuality, the ultimate task at hand

Potenza *and* Différance   99

is to break the sovereign structure that holds us in ban of being, to "think the existence of potentiality without any relation to Being in the form of actuality" (*HS* 47). Clearly not the project of Aristotle's *Metaphysics*, this is nevertheless about as near as one could get to a concise description of Agamben's own first-philosophical project, which, as mentioned before, he calls a "coherent ontology of potentiality," and which we might also call a "dunamology" or "potentiology." The polemical context in which Agamben is writing is, then, a very different one from Aristotle's, and as I hope to show in the remaining pages of this chapter, Agamben's primary interlocutor on the question of potentiality is not in fact Heidegger, but Derrida.

WRITING AND POTENTIALITY

From infancy to Voice, the point arrives toward the end of the 1980s where potentiality presents itself as the first principle of Agamben's philosophy. What, in these critical years, is the status and nature of Agamben's debate with deconstruction? My thesis is that Agamben not only had kept deconstruction on his horizon, but that the foregoing theory of potentiality is in large part determined by the debate with Derrida. Or to put this in rather stark terms, Agamben's concept of (im)potentiality presents itself as a response and counterconcept to Derrida's central concept of *différance*.

But perhaps that is putting it a bit too bluntly, for in this period the concept of potentiality emerges not simply as an opposing or a polemically antagonistic riposte; in fact, in his 1990 essay on Derrida called "*Pardes*: The Writing of Potentiality," potentiality is presented, as the title suggests, as if it were a coherent development out of Derrida's thought. As we have seen, Agamben had earlier suggested that Derrida had rigorously exposed the limits of the metaphysical system, but conspicuously failed to breach them; in this essay, however, Derridean "writing" appears to offer the possibility of precisely such a breach and opening onto potentiality. Indeed, Agamben here describes Derrida's concept of the "trace" as "nothing other than the most rigorous attempt to reconsider—against the primacy of actuality and form—the Aristotelian paradox of potentiality.... The trace ... is not a form, nor is it the passage from potentiality to actuality; rather, it is a potentiality that is *capable* and that experiences itself " (*P* 216). But if that is the experience of the trace, then how far is Agamben distancing himself from deconstruction? Is he offering a contesting version of the critique of metaphysics, or a further development of the Derridean critique?

Perhaps the best way to begin to understand the status of the debate here is to note that Agamben's reading of the logic of the trace in "*Pardes*" operates by translating the Derridean vocabulary into his own vocabulary of potentiality. In many ways, terminology is the central issue in this essay. Citing, as he does in a number of essays, Deleuze's saying that "terminology is the poetic moment of thought," Agamben suggests that in contemporary philosophy, the "referential character [of philosophical terms] can no longer be understood simply according to the traditional scheme of signification; it now implies a different and decisive experience of language. Terms, indeed, become the place of a genuine *experimentum linguae*" (P 208). While this suspension or alteration of the referential function of philosophical terminology characterizes, for Agamben, the situation of contemporary philosophy in general—an intriguing assertion that would merit further investigation—"Jacques Derrida is the philosopher who has perhaps most radically taken this situation into account" (P 208). More specifically, Agamben asserts that "Deconstruction suspends the terminological character of philosophical vocabulary; rendered inde-terminate, terms seem to float interminably in the ocean of sense" and this "constitutes deconstruction's insuperable contemporaneity" (P 209). The focus of the essay, then, falls on the ambiguous function of Derrida's terminology, and the burden of the argument is to decipher or elucidate the unusual philosophical logic that animates this indeterminate vocabulary.

The prime example from "*Pardes*" is the Derridean term "trace." In Derrida's presentation of the way a given sign (reconceived as the trace) signifies within the differential semiological system, the residue or resonance of the other sign (indeed, all the other signs) is contained within the sign as part of its graphic nature—that is to say that, by virtue of its difference and absence, sign B leaves its trace in sign A, which itself *is* nothing but the trace of the sign B's absence, which in turn is nothing but the trace of other absent signs in an interminable play of traces. In "*Pardes*," however, this Derridean rewriting of the semiological function into the graphic vocabulary of the trace, tracing, etc.—with all of its material metaphorics and with all of the deconstructive consequences that follow from it—is strategically retranslated by Agamben back into what appears to be a more traditional (indeed, classical and medieval) vocabulary of reference, which, he suggests, enables us to break a certain impasse that the rhetoric of the trace creates or reinforces.

Agamben states that there are two distinct types of reference identified in medieval logic—an *intentio prima* and an *intentio secunda*. An *intentio prima* is the rather commonsense version of linguistic reference in which a sign stands for an object or concept; but an *intentio secunda* is, as the name suggests, a sort of second-order reference, a sign that stands not for an object, but for an *intentio prima*. As Agamben puts it: "In the semiotic scheme by which *aliquid stat pro aliquo*, A stands for B, the *intentio* [*secunda*] cannot indicate the first *aliquid* or the second; it must, rather, above all refer to the 'standing for' itself" (P 212). Or in other words, in an *intentio secunda*, which in fact characterizes all signs insofar as they are recognized as signs, "it is necessary that the term signify itself, but *signify itself only insofar as it signifies*" (P 212). Agamben accepts the distinction between these two types of reference or *intentio*, which stands to reason since, as we've seen in the previous pages, self-reference and deixis constitute a distinct and privileged linguistic sphere for him, and one that he feels the semiotic structuralism of the post-Saussurian tradition has overlooked or remained blind to. Certainly for Agamben, Derrida errs in not recognizing the distinctiveness of the two types of reference, since he collapses the *intentio secunda* into an *intentio prima* and thus renders unintelligible—or bars the inquiry into—the nature of *intentio secunda*, the indestructible and persistent self-reference of signs that enables them to be signs, and arrives again at an impasse where deconstruction sets up camp. He writes: "The aporia of Derrrida's terminology is that in it, one *standing for* stands for another *standing for*, without anything like an objective referent constituting itself in its presence. But, accordingly, the very notion of sense (of 'standing for') then enters into a state of crisis. This is the root of the particular terseness of Derrida's terminology" (P 212). Another way to put this is that the grammatological project throws into crisis the semiological model of *intentio prima*, but insofar as Derrida accepts *intentio prima* as the "irreducible character of signification" (P 212), there is no path out of this impasse.

For Agamben, on the other hand, all signs qua signs have something like this second-degree *intentio* in them, but *intentio secunda* is a force or function that cannot be reduced to or identified with the *intentio prima* of A stands for B. These two types of reference or signification are distinct from one another, even though they are inseparable in any sign. *Intentio prima* (semiology) depends on *intentio secunda* for its functioning (insofar as in order to be more than an inert mark or object it must be an effective sign and this effectiveness is the result of the *intentio secunda*), but this *intentio secunda*, in a paradoxical giving-in-the-act-of-withdrawal that we have seen in various modulations so far in these pages, cannot be made to coincide with or even touch the *intentio prima*. As it is put in Frege's paradox, which Agamben glosses here, "*a term cannot refer to something and, at the same time, refer to the fact that it refers to it*" (P 213). Thus, the naming function of the term cannot be named by the term that is its instantiation, and this creates a topological restlessness where the place of the sign is ceaselessly displaced by the inability of the sign to name its own ground. "What is unnameable is *that there are names* ('the play which makes possible nominal effects' [M 26]); what is nameless yet in some way signified is the name itself. This is why the point from which every interpretation of Derrida's terminology must depart . . . is its self-referential structure" (P 211).

It is a powerful account of the Derridean position, and indeed resonates closely with Derrida's own presentation of the question, though Agamben draws conclusions with which Derrida will decidedly not be in agreement. In "Différance," Derrida writes:

> Since the trace is not a presence but the simulacrum of a presence that dislocates itself, displaces itself, refers itself, it properly has no site—erasure belongs to its structure And not only the erasure which must always be able to overtake it (without which it would not be a trace but an indestructible and monumental substance), but also the erasure which constitutes it from the outset as a trace, which situates it as the change of site, and makes it disappear in its appearance, makes it emerge from itself in its production. (M 24)

Self-erasure is constitutive of the trace because, as Frege's paradox indicates, the name cannot name its own naming, or in the topological terms of these passages, the site of the name is unnameable and thus must be figured as an originary erasure of the name. What is indicated and oddly reaffirmed here, then, is the negative ground discussed at some length in the previous chapter. For Agamben, this paradox is at the root of Derrida's problematic, and indeed of his evacuated terminology: "In Derrida, the irreducible character of signification implies the impossibility of the 'extinction of the signifier in the voice' grounding the Western conception of truth. 'Trace' names precisely this inextinguishable instance of *repraesentamen* in every presence, this excess of signification in all sense" (*P* 212).

Another way to illustrate this topological problematic is with Derrida's well-known claim that "*différance* is literally neither a word nor a concept" (*M* 3) (which Agamben invokes on *P* 213), for it, too, is based on the aporias of signification conceived as *intentio prima*. To see this, one must, however, return to the context in which Derrida made this claim and clearly identify his terms "word" and "concept" as the technical polar terms in the Saussurian model of the sign as presented in the *Course*, where they are rendered first as "sound-image" and "concept" and then refined into "signifier" and "signified";[26] Derrida's statement can therefore be glossed as "*différance* is literally neither a signifier nor a signified." The two poles of the sign "arbor," for example, consist in the signifier "arbor" and the concept of *tree* (figured in Saussure's diagram with an image of a tree). Bound together in the split-yet-unified sign, these two elements instantiate the logic of the *intentio prima*, insofar as the signifier "arbor" *stands for* the signified *tree*. Neither of these, however, is a free-standing and independently functioning element because the sound "arbor" without the concept of *tree* would be an "indestructible and monumental substance," inert and without signification, while conversely the concept of *tree* without the signifier "arbor" would be unthinkable and formless; it would be a vague and nebulous shadow in the "indefinite plane of jumbled ideas" that the *Course* illustrates with a sort of fluid wave or cloud.[27] The "linguistic fact" consists precisely in the mysterious conjunction of these two elements in the sign, a nexus without which neither would be much of anything. But this means that the mystery of the linguistic fact consists precisely in this "standing for" which conjoins these two elements, but which neither the word nor the concept would be able to indicate, since they constitutively stand on either side of that conjunction.

Différance, in this context, is neither a word nor a concept because it attempts to catachrestically name this nexus between the two, and Derrida's brilliant neologism inscribes that catachresis within the (non)word itself. *Différance* is not a word because the inaudible orthographical disruption renders it irreducible to the spoken signifier, which, on Derrida's reading of Saussure, is the very essence of the "word." And it is not a concept because as the name for the systematic play of differences that enables the "possibility of conceptuality" (*M* 11), it escapes or always antedates the sphere of conceptuality. This is a well-known argument that has had an ample critical afterlife, but to translate it into the terms Agamben employs in "Pardes," we could say that *différance* is a word that does not *stand for* any "objective referent constituting itself in its presence" but rather stands for the "standing for" itself. It is *intentio secunda*, though conceived in such a way that it is made to adhere to the logic of *intentio prima* (A stands for B), which leads to the inevitable aporia of self-reference. Or as Agamben also puts it: "there can [in Derrida's extreme semiology] be neither an *intentio prima* nor an *intentio secunda*; every intention is always *secundo-prima* or *primo-secunda*, such that in it intentionality always exceeds intent and signification always anticipates and survives the signified" (*P* 212).

For Agamben, the exposure and *insistence* on this structure—or infrastructure—of *différance* and the trace constitutes "the specific achievement of Derrida's thought" (*P* 214), and it separates him from logicians like Russell and Tarski who when faced with similar insights into the aporias of sense sought "expedients [e.g., the theory of types or metalanguage] to avoid the consequences of this radical anonymity of the name" (*P* 214). Instead, Derrida "does not limit himself to reformulating logical paradoxes ... [but rather] makes these paradoxes into the place of an experiment in which the very notion of sense must be transformed and must give way to the concept of trace" (*P* 214). Indeed, Derrida's critique of logocentric metaphysics is part and parcel of his fixing his gaze—at least up to a certain point—squarely on this impasse of sense.

But the decision to set up camp here and dwell at this crossroads is, for Agamben, not the only strategy or option presented by this insight into the aporetic structure of the sign. Indeed, Agamben suggests that the progress from grammatology to deconstruction entails a step backward or a recoiling away from the true insight that Derrida's early grammatological inquiry enabled: "Grammatology was forced to become deconstruction in order to avoid this paradox (or, more precisely, to seek to dwell in it correctly); this is why it renounced any attempt to proceed by decisions about meaning. But in its original intention, grammatology is not a theory of polysemy or a doctrine of the transcendence of meaning; it has as its object ... a radicalization of the problem of self-reference that calls into question and transforms the very concept of meaning grounding Western logic" (*P* 213).

The translation of the problematics of sense into the graphematic language of the trace is, for Agamben, "the specific achievement of Derrida's thought" (P 214). But why, he asks, is the terminology of the language of intention and sense necessarily translated into that of the trace and of writing? "What is the nature of Derrida's *experimentum linguae*, if it must have the form of writing?" (P 214). This is where the proximity between Derrida's thought of writing and Agamben's thought of potentiality is most forcefully presented.

Agamben suggests that there is a sort of historical unconscious at work here, wherein Derrida's evocation of writing is determined by the tradition that originates with Aristotle's doctrines of interpretation and potentiality. In simple terms, Agamben's basic claim about the Derridean graphematic rhetoric is that in writing about writing one is always implicitly writing about potentiality, as if it were potentiality that had long been repressed by graphocentrism rather than writing repressed by logocentrism. Here Agamben rehearses an argument concerning a phrase that can be traced back (through Isidore and Bede) as far as Cassiodorus, who says: "When he wrote *De interpretatione*, Aristotle dipped his pen in thought [*calamum in mente tingebat*]" (P 214; *Institutiones* 2.3.11). This image, and the historical persistence of this "quaint saying,"[28] provide Agamben with a rhetorically forceful—and quasi-historical—strategy for retranslating once again the Derridean terminology of writing into one of linguistic self-reference and ultimately of potentiality. As he writes: "According to this tradition, the work grounding the Western conception of linguistic signification and its link to thought was written 'by dipping a pen in thought.' Thought was able to write about the relation between language and thought and between thought and the world only by referring purely to itself, filling its pen with the ink of its own opacity" (P 214–15). What then, for Agamben, is the opaque ink (thought, *mente*, *nous*) filling the scribe's pen? And what, if anything, in the Aristotelian text could justify or give rise to this long-lived characterization of Aristotle as writing with the ink of *nous*?

This "striking metaphor," Agamben tells us, has its origin in "the famous passage from *De anima* (430a 1) in which Aristotle likens the potential intellect to a writing tablet (*grammateion*) on which nothing is written" (P 215), or more precisely, "its *epitedeiotes*, that is, the light layer of wax covering it, on which the stylus inscribes letters (in the terms of the Latin translators, not a *tabula rasa* but a *rasura tabulae*)" (P 245).[29] In establishing the

106   *First Principles*

provenance and original significance of this metaphor, Agamben can then assert that there is from the beginning an implicit priority of potentiality over writing inscribed, so to speak, within the very metaphor itself, though one that has been obscured by centuries of grammo- and graphocentric translations and interpretation. What Aristotle's *grammateion* (and its *epitedeiotes*) shows us is that "The apothegm on the scribe of nature who dips his pen in thought . . . acquires its proper sense as the image of a *writing of potentiality*. Aristotle could write his logical works . . . only by dipping his pen in *nous*, that is, in pure potentiality" (P 216). And further, in a condensed summary of Aristotle's doctrine of *nous pathetikos*, he writes: "The nature of the [potential or passive] intellect is such that it is pure potentiality (429 a21–22). . . . *Nous* is thus a potentiality that exists as such, and the metaphor of the writing tablet on which nothing is written expresses the way in which a pure potentiality exists" (P 215).

As we saw in the previous sections, the existence of a potentiality as such, indifferent to or independent of any actuality, is the prime object of Agamben's first-philosophical thought, and here one can see the extreme proximity Agamben is suggesting between his potentiology and the early Derrida's thought of the trace ("the most rigorous attempt to reconsider— against the primacy of actuality and form—the Aristotelian paradox of potentiality"). This claim of proximity is based on the idea that there is a potentiological repressed in Derrida's grammatological discourse—or that at least "It is in the context of this writing of the potentiality that no one writes that we must situate Derrrida's concept of the trace and its aporias" (P 216). And once we have placed the thinking of the trace within that broader context, Agamben suggests, we might discover paths other than the one that led from grammatology's "radicalization of the problem of self-reference" to deconstruction's dwelling in exile in the aporias of signification. Indeed, for Agamben (following Aristotle), "this pure potentiality (the *rasum tabulae*) is itself intelligible; it can itself be thought; 'it [the intellect] is intelligible like other intelligibles' (*De anima* 430a 2)" (P 215). Or to be more precise, pure potentiality is intelligible just as other intelligibles are, but only through a fundamentally different mode of intellection that remains to be defined.

Agamben rehearses the above argument concerning the Aristotelian *nous* and *grammateion* in similar, slightly more detailed terms in the essay devoted to Bartleby (see P 243–45), and Melville's foundling scrivener is certainly the most famous scribe in Agamben's dramatis personae. But if Bartleby makes something of a cameo appearance in *"Pardes,"* the essay actually has a different cast of characters, which includes, of course, the rabbis Aher and Akiba (proxies for Derrida and Agamben respectively, as a number of commentators have noted) as well as a certain *"Khōra"* who appears in the essay's closing pages. In *"Pardes,"* Agamben cites passages from Derrida's texts *"Différance," "Positions," "Ousia* and *Grammē,"* and *Of Grammatology*, all of which appeared between 1967 and 1971.[30] And though it is not mentioned explicitly, one might also hear distinct echoes from Derrida's discussion of Freud's "A Note upon the 'Mystic Writing-Pad'" in "Freud and the Scene of Writing" (1966). But I would suggest that the Derrida text Agamben has in mind—and to which he is responding most closely, without naming it—is the 1987 essay *"Khōra."*

Written for a collection of essays in honor of Jean-Pierre Vernant, Derrida's essay examines the moment in the middle of Plato's *Timaeus* in which the enigmatic figure of *"khōra"* appears. I choose to call *khōra* a "figure" rather than a "thing" or "character" here because, as Derrida emphasizes in his essay, it is not clear what—or who—this *khōra* is. Indeed, Derrida exploits the indistinction between personal and impersonal pronouns in French (*il* and *elle* are used for both things and people) to suggest that *"Khōra"* may be taken not only as the name of a thing but also as a personal name, the name of a woman.[31] For our purposes, however, the most important characteristic of the word *"khōra"* in Derrida's analysis is that it also turns out to be the name of a rhetorical figure, or more precisely the name of a figure for the "radical anonymity of the name," a name that is "literally neither a word nor a concept."

In Plato's rather one-sided dialogue, Timaeus relates an intricate cosmology and myth of creation. While the *Timaeus* is an important source for information about Greek science, myth, and mathematics, the salient point of Timaeus's speech for the present discussion is the way his cosmology operates explicitly on the well-known Platonic division between the eternal, unchanging, and insensible Forms or Ideas on the one hand, and the fleeting and sensible world of change on the other. Indeed, in his opening gestures, Timaeus presents this structure quite clearly and in terms that map closely onto those that have been informing the discussion of the present chapter: "[W]e must begin," Timaeus says, "by making the following distinction: What is *that which always is* and has no becoming, and what is *that which becomes* but never is? The former is grasped by understanding, which involves a reasoned account. It is unchanging. The latter is grasped by opinion, which involves unreasoning sense perception" (27d–28a).[32] Thus we have an exposition of the division between the intelligible and the sensible, and this polarity organizes Timaeus's discourse on the creation and structure of the universe for a number of dense pages. At a certain point, however, he pauses and decides to begin again with a new account, one that is "more complex than the earlier one":

> Then we distinguished two kinds, but now we must specify a third, one of a different sort. The earlier two sufficed for our previous account: one was proposed as a model, intelligible and always changeless, a second as an imitation of the model, something that possesses becoming and is visible. We did not distinguish a third kind [*triton genos*] at the time, because we thought that we could make do with the two of them. Now, however, it appears that our account compels us to attempt to illuminate in words a kind that is difficult and vague. What must we suppose it to do and to be? This above all: it is a *receptacle* of all becoming—its wet-nurse, as it were. (48e-49a)

Who or what is this receptacle or wet nurse? And why is she/it so "difficult and vague"? There are two or three things we know about her. Timaeus tells us, for example:

> We must always refer to it by the same term, for it does not depart from its own character in any way. . . . Its nature is to be available for anything to make its impression upon, and it is modified, shaped, and reshaped by the things that enter it. . . . [And] if it is to do so successfully, then it ought to be devoid of any inherent characteristics of its own. (50 c–51a)

> [I]f we speak of it as an invisible and characterless sort of thing, one that receives all things and shares in a most perplexing way in what is intelligible, a thing extremely difficult to comprehend, we shall not be misled. (51b)

And finally, of course, we know its/her name:

> [T]he third type is *khōra*, which exists always and cannot be destroyed. It provides a fixed state for all things that come to be. It is itself

apprehended by a kind of bastard reasoning that does not involve sense perception [or "that involves the absence of perception" (see below)], and it is hardly even an object of conviction. (52a–b)

Given the extremely strange status of *khōra* itself, standing in the space—indeed, constituting the space—between the intelligible and the sensible and thus being an object neither of sense perception nor of intellection ("*khōra* is neither sensible nor intelligible" [*K* 96]), what sort of entity does the term "*khōra*" name? Does it even make sense to call "*khōra*" a name or a word at all? Like its synonym—or pseudonym—"*différance*," "*khōra*" is neither a word nor a concept, and for precisely the same reasons. Derrida writes: "We would never claim to propose the exact word, the *mot juste*, for *khōra*, nor to name it, *itself*, over and above all the turns and detours of rhetoric.... Its name is not an exact word, not a *mot juste*. It is promised to the ineffaceable even if what it names, *khōra*, is not reduced to its name" (93–94). And what is more, this non-naming or nicknaming strategy proves to inform the terminological strategy adopted by Plato himself, or at least Timaeus: "[I]f Timaeus names it as a receptacle (*dekhomenon*) or place (*khōra*), these names do not designate an essence, the stable being of an *eidos*, since *khōra* is neither of the order of the *eidos* nor of the order of mimemes, that is, of images of the *eidos* which come to imprint themselves in it—which thus *is not* and does not belong to the two known or recognized genera of being" (*K* 95). Thus we have the *name* "*khōra*" but there is nothing to which it refers: "There is *khōra* but *the khōra* does not exist" (*K* 97).

Agamben's insistence of the odd status of terms in Derrida finds a close corroboration in passages such as these from "Khōra." Like *différance*, trace, etc., which in Derrida's usage are both names and non-names (or terms that suspend their own naming power), *khōra* is a sort of catachresis, a figurative name for that which has no other name, and which thus does not entail the transport of meaning or sense from one sphere (say, the proper or literal) to another (say, the improper or figurative). It is worth emphasizing how this kind of figure is distinct from metaphor, as Derrida does here, though he does not refer to catachresis by name and only implicitly alludes to his discussion of metaphor and catachresis in "White Mythology" (see especially *M* 245–57). In discussing previous work on the *Timaeus*, particularly that by Albert Rivaud and Luc Brisson, Derrida notes that the commentators "speak tranquilly about metaphors, images, similes. They ask themselves no questions about this tradition of rhetoric which places at their disposal a reserve of concepts which are very useful but which are all built upon this distinction between the sensible and the intelligible, which is precisely what the thought of the *khōra* can no longer get along with" (*K* 92).

This specification is illuminating to the point of clearly stating the basic claim of Derrida's reading of the *Timaeus*. "*Khōra*" splits—or lies between—the two poles of the logic of signification and never lends itself to subsumption into either of them; indeed, *khōra* constitutes the splitting or the spacing itself, which is the very condition of possibility for the proper/literal and the improper/figural and can therefore belong to neither. The term *khōra*, thus, circulates in the text as a mobile marker of an excess over the economy of signification, which in turn puts into question not only the logics of signification and metaphor, but also the logics of all metaphysical binaries and oppositions. In his critique of the commentators' "tranquility" concerning the rhetoric of the text, Derrida specifies that

> it is not a question here of criticizing the use of the words *metaphor, comparison*, or *image*. It is often inevitable.... But there is a point, it seems, where the relevance of this rhetorical code meets a limit and must be questioned as such, must become a theme and cease to be merely operative. It is precisely the point where the concepts of this rhetoric appear to be constructed on the basis of "Platonic" oppositions (intelligible/sensible, being as *eidos*/image, etc.), oppositions from which *khōra* precisely escapes. (*K* 147n1)

As a catachresis, as a "carrying over" that neither begins in the proper/literal nor ends in the improper/figural, but is something like *pure carrying over, Khōra* is thus the breach that undermines and ultimately unravels the text of the *Timaeus*, as well as the entire metaphysical logic that both organizes and arises out of the text. Derrida writes:

> [W]ith these two polarities [i.e., metaphorical sense and proper sense], the thought of the *khōra* would trouble the very order or polarity, of polarity in general, whether dialectical or not. Giving place to oppositions, it would itself not submit to any reversal. And this, which is another consequence, would not be because it would inalterably be *itself*

beyond its name but because in carrying beyond the polarity of sense (metaphorical or proper), it would no longer belong to the horizon of sense, nor to that of meaning as the meaning of being. (*K* 92–93)

Extrinsic to the horizon of sense conceived according to the Platonic polarity between the intelligible and the sensible, *khōra* is also eccentric to the organizing differential structure of the fundamental ontology that appears at the twilight of Western metaphysics, the difference between being and beings, the ontological difference. Thus Derrida's "questions are also addressed to certain decisions of Heidegger and to their very horizon, to what forms the horizon of the question of the meaning of being and of its epochs" (*K* 120). Derrida's "*Khōra*" therefore presents itself as an exemplary deconstructive reading, not only because of the clarity and programmatic nature of his argumentation, but perhaps most of all because of the schematic metaphysical structure of the *Timaeus* itself, which, after all, is part of the Platonic corpus that in large part laid out the structure of Western philosophical thought at its origin and determined its questions up until its twilight.

However, in what appears to be an unclearly motivated (and oddly brusque) aside at the end of the essay, Derrida turns from Plato to Aristotle and states: "[*hulē*—matter—is] a word that Plato never used to qualify *khōra*, let that be said in passing to announce the problem posed by the Aristotelian interpretation of *khōra* as matter" (*K* 127). Since the Aristotelian interpretation of the *khōra* as *hulē* (in *Physics IV*) had not been an issue in the essay, this is a slightly puzzling moment in its penultimate sentence. Very likely Derrida's intention here is to dismiss the possibility that *khōra* can be thought of as a simple, solid material substance, though as he knows, this would not do justice to the Aristotelian concept of *hulē*. Derrida is, nevertheless, right to note that Plato never used the term *hulē* to qualify *khōra*, or in any sense other than the literal one of wood or building material, as indeed it is Aristotle who first employed term *hulē* to mean "matter" in this more abstract sense. However, the fact that Plato never used the term in this way does not lay the issue to rest, and there has been considerable debate over the justness of Aristotle's reading of *khōra* as *hulē*.[33] That debate will not be settled here, but Derrida's aside does serve to throw into relief the differing approaches he and Agamben will take to the question of *khōra*, for in contrast to Derrida, Agamben appeals directly to the Aristotelian elaboration of the Platonic concept and, as Adam Thurschwell rightly notes, "endorses [it] wholeheartedly."[34] What, then, is the position that Agamben endorses here? It is not only that for Aristotle *khōra* is *hulē*, but that *hulē* is *dunamis*.

In *Physics IV*, Aristotle claims that "Plato in the *Timaeus* says that *hulē* and *khōra* are the *same*" (209b), and for his part Agamben affirms that "Aristotle develops his theory of matter as potentiality on the basis of Timaeus's *khōra*" (P 218). While this allusion is left unelaborated in "Pardes," Agamben had in fact dealt with this question in a chapter of *Idea of Prose* titled "The Idea of Matter," where we read:

> The decisive experience, so difficult to talk about, it is claimed, for those who have had one, is not even an experience. It is nothing more than the point at which we touch the limits of language [*linguaggio*]. But what we touch there is obviously not a thing so new and awesome that we lack the words to describe it; it is, rather, matter [*materia*], in the sense in which one says, "the Matter of Britain" or "going into the matter," or even "subject matter index." Whoever touches on his own matter, in this sense, simply finds the words to say. Where language [*linguaggio*] ends, what begins is not the unsayable but the matter of the word [*parola*, also "speech"]. He who has never reached, as in a dream, this wood-like [*lignea*] substance of language [*lingua*], which the ancients called *selva*, remains, even if he keeps silent, a prisoner to representations. (*IP* 37, modified)

Like "the grammarians and the nihilists" of Nagarjuna's parable, those who do not reach the substance of language remain constrained and imprisoned by representation, by a view of language *as* representation. But what, then, is language if it is not representation? And how could one conceive of language in a way that escapes the paradoxes of representation and the sign?

I have modified and glossed this translation in order to bring out certain intricacies that are pertinent to the present discussion and that should make more visible how this passage fits into Agamben's theory of language. The first point to note is the emphasis Agamben places on the differences among (1) *linguaggio* (French: *langage*), language in general or the faculty of language; (2) *parola* (Fr: *parole*), the word or speech; and (3) *lingua* (Fr: *langue*), language or *a* language. The decisive experience Agamben describes in this passage is that in which we "touch the limits of *linguaggio*," the moment when we reach the point where language, or our capacity for speaking, tarries on the edge of speechlessness before we are able to "find the words to say." These words, however, are not particularly extraordinary ones nor are they the names of inexpressible or ineffable things; they are ordinary words like "King Arthur," or "transitor," or "quilts." Agamben suggests that words such as these—and all the others—materialize out of the encounter with the elusive matter of language, which comes to light as such in the moment of difficulty.[35]

The fact that the matter-*hulē* of language is precisely what is at stake in this passage is suggested by the cryptic allusion made with the word *lignea*. *Lignea*, wood-like, is a more or less direct reference to the Platonic and Aristotlelian term *hulē*, which, in its translation from Greek into Latin via Calcidius's fourth-century commentary on the *Timaeus*, was first rendered as "wood" (*silva*) and eventually as "matter" (*materia*).[36] The philosophical importance of these etymological issues, both in the Greek itself and in its translation into Latin, have been commented on elsewhere.[37] Suffice it here to say that in this reference to the wood-like substance of language, Agamben elliptically equates this substance with potentiality itself. For as Aristotle affirms, matter, *hulē*, is "that which exists in virtue of its potentiality" (*Physics* I 9, 192a 27); "what exists potentially is matter" (*Metaphysics* XII 5, 1071a 10); and most forcefully, "matter is potentiality (*On the Soul* II 1, 412a 9). Having already reviewed Agamben's reading of Aristotle's doctrine of potentiality in some detail, the point to make here is that though it is named rather obliquely, "potential" is the exact significance of the word *lignea* in this passage. If this is true, then the argument would be roughly that in experiencing the failure of language (its limit) what we encounter is an index not of an inherent semiological errance or displacement, but of language's matter, which is nothing more substantial than, indeed nothing other than, its anterior and continuing potentiality.

Beyond the "quotation without quotation marks" of Aristotle in this passage, there is also an allusion to another of Agamben's master-thinkers; indeed, this entire passage is something of a gloss on the moment in the lectures on "The Nature of Language" in which Heidegger locates the supremely significant moment (he, too, calls it the "decisive experience") when, in attempting to speak, we find we lack the words to express ourselves.

In this series of three lectures from the late 1950s, Heidegger argues that language makes itself available to us in the very act by which it withdraws from us as such. Everyday language, communicative language, the language that we employ unproblematically and unself-consciously to speak and say things, is only given to us on the condition of language itself, language as such, receding. "Only because in everyday speaking language does *not* bring itself to language but holds back, are we able simply to go ahead and speak a language, and so to deal with something and negotiate something by speaking."[38] That is to say, the language that we know is not language in its most fundamental state; rather, it is simply the effect or residue of language, which conceals itself as such. Everyday spoken language is in fact the concealment of language. And yet even though our spoken language is constituted precisely by language's withdrawal, we are not without access, however fleeting, to this language as such, for it flashes up in the interstices of discourse. "[W]hen does language speak itself as language? Curiously enough, when we cannot find the right word for something that concerns us, carries us away, oppresses us or encourages us. Then we leave unspoken what we have in mind and, without rightly giving it thought, undergo moments in which language itself has distantly and fleetingly touched us with its essential being."[39] And it is precisely toward preparing the way for "an experience with language"—with this language as such—that Heidegger's analysis here and in numerous other pieces of this period is directed.[40]

While Heidegger's lectures on "The Nature of Language" are (just) below the surface of "The Idea of Matter," Agamben draws on them directly and explicitly in "*Experimentum linguae*," the belated introduction to *Infancy and History*, where he writes: "We have this experience [with language] only where we lack names, where speech breaks on our lips. This breaking of speech is [for Heidegger] the 'backward step on the road of thought'" (*IH* 6). While thus acknowledging the Heideggerian provenance of this problematic, Agamben then proceeds to distinguish his thought from Heidegger's in suggesting that the matter that he is attempting to isolate in this decisive experience is more graspable in its content—or at least thinkability—than what Heidegger has in mind in the moment of speechlessness. In distinction (but also in debt) to Heidegger's analysis, Agamben therefore affirms "the possibility that there is an experience of language which is not merely a silence or a deficiency of names, but one whose logic can be indicated, whose site and formula can be designated, at least up to a point" (*IH* 6). The site of this scarcely mapped "transcendental experience" (*IH* 6) corresponds to—or better, occupies the same *space*—as Derrida's *différance*. Indeed, to return to the two contesting essays at hand, matter/(im)potentiality and *différance* share not only the same space but also the same nickname: space, *khōra*.

While there can be no doubt that Agamben's argument concerning *khōra* is firmly grounded in Aristotle's identification of *hulē* with both *khōra* and (im)potentiality, at a critical moment toward the end of "*Pardes*," in a discussion of one's persistent capacity to sense even in the absence of all stimuli, Agamben turns from Aristotle to the greatest of the neo-Platonists, Plotinus, and his question of how it is "possible to conceive of a non-form (*amorphon*) and an indetermination (*aoristia*)?" (P 217).[41] Or, as this question is put in "On Potentiality," "How ... can a sensation exist in the absence of sensation? How can an *aisthēsis* exist in the state of *anesthesia*?" (P 178). What is our feeling of being-able-to-see even when we cannot see anything?[42] For Agamben, such an experience, insofar as it is an experience of a potentiality or capacity in a state of unrealization, brings to sensibility the very impotentiality that is the "cardinal secret" of Aristotle's theory of *dunamis*. "In the dark," Agamben writes, "the eye does not see anything but is, as it were, affected by its own incapacity [*impotenza*] to see; in the same way, perception [in Plotinus's argument] is not the experience of something—a formless being—but rather perception of its own formlessness, the self-affection of potentiality" (P 217). That is to say, what is being perceived or experienced here is the unactualized potentiality to be or to do—(im)potentiality as such. And thus what is "materialized" or made intelligible in this experience is something that must be thought of outside—or between—the logics of the sensible and the intelligible. For Agamben, this is the very space in which Derrida's trace operates: "Between the experience of something and the experience of nothing there lies the experience of one's own passivity. The trace (*tupos, ikhnos*) is from the beginning the name of this self-affection, and what is experienced in this self-affection is the event of matter" (P 217). *Hulē* is the materialization—not the realization—of potentiality as such, the bringing to experience of potentiality, which is neither intelligible nor sensible, but accessible by a third kind of intellection. This event is the experience involved in the *experimentum linguae*.

Even though the logic of the trace and of Derrida's suspended terminology bring to light that event, this nevertheless is not the end point and absolute limit of thought.

> The aporias of self-reference ... do not find their solution here; rather, they are dislocated and (according to the Platonic suggestion) transformed into *euporias*. The name can be named and language can be brought to speech, because self-reference is displaced onto the level of potentiality; what is intended is neither the word as object nor the word insofar as it *actually* denotes a thing but, rather, a pure potentiality to signify (and not to signify), the writing tablet on which nothing is written. (P 217–28)

But if the aporias of self-reference have required—or better, enabled—us to be *displaced* from the level of actuality and ontology onto the level of potentiality, what, then, is the mode of thought by which one could think or perceive this pure potentiality? What is the mode of thought involved in the *experimentum linguae*?

This is the point in "*Pardes*" where Agamben turns to Aristotle's reading of *khōra* as *hulē*:

> In the *Timaeus*, Plato gives us the model of such and experience of matter. *Khōra*, place (or rather nonplace), which is the name he gives to matter, is situated between what cannot be perceived (the Idea, the *anaisthēton*) and what can be perceived (the sensible, perceptible as *aisthēsis*). Neither perceptible nor imperceptible, matter is perceptible *met' anaisthēsias* (a paradoxical formula that must be translated as "*with the absence of perception*").⁴³ *Khōra* is thus the perception of an imperception, the sensation of an *anaisthēsis*, a pure taking-place (in which truly noting takes place other than the place). (P 218)

This paradoxical perception by means of the absence of perception is the "bastard form of reasoning" Timaeus says is required for thinking *khōra*'s "third kind" (*triton genos*), which is neither sensible nor intelligible. It is with a consideration of this bastard form of reasoning that this chapter will end.

As noted earlier, Timaeus interrupts his discourse halfway through to introduce the figure of *khōra* into the schematic polarity of the sensible and the intelligible. *Khōra* spaces the two apart, and gives space to the becoming of the sensible, which is a copy of the ideal form. *Khōra* is the wet nurse or receptacle of all that comes to be, receiving its characteristics while possessing none intrinsically of her own. Thus after proceeding with a myth of

Potenza *and* Différance   117

the origin of the universe and a description of its elements and processes, Timaeus doubles back and recommences from a beginning that is not the same as the first. For Derrida this means that "We will not go back... to first principles or elements of all things (*stoikheia tou pantos*). We must go further onward, take up again everything that we were able to consider hitherto as the origin, go back behind and below [*en decà*] the elementary principles, that is, behind and below the opposition of the paradigm and its copy" (*K* 125). This place that lies further onward from philosophy—certainly further onward from the "philosophy-of-Plato" and "*philosophy* as the Platonic thing" (*K* 119)—is made intelligible by precisely the "bastard reasoning" necessitated by the third type that is *khōra*. But what does "bastard" imply? For Derrida, it implies contamination and impurity, which are valorized because they introduce into philosophy, right at the origin of philosophy, philosophy's other, nonphilosophy. "Let us take things up again from farther back [Timaeus suggests], which can be translated thus: let us go back behind and below the assured discourse of philosophy. . . . We must go back toward a preorigin which deprives us of this assurance and requires at the same time an impure philosophical discourse, threatened, bastard, hybrid. These traits are not negative" (*K* 125–26).

While the significance of this reading remains unelaborated in Derrida's text, Adam Thurschwell has persuasively filled out the implications of this gesture at the end of "*Khōra*." In his incisive commentary, he notes that this contamination of philosophy constitutes a breach in philosophy's pure discourse of truth by the alterity—the relation to the Other—that precedes and antedates philosophy. He writes: "By naming, and then opposing *khōra* to the 'ontologic' of ontology, Derrida asks, *in fine*, what if the truth of the Being of beings were a woman? And not just truth in general, but the truth (and the necessity) of philosophy; and not just 'a' woman in the sense of 'any woman' or 'some woman,' but a particular woman, a singular woman with a name ('*khōra*')? Not, that is, the 'other' (*l'autre*) of philosophy and its binary oppositions, but the personal Other (*l'Altrui*) of Levinasian ethics."[44] Thus, as Thurschwell's commentary makes clear, the bastard reasoning to which Timaeus refers is an impure philosophical thought, or better, a thought of the impurity of philosophy. Insofar as *Khōra* is not only a space (or the giving of place), but also and above all a proper name, the name of a woman, the contamination of philosophy that she marks as she circulates around this text is precisely the ethical relation to the Other.

In addition to clarifying this gesture toward the ethical in Derrida's reading of the *Timaeus*, Thurschwell also suggests that this original hybridity and impurity of philosophy is the source of an anxiety animating Agamben's response to Derrida (though Thurschwell does not quite suggest that Agamben is writing in direct response to this particular essay).[45] For Thurschwell, Agamben "loves philosophy a little too much," and is engaged in a project of saving philosophy from its contamination by the bastard and nonphilosophical ethical Other.[46] However, though he rightly identifies a fundamental split between Derrida's ethical thought and Agamben's on the question of *khōra*, his conclusion that Agamben is attempting to save philosophy from ethics is based on a characterization of Agamben's thought as a fundamental ontology and not as the dunamology that the previous pages of this chapter have sought to clarify.

For Agamben, neither Plato nor Aristotle has in mind some sort of solid substance or "stuff" when they speak of *khōra* or *hulē*. And on this key point Thurschwell's excellent analysis of these texts misses the mark, for he seems to suggest that Agamben ultimately equates *khōra* (in Plato, Aristotle, and Derrida) with actualized, solid "matter" in the vulgar sense.[47] While it is true that Agamben describes Derrida's trace as "truly something like the experience of an intelligible matter" (*P* 218) and that Derrida precisely specifies that "*khōra* is neither sensible nor intelligible" (*K* 96), all of these terms must be qualified and, as it were, suspended. When Derrida says that *khōra* is neither sensible nor intelligible, he means that, like *différance*, it is neither a word nor a concept in the sense discussed above; indeed *khōra* divides and collapses these two constitutive poles of the metaphysical structure of signification, and thus cannot be thought or experienced or named by way of either *aisthēsis* or pure intellection. *Khōra* is the catachrestic breach in the structure that leads it to its internal impasse and self-deconstruction. However, at stake in Agamben's claim about the trace as "intelligible matter" is anything but solid "stuff" or a mode of *aisthēsis* as traditionally understood, and neither does Agamben attribute this understanding of the problem to Derrida. Like Derrida, Agamben locates both *khōra* and *hulē* not on the side of the sensible, but rather precisely between the sensible and the intelligible, and so the mode of "intelligibility" of this "matter" (both in scare quotes) must be sought according to a different, nonmetaphysical logic, a "bastard reasoning." Though profoundly familiar with Agamben's project, Thurschwell does not in this case do justice to what Agamben means by "intelligible matter," and thus too easily repositions Agamben within the metaphysical/ontological project.

What then *does* Agamben think *khōra* is? And what is the bastard reasoning it requires of us? As a continuation of the project of "The Human Voice," wherein the concept of infancy was "staked on the possibility that there is an experience of language which is not merely a silence or a deficiency of names, but one whose logic can be indicated, whose site and formula can be designated, at least up to a point," the thinking of *khōra* here returns to that site and further penetrates into that elusive logic, though armed now with the theoretical apparatus of potentiality-impotentiality. Thus *khōra* is not a catachrestic nickname for this nameless space; rather it is "the perception of an imperception, the sensation of an *anaisthēsis*, a pure taking-place (in which truly nothing takes place other than the place)" (*P* 218). Like the alpha-privative in *adunamia*, the negations in "imperception" and "*anaisthēsis*" here must be understood in a "privative mode," and thus might be more clearly rendered as "the perception of potentiality not to perceive." *Khōra* and matter may indeed be names for the trace, but the trace is "nothing other than the most rigorous attempt to reconsider—against the primacy of actuality and form—the Aristotelian paradox of potentiality" (*P* 216). The trace is the "writing of potentiality" because, in being neither perceptible nor imperceptible, in belonging to the order neither of the sensible nor of the intelligible, in being a "pure taking-place" (*P* 218), it, too, is intelligible only by means of the bastard reasoning of *anaisthēsias*, "the absence of perception." The trace is the writing of potentiality not because it is the realization of a potentiality into an actuality, but because it is the materialization of pure potentiality, a matter that brings the sphere of pure *dunamis-adunamia* to thought. Thus, for Agamben, the "*experimentum linguae* that is at issue in grammatological terminology does not (as a common misunderstanding insists) authorize an interpretive practice directed toward the infinite deconstruction of a text. . . . Rather, it marks the decisive event of matter, and in doing so it opens onto an ethics" (*P* 218–19).

Thurschwell has suggested that Agamben "fails or declines to recognize the ethical (in the Levinasian sense) origin of philosophy's presuppositional drive toward its own (pre)origins," and in precisely locating the site of this debate at the point where the ethical breaches the philosophical, he has rightly identified a major term in this debate.[48] It would, however, be more accurate to say here that Agamben offers a contesting concept of the ethical or of ethos, the experience of which is precisely the stake in the *experimentuim linguae* that is the event of matter. Agamben writes, in terms that directly recall "The Idea of Matter" cited earlier: "Whoever experiences this ethics and, in the end, finds his matter, can then dwell—without being imprisoned—in the paradoxes of self-reference, being capable of not not-writing" (219).

"Thanks to Aher's [Derrida's] obstinate dwelling in the exile of the Shechinah, Rabbi Akiba [Agamben] can enter the Paradise of language and leave unharmed" (219). While Aher and his "interpretive practice directed toward the infinite deconstruction of a text" remain on this side of the metaphysical impasse, his obstinate dwelling there allows Akiba to recognize the trace as "decisive event of matter" and thus pass into the Paradise of language, the ethos that is opened up in the breach between the intelligible and the sensible, into *Khōra*'s arms. Whether one views Agamben's Talmudic allegory as playful or cloying will depend on one's temperament and sympathies, but at the level of argumentation, "*Pardes*" represents the moment when Agamben claims the greatest proximity and compatibility between his and Derrida's projects, a claim that, once unpacked, would seem unlikely to convince many in the Derridean camp. It also represents a moment after which we will see Derrida responding (albeit sparsely) to Agamben's challenge. It is to the texts of this period that we will turn in the second half of this book, beginning with Agamben's most famous and influential text, *Homo Sacer*, in which, after this ambivalent gesture of rapprochement in "*Pardes*," the engagement with Derrida will once again assume a more stridently polemical tone. And in a fashion perfectly consistent with the topographical metaphorics of impasse and exile with which "*Pardes*" ends, this polemic will most strikingly assume the form of two contesting readings of the threshold before the door of the law—the image with which the first chapter of this book began, and to which it will now return.

PART TWO

Strategy without Finality or Means without End

4

SOVEREIGNTY, LAW, AND VIOLENCE

> Justice? —You get justice in the next world, in this world you have the law.
> —WILLIAM GADDIS, *A FROLIC OF HIS OWN*

The second half of this book is dedicated to periods in Agamben's and Derrida's careers that have both been described as turns from their first-philosophical work toward more overtly political theory. In the case of Derrida, this turn is often located at *Specters of Marx* (1993), while for Agamben it is located perhaps at *The Coming Community* (1990), but most certainly by the time he begins his magisterial and, at this writing, ongoing *Homo Sacer* project (1995–). There is, of course, good reason for this view of things. To be sure, Derrida's book on Marx, which will be discussed in chapter 6 below, derives from a lecture delivered at a conference devoted to the question "Whither Marxism?" at the University of California at Riverside in 1993 and thus addresses, more thoroughly and concertedly than he had ever done before, this dominant body of leftist political thought in the immediate wake of the collapse of the Soviet Union in 1991. While Marx and Marxism do not continue to be particularly notable touchstones for Derrida's thinking over the next decade, the concern for overtly—and often topically—political questions nevertheless remains a distinct feature of his work from this last period of his life.

In Agamben's case, *The Coming Community* marks the consolidation of a number of terms and figures from what would, in the years following, become his distinctive political lexicon: "whatever being," "exemplarity," Bartleby, and even "*homo sacer.*" This last term, of course, leads directly to what can be considered Agamben's true entry into political theory, *Homo Sacer: Sovereign Power and Bare Life*, to which we will turn in a moment.

Nevertheless, even in its aphoristic mode, which contrasts so strongly with the systematic presentation of *Homo Sacer*, *The Coming Community* gestures unmistakably toward the nonsovereign, antinomian, messianic politics that Agamben would develop in the 1990s and 2000s, as is clear from one particularly striking passage from a chapter devoted to the Tiananmen Square protests of 1989. Seeing something like the ultimate stakes of political struggle revealed precisely in the lack of concrete demands on the part of the peaceful protesters and the violent reaction on the part of the Chinese authorities, Agamben writes: "*The novelty of the coming politics is that it will no longer be a struggle for the conquest or control of the State, but a struggle between the State and the non-State (humanity), an insurmountable disjunction between whatever singularity and the State organization*" (CC 85).

In both Agamben's and Derrida's cases, then, the seismic shift in continental leftist political thought during and following the Gorbachev period of the Soviet Union and the late Deng Xiaoping period in China appears to have been an impetus for their development of a new political idiom and philosophy, and indeed goes a long way toward accounting for the significant influence of these two non-Marxist thinkers in the sphere of contemporary political theory. Nevertheless, for all of their power as political thinkers, and for all the influence they have had on political thought of the last two decades, the view taken here is that both Derrida and Agamben are always doing first philosophy. This is not to say that their work does not have any bearing on political questions, quite the contrary, but rather that for both thinkers, political questions are always addressed and ultimately referred to the first philosophical "systems" that they outlined earlier in their careers. Another way to say this is that one cannot fully understand their political interventions without understanding their first-philosophical work—that is, the work on which their political thought is firmly grounded.

ABANDONING THE LOGIC OF THE BAN

Though a political valence has been present to some degree in Agamben's work from its earliest period, and indeed emerges as the guiding concern in *The Coming Community*, it is with *Homo Sacer: Sovereign Power and Bare Life* that Agamben's turn toward a properly political philosophy is decisively made. And this decisive turn can be located in the introduction of what can be called Agamben's signal political concepts, most of which are actually present in the book's title: *homo sacer*, sovereignty, bare life. All three of those concepts have attracted a good deal of commentary since the book's publication. Yet there is a still more fundamental concept that, while it has certainly not gone unnoticed, has not received as much attention in discussions either of Agamben's political thought or of biopolitics more generally. That concept is "abandonment" or the "ban." Because it is the fundamental structural element that links the first three concepts together, and thus emerges as a sort of first political-philosophical principle, the logic of the ban must therefore be examined as the groundwork for Agamben's political theory; but it is also of particular relevance to the present discussion because, among all of Agamben's political terms, it is the most evidently "deconstructive" in its derivation and function. As Agamben notes quite unambiguously, he adopts this concept of the ban—or of *abandonment*—from the work of Jean-Luc Nancy. Here is not the place to examine Nancy's own close but complex relation to Derrida, but the, so to speak, deconstructive provenance of what has become a key Agambenian term must be kept in mind as we consider its development and significance in Agamben's thought. Indeed, in keeping with the tenor of Agamben's long engagement with deconstruction, the ban represents both the opening toward and a barrier to the new philosophical and political sphere toward which his thinking is striving. What, then, is the ban, and what is its structure?

Perhaps the best place to start in answering these questions is Nancy's 1981 text "Abandoned Being." Notwithstanding its brevity, Nancy's text is wide-ranging in its reference and often rather elliptical in its argumentation (Agamben calls it "extremely dense" [*HS* 58]). Among the most straightforward portions of this text, however, are the passages that concern the way "abandonment" constitutes the fundamental way in which one is subjected to the law. Rather than by a direct and coercive exertion of force on the part of the law or even by a collective agreement along the lines of the social contract, Nancy argues that the individual becomes subject to the law by virtue of his or her paradoxical *abandonment* by and to the law: "The origin of 'abandonment' is a putting at *bandon*. *Bandon* (*bandum, band, bannen*) is an order, a prescription, a decree, a permission, and the power that holds these freely at its disposal. To *abandon* is to remit, entrust, or turn over to

Sovereignty, Law, and Violence 127

such a sovereign power, and to remit, entrust, or turn over to its *ban*, that is, to its proclaiming, to its convening, and to its sentencing."[1] In a somewhat nuclear form, Nancy has here proposed an oblique definition of sovereignty as Agamben will go on to employ it, since it is precisely by virtue of this ban-relation and the "exceptional" space it creates that the sovereign wields its legal power to proclaim, convene, and sentence. Or to put this another way, the sovereign-juridical order, the law itself, is founded on the obscure and seemingly nonlegal mechanism of abandonment. In a passage that recalls, once again, Kafka's man from the country, Nancy writes:

> Abandonment does not constitute a subpoena to present oneself before this or that court of the law. It is a compulsion to appear absolutely under the law, under the law as such and in its totality. In the same way—it is the same thing—to be *banished* does not amount to coming under a provision of the law, but rather to coming under the entirety of the law. Turned over to the absolute of the law, the banished one is thereby abandoned completely outside its jurisdiction. The law of abandonment requires that the law be applied through its withdrawal. The law of abandonment is the other of the law, which constitutes the law.[2]

From this brief but crucial passage a line could be drawn more or less directly to Agamben's exposition of the "paradox of sovereignty" in the first chapter of *Homo Sacer*. Agamben opens this discussion, however, not with the situation of the abandoned being, whose subjection to the totality of the law is part and parcel of its being abandoned by the law, but rather with the figure of the law itself, embodied in the person of the sovereign. Just as Nancy notes how the abandoned being is subjected to the law by virtue of its exclusion from the sphere of law, so Agamben begins his account of the paradoxical logic of sovereignty by noting that "the sovereign is, at the same time, outside and inside the juridical order" (*HS* 15). This is because, as Carl Schmitt famously argues, the sovereign is by definition "he who decides on the exception," that is to say, decides that the entire juridical order—rights, laws, legal protections and procedures, etc.—is to be suspended in the face of an emergency.[3]

The resulting "state of exception," or *Ausnahmezustand*, thus constitutes, for as long as it lasts, a legal vacuum wherein the statutes of the law are no longer applicable. The sovereign is the being whose juridical supremacy consists precisely in the ability to suspend the law by declaring the state of exception. In this state of sovereign exception, however, the law is not simply effaced and eliminated. Indeed, it persists precisely in the figure of the sovereign, who embodies the juridical order in a virtual, one might say absolute, state; the sovereign is thus both outside and inside the law. In a symmetrical inversion, then, the paradoxical and obscure location of Nancy's abandoned being is seen under this Schmittian lens to be structurally the same as (or at least congruent with) that of the sovereign. Thus the abandoned being and the sovereign appear to occupy a unique ambiguous space that bleeds across the blurred borders of the legal and extralegal spheres. As Thanos Zartaloudis has put it, "the state of exception does not form a limit between an inside and an outside of the law, but rather forms *on* the limit, on the threshold where the two cannot be distinguished."[4] This "zone of indifference" or "zone of indistinction" is the terrain on which the juridical order founds and legitimizes itself, and it is the terrain on which Agamben seeks to undermine and ultimately dismantle the legal sphere itself.

The relation between the sovereign and the subject in the state of exception (that is, between the suspended law and the abandoned being) is what Agamben calls the "*relation of exception*" (HS 18) or, following Nancy, the "*ban*" (HS 28), and it is in the precise logic of this relation that the difference between Agamben's and Nancy's analysis of the foundation of the juridical order emerges. On the one hand, it is worth noting (since this will become an important issue later in this book) that Agamben specifies that the anomic state of exception is not a return to an originary, prejuridical space (such as a Hobbesian or a Rousseauian "state of nature"); it is "not the chaos that precedes order but rather the situation that results from its suspension" (HS 18). On the other hand, and more to the present point, the relation of exception is the fundamental mechanism—what Agamben will later call the *fictio iuris* par excellence—that binds the subject to the legal order, the mechanism by which, in other words, the juridical order is founded and law attains its force and validity. The sovereign exception is more that just a raw exertion of violent or coercive force over an extrajuridical sphere, and it is more than just an expulsion or exclusion of certain beings and actions from the sphere of the law. Indeed, it is precisely a combination of the two, an "inclusive exclusion." Agamben writes: "Here what is outside is included not simply by means of an interdiction or internment, but rather by means of the suspension of the juridical order's validity—by

Sovereignty, Law, and Violence

letting the juridical order, that is, withdraw from the exception and abandon it.... The particular 'force' of law consists in this capacity of law to maintain itself in relation to an exteriority" (*HS* 18). Or as he puts it a few lines later, "What is at issue in the sovereign exception is not so much the control or neutralization of an excess as the creation and definition of the very space in which the juridico-political order can have validity" (*HS* 19).

The sovereign ban is thus an *articulating* device, one that binds, by a very peculiar mechanism, living beings to the law, thus giving the latter validity and "force." This is the key point to make here about Agamben's analysis, for it is what ultimately distinguishes his understanding of law from Derrida's, as we will see in greater detail in the following section. As is the case with the Derridean "differantial" structure, the Agambenian ban entails a minimal but irreducible difference between two elements (say, the law and the living being), but at the point where the two meet—or rather, do not meet—Agamben discerns not an uncontrollable and directionless cross-pollination or contamination or even proliferation of decentered differences, but rather a strategic articulation across an obscure fictional nexus. For Derrida, the purity and autonomy of any given element is a fiction while the truth of that element consists in nothing but the traces it bears of all the others in a given structure; for Agamben, the articulating mechanism of the ban, in which the living being is subjected to the law by means of a sort of obscure *trace* of the law inscribed in the abandoned being's living body, is *itself* the constitutive fiction of the juridical order and the source of its force. In other words, for Agamben the yoking together of the living being and the law by means of a ban-structure is, as in Derrida and Nancy, the foundation of legal force, but this is precisely the fiction to be exposed and neutralized—the "Gordian knot" (*HS* 48) to be severed.

It would be difficult to overstate the importance of the logic of the ban in Agamben's work from *Homo Sacer* on. This logic is, for example, the linchpin of his biopolitical theory, since it is by virtue of the ban-structure that *zōē* is excluded-and-included in the juridico-political body of the human, thus becoming "bare life." Agamben's thesis concerning the historical and theoretical distinction between *bios* and *zōē*, and Derrida's critique of this thesis, will be discussed in more detail in the next chapter, but here it useful to review Agamben's argument with close attention to the way it is grounded in the inclusive-exclusive logic of the ban-structure. Such an example, furthermore, is fortuitous for our present purposes because in the particular mechanism by which *bios* and *zōē* are distinguished and articulated we can see that the "relation" between these two terms in the ban-structure is not the same of the "relation" of difference that defines the infrastructure of *différance*.

As is well known, Agamben argues that, at least as early as the Greeks, Western thought has operated with a dual conception of life. Indeed, he begins the introduction to *Homo Sacer* by noting that "The Greeks had no single term to express what we mean by the word 'life'" and that this terminological division corresponds to the split between two distinct notions of life. *Zōē* names "the simple fact of living common to all living beings," while *bios* names "the form or way of living proper to an individual or a group" (*HS* 1). Within this scission lies, for Agamben, the most fundamental structure of Western politics, for according to his reading (especially of Aristotle), Greek politics itself is constituted by the relegation of *zōē* to the *oikos* as excluded from the *polis*. With the home conceived as the sphere in which "reproduction and the subsistence of life [i.e., *zōē*]" (*HS* 2) occurs, the *polis* is the sphere in which the *bios politikos*, the political life, of the community is carried out. While Agamben suggests that in the Greek city-state this division between biological life and political life functioned more or less smoothly, since Greek politics remained largely indifferent to questions of biological life, later developments in the political history of the West reveal retroactively that the constitutive biopolitical structure of Western politics had lain precisely (albeit obscurely) in this distinction. Drawing on Foucault's analyses in *The History of Sexuality* and elsewhere, he recalls Foucault's argument that "at the threshold of the modern era, natural life begins to be included in the mechanisms and calculations of State power, and politics turns into *biopolitics*" and "the species and the individual as a simple living body become what is at stake in a society's political strategies" (*HS* 3). While it is beyond the scope of the present discussion to follow the issue further, it is worth noting that one difference between Foucault's and Agamben's accounts of biopolitics is that for the latter, biopolitics is not a relatively recent development, but rather the "truth" about Western politics from its beginnings. If anything, for Agamben the modern development of biopolitics is simply the historical fulfillment of the originary biopolitical vocation of the West. However that may be, the *bios-zōē* split is, at least within his biopolitical theory, Agamben's privileged example of the mechanism of the sovereign ban.

In becoming a subject to politics, the human is subject to a, so to speak, vital internal division between two types of life. *Zōē* is excluded from the sphere of political life, and yet this "simple fact of living" is, of course, not eliminated from the *bios politikos*. Rather, within the sphere of politics and law this *zōē* persists in the state of abandonment; it is included in the sphere of politics precisely in the form of its exclusion. This is to say that in attaining the "form" of *bios*, human life necessarily contains an internal rift whereby *zōē* is held in an obscure yet determinative relation of inclusive exclusion in/from *bios*. In becoming political, in becoming juridical, the human being is subjected to this fundamental vital division between *bios* and *zōē*, and indeed for Agamben the very conceptual/lexical division of these two senses of life is the marker of the original sovereign constitution of the political-juridical order. As he writes, "the inclusion of bare life in the political realm constitutes the original—if concealed—nucleus of sovereign power. *It can even be said that the production of a biopolitical body is the original activity of sovereign power*" (HS 6).

This passage furnishes the opportunity to clarify a common misunderstanding concerning *bios*, *zōē*, and bare life in Agamben's biopolitical theory. For Agamben, bare life is not natural, biological life or *zōē*; it is precisely the politicized *zōē* that has been identified and inclusively excluded in the body of the human subjected to sovereign power. Indeed, in Agamben's biopolitical schema, sovereign power can be identified as the power that makes this inclusive exclusion of the *zōē* that thus becomes bare life. *Bare life is therefore the materialization of the relation of ban*, and since the juridical order is founded on the inclusive exclusion of abandonment, bare life is the ultimate stake of politics, the political *prima materia* par excellence. This is life in the sovereign ban, life in the state of sovereign exception, the life of the Roman *homo sacer* who, as Agamben's well-known argument explains, is both excluded from the law's protection and utterly included in the law's power since all violence against him is de facto legal: "It is in this sense that the paradox of sovereignty can take the form 'There is nothing outside the law.' *The originary relation of law to life is not application but Abandonment.* The matchless potentiality of the *nomos*, its originary 'force of law,' is that it holds life in its ban by abandoning it" (HS 29).

While the logic of the inclusive-exclusive ban-structure is central to Agamben's thought in *Homo Sacer*, it is enough to note the similarity between the ban mechanism and the logic of "removal" in Agamben's earlier analysis of the "Voice" to see that his argument concerning sovereignty has a long genealogy in his work. And indeed, in a key passage of *Homo Sacer*, he sketches a conceptual itinerary that will recall the central issue discussed in chapter 2 of this book:

> The link between bare life and politics is the same link that the metaphysical definition of man as "the living being who has language" seeks in the relation between *phōnē* and *logos*.... The living being has *logos* by taking away and conserving its own voice in it, even as it dwells in the *polis* by letting its own bare life be excluded, as an exception, within it. Politics therefore appears as the truly fundamental structure of Western metaphysics insofar as it occupies the threshold on which the relation between the living being and the *logos* is realized. (*HS* 7–8)

In the ban-structure that includes and excludes *zōē* within/without *bios* or political life, Agamben sees a repetition or modulation of the very same structure by which the human Voice is constituted by the primary removal of the animal voice. And just as the analysis of the Voice led Agamben in the following years to the analysis of (im)potentiality, so, too, does Agamben draw on his theory of (im)potentiality for his analysis of the biopolitical/sovereign ban.

As discussed in detail in chapter 3, in his acccount of the way potentiality passes into act Agamben argues that the "cardinal secret" of Aristotle's doctrine is that actuality is as much a product of the potentiality-not-to (*adunamia*) as of the potentiality-to (*dunamis*). In fact, what happens in the passage to act is not so much a realization of that toward which *dunamis* tends, but above all an operation worked on *adunamia*, an operation—a "setting aside"—that is structurally the same as the removal of the voice in the Voice and the inclusive exclusion of the sovereign biopolitical ban. "What is potential," Agamben writes, "can pass over into actuality only at the point at which it sets aside its own potential not to be (its *adunamia*). To set im-potentiality aside is not to destroy it but, on the contrary, to fulfill it, to turn potentiality back upon itself in order to give itself to itself" (*HS* 46). The key point of this analysis in the present context is the way that even in actuality there is what Aristotle calls a "preservation [*sōtēria*, salvation] of what is in potentiality by what is in actuality and what is similar to it" (*De anima* 417b 3–4; qtd. in *HS*: 46). For Agamben, this mechanism is the fundamental structural problematic not only of the Western ontological tradition, but also the Western political and juridical tradition:

> In thus describing the most authentic nature of potentiality, Aristotle actually bequeathed the paradigm of sovereignty to Western philosophy. For the sovereign ban, which applies to the exception in no longer applying, corresponds to the structure of potentiality, which maintains itself in relation to actuality precisely through its ability not to be. Potentiality (in its double appearance as potentiality to and as potentiality not to) is that through which Being founds itself *sovereignly*, which is to say, without anything preceding or determining it (*superiorem non recognoscens*) other than its own ability not to be. (HS 46)

In its, so to speak, juridical guise, (im)potentiality is the sovereign power that gives being in withdrawing itself, gives being as a precipitate of that sovereign withdrawal. At both the ontological level and the juridical level (and, as we will see in the following chapters, at the "anthropogenetic" level and the "chronogenetic" level), the mechanism of the sovereign ban is the fundamental structuring—and more specifically, *articulating*—device that holds the edifice together and gives it validity and force. Agamben's biopolitical theory, which centers on the sovereign separation and articulation of *bios* and *zōē* and the production thereby of bare life, is thus a modulation of his first-philosophical thought, and must be understood as part of the same project. Among other things, this means that Agamben's goal of a pure "potentiology," as described in chapter 3, is equally the goal of his biopolitical theory. In *Homo Sacer*, he asserts the common desideratum of his first-philosophical and biopolitical thought in terms that are notable not only for their clarity but also, especially for the purposes of the present discussion, for their polemical tone:

> [O]ne must think the existence of potentiality without any relation to Being in the form of actuality—not even in the extreme form of the ban and the potentiality not to be, and of actuality as the fulfillment and manifestation of potentiality—and think the existence of potentiality even without any relation to being in the form of the gift of the self and of letting be. This, however, implies nothing less than thinking ontology and politics beyond every figure of relation, beyond even the limit relation that is the sovereign ban. Yet it is this very task that many, today, refuse to assume at any cost. (HS 47)

Although Agamben surely has others in mind here as well, Derrida is undoubtedly the foremost among those "many" who refuse to take on the task of severing the Gordian knot of ontology by thinking beyond the figure of relation.

Indeed, it is at precisely this point of *Homo Sacer* that Agamben introduces (in the chapter "Form of Law") his polemic with Derrida concerning the status of the law in Kafka's parable "Before the Law." I discussed this reading in some detail in the opening pages of this book, but it is worth recalling here how, for Agamben, Derrida's emphasis on the eternal deferral of the man from the country's contact with the law—the *événement qui arrive à ne pas arriver*—is a figure for the irreducible and endless deferral of the *différance* that governs, as absent origin, the text of the law just as it governs all texts. For Agamben, this constitutes an unwarranted hypostasis or absolutization of the "Oedipal" semiological logic of the text of the law and places an injunction on any attempt to surpass or bypass the law's rule, or to see it "from the point of view of the Sphinx." By contrast, on Agamben's rather joyous reading of the tale, the man from the country's lifelong sojourn before the gate of the law is a cunning and patient strategy to have the law finally and definitively neutralized and its dominion over (that is to say its fictional articulation to) extralegal life finally broken, a sign of which Agamben sees in the fact that at the end of the tale the gatekeeper moves to close the gate of the law. In both Agamben's and Derrida's readings of the parable, the state in which the man from the country encounters the law could be described as "state of suspension" or indeed in a "state of exception" insofar as there is no positive content of this law discernable to the man from the country. The man from the country encounters the law "in the extreme form of the ban and the potentiality not to be," which is the mythic origin of the law and the source of its binding force. And yet, for Derrida the countryman fails before the law, while for Agamben he triumphs over it. Do Derrida's and Agamben's readings, then, truly envision two different origins of law, two different "states of exception," and two different strategies for thinking at the limit of the legal order? They do.

MEANS AND ENDS: READING THE "CRITIQUE OF VIOLENCE"

About halfway through the second chapter of *State of Exception*, titled "Force-of-Law," Agamben briefly evokes Derrida's 1989 lecture "Force of

Law: The 'Mystical Foundation of Authority,'" noting that it "in truth was a reading of Benjamin's essay 'Critique of Violence'" (*SE* 37).[5] In this chapter, Agamben does not overtly engage Derrida's essay much beyond suggesting that it fails to pursue the very issue its title raises, namely, the nature of "force of law" (and indeed, as we will see in a moment, Derrida's essay is more interested in the second phrase of its title, the "mystical foundation of authority"). Nevertheless, in the pages surrounding this invocation of Derrida's text, Agamben offers a reading of Benjamin that stands in stark contrast to the one that Derrida proposes.

In his essay, Derrida identifies, and applies pressure on, a number of troubled distinctions that appear to organize Benjamin's text, including, most importantly, those between natural and positive law, and lawmaking and law-preserving violence. But beyond the establishment and analysis of these distinctions, the real aim of "Critique of Violence" is, on Derrida's reading, the identification of an originary violence, a grounding or founding violence that would serve to structure all of the historical modulations of violence that are in turn evoked and analyzed in the essay. This is to say that for Derrida, the "Critique of Violence" is fundamentally oriented toward finding an originary violence that stands in a prehistoric or ahistoric space undergirding juridical violence's historical modulations and manifestations. Derrida's reading, then, which the following pages will examine, fits cleanly into a general deconstructive strategy, and so shows itself to be a perfectly programmatic (which is not to say dull or without surprises) "exercise in deconstructive reading" (*FL* 264).

Agamben's reading is programmatic as well. For Agamben, what is at stake in Benjamin's "Critique of Violence" is not the origin of violence, but the affirmation of a violence that exists outside of a juridical framework. Like Derrida, Agamben traces a series of oppositions in the essay, most importantly that between lawmaking and law-preserving violence, but rather than reading them as deconstructable binaries that contaminate each other, he examines the strategic ways in which the modalities of violence are articulated together and how Benjamin, in exposing the jagged seam, or better, the noncoincidence of these spheres of violence, reveals a vacuum at the center of every articulation and a sovereign-exceptional decision that every time attempts to hold them together at this fictitious juridical nexus point.

This difference in perspective reveals how the goals of their readings differ fundamentally. For Derrida, the unstoppable oscillation and contamination between the polar terms holds the binary system in an differantial topology that can never settle on a final or originary ground (except the nonground of ethical alterity and the responsibility to the Other). This oscillation also reveals the concept of origin itself to be embedded in a logic of iterability. For Agamben, by contrast, the point of Benjamin's analysis—and of course, of his own effort—is to definitively separate what has been forcibly (sovereignly) articulated together in order to open a new nonjuridical space for human action. This postjuridical space is the sphere of what Agamben calls "use" or "play," which I will examine in the conclusion of this book.

In "Force of Law" Derrida describes his reading of "Critique of Violence" as a programmatically deconstructive one, but perhaps more crucial than this is his assertion that Benjamin's *own* essay "lends itself" (*FL* 264) to a deconstructive reading. That is to say, the deconstructive reading strategy that Derrida adopts here is presented as the immanent logic of Benjamin's text itself, as if the intention of the essay's rhetorical strategies and structures were to deconstructively undermine their own overt architecture. As Derrida puts it: "This deconstruction does not *apply itself* to such a text. . . . It is in some way the operation or rather the very experience that ["Critique of Violence"], it seems to me, first does itself, by itself, on itself" (*FL* 264). Even though deconstruction is the case with every text, the "Critique of Violence" proves to be "exemplary" (*FL* 264) in this way.

Of the key distinctions that Derrida identifies as structuring the essay, we will focus here on two. The first is that between natural law and positive law. The second, which in some ways derives from the first, is that between what Benjamin calls "lawmaking violence" (*die rechtsetzende Gewalt*) and "law-preserving violence" (*die rechtserhaltende Gewalt*). Let us review the two in order.

(1) *Natural and positive law.* The ostensible aim of Benjamin's essay is a critique of violence *in itself.* That is to say, an evaluation or anatomy of violence not as a means to an end but as a distinct phenomenon in its own right. Benjamin notes that the reason such a critique of violence is so difficult is that the two dominant schools of legal thought—natural law and

Sovereignty, Law, and Violence 137

positive law—view the question of violence exactly as one of means and ends, and thus make it all but impossible to raise the question of the nature of violence *itself*. A quick gloss on natural and positive law may help to clarify Benjamin's point here.

For a concise definition of natural law, we can turn to a late text by Leo Stauss: "By 'natural law' is meant a law that determines what is right and wrong and that has power or is valid by nature, inherently, hence everywhere and always."[6] This definition is especially useful to us here because it identifies the two questions at issue in the present discussion, namely, the law's relation to justice ("what is right and wrong") and the law's force or violence (*Gewalt*) ("has power or is valid"). In natural law, the justice of a law is inherent to the law and is part and parcel of its force. There is no substantial scission, at least theoretically, between a law's rightness and its applicability or enforceability; the violence of the law is the law's "right" because it is its natural or divinely granted power to enforce itself. As Benjamin puts it, natural law "perceives in the use of violent means to just ends no greater problem than a man sees in his 'right' to move his body in the direction of a desired goal."[7] As a result of this assumption, questions of natural law are not centered around the problem of its *Gewalt* as the means of achieving its ends, but rather around the ends themselves, whether the ends of a given law are just and in keeping with the precepts of the natural law, the discovery of which is the task of legal reasoning.[8]

On the other end of the theoretical spectrum, positive law is a fundamentally historicizing and constructivist mode of thinking about law. For positive law theorists, the law is a formal construct, the result of historically contingent and conventional legislative decisions and agreements. The task of legal thought in positive law is the study of the historical evolution and formal consistency of certain legal and constitutional orders, not the discovery of eternal and natural principles of justice that the juridical order should model. What this means is that the question of *justice* is not a properly legal, but rather political and moral, question, and that legal thought proper has very little to do with the question of justice in the natural law sense. In the words of Hans Kelsen, whose work in the first half of the twentieth century contributed greatly to the ascendancy of positive law in our current legal culture: "Law and justice are two different concepts. Law as distinguished from justice is positive law."[9] And yet, the concept of justice is not totally absent from positive law, although the form it takes is substantially different from the one found in natural law. For the question of justice enters into positive law not at the level of the *ends* of law (i.e., whether the ends of a given set of laws are just) but precisely at the level of the law's application, its means, that is to say, the legal application of violent legal force. To mark this difference, Kelsen uses the term "legality" rather than "justice": "Justice, in the sense of legality, is a quality which relates not to the content of a positive order [i.e., the statutes themselves and the ends they aim to achieve], but to its application.... 'Justice' means that maintenance of a positive order by conscientious application of it."[10] This is to say that in positive law, justice/legality is a question of how the *Gewalt* of law is employed, and whether this application is a just (i.e., consistent, fair, unbiased) or unjust (i.e., capricious, arbitrary, motivated) one. Thus, in natural law, the law's *Gewalt* is an unproblematic and inherently just datum of the law, whose ends are the object of legal critique; in positive law, conversely, the application of the law's *Gewalt* is the unique locus of the question of justice or legality within a formal legal order, which in itself is subtracted from the realm of justice. Benjamin summarizes the difference between these two schools in precisely these terms: "If justice is the criterion of ends, legality is that of means.... Natural law attempts, by the justness of the ends, to 'justify' the means, positive law to 'guarantee' the justness of the ends through the justification of the means."[11]

The implications of these divergent schools of thought are, of course, vast, but what these two camps of legal theory share, and what is relevant for the present discussion, is an inability to think of violence as a means without regard to an end, that is to say, to think about *Gewalt* as such. In both cases, the question of violence is framed by the relation between violence and the ends of law, whether it be a natural attribute of the law in its essence or the object of scrutiny in the modalities of the law's application. As Benjamin puts it, "Notwithstanding [their] antithesis ... both schools meet in their common basic dogma: just ends can be attained by justified means, justified means used for just ends."[12] And as Derrida puts it, "the two traditions share the same dogmatic presupposition, namely, that just ends can be attained by just means" (*FL* 266). This shared presupposition, that there is some sort fundamental nexus between law and *Gewalt*, is what makes the object of Benjamin's study—an extrajuridical violence or a violence understood *as such*—so threatening to both camps. In this regard, Benjamin suggests that "the law's interest in a monopoly of violence vis-à-vis individuals is explained not by the intention of preserving legal ends but, rather, by the intention of preserving the law itself; that violence, when not in the hands of the law, threatens it not by the ends that it may pursue but by its mere existence outside the law."[13] Benjamin had opened this essay by asserting that the "task of a critique of violence can be summarized as that of expounding its relation to law and justice," and it is now clear that the essential point about that "relation" is precisely that it *is* a relation and not an identification, that contrary to the assumptions of both the natural and the positive law traditions, *Gewalt* can be separated from the law and, in this sense, conceived as a "pure means"—a pure violence.[14]

(2) *"Lawmaking" and "law-preserving" violence.* Both of the great schools of legal thought, then, show themselves to be in solidarity concerning this question of an extrajuridical or "pure" violence. As important as this assertion is for his analysis, Benjamin does not continue his inquiry in this precise direction, but rather redirects it toward a derivative or perhaps analogous problem that will organize the bulk of his essay. Indeed, upon the presupposed exclusion of an extrajuridical violence is constructed the additional and, as Derrida and Agamben will go on to show, extremely fraught distinction of lawmaking and law-preserving *Gewalt*. For the legal tradition, Benjamin writes, "All violence as a means [i.e., to an end] is either lawmaking or law-preserving," which is to say that it sees all *Gewalt* as contained within the legal order under one of these two forms.[15] The latter category refers to the application of existing law, and is relatively unproblematic; the law exerts *Gewalt* in the application or enforcement of its own statutes, and in doing so acts to preserve its own order. But this modality of legal force is relevant only to the enforcement of an established set of laws. What about the violence that is exerted in the establishment of that order itself? It is with regard to this question that legal thought pushes up against the possibility of an extralegal violence and attempts to incorporate it into a juridical sphere under the concept of lawmaking violence. This is where Benjamin—and after him Derrida and Agamben—will direct their readings and our attention.

What is the nature of a violence—for example, revolutionary violence—that overturns one juridical order and establishes a new one? This is not an easy question to answer. Does it belong to the established and dying legal regime, which it is in the process of destroying, or to the nascent future one, which does not yet exist in the moment of the revolutionary action?

From the perspective of the dying legal order, this violence would be a criminal act that it would obviously seek to quash and punish, thus preserving the integrity and dominion of its rule. From the perspective of the not-yet-existent legal order, this violence would at the very least present a difficult temporal problem, since insofar as this violence itself gives rise to the new order, it cannot easily be seen as deriving from and existing within that order. The contradictory and ambiguous nature of these categories is seen in two examples that Benjamin discusses at some length, the general strike and the police. These two examples, indeed, seem chosen to show the difficulty of keeping the two forms of legal violence apart, insofar as they represent a sort of diametrically opposed pair of actions that lie at the outer limit of the juridical order, where the consistency and omnicomprehensiveness of the law appear to break down.[16] Another way of saying this is that both the strike—and in particular the workers' guaranteed legal right to strike—and the police are legal phenomena that extend just beyond the legal order and touch on a violence that is extrajuridical.

Take the case of the strike. Benjamin, following Georges Sorel, notes the difference between a "political strike" and a "proletarian general strike" or "revolutionary general strike."[17] In the former case, the strike is conducted within the general framework of the constitutional and legal order, and the antagonists involved—say, a factory and the workers—are equally subjected to the legal strictures and remedies provided by the legal state, which presides over the dispute and can, with law-preserving violence, intervene if necessary. State power, in other words, is neither targeted nor threatened by the event of the "political strike." However, as Benjamin writes, "In contrast to this political general strike . . . the proletarian general strike sets itself the sole task of destroying state power."[18] Commenting on this danger to the state, Derrida writes: "The general strike thus provides a valuable guiding thread, since it exercises the conceded right to contest the order of existing law and to create a revolutionary situation in which the task will be to found a new law, if not always . . . a new state" (*FL* 269). In granting the right to strike, the constitutional order places itself in an ambivalent position, having provided for a violent action that can, under rather easily imaginable conditions, end up becoming an extrajuridical violence that threatens that order's very existence. This troubling extremity of the constitutional order is paired, in an almost symmetrical fashion, with Benjamin's example of the police.

Unlike the extrajuridical violence of the revolutionary general strike, which arrives from outside of the law and attacks it, modern policing represents an extrajuridical violence that seems to come from within (and is exerted by) the legal order. For Benjamin, the ambiguity of police violence is that "in this authority the separation of lawmaking and law-preserving violence is suspended.... It is lawmaking, because its characteristic function is not the promulgation of laws but the assertion of legal claims for any decree, and law-preserving, because it is at the disposal of these ends."[19] That is to say, insofar as the police most characteristically work toward the ends of "decrees" (Benjamin does not say "laws" here), which it itself has asserted the legal claims for, both the lawmaking and law-preserving function are collapsed into each other. The police "intervene 'for security reasons' in countless cases where no clear legal situation exists" and thus "[i]ts power is formless, like its nowhere-tangible, all-pervasive, ghostly presence in the life of civilized states."[20] The pertinent example here of just such a police intervention "for security reasons" would, of course, be the case of a political strike escalating and transforming itself into a revolutionary strike, an emergency situation in which the state calls upon an ambivalently legal violence to meet an equally, if symmetrically opposite, legally uncertain violence.

The legal gray zone imagined here—roughly speaking, the state of exception—is particularly relevant for Agamben's analysis, about which more in a moment. Let us, though, return to the problem of the relation of lawmaking (or revolutionary) violence and its noncoincidence with the legal order that it establishes, for this is where Derrida will focus his lens. "All revolutionary situations," he writes, "all revolutionary discourses, on the left or on the right (and from 1921, in Germany, there were many of these that resembled each other in a troubling way, Benjamin often finding himself between the two) justify the recourse to violence by alleging the founding, in progress or to come, of a new law, of a new state" (*FL* 269). Keeping in mind that what is at stake here is less the justification—in good or bad faith—of revolutionary actors' actions than the way the legal tradition conceives of violence exclusively as lawmaking or law-preserving violence (and excludes the possibility of another *Gewalt* over which it has no jurisdiction), we note that Derrida focuses on the temporal problematic involved in defining revolutionary violence as "lawmaking." And this, in turn, quickly becomes a question of the temporal status of the event that we might call the *origin of law*.

What is the temporality of the act of "lawmaking *Gewalt*," which takes place when the law-in-the making is only an uncertain future possibility (for, of course, not all revolutions or lawmaking efforts are successful and lead to actual new states or laws)? Such lawmaking violence can only be conceived as such when the future consequential event will have taken place. That is, only from the retrospective point of view of the future will such a violence have been lawmaking. Derrida identifies the temporal problem in a way that immediately incorporates the discussion into his own canonical conceptual terms: "In these situations said to found law or state, the grammatical category of the future anterior all too well resembles a modification of the present to describe the violence in progress. It consists, precisely, in feigning the presence or simple modalization of presence. Those who say 'our time,' while thinking 'our present' in light of a future anterior present do not know very well, by definition, what they are saying. It is precisely in this nonknowledge that the eventness of the event consists, what one naively calls its presence" (*FL* 269).

This is the point Derrida presses here, showing that the grounds for the intelligibility (which is to say, legality) of this violence lie nowhere in any supposed presence or present of the violent act. This displacement of intelligibility from any "present" in which the act takes place is what makes such violence always, so to speak, "senseless," which is part of what makes it so troubling; it is also what makes this lawmaking violence "mystical." Derrida writes: "These moments, supposing we can isolate them, are terrifying moments because of the sufferings, the crimes, the tortures that rarely fail to accompany them, no doubt, but just as much because they are in themselves, and in their very violence, uninterpretable or undecipherable. This is what I am calling the 'mystical'" (*FL* 269). Inherent in the ambiguous unfolding of this violence is the displacement toward a future that will render it intelligible, which is to say that the essence of this founding act of violence is always absent and displaced into fundamentally unknowable future, making this pure futurity the paradoxical (non)ground on which the originary foundation of the juridical order takes place. For this reason, "Only the 'to-come' [*avenir*] will produce the intelligibility or the interpretability of this law" (*FL* 270).

On the one hand, the temporal ungroundedness of this action or act is a figure for what Derrida above called the "eventness of the event," and his argument gestures toward the discussion of temporality in such texts as *Specters of Marx*, to which we will turn in chapter 6. But on the other, and most relevantly to the present discussion, Derrida here evokes, in terms that anticipate Agamben's analysis of the state of exception, the way this revolutionary lawmaking violence founds the law precisely by suspending it:

> As Benjamin presents it, this violence is certainly legible, even intelligible since it is not alien to law, no more than *polemos* or *eris* are alien to all the forms and signification of *dikē*. But it is, in law, what suspends law. It interrupts the established law to found another. This moment of suspense, this *epokhē*, this founding or revolutionary moment of law is, in law, an instance of nonlaw [*dans le droit une instance de non-droit*]. (FL 269)

The "foundation of the law" takes place not in the presence of the law, but rather in its absence or irreducible negativity; it is "suspended in the void or over the abyss" (FL 270), and this radically separates this foundation in its origin from any temporal or chronological continuity and from any "referential" appeal to the past or present constitutional order on the model of constative language use. Instead, Derrida suggests, the logic that this act of revolutionary *Gewalt* resembles—or instantiates—is that of the performative enunciation in its most extreme and pure form. Continuing the analogy between a legal actor and a speaker, the former "using" the law (in the sense of the constitutional text) in the way that the speaker "uses" language (in the sense of *langue* or *lingua*), Derrida writes that in the situation of revolutionary violence, "The supposed subject of this pure performative would no longer be before the law [*devant la loi*], or rather he would be before a law [*loi*] still undetermined, before the law as before a law still nonexisting, a law still ahead, still having to and yet to come [*une loi encore devant et devant venir*]" (FL 270).

As we have seen in the opening chapter of this book this is the sense Derrida gives to Kafka's parable "Before the Law." There we saw that in Derrida's reading of Kafka's story, the upshot of the gatekeeper's endless deferral is that an event "happens not to happen [*arrive à ne pas arriver*]," that the man from the country, who wants to touch the law as if it were a graspable and present "thing," is denied such an experience because there is ultimately no origin or essence of the law to be grasped. At most what there is of the law is there to be read as a text. Recalling at this point his own earlier essay "Before the Law," Derrida writes that Benjamin's figure of this temporally ungraspable lawmaking moment reproduces the aporias dramatized in Kafka's text:

> [T]he being "before the law" that Kafka talks about resembles this situation, both ordinary and terrible, of the man who cannot manage to see or above all to touch, to catch up with the law [*loi*]: it is transcendent in the very measure that it is he who must found it, as yet-to-come [*comme à venir*], in violence. One "touches" here without touching on this extraordinary paradox: the inaccessible transcendence of the law [*loi*], before which and prior to which "man" stands fast, only appears infinitely transcendent and thus theological to the extent that, nearest to him, it depends only on him, on the performative act by which he institutes it.... The law [*loi*] is transcendent and theological, and so always to come, always promised, because it is immanent, finite, and thus already past. Every "subject" is caught up in this aporetic structure in advance. (*FL* 270)

This temporally aporetic structure—the performative structure of the "promise"—is the originary ground on which the law is established, and thus the always renewed and reaffirmed ground upon which and "before" which it exerts law-preserving violence.

In a characteristic gesture, then, Derrida forces the phrase "before the law" to manifest its two incompatible senses. Both standing in front of the law to which it is bound, and existing before there is yet the law, the subject before the law (say, the man from the country) represents an aporetic collapse of both forms of legal *Gewalt*. This co-implication of the two forms of legal *Gewalt*, which Benjamin attempts rigorously to separate, provides Derrida a further foothold in his reading—against the grain—of Benjamin's text, a reading that will ultimately assert that any concept of the origin or essence of law will collapse as it succumbs to the logic of iterability.

The violence of the established law (law-preserving violence) stands upon the violence of the founding of law (lawmaking violence) as its source and legitimation. For Derrida, Benjamin structures his critique of violence on the opposition—or at least distinction—between lawmaking and law-preserving violence that is here made to tremble as the undecidability and ambiguity of the former calls into question the integrity of the latter. Earlier we had seen how Derrida problematizes the definition of lawmaking violence on the basis of its temporal noncoincidence with the legal order; here, in a second gesture, he places that damaged concept of lawmaking violence into relation to law-preserving violence, which implicitly depends on it for its conceptual coherence. In doing so, Derrida is, in a characteristically ambiguous gesture, reading both with and against Benjamin's text, to which, as noted above, he seems to want to grant some awareness of its own self-immolating structures. Though Derrida's reading is expansive and often elusive, its nucleus is summarized in a passage that merits being quoted at length:

> [B]eyond Benjamin's explicit purpose, I shall propose the interpretation according to which the very violence of the foundation or *positing of law* (*rechtsetzende Gewalt*) must envelop the violence of the *preservation of law* (*rechtserhaltende Gewalt*) and cannot break with it. It belongs to the structure of fundamental violence in that it calls for the repetition of itself and founds what ought to be preserved, preservable, promised to heritage and to tradition, to partaking [*partage*]. A foundation is a promise. Every positing (*Setzung*) permits and promises, posits ahead [*permet et pro-met*]; it posits by setting and promising [*en mettant et en promettant*]. And even if a promise is not kept in fact, iterability inscribes the promise as guard in the most irruptive instant of foundation. Thus it inscribes the possibility of repetition at the heart of the originary. Better, or worse, it is inscribed in this law [*loi*] of iterability; it stands under its law or before its law [*sous sa loi ou devant sa loi*]. Consequently [*du coup*], there is no more pure foundation or pure position of law, and so a pure founding violence, than there is a purely preserving violence. Positing is already iterability, a call for self-preserving repetition. Preservation in its turn refounds, so that it can preserve what it claims to found. Thus there can be no rigorous opposition between positing and preserving, only what I will call (and Benjamin does not name it) a *differential contamination* between the two, with all the paradoxes that this may lead to.... Deconstruction is also the thought *of* this differential contamination—and the thought *taken by* the necessity of this contamination. (FL 272)

Several points come to the fore in this passage. First, the oscillation between lawmaking and law-preserving violence works a fatal destabilization of the originariness of lawmaking violence, and thus calls into question any appeal to a presence or essence of the "Law." This lack of presence is, in Derrida's reading of Kafka's parable, what the man from the country discovers. The positing of law, which Derrida likens by virtue of its performativity and futurity to the promise, posits itself ahead ["*pro-met*"] and thus affirms the necessity of a future repetition of itself in any juridical act of law-preserving violence. This in turn leads to Derrida's second point, that before the law there is another, more originary and more fundamental law, the "law of iterability," which is itself irreducible to any originary presence. Thus the mutual differential contamination of Benjamin's rigorously separated organizing structures reduces the entire architecture of the text to iterability, repetition, and infinite regress. As Derrida writes, "What threatens the rigor of the distinction between the two types of violence—and which Benjamin does not say, excluding it or misrecognizing it—is, at bottom, the paradox of iterability. Iterability makes it so that the origin must [*doit*] repeat itself originarily, must alter itself to count *as origin*, that is to say, to preserve itself" (*FL* 277–78). Here Derrida suggests that Benjamin excludes or misrecognizes this "ruinous" (273) contamination; elsewhere he implies that Benjamin seeks to repress it and for this reason we can "witness an ambiguous and laborious movement on Benjamin's part to save at any cost a distinction or a correlation without which his whole project could collapse" (*FL* 274). And yet, as noted above, at other points in the essay he suggests instead that this uncontrollable movement of the rhetorical structures of the text is in fact Benjamin's intended strategy. Clues to this intention are scattered about the text, and they are always oblique. One thing that they tend to have in common, though, is that they employ the vocabulary of *spectrality*.

One way of seeing Derrida's essay is as a reading of the rhetoric of spectrality as it traverses, and, so to speak, *haunts* Benjamin's text. As he notes: "this text tells a ghost story, a history of ghosts" (*FL* 278), and these ghosts always appear at this ambiguous nexus point of the two types of violence, especially as it is embodied in the figure of the police. See, for example, this selection of passages from Derrida's essay:

- [W]hat today testifies to this in a manner that is even more "spectral" (*gespenstische*) by mixing the two forms of violence (preserving and founding) is the modern institution of the police. This is a mixture of

Sovereignty, Law, and Violence 147

two heterogeneous violences, "in a kind of spectral mixture (*in einer gleichsam gespenstischen Vermischung*)," as if one violence haunted the other. (*FL* 276)

- Such discourse [of a new critique of violence] Benjamin would like either to found or to preserve, but in all purity he can do neither. At most, he can sign it as a spectral event. Text and signature are specters, and Benjamin knows it. (*FL* 277)

- [T]he police [is an] index of a ghostly violence because it mixes foundation which preservation and becomes all the more violent for this. (*FL* 278)

- [T]he police is nowhere graspable (*nirgends fassbare*). In so-called civilized states the specter of its ghostly apparition is all pervasive (*allverbreitete gespenstiche Erscheinung im Leben der zivilisierten Staaten*). (*FL* 279)

Above all, however, this ghostly revenant that haunts the law is indicated by Benjamin's insight that there is "something rotten in the law (*etwas Morsches im Recht*)."[21] "There is," Derrida elaborates, "something decayed or rotten in law, which condemns it or ruins it in advance" (*FL* 273).

There is also something rotten in the state of Denmark. Though Hamlet is not mentioned in Derrida's essay, the vocabulary and thematics of specters and haunting—a very *hauntological* reading of Benjamin—cannot but remind us now of *Specters of Marx*, which would appear three years later in 1993. In the prologue to "First Name of Benjamin," Derrida promises what was then to come, stating how in his reading of Benjamin's text he will attempt to demonstrate that "it is haunted by haunting itself, by a quasi-logic of the ghost which, because it is the more forceful one, should be substituted for an ontological logic of presence, absence or representation" (*FL* 259). That hauntology will be more fully developed in *Specters of Marx*, to which we will turn in chapter 6, but even here, its ghostly demarcations begin to emerge around the figures of the *Gespenst*, iterability, the "mystical." Irreducible iterability is what is rotten in the law, rotten like an old rope or chain tenuously holding violence and law together. Iterability is the structure of the temporal slippage that deconstructs any originary presence of the law, leaving only a topological displacement between juridical orders that, by virtue of their spectral or "mystical" origin, are shown to rest on a hauntological ground rather than an ontological one. This haunting is both the "force of law" and the "'mystical' origin of authority" of Derrida's title.

With this exposition of Derrida's reading of the "Critique of Violence," we are now in a better position to understand the grounds and the implications of Agamben's emphatic rejection of this reading.

State of Exception begins with a historical and theoretical exposition of "the state of exception as a paradigm of government."[22] The focus of this opening chapter of the book is stated in its first sentence, where Agamben asserts that there is an "essential contiguity between the state of exception and sovereignty" (*SE* 1) and credits Schmitt with having established this fact in his 1922 book *Political Theology*. This introductory gesture precisely identifies the link and progression between the analysis of *Homo Sacer* and that of *State of Exception*, and gives a first indication of how Agamben's analysis in the *Homo Sacer* project is moving more deeply into concrete historical, legal, and political terrain. Of course, all of these aspects of the issue are co-implicated with one another, and ultimately constitute a single object of inquiry, an inquiry whose stakes, Agamben suggests, are extremely high. While sovereignty (the logic of which is largely the subject of *Homo Sacer*) is "contiguous" with the state of exception, and "the law employs the exception—that is the suspension of law itself—as its original means of referring to and encompassing life" (*SE* 1), the rigorous analysis of this space of sovereign exception that this book undertakes may, he suggests, lead us to the great desideratum of Western political thought:

> Only if the veil covering this ambiguous zone is lifted will we be able to approach an understanding of the stakes involved in the difference—or the supposed difference—between the political and the juridical, and between law and the living being. And perhaps only then will it be possible to answer the question that never ceases to reverberate in the history of Western politics: what does it mean to act politically? (*SE* 2)

Rather than an originary violence or foundation of law, what this text seeks to illuminate and define is political action, what Agamben later will call "a truly human action." In *State of Exception*, this action has its index in Benjamin's notion of "pure *Gewalt*."

As we saw above, both the positive and natural law traditions have difficulty grappling with the phenomenon of a *Gewalt* that lies outside of the juridical order. With the figure of lawmaking violence, legal theory attempts to incorporate what can appear to be an anomic violence into a more or less coherent legal category. In anticipation of his reading of Benjamin's "Critique of Violence," Agamben spends some time in the opening chapter of *State of Exception* reviewing the debates within legal theory concerning the place of constituent power (a rough synonym for lawmaking violence) and revolutionary violence.

Distilled into its most basic form, the question can be put thus: Can (or should) a constitution regulate the lawmaking violence to which it owes its own existence? Or to put this more abstractly: Is lawmaking violence "legal"? On the one hand, some legal theorists advocate (and some constitutions provide for) a type of exceptional, quasi-extrajuridical violence that would nevertheless be subsumed into the constitutional order in the form of a declared right of resistance or, conversely, the natural right of the constitutional order to defend and preserve itself in extreme situations. Such models see the state of exception as ultimately included within the juridical order, whether that be through explicit norms and statutes providing for such rights or by reference to a deeper, even prenormative stratum of the legal sphere. On the other hand, some theorists affirm that the state of exception or emergency, in which violence is enacted in the suspension of the legal order, is the manifestation of an essentially extrajuridical, purely factual sphere of action. This extrajuridical sphere, however, would then be the stage on which fundamental lawmaking violence would take place in the establishment of a new legal order, and thus the problem of the intimate relation between the legal and extralegal remains unresolved. As Agamben notes, "[t]he simple topographical opposition (inside/outside) implicit in these theories seems in sufficient to account for the phenomenon it should explain" (*SE* 23). And notwithstanding the differences among these positions, ultimately, for Agamben, "The essential point . . . is that a threshold of undecidability is produced at which *factum* and *ius* fade into each other" (*SE* 29).

Not unlike the Heideggerian principle according to which the pure presence-at-hand of tools becomes manifest when they break or become unusable, here the essentially fractured structure of the juridical order (that is, fractured between the law and its *Gewalt*) comes into view in the extreme situation in which it must suspend itself in order to affirm and preserve itself.[23] What is revealed in these extreme situations, for Agamben (as well as for Schmitt, who asserted that "the rule as such lives off the exception alone"), is that the juridical order is constitutively fractured by a split between norms and their application or enforcement, and that the state of exception is the strategic device by which the law confronts the breakdown of its normal functioning order.[24] While both natural and positive law attempt to incorporate *Gewalt* into the juridical order in the ways discussed above, when viewed without a juridical or normative bias, the extreme situation puts the lie to this fiction concerning the "force of law." In the emergency, the fracture is seen plain, and the fundamental question of law and its force must be posed in such a way that they cannot be welded together by any ruse of natural or positive law. As Agamben's historical and theoretical exposition of emergency law seeks to demonstrate, the juridical order consistently confronts the irruption of extrajuridical violence by sovereignly declaring a state of exception and exerting a "legal" extrajuridical violence until normal conditions can be reestablished and the fictional unity of law and *Gewalt* can reassert itself. "It is," Agamben writes, "as if the juridical order [*il diritto*] contained an essential fracture between the position of the norm and its application, which, in extreme situations, can be filled only by means of the state of exception, that is, by creating a zone in which application is suspended, but the law [*la legge*], as such, remains in force" (*SE* 31). As we saw in the first section of this chapter, for Agamben this sovereign exception is the true and so to speak originary foundation of the juridical order, and it is the fiction by which the law asserts its dominion over life and human action.

The ghostly nature of the law in the state of sovereign exception, a zone in which the law remains *in force without application*, is perhaps the central concern of *State of Exception*; it is, in any case, certainly the central issue in Agamben's polemical engagement with Derrida in this text.[25] Focusing on the phrase "force of law," Agamben asserts that in both ancient and modern legal doctrine, the term refers not to the force that inheres in the law, but rather to the law-like force that "the executive power can be authorized to issue in some situations, particularly in the state of exception" (*SE* 38). That is to say, in the precise usage of the phrase "force of law," a violence that the law claims as its own (and indeed *names* as its own) is revealed to be detachable and autonomous from the law. The condition under which this nonidentity of force and the juridical order comes to light, of course, is the emergency in which the executive—acting as the sovereign—is the sole maker of "decrees, provisions, and measures that are not formally laws [but] nevertheless acquire their force" (*SE* 38). Once again, the stability and coherence of the juridical order is shown to be founded on the sovereign reincorporation of the extralegal into the legal by virtue of the sovereign's decision on the exception. Faced with the collapse of law, the sovereign occupies the blurred space between the two and strategically captures anomic violence and rearticulates it with the juridical order. Agamben's primary concern here, however, is that this sovereign articulation is a *strategic fiction*, aimed at preserving and protecting the rule of law; it is also Derrida's "mystic foundation." As Agamben writes,

> in extreme situations "force of law" floats as an indeterminate element that can be claimed both by the state authority . . . and by a revolutionary organization. . . . The state of exception is an anomic space in which what is at stake is a force of law without law (which should therefore be written: force-of-l̶a̶w̶. Such a "force-of-l̶a̶w̶" in which potentiality and act are radically separated, is certainly something like a mystical element, or rather a *fictio* by means of which law seeks to annex anomie itself. (*SE* 38–39)

What comes into clear view here, then, is the proximity of Agamben's analysis to Derrida's, as well as the ultimate distance Agamben will take from the deconstructive position. Whereas Derrida sets out to deconstruct the appeal to an originary essence implicit in the concept of pure violence, Agamben sees the task presented in Benjamin's essay as the transposition of the historically given apparatus of the law into a new condition. Though both the deconstruction of legal origins and the raising of the law to a postlegal dimension can be seen as forms of philosophical antinostalgia, there is clearly a fundamental difference in their orientations, to which Agamben draws our attention in overt and implicit ways. For Agamben, Derrida's maintenance of an undecidability between law and force, or between originary, lawmaking violence and law-preserving violence, amounts to a maintenance of this *fictio*, a fiction that is aimed at the strategic preservation of the juridical order.

As we will see in a moment, the choice between the maintenance or the deactivation of that *fictio iuris* is precisely the stake of the debate on the state of exception between Benjamin and Schmitt, which Agamben reconstructs in both its exoteric and esoteric contours in the chapter titled "Gigantomachy Concerning a Void." Before turning to that chapter, however, it is worth examining an analogy that both Agamben and Derrida draw between law and language, where we see most clearly how integrally connected Agamben's and Derrida's legal-theoretical work of the 1990s is to their first-philosophical and linguistic thought developed in the decades preceding.

As noted in chapter 1, the Saussurian *epokhē* posits the system and structures of *langue* (as opposed to both *langage* and *parole*) as the sole object of "general linguistics" (as opposed to, say, a "linguistics of speaking"). The wide-ranging implications of this insight need not be reviewed here; it is, however, worth noting this methodological principle in considering the analogy Agamben proposes between the ambiguous relation of priority between *langue* and *parole* and between law (*legge, loi*) and its application. As Agamben puts it:

> Just as linguistic elements subsist in *langue* without any real denotation, which they acquire only in actual discourse, so in the state of exception the norm is in force without any reference to reality. But just as concrete linguistic activity becomes intelligible precisely through the presupposition of something like a language, so is the norm able to refer to the normal situation through the suspension of its application in the state of exception. (*SE* 36)

A body of law—say, a constitution—exists as a fixed system of rules and statutes much in the same way a *langue*—say, English or Italian—is a fixed system of words and grammatical rules. This structuralist model, however, leads to certain quandaries once we have clearly identified a separation of language or law from its use or application. That is, the passage between system and use proves difficult indeed once we have separated language from its enunciation and law from its *Gewalt*.

On Agamben's reading, this aporia has remained largely insoluble because of the influence not only of the semiological model, but also of the Kantian theory of determinate judgment, in which the body of law is seen as a general rule into which the particular case must be logically subsumed. For Agamben, however, what is at stake is not a logical or semiological operation, but a practical and "political" one, which the dominance of the theory of judgment hopelessly obscures. As he writes, continuing the analogy with language:

> In the relation between the general and the particular (and all the more so in the case of the application of a juridical norm), it is not only a logical subsumption that is at issue, but first and foremost the passage from a generic proposition endowed with a merely virtual reference to a concrete reference to a segment of reality (that is, nothing less that the question of the actual relation between language and world). This passage from *langue* to *parole*, or from the semiotic to the semantic, is not a logical operation at all; rather, it always entails a practical activity, that is, the assumption of *langue* by one or more speaking subjects and the implementation of that complex apparatus that Benveniste defined as the enunciative function. (*SE* 39)

As we saw in the previous section, Derrida draws virtually the same analogy between law and language, though there his point is to deny the coherence of conceiving legal action on the model of the constative utterance. Where Derrida goes on to argue for a "performative" understanding of the act of *Gewalt*, however, Agamben describes such a violent legal action on the model of enunciation; indeed, for Agamben, performatives—like every enunciation—are included within the sphere of the "practical activity" of language use. The different directions Agamben and Derrida take the same analogy illuminates the fundamental difference in their first principles. As has been argued in previous chapters, for Agamben the logic of enunciation (Benveniste's development of Saussure's glimpse of language "from the point of view of the Sphinx") brings us outside of the logic of semiology and into a sphere of action (or "speaking") that exceeds or precedes the edifice of structural linguistics. Following this analogy, we can see that here, too, this "violent" and extrajuridical human action stops the machine of law in its tracks, freezes its structures and suspends its movement, and unfolds in a "purely" (in a sense we will discuss in a moment) anomic space. The distinction between remaining within and moving beyond (or beside) the sphere of law is the precise issue in the debate (both exoteric and esoteric) that Agamben excavates between Benjamin and Schmitt, to which we will now turn.

In addition to being an extraordinary reading of the intellectual *polemos* between these giants of the Weimar and Nazi eras in Germany,

Agamben's account of their debate is also a sort of allegorical representation of the *polemos* between himself and Derrida. And it will come as no surprise that in this allegory Benjamin represents Agamben's position while Schmitt represents Derrida's. The former therefore seeks "to ensure the possibility of a violence . . . that lies absolutely 'outside' (*ausserhalb*) and 'beyond' (*jenseits*) the law and that, as such, could shatter the dialectic between lawmaking violence and law-preserving violence" (*SE* 53), while the latter constantly "tries to capture Benjamin's idea of a pure violence and to inscribe anomie within the very body of the *nomos*" (*SE* 54). Although the "exoteric dossier" of the Benjamin-Schmitt exchange is well enough known (though contested and controversial), Agamben makes a significant contribution to the scholarship with his pursuit of the traces of an esoteric, that is to say, barely attested intellectual back-and-forth between the two. While Agamben's discovery of this close exchange may not "blow to pieces our conception of the intellectual history of the Weimar period" (qtd. in *SE* 53), as Jacob Taubes suggested Benjamin's 1930 letter to Schmitt might, it nevertheless drastically alters a common understanding of Benjamin's and Schmitt's intersecting intellectual itineraries.

Agamben begins to uncover the esoteric Benjamin-Schmitt dossier by scrutinizing the famous theory of sovereignty proposed in *Political Theology*, which he persuasively argues is a "precise response to Benjamin's ['Critique of Violence']" (*SE* 54). To support this claim, Agamben points to Schmitt's footnotes and references to contemporary periodicals that suggest Schmitt almost certainly would have read the issue of the *Archiv für Sozialwissenschaften und Sozialpolitik* in which Benjamin's essay had appeared (see *SE* 52).[26] On this basis, Agamben proceeds to show how the function of the sovereign in Schmitt's theory, that is, the declaration of the emergency aimed at the preservation of the juridical order, is directed precisely at the extrajuridical (whether "pure," "revolutionary," or "divine") violence that Benjamin's "Critique" seeks to guarantee.[27] In the face of the emergency (the irruption of revolutionary violence), the sovereign decides on the exception, exerts his own quasi-extrajuridical violence to quash or capture that other violence, and thus restores the integrity and wholeness of the juridical order.

"If these premises are accepted," Agamben writes, "then the entire exoteric debate between Benjamin and Schmitt appears in a new light" (*SE* 55). Indeed, this initial parry appears to be the first in a series of moves and countermoves that lasts for two decades. The sovereign's inability to decide in the *Origin of German Tragic Drama* (1925), for example, is now seen as a response to Schmitt's sovereign decision, and the worldliness and creaturely nature of Benjamin's baroque sovereign is a rebuttal to the quasi-divine nature of Schmitt's sovereign decider (see *SE* 55–57). But most crucially altered by this new perspective is our understanding of the stakes involved in Benjamin's famous but obscure claim, in the eighth thesis on the philosophy of history (1940), that "[t]he tradition of the oppressed teaches us that the 'state of exception' in which we live is the rule. We must attain to a concept of history that accords with this fact. Then we will clearly see that our task is to bring about the real [*wirklich*] state of exception, and this will improve our position in the struggle against fascism."[28] In response to Schmitt's consistent efforts to incorporate anomic violence back into the juridical order, and most pointedly his efforts to do so in the face of the permanent state of exception established by the Nazi regime (of which by this time he had become an illustrious member), Benjamin's distinction between the "state of exception in which we live" and a "real state of exception" that it is our task to bring about recalls yet again, though with ever-increasing urgency, his affirmation of a purely anomic violence and purely extrajuridical space for human action. As Agamben writes, "at issue in the anomic zone is the relation between violence and law—in the last analysis, the status of violence as a cipher for human action. While Schmitt attempts every time to reinscribe violence within a juridical context, Benjamin responds to this gesture by seeking every time to assure it—as pure violence—an existence outside of the law" (*SE* 59).

On this reading, the eighth thesis, then, also contains an ambiguous claim about both the Nazi regime and Schmitt's thought. Schmitt's efforts of the mid-1930s to define the shape of a new constitution to replace the Weimar constitution were destined to fail in the face of the Nazi "emergency" because this emergency was precisely not temporary and not aimed at the restoration of a normally functioning constitutional order. Instead, from 1933 to 1945, when an end was put to it by force, the Nazi period functioned as a permanent state of exception in which exception and rule had become, as Benjamin clearly puts it, one and the same. Schmitt's efforts to reinscribe anomie into the juridical order can only fail in such a context because he evidently misunderstands or denies the very nature of the Nazi emergency, viewing it in the terms he had earlier developed to describe the various kinds of dictatorship and emergency regimes, all of which are ultimately grounded in and committed to some sort of juridical, constitutional order, whether that be the existing one (in the case of "commissarial dictatorship") or the one to come (in the case of "sovereign dictatorship"). Both of these modalities of exceptional sovereign power, however, are revealed as juridical fictions in the face of the Nazi state, in which the distinction between exception and rule collapses permanently. As Agamben writes:

> Every fiction of a nexus between violence and law disappears here: there is nothing but a zone of anomie, in which a violence without any juridical form acts. The attempt of state power to annex anomie through the state of exception is unmasked by Benjamin for what it is: a *fictio iuris* par excellence, which claims to maintain the law in its very suspension as force-of-law. What now takes its place are civil war and revolutionary violence, that is, a human action that has shed [*deposto*] every relation to law. (*SE* 59)

Another way to say this is that the extreme situation of the Nazi state forces into the light the hidden articulation between rule of law and the extrajuridical, and shows that articulation to be a purely strategic, political, and fictional nexus. For Schmitt the jurist, who sees the fundamental problem of law in terms precisely of this structure, the task at hand is always the protection of the juridical order from the threat of collapse, and his state of exception is always a matter of reestablishing this *fictio iuris*. From this point of view, the foundation of the law is the sovereign and the exception that he declares in this evacuated legal limbo in order to protect and preserve the juridical order. For Benjamin the antinomian, however, the task at hand is to bring about the "real" state of exception, the definitive shattering of the sovereign dialectic between lawmaking and law-preserving violence, in order to, as he puts it in "Critique of Violence," "[found] a new historical epoch."[29]

This reading of Schmitt's theory of sovereignty as a response to Benjamin's pure, anomic violence must be taken into account if we are to understand Agamben's appropriation of Schmitt. As discussed in the first section of this chapter, Agamben's analysis of sovereignty and bare life—and his theory of biopolitics more generally—are probably unthinkable without Schmitt. However, the fact that Schmitt, in Agamben's reconstruction, comes out as the "loser" of the gigantomachy with Benjamin, as well as Agamben's clear declaration that Schmitt's theory is "fallacious" (*SE* 50), suggest the degree to which Agamben's debt to and appropriation of Schmitt's thought are really an appropriation and affirmation of Benjamin. This should, of course, not come as much of a surprise, given the profound influence Benjamin has always had on Agamben. Here, however, insofar as Agamben casts Benjamin and Schmitt as figures for himself and Derrida respectively, the reconstructed gigantomachy concerning a void—that is, concerning the state of exception—also shows how proximate and yet distant Agamben understands his own position to be from Derrida's. In this, so to speak, allegorical register, Derrida's affirmation of an irreducible undecidability with regard to questions of law and justice entails dwelling within the limbo of the sovereign *fictio* at a sort of zero degree, a pure decision/indecision that has no decisive content other than the function of maintaining the law in a virtual, though empty, state. "The undecidable," he writes, for example, "remains caught, lodged, as a ghost at least, but an essential ghost, in every decision, in every event of decision. Its ghostliness [*sa fantomaticité*] deconstructs from within all assurance of presence, all certainty or all alleged criteriology assuring us of the justice of a decision, in truth of the very event of a decision" (*FL* 253).

Such a deconstruction of the origin and presence of the law into the undecidability of "justice," which Derrida proposes as a near-synonym for *différance,* and thus as nonpresence itself, leads deconstructive legal thought to an affirmation of what Derrida had more than twenty years earlier, in "Différance," called "strategy without finality" (*M* 7). As incalculable "justice" irrupts into the juridical and causes all legal finalities and complacencies to deteriorate, the law unravels like the text that, for Derrida, it ultimately is. This textuality requires legal thought to follow the path of deconstructive reading and reasoning that he has pursued from his earliest work. Just as in the case of the literary or philosophical text, here, too,

> [i]n the delineation of *différance* everything is strategic and adventurous. Strategic because no transcendent truth present outside the field of writing can govern theologically the totality of the field. Adventurous because this strategy is not a simple strategy in the sense that strategy orients tactics according to a final goal, a *telos* or theme of domination, a mastery and ultimate reappropriation of the development of the field. Finally, a strategy without finality, what might be called blind tactics, or

> empirical wandering if the value of empiricism did not itself acquire its entire meaning in its opposition to philosophical responsibility. If there is a certain wandering in the tracing of *différance*, it no more follows the lines of philosophical-logical [and here we can add "-legal"] discourse than that of its symmetrical and integral inverse, empirical-logical discourse. The concept of *play* keeps itself beyond this opposition, announcing, on the eve of philosophy and beyond it, the unity of chance and necessity in calculations without end. (*M* 7)

While the context for this 1968 text is quite different from that of the 1989 essay on the "Critique of Violence," and while certain directions in which this passage would lead us cannot be followed here, it nevertheless should suffice to illustrate the rigorous consistency between the foundational early texts of Derrida's oeuvre and the later, more overtly political—and in this case, legal—debates. The deconstructive reading argues that this ghostly noncoincidence of law and violence is the sphere of—or *is*—"justice" as the "to come" itself, the pure promissory structure of the ethical relation to the other. And from this space, or spacing, of juridical *différance* deconstructive legal reasoning takes its course (or, as Agamben unsympathetically puts it, "sets up its factory"). On Agamben's reading of "Critique of Violence," however, Benjamin's entire argumentation as well as his exoteric and esoteric debate with Schmitt are aimed at definitively halting the oscillation of this juridical machine and, as Benjamin puts it, "[founding] a new historical epoch."[30] This, for Agamben, is the decisive step that Derrida and deconstruction do not take.[31]

If there is a valorized concept of justice in Benjamin's thinking on law, it is not to be found within the juridical machine, and not even in the deconstructed differantial interstices of its temporal structures. For Agamben, Benjamin does give some indications of his conception of justice in the "new historical epoch," but this, too, must be strictly contrasted with Derrida's reading of the same concept. Indeed, while for Derrida justice as *différance* is the central focus of the essay (whether wittingly or unwittingly on Benjamin's part), Agamben pointedly notes that "the topic of justice in the essay is, in fact, discussed only in relation to the ends of law" (*SE* 61), which is to say that it is a functioning category only within the ends-oriented spheres of positive and natural law, both of which Benjamin seeks explicitly to move beyond. And furthermore, the idea of justice would be

Sovereignty, Law, and Violence 159

a problematic category for Agamben in any case, given how closely associated it is in its essence with the juridical; as a concept, "justice" is, Agamben might say, "contaminated by law" (*SE* 64).

This latter question of contamination—and is counterpart, "purity"—leads us finally to what, for Agamben, is the true desideratum of Benjamin's essay, and perhaps of his thought generally. If the concept of justice in "Critique of Violence" is associated with the positive and natural law traditions, that is to say, with the mytho-juridical order itself, what, then, is the ultimately valorized term of the essay? The answer, Agamben suggests, can be found in "the topic—which flashes up in the text only for an instant, but is nevertheless sufficient to illuminate the entire piece—of violence as 'pure medium,' that is, as the figure of a paradoxical 'mediality without ends'—a means that, though remaining such, is considered independently of the ends that it pursues" (*SE* 61–62).

Benjamin began his essay by stating that "The task of a critique of violence can be summarized as that of expounding its relation to law and justice."[32] Given that the ultimate object of that critique is explicitly "pure violence," this is in effect a rather odd assertion, since in its most common usage "purity" tends to denote the absolution of all relationality or, as Derrida might insist, contamination. The assumption that legal violence is a means to an end is a fundamental assumption of positive and natural law, so in attempting to identify and valorize a "pure" violence, what step beyond the legal conception of *Gewalt* is Benjamin taking? For Derrida, the question of a pure violence leads Benjamin to the problematic search for an originary violence that is logically or chronologically subtracted from the historical modulations of legal violence. But this is precisely where Agamben and Derrida will diverge most fundamentally in their readings of "Critique of Violence," for on Agamben's account the purity of pure violence—of a pure means—has nothing to do with originality:

> [P]ure violence (which is the name Benjamin gives to human action that neither makes nor preserves law) is not an originary figure of human action that at a certain point is captured and inscribed within the juridical order (just as there is not, for speaking man, a prelinguistic reality that at a certain point falls into language). It is, rather, only the stake in the conflict over the state of exception, what results from it and, in this way only, is supposed prior to the law. (*SE* 60)

This reading of the concept of "pure violence"—"the essential technical term of Benjamin's essay" (*SE* 60)—depends on a precise understanding of the specific meaning of "purity" in Benjamin's lexicon. Citing a 1919 letter from Benjamin to Ernst Schoen, Agamben demonstrates that "purity" does not name an inherent and absolute quality of a given being or object, but rather (paradoxically) a relational one. As Benjamin writes, "The purity of a being is *never* unconditional or absolute; it is always subject to a condition. . . . [T]his condition *never* inheres in the being itself."[33] And even more decisively, in the 1931 essay on Karl Kraus, he writes that "at the origin of the creature stands not purity [*Reinheit*] but purification [*Reinigung*]" (qtd. in *SE* 61).[34] This is to say that, even when it is a matter of "origin," the purity at stake here is not an originary and absolute essence, but the result of a process or operation: *purification*. In the case of pure violence (as pure means), this would be a process or operation worked on the mediating juridical violences of positive and natural law. The "mediality without ends" or "pure violence," then, is not originary in any chronological or generative sense, but rather the result of a "purification" whose significance and mechanics Agamben will go on to elaborate in terms that embed the concept not only in Benjamin's broader oeuvre but also Agamben's own.

In a key passage that draws together his reflections on both law and the *experimentum linguae*, Agamben writes:

> The [pure] medium does not owe its purity to any specific intrinsic property that differentiates it from juridical means, but to its relation to them. In ["On Language as Such and on the Language of Men"], pure language is that which is not an instrument for the purpose of communication, but communicates itself immediately, that is, a pure and simple communicability; likewise, pure violence is that which does not stand in a relation of means toward an end, but holds itself in relation to its own mediality. And just as pure language is not another language, just as it does not have a place other than that of the natural communicative languages, but reveals itself in these by exposing them as such, so pure violence is attested to only as the exposure and deposition of the relation between violence and law. (*SE* 62)

This analysis of pure violence—conceived now as a mediality without ends—is fundamentally at odds with Derrida's reading of pure violence as an (illusory) origin of legal and historical violence. As the passage above

Sovereignty, Law, and Violence 161

shows, there is no question of recovering an uncontaminated, metaphysical, absolute violence that serves as the ground on which the juridical machine produces law or justice. Neither, however, is there a justice conceived as the differantial structure that is the condition of possibility for legal conceptuality. Instead, for Agamben the stakes of Benjamin's essay are located in a different historical register: not prehistory, but that "new historical epoch" that Benjamin suggested may only come with the halting of the juridical machine.

In these contesting readings of Benjamin's essay, a great deal rests on the precise definition of "purity." Derrida finds, and affirms, contamination and irreducible *différance* in the fundamental structures of the law. This for him is the promissory space of justice that is somewhat secretly harbored within the law. Agamben, too, identifies such a problematic displacement (or fiction) at the center of the legal order, one that remains implicated within the polarized relation between the law and its application. However, in a gesture with which we are by now quite familiar, the point for Agamben is not to hypostatize—or volatilize—that irreducible oscillation, declaring it to "be" justice, but rather to halt and deactivate the very workings of the juridical machine. Two points must be emphasized here. First, for Agamben that displacement is not the unstoppable working of pure *différance* but rather the function of the sovereign ban-structure. Second, having replaced "purity" with "purification," Agamben (following Benjamin) proposes a different concept of origin: as a paradoxically *relational* concept, pure violence begins with the fictional articulations of the juridical machine as the, so to speak, historically a priori givens from which a "truly political" (*SE* 88) thought must commence. Describing what may be called a historical-methodological *epokhē*, Agamben writes: "Life and law, anomie and *nomos*, *auctoritas* and *potestas*, result from the fracture of something to which we have no other access than through the fiction of their articulation and the patient work that, by unmasking this fiction, separates what it had claimed to unite. But disenchantment does not restore the enchanted thing to its original state: According to the principle that purity never lies at the origin, disenchantment gives it only the possibility of reaching a new condition" (*SE* 88).

This is the background for Agamben's call (and this is perhaps his most concrete political imperative) to "halt the machine, to show its central fiction," which is possible "because between violence and law, between life and norm, there is no substantial articulation" (*SE* 87). Between them there is in fact only the inclusive exclusion of the sovereign ban. Here, too, we can hear a critique of the deconstructive position, for in asserting that there is no "substantial" connection between the polar components of the juridical machine, and that this non-nexus is revealed—and more importantly, affirmed—in the "real" state of exception, Agamben departs from Derrida's strategy without finality, which for him amounts to maintaining the law in its ghostly and virtual state as pure form of law, or the fictional state of exception. Instead, he understands pure violence as that which decisively deposes the law, deactivates it, and leads us to a "new condition" of mediality without end.

Agamben takes this to be the nearly self-evident significance of Benjamin's figure of a deposed and deactivated law that is studied by Kafka's "new attorney." In a passage that returns us to the man from the country standing before the door of the law, Agamben writes:

> Obviously, it is not a question here of a transitional phase that never achieves its end, nor of a process of infinite deconstruction that, in maintaining the law in a spectral life, can no longer get to the bottom of it. The decisive point here is that the law—no longer practiced, but studied—is not justice, but only the gate that leads to it. What opens a passage toward justice is not the erasure of law [and thus a return to a pure, pre-juridical paradise], but its deactivation and inactivity [*inoperosità*]—that is, another use of the law. (*SE* 64)

In passages such as this one, we can see not only the terms of the polemic with Derrida, but also the way in which charges that Agamben is a more or less Heideggerian nostalgist, seeking forever the lost plenitude of a golden age, seeking forever to unforget being, are misplaced.[35] While Derrida deconstructs what he finds to be a nostalgic and metaphysical appeal to an "originary" violence in "Critique of Violence," Agamben's reading is founded on the historical *epokhē* in which the question of origin is reconceived or bracketed off. At the very least, such a search for origins is explicitly not the aim and not the stake of Agamben's programmatic reading of Benjamin's essay and of the sovereign logic that fictionally unites the polar terms around which that essay is organized. As he writes, "If it is true that the articulation between life and law, between anomie and *nomos*, that is produced by the state of exception is effective though fictional, one can still not conclude from this that somewhere either beyond or before juridical apparatuses there is an immediate access to something whose fracture and impossible unification are represented by these apparatuses" (*SE* 87). There is no *before* to be recovered; what we have are the historical apparatuses of the law, and these are the paradoxically historical a priori givens from which thought is bound to begin. Certainly this can be seen in Agamben's signal concept of bare life, which, though sometimes misunderstood, is anything but pure, prejuridical, and prehistorical natural life (*zōē*). As with pure violence, "[b]are life is a product of the machine and not something that pre-exists it" (*SE* 87–88).

No search for a lost origin, then, since one is not necessary to found law. The point, rather, is to halt the juridical machine by exposing the void that lies at the center of its articulating mechanism, the central fiction that holds the machine together and keeps it running. Another way to put this might be that in Agamben's political-philosophical project there is a strategy *with* a finality: "To show law in its nonrelation to life and life in its nonrelation to law [and thereby to] open a space between them for human action, which once claimed for itself the name of 'politics'" (*SE* 88). This exposure and halting of the machine, however, does not entail wholly eliminating or effacing the machine, but rather deactivating it, rendering it inactive or inoperative, *inoperosa* or *désoeuvrée*. This is precisely what, in the Benjamin essay, pure violence does to the machine of the juridical order, whose ends are always the preservation or the positing of law and whose means are *Gewalt*: "pure violence exposes and severs the nexus between law and violence and can thus appear in the end not as violence that governs or executes (*die schaltende*) but as violence that purely acts and manifests (*die waltende*)" (*SE* 62).

Pure violence is the violence that deactivates the machine, but a stopped machine is still there. Can it be put to a new use? What is the nature of a postjuridical human action, and what—if anything—does it have to do with the remnants of the broken apparatuses of the legal machine? With these questions, Agamben's analysis leads to an issue that I will take up in greater detail in the conclusion of this book. It will be helpful, however, to anticipate that discussion with a brief review of the indices Agamben offers in *State of Exception*. Recalling Benjamin's assertion, in his essay on Kafka, that "[t]he law which is studied but no longer practiced is the gate to justice," Agamben focuses in on the significance of this "study," and in doing so finds one of his most compelling images for the nature of human action that has moved beyond the now definitively deactivated apparatuses of the law.[36] "In [Benjamin's] Kafka essay," he writes, "the enigmatic image of a law that is studied but no longer practiced corresponds, as a sort of remnant, to the unmasking of mythico-juridical violence effected by pure violence" (*SE* 63). This deactivated or deposed law, which is no longer in force and has no applicability, is what Kafka's "new attorney" pursues in his study, just as do his co-players on Kafka's stage: "Kafka's characters . . . have to do with this spectral figure of the law in the state of exception; they seek, each one following his or her own strategy, to 'study' and deactivate it, to 'play' with it" (*SE* 64).

What is pursued here is not a lost essence—whether that be absolute, "pure," or originary—but rather a new condition in which a postjuridical human action resembles nothing so much as play. As Agamben writes in the paragraph that concludes his chapter on the Benjamin-Schmitt (and Agamben-Derrida) gigantomachy:

> One day humanity will play with law just as children play with disused objects, not in order to restore them to their canonical use but to free them from it for good. What is found after the law is not a more proper and original use value that precedes the law, but a new use that is born only after it.. . . . This liberation is the task of study, or of play. And this studious play is the passage that allows us to arrive at that justice that one of Benjamin's posthumous fragments defines as a state of the world in which the world appears as a good that absolutely cannot be appropriated or made juridical. (*SE* 64)

In such a postjuridical and truly anomic space there may indeed be the remnants of the juridical machine; there is, however, no longer any need to endlessly "negotiate with the law" (*SE* 88), but rather the possibility for a human action or praxis—conceived along the lines of a child's "play," the new attorney's "study," and a noninstrumental "use"—that Agamben defines most broadly as a means without end.

In the essay "In Praise of Profanation," which is one of Agamben's most concerted and evocative presentations of this concept of a "new use," he offers still another figure for what use or action might look like in the "new historical epoch" inaugurated by the general *désoeuvrement* of the apparatuses that govern Western culture. Oddly enough, however, it is not

Sovereignty, Law, and Violence

a human figure; it is a cat. "The cat," Agamben writes, "who plays with a ball of yarn as if it were a mouse . . . knowingly uses the characteristic behaviors of predatory activity . . . in vain. These behaviors are not effaced, but . . . deactivated and thus opened up to a new, possible use" (*Prof* 85). But what type of use might this postdeactivation action be? What is the relation between this new use and the old use that it mimics? What is the point of the cat's *play*? "The game with the yarn," Agamben suggests,

> liberates the mouse from being prey and the predatory activity from being necessarily directed toward the capture and death of the mouse. And yet, this play stages the very same behaviors that define hunting. The activity that results from this thus becomes a pure means, that is, a praxis that, while firmly maintaining its nature as a means, is emancipated from its relationship to an end; it has joyously forgotten its goal and can now show itself as such, as a means without an end. The creation of a new use is possible only by deactivating an old use, rendering it inoperative. (*Prof* 86)

The point of this passage is not to call for an end to predation in the animal kingdom, but rather to offer an image of a distinctive and discrete activity that has been detached from its "natural" end and becomes a mimicry and substitution that manifests itself "purely" (in the technical sense discussed above) as "play." This important concept of "play" will be discussed further in the conclusion to this book, but before that, let us stay for a while with the cat, and with "the animal" more generally.

5

TICKS AND CATS

> For his tongue is exceeding pure so that it has in purity what it wants in music.
> —CHRISTOPHER SMART, *JUBILATE AGNO*

In the years around the turn of the century, Agamben and Derrida both focused their attention on the question of the animal and its relation to the human. Though Derrida's book *The Animal That Therefore I Am* [*L'animal que donc je suis*] was published in French in 2006, two years after his death, the component parts of that book have a slightly complicated publication history that is worth briefly reviewing here not least because this will establish the timeline of these texts' appearance in relation to Agamben's book *The Open: Man and Animal*. As recounted in Marie-Louise Mallet's foreword to *The Animal That Therefore I Am*, as well as the opening pages of Derrida's text itself, the material of this book was first presented at a ten-day conference devoted to Derrida's work at Cerisy-la-Salle in 1997. The section that now forms the book's first chapter appeared in print in the published conference proceedings in 1999, and the book's third chapter appeared in an issue of *Les Cahiers de L'Herne* in 2004.[1] *The Open*, on the other hand, was published in Italian in February 2002, though Agamben had been presenting material from it in seminars the previous year. Agamben's seminars on the animal would thus have taken place a few months before Derrida began, in December 2001, his own series of lectures on "The Beast and the Sovereign," which, as we will see, polemically engage Agamben.[2]

Both Agamben's and Derrida's texts on the animal have been very influential in recent debates concerning animal ethics and philosophy. That context and those debates, however, remain outside the scope of the present chapter, which will instead be concerned with how Agamben's and Derrida's texts on the question of the animal resonate with each other, and how they sit within the oeuvres that the present study has been reading in tandem. Indeed, Dominick LaCapra is right when he notes that, notwithstanding Agamben's recent influence in the field of animal studies, in truth "*The Open* has virtually nothing specific to say about other-than-human animals or their lives," and this could also be claimed about *The Animal That Therefore I Am*.[3] Both Derrida and Agamben trouble the division between the human and the animal, and yet in both cases, even though they each evoke the terrible misfortune of animal life that is born under the dominion of, for example, modern biobusiness and factory farming, the center of interest of their texts themselves lies elsewhere.[4] Their focus, instead, is on the ontological and anthropogenetic function of that all-important distinction and exclusion of the animal from the human. As the following pages will show, while Derrida makes this a multiple, mutable, and thus doubtful boundary—that is to say, while he deconstructs the fateful division between *the* human and *the* animal—Agamben presents the line dividing the human and the animal as an internal one that passes within man. For Agamben the man-animal divide is ultimately determined not by alterity and difference (or *différance*) but by the exceptional separation, the inclusive exclusion, the logic of which was outlined in the previous chapter.

MACHINES

On first glance, *The Open* appears to be divided into two roughly equal halves. The first half of the book presents a series of episodes in the intellectual and scientific history of humanism in which attempts are made to find a definitive line or criterion of separation between man and animal. In chapter 4, we examined the logic and mechanics of the sovereign ban and its inclusive-exclusive topological structure. *The Open* extends that argument into the sphere of human self-definition against the animal. As the next few pages will show, all of the efforts to define the human are driven by what Agamben—borrowing a term from Furio Jesi—calls the "anthropological machine of humanism" (*O* 29), a mechanism or device that is ceaselessly deployed, though in various guises, to produce the human by *banning* or *ab-bandoning* the life (*zōē*) not only of the nonhuman animal other, but more importantly of the "anthropophorous" animal that is the human's living body. Matthew Calarco puts it well: the anthropological machine "can best be understood as the symbolic and material mechanisms at work in various scientific and anthropological discourses that classify and distinguish humans and animals through a dual process of inclusion and exclusion."⁵ In the first half of *The Open*, Agamben writes a history of the anthropological machine of humanism as a history of (1) defining the life (*zōē*) of the human as animality, and (2) identifying animals exclusively with this banned—or bare—life. Another way of saying this is that in the first half of *The Open*, Agamben sketches a biopolitical history of the human-animal distinction.

These vignettes, however, cease about halfway through the book and give way to a series of densely argued chapters on Heidegger that make up the bulk of the remaining pages. The style and mode of argumentation of these later chapters, as well as their extended engagement with a single thinker, seem to suggest that they have a different status in the arc of the book's argumentation, that perhaps with Heidegger we move beyond the biopolitical and "anthropological" foundations of the humanist tradition. But as will be discussed toward the end of this chapter, the Heidegger chapters of *The Open* do not in fact start a new movement in the text. Rather they can be seen as the culmination or conclusion of the survey of attempts to define the human over against (and above) the animal. The latest and deepest and most subtle effort to think the human not in terms of an excluded-included animality, Heidegger's thought nevertheless still falls into the machinery of the anthropological machine and thus represents a limit point at the end of the metaphysical tradition of humanism.

The first half of *The Open* is made up of a series of elegantly presented vignettes in the history of philosophy, theology, and natural history in which Agamben observes and demonstrates the operations of the anthropological machine at work. For example, in the chapter titled "Physiology of the Blessed," Agamben sketches the way medieval theologians attempted to deal with the difficult problem of what happens to the physical bodies of those who have been resurrected and are in Paradise. If the entry into the afterlife entails the integral resurrection of the body, then a number of inconvenient—and somewhat comical—questions arise, such as: In whose body is Adam's rib resurrected? What about a lifetime's worth of hair and fingernail cuttings, and bodily secretions—are these part of the resurrected body? What about the contents of the intestines? Do we have to eat in paradise? If so, what do we eat, and do we then digest and defecate? And if we do, then where does the excrement go? If the body is integrally resurrected, then is there sexuality in Paradise? Reproduction? Sex without reproduction—just for fun? In short, what happens to all of the animal functions of the redeemed body in the afterlife?

Though the many vicissitudes of what is, of course, a voluminous and varied theological corpus are alluded to in this brief chapter, Agamben centers on Aquinas's representative position on the issue, namely, his definitive "exclusion of the *usus venereorum et ciborum* from Paradise" (*O* 19).[6] Just as animals and plants, for Aquinas, are barred entry into Paradise, so, too, is the animal life of the human excluded from the glorious body as a condition for its redemption. "In the body of the resurrected," Agamben writes, "the animal functions will remain 'idle and empty' exactly as Eden, according to medieval theology, remains empty of all human life after the expulsion of Adam and Eve. All flesh will not be saved, and in the physiology of the blessed, the divine *oikonomia* of salvation leaves an unredeemable remnant" (*O* 19). The question of the bodily condition of redeemed humanity thus lays bare the internecine war within the living human, the ceaseless border strife between the human being and the animal body to which it remains attached. Indeed, what the Christian tradition takes to be the most essential and defining characteristic of humanity, that we are created and destined for salvation, entails an aporetic (or more precisely "ab-bandoned") articulation with our animal bodies, an inclusive exclusion of our animality, that the doctrine of the resurrection cannot overcome. And Aquinas's argumentation shows this nexus point to be a perfectly "idle and empty" space.

Agamben's chapter on "Taxonomies," which jumps ahead several hundred years, and across disciplines, focuses on Linnaeus and early primatology. Linnaeus, Agamben tells us, "had a weakness for apes" (*O* 23) and indeed dismissed Descartes's belief (about which more later) that apes, along with all the other animals, were essentially nothing more than complex machines lacking souls and the capacity to truly think. Whether it was owing to his personal fondness for these creatures or the results of meticulous research (both, surely), Linnaeus never was able to settle on a solid—or at least physiological—criterion for distinguishing between them and humans. Citing a text titled "Man's Cousins," in which Linnaeus admits that he "hardly knows a single distinguishing mark which separates man from the apes (qtd. in *O* 24), Agamben goes on to review the evidence of Linnaeus's doubt that the human is the exceptional creature among all the others. Not only does Linnaeus place *Homo* within the order of *Anthropomorpha* or *Primates* in the *Systema Naturae*, but he does not, Agamben tells us, "record—as he does with the other species—any specific identifying characteristic next to the generic name *Homo*, only the old philosophical adage: *nosce te ipsum* [know yourself]" (*O* 25).[7] On Agamben's reading, what "the founder of modern scientific taxonomy" (*O* 23) intends by this cryptic note is that "man has no specific identity other than the *ability* to recognize himself" (*O* 26), that the status of man as man is determined by nothing natural or physical but rather by an ability and, most crucially, that *activity* of self-recognition. This characteristic and self-defining activity determines *Homo* as "*the animal that must recognize itself as human to be human*" (*O* 26). And in a passage in which he introduces the book's central concept of the "anthropological machine," Agamben writes: "*Homo sapiens*, then, is neither a clearly defined species nor a substance; it is, rather, a machine or device for producing the recognition of the human" (*O* 26).

In the chapter titled "Without Rank," Agamben juxtaposes the "humanist discovery of man," represented here by Pico della Mirandola's *On the Dignity of Man* (1486), with the fascination and confusion provoked among intellectuals in the eighteenth century by the increasingly frequent appearances of "feral children," children who had evidently grown up alone in the woods, entirely outside of civilization, and who appeared incapable of precisely such self-recognition. Agamben argues that in his oration Pico, like Linnaeus, assigns to man no proper and definitive characteristics, but rather the ability to take any form—and assume whatever rank in the hierarchy of created beings—that he makes for himself. For Pico, "since [man] was created without a definite model (*indiscretae opus imaginis*), he does not even have a face of his own (*nec propriam faciem*) and must shape it at his own discretion in either bestial or divine form" (*O* 29). The human is thus a fluctuating and transient being, one whose position moves up and down on the ladder of creation according to its own self-fashioning activity. And with the birth of Linnaean taxonomy 250 years later, members of humanity on the lower rungs of the ladder get a name, *Homo ferus*, who, the *Systema naturae* tells us, walks on all fours, is without language, and is covered with hair. This mysterious, half-animal branch of humanity is not a figure of pure speculation on Linnaeus's part, for later editions of the *Systema* tell us whom he has in mind. The 1758 edition list five examples of feral children who had appeared in disparate parts of Europe between 1717 and 1731.[8] The fascination that these wild children held for so many thinkers of the age of reason and the "passion with which the men of the Ancien Régime try to recognize themselves in them and to 'humanize' them" is, Agamben argues, evidence of "how aware they are of the precariousness of the human" (*O* 30) and of how uncertain the position of *Homo sapiens* is in the hierarchy of creatures. As Lord Monboddo writes in a passage from an obscure (though perfectly chosen) introduction to one of these accounts, "*reason* and *animal sensation*, however distinct we may imagine them, run into one another by such insensible degrees, that it is as difficult, or perhaps more difficult, to draw the line betwixt these two, than betwixt the *animal* and *vegetable*" (qtd. in *O* 31).

What gradually comes into view in the striking vignettes of the first half of *The Open*, then, is the working of what Agamben calls the "anthropological machine," which is also the title of the book's ninth chapter. The specific historical figure of this chapter is the nineteenth-century debate surrounding the "missing link" between man and the other primates. While evolutionary theorists and paleontologists (such as Thomas Huxley, Eugen Dubois, and above all Ernst Haeckel) sought to discover evidence of the transitional creature between man and a prehuman primate in the fossil record, Agamben suggests that the paleontological/physiological search for the missing link is posed in terms that make it impossible that such a task could ever succeed. After briefly reviewing how late-nineteenth-century naturalists attempted to "[reconstruct] the evolutionary history of man on the basis of both the results of comparative anatomy and the findings of paleontological research," Agamben argues that the ambiguous nature of this transitional ape-man is in truth always implicitly defined and determined "by subtracting an element that had nothing to do with either one, and that instead was presupposed as the identifying characteristic of the human: language" (*O* 34). Haeckel's quest for the missing link, whom he indeed names *Homo alalus* or the *sprachloser Urmensch*, is less a search in the fossil record than a speculation about the origin of human language. That is to say, what ultimately makes the *Urmensch* a transitional creature is not a physical or physiological difference from *Homo sapiens*, but its inability to speak. In other words, Haeckel's *Homo alalus* is the speculative result of a conceptual paradox; its unspeaking nature is derived from a pure presupposition about the nature of speaking man, to whom it in turn is supposed to give rise. Or as Agamben puts it, such a nonspeaking man is "only a shadow cast by language, a presupposition of speaking man, by which we always obtain only an animalization of man (an animal-man, like Haeckel's ape-man) or a humanization of the animal (a man-ape [such as the feral child]). The animal-man and the man-animal are the two sides of a single fracture, which cannot be mended from either side" (O 36).

The irresolvable paradox and circularity of Haeckel's (and his peers') speculations about the missing link—just like the contradictions that lie at the center of virtually all of the man-animal distinctions that Agamben reviews in this first half of the book—constitute what might be considered the motor of the anthropological machine of humanism, whose central mechanism is none other than the inclusive exclusion of the ban-structure, the space of exception, which is the articulating non-nexus of the opposing terms human and animal. As Agamben writes:

> Insofar as the production of man through the opposition man/animal, human/inhuman, is at stake here, the machine necessarily functions by means of an exclusion (which is also always already a capturing) and an inclusion (which is also always already an exclusion). Indeed, precisely because the human is already presupposed every time, the machine actually produces a kind of state of exception, a zone of indeterminacy in which the outside is nothing but the exclusion of an inside and the inside is in turn only the inclusion of an outside. (O 37)

According to Agamben's analysis, the human is presupposed in order to articulate a relation with its supposedly nonhuman other, but this space of exclusion and articulation is the purely fictitious and virtual nexus established by the ban or exception. The category of the human, that is to say, is produced entirely by virtue of this empty space. The upshot is that neither term is truly separated from the other—and thus neither term ever really comes wholly into being as such; rather, what is produced is a (fictitious) zone of exception that establishes the dominion of the valorized term (the human in this context, *bios* in others) on the condition that the inferior term (the animal, *zōē*) be subjected to the condition of ab-bandonment and be produced not as pure and independent *zōē* but as bare life. In the effort to identify, define, and produce "the human" as such, that is, the human as wholly distinct from the animal, the anthropological machine instead ceaselessly generates a space of sovereign exception. This space, "[l]ike every space of exception . . . is, in truth, perfectly empty, and the truly human being who should occur there is only the place of a ceaselessly updated decision in which the caesurae and their rearticulation are always dislocated and displaced anew. What would thus be obtained, however, is neither an animal life nor a human life, but only a life that is separated and excluded from itself—only a *bare life*" (O 38). It is in this context that Agamben's calls to halt or "render inoperative" (O 92; see also 38) the anthropological machine become understandable, especially when considered as a modulation of his Benjaminian call to bring about the "real state of exception." Agamben's attempt to halt the machine is not aimed at valorizing one or the other of the two poles, or at reestablishing a hypothetically neutral criterion for the division (which for Agamben would be impossible and amount to an act of bad faith). Rather, it is aimed at separating them definitively, thus breaking the machine and rendering it inoperative. Just as moving from the fictitious state of exception to the real state of exception entails truly breaking the (non-)nexus that binds life to the law in the sovereign ban, here a "real" division between the human and the animal would entail rupturing the virtual articulation that is at work in all of the models of human auto-definition. In every case, Agamben's analysis shows the articulation to be fictional, virtual, and "empty." Halting the machine would therefore mean exposing that central emptiness on which the human is (self-)constructed and guaranteed.

It is, however, interesting to note that Agamben's call to stop the machine (O 38) comes at a point in the text where the argument appears to be changing directions. Indeed, it comes precisely where the text begins to move into its extended analysis of Heidegger. As will be discussed below, Agamben goes on to ague that Heidegger's thought, too, gets caught up in the workings of the anthropological machine. However, before Agamben enters fully into his reading of Heidegger's texts, he presents a sort of two-chapter interlude (chapters 10 and 11, "*Umwelt*" and "Tick") concerning the work of the zoologist Jakob von Uexküll that serves as both overture and transition to the discussion of Heidegger. In these chapters, Agamben suggests, by means of a very cryptic figure, a direction for thought that perhaps "neither Uexküll nor Heidegger was prepared to confront" (O 70).

That figure is the tick that Uexküll reports was held in a sort of suspended animation in a laboratory for eighteen years, a figure that, as we will see, Agamben presents as a sort of third term, between or beyond (in any case outside of) the system of the anthropological machine.

A fuller discussion of Agamben's reading of Heidegger will, however, have to wait for a moment while we turn to Derrida's treatment of the human-animal distinction. Though *The Animal That Therefore I Am* is Derrida's first long text devoted entirely to the question of the human and the animal, he nevertheless notes there the striking menagerie of animals that have populated his texts in the past: ants, hedgehogs, silkworms, spiders, bees, serpents, wolves, horses, crustaceans, steers, sheep, pigs, asses, moles, hares, swans, birds, hens, fish, chimeras, eagles, dogs, swallows, shrimp, oysters, sponges. Remembering this menagerie less as a Noah's Ark than as a circus, "with an animal trainer having his sad subjects, bent low, file past" (*Animal* 39), Derrida evokes here not only the persistence of the animal figure on the stage of his thought, but also the sublime scale of that stage itself. With *The Animal That Therefore I Am*, this animal drama moves into the spotlight.

The central strategy of *The Animal That Therefore I Am* can be discerned in its title, which includes a typically ingenious pun that puts the entire argument into motion. And the pun is difficult to translate. "L'animal que donc je suis" can be understood as both "the animal that therefore I am" and "the animal that therefore I follow," since "suis" is also the first-person present indicative of the verb "suivre." Over the course of the text, David Wills, its translator, has recourse to a number of shrewd and inventive devices for marking this play on words in English, but in general wherever one reads "I am" in the text, one must also hear "I follow" (and vice versa).[9] The indistinction between "je suis" (I am) and "je suis" (I follow) in French is the rhetorical performance of what Derrida will go on to argue is the troubling ambiguity that runs like a fault line through all of the philosophical texts on the human and the animal (by Descartes, Kant, Heidegger, Levinas, Lacan) that he examines over the course of the lecture, for at this uncertain border, every affirmation concerning the essence or "being" of the human, every affirmation concerning what the living human *is*, shows itself to be an affirmation (more or less untenable) of an essential difference between the human and all other (inferior) forms of life, which in turn get assimilated together under the general rubric of "the animal." Being and following—that is to say, what one *is* and what one *comes after*—get collapsed into one another in a process that deconstructs every grand edifice of philosophical (as well as scientific, anthropological, theological, etc.) argumentation concerning "man." What is therefore at stake in Derrida's survey of key philosophical texts on the human/animal is the way the being ("être") of the human is inextricably bound up with the human's proximity to, distinction from, and following after ("suivre") the animal.

Another allusion in the title of the text is, of course, to Descartes's famous phrase "I think therefore I am" ("je pense donc je suis," "cogito ergo sum") in the *Meditations on First Philosophy*, to which Derrida devotes his attention primarily in the second section of the book. Here Derrida focuses his lens on how Descartes's question, *Qui suis-je?* or *Que suis-je?* ("Who or what am I (following)?"), complicates the great conclusion of the method of radical doubt—namely, that *I am*—and forces the question of the animal into the terrain of the *cogito*. As Derrida slyly (like a fox?) writes in a passage where the ambiguity of the word *suis* is on full display,

> I thought I had simply invented this innocent and at the same time perverse game of homonymy, this double usage of the little thing, of the powerful little word *suis*. . . . I don't remember having ever encountered it in the consequential form of the demonstration that I am undertaking: namely, that previously (before, but before what time, before time?), before the question of (the) *being* as such, of *esse* and *sum*, of *ego sum*, there is the question of following, of the persecution and seduction of the other, what/that I am (following) or who is following me, who is following me while I am (following) it, him, or her. (*Animal* 64–65)

This innocent little word at the center of the question *Qui* or *Que suis-je?*, then, is Derrida's point of entry into Descartes's text and what he calls the "original moment . . . the first version of this sentence, which in French is already a translation: 'But as for me, who am I . . .'" (*Animal* 69).[10]

Descartes, of course, answers this question by determining that he is a "thing that thinks."[11] Furthermore, from the impossibility of doubting that such thinking is taking place he draws the famous conclusion that "I am, I exist—that is certain."[12] And yet, the irreducibility of the "I am" that is discovered and verified by the method of radical doubt is unwittingly predicated, Derrida argues, on an insufficiency of doubt regarding the capabilities of the animal/other that "I am following." Even though Descartes "doubted to the level of hyperbole," he nevertheless "never doubted . . . that the animal was only a machine, even going so far as to make of this indubitability a sort of condition for doubting, that of the *ego* as such, as *ego dubito*, as *ego cogito*, and therefore as *ego sum*" (*Animal* 75–76). There is, of course, a great deal to say about the implications of the mechanistic worldview in Descartes's thought, and indeed his early texts such as *The World* and the *Treatise on Man* (1629–33)—which he suppressed for fear of disapproval by the church but which strongly inform (and are alluded to in) the *Discourse on Method*—suggest the extent to which Descartes was able to imagine the physical world, and above all the human body, as a machine.[13] But the issue at hand here is "thinking," and in particular the kind of thinking that can serve as the guarantor of existence. What, then, is the difference between human thinking and the sort of mental activity and capabilities that animals, and even certain machines, evidently engage in or are endowed with? The answer, for Descartes, is that machines, automatons, and animals cannot "respond."

In the fifth part of the *Discourse on Method*, Descartes deals at some length with the question of the "difference between man and beast."[14] The entire demonstration of the human's distinctive essence, its rationality, is based here on the assertion that animals are no more than reactive machines, mechanisms that differ from man-made automatons only in that their extraordinary complexity could only be achieved by the hand of God. Referring to the earlier demonstration undertaken in the *Treatise on Man*, Descartes argues that if we were to be presented with a machine so meticulously constructed that it "had the organs and outward shape of a monkey or of some other animal that lacks reason, we should have no means of knowing that they did not possess entirely the same nature as these animals."[15] A claim such as this indeed suggests that Descartes is rather overly credulous concerning the limited capacities of the animal; it also reminds one of Linnaeus's remark, which Agamben cites as an epigraph to the chapter "Taxonomies" in *The Open*, that "surely Descartes never saw an ape" (*O* 23). However that may be, Descartes invokes this hypothetical animal automaton in order to illustrate by contrast one kind of automaton that could never fool us into thinking it was the real thing, for "if any such machines bore a resemblance to our bodies and imitated our actions as closely as possible for all practical purposes, we should still have two very certain means of recognizing that they were not real men."[16] What are these two means? "The first is that they could never use words, or put together other signs, as we do in order to declare our thoughts to others."[17] The second is that though such machines might be able to perform certain tasks very well indeed, even better than a human might, they could never perform *all* the myriad tasks that we can; they could never improvise within, adapt to, or learn from "all the contingencies of life," and this "would reveal that they were acting not through understanding but only from the disposition of their organs."[18] For Descartes, this thought experiment about animals, automatons, and humans "shows not merely that the beasts have less reason than men, but that they have no reason at all."[19]

Descartes also puts this in another way: animals, like machines, cannot *respond*. Citing a letter of March 1638 (sadly not included in the English edition of the *Philosophical Writings*), Derrida draws out Descartes's link between human reason and the ability to respond. In this letter Descartes restates his two "very certain means" for distinguishing automatons from real humans:

> [O]ne is that never, unless it be by chance, do these automatons *respond*, either with words or even with signs, concerning what is *asked* of them [*ce dont on les* interroge]; and the other that although the movements that they make are often more regular and more certain that those of the wisest men, they nevertheless *lack* several things that they should do in order to imitate us, more than would the most senseless of men." (qtd. in *Animal* 82; Derrida's italics)

The animal's and the automaton's physiological or preprogrammed reaction to given stimuli is in no way a true response. It is simply—even in the case of an animal "cry[ing] out that you are hurting it"—a matter of movements among the pulleys and gears that make up their mechanical/physiological structures.[20]

Now, this description of the animal's reactions to stimuli as mere mechanical effects leads Derrida to what is the most important point for our purposes here. By a striking associative-analogical leap, Derrida links the animal's inability to respond to the inability of writing, of the written word, to respond. It is in this movement that Derrida connects his critique of Descartes's denial of the animal's ability to respond—and correlatively, of the dubious affirmation of the human's ability to respond—to his own philosophical first principles and the grammatological dismantling of phono-logo-centrism.

In the opening moments of his discussion of Descartes, Derrida not only poses the question "But as for me, who am I (following)?," but also notes that he is quoting it from the *Second Meditation*. That this question, asked more or less in earnest, is nevertheless a repetition of a phrase written in (the French translation of) the *Meditations of First Philosophy*, leads Derrida to write:

> I repeat it, I can reproduce it mechanically, it has always been capable of being recorded, it can always be mimed, aped, parroted by these animals, for example, those apes and parrots about which it is said that they can imitate (even though Aristotle denied them mimesis) without understanding or thinking, and especially without replying to the questions they are asked. According to many philosophers and theoreticians, from Aristotle to Lacan, animals do not respond, *and they share that irresponsibility with writing*, at least in the terms in which Plato interprets the latter in the *Phaedrus*. What is terrible (*deinon*) about writing, Socrates says, is the fact that, like painting (*zōgraphia*), the things it engenders, although similar to living things (*hōs zōnta*), do not respond. No matter what question one asks them, writings remain silent, keeping a most majestic silence or else always replying in the same terms, which means not replying. (*Animal* 52; my italics)

At issue in this passage are several related anthropo-logo-centric theses that Derrida will dismantle over the course of his text: (1) even though animals *may* indeed be able to speak (i.e., parrots talking, apes using sign language), they nevertheless cannot truly respond, and it is in *this* particular sense that the animal is deprived of language; (2) the unresponsive cry or voice of the animal is a matter of physical, mechanical reactions to stimuli, making the animal indistinguishable from a complex machine; (3) the human word is by contrast nonmechanical and is therefore invested with a variety of valorized qualities like spirit, thought, soul, reason, etc. The central assertion in this passage, however, is that there is an analogy—or identification—between the lifeless, mechanical, repetitive word of the animal and the lifeless, mechanical, repetitive word of writing in contrast to the vital, unique, original, and responsive word of the thinking and speaking human. This opposition can be schematized, as Derrida does, as that between writing and the voice, or in the most general terms, between *différance* and presence. Among all of the byways and meanders of the wide-ranging readings offered in this complex book, this analogy structures the argument throughout.

Can the animal respond? Derrida begins his text with a sort of anecdote, a scene of himself caught naked for a moment by the gaze of a cat—*his* cat—before whom he feels suddenly and surprisingly ashamed. Crucial to this introductory tale is that this encounter really did happen between Derrida and his cat, and that neither he nor his cat is a representative or a figure for a class of beings. Derrida's cat is no "exemplar of a species called 'cat,' even less so or an 'animal' genus or kingdom.... [The cat] comes to me as *this* irreplaceable living being that one day enters my space, into this place where it can encounter me, see me, even see me naked" (*Animal* 9). And neither is this cat a figure for any of the other literary and philosophical cats Derrida enumerates: Hoffmann's, Montaigne's, Rilke's, Buber's. Least of all is she the same as the little cat whom Alice, in *Through the Looking Glass*, decides one cannot speak with "on the pretext that it doesn't reply or that it always replies the same thing" (*Animal* 8). Alice's conclusion is, as Derrida will go on to show, Cartesian to the core, for in their mechanical repetition or reaction that is not a true response, in the way no matter what you say to them they "*always* purr . . . *always* say the same thing," cats remain, for this very Cartesian Alice, on the far side of that dividing line between the human and the nonhuman. Animals cannot respond to you, cannot answer what you ask them, and thus are deprived of the human word.[21]

Or in other words, the animal's inability to respond corresponds to its incapacity to speak in the first person. For the majority of the scientific and philosophical tradition, the animal does not have the capacity to think or say "I." The implications, for both Derrida and Agamben, of the ability to utter the first-person pronoun were discussed at some length in chapter 2, but here what is most crucial to note is the way Derrida modulates his critique of the self-present voice (developed most concertedly, as we saw, in his readings of Husserl) into a deconstruction of what he takes to be the complacent self-assurance of the speaking (i.e., human) subject. Above all, being able to *respond*—rather than mechanistically react to stimuli—correlates to having a living voice, to being a conscious "I" existing in a vocal medium, an *ego* that can say "I think." From Descartes to Kant to Husserl and beyond, "This capability, this power to have [*pouvoir-avoir*] the 'I' takes the high ground; it erects, it raises (*erhebt*) man infinitely (*unendlich*) above all the other beings living on earth" (*Animal* 92). Speaking here specifically of Kant's thinking subject, though as a "reprise of the Cartesian *cogito*" (*Animal* 92), Derrida illustrates the intimate relation of the ability to say (or think) "I" with the ability to respond, both of which capacities are the defining abilities of the human against the animal. "Every human language," Derrida writes, "has at its disposal this self 'as such,' even if the word for it is lacking" (*Animal* 93). And citing a passage in which Kant argues that "All languages must think it when they speak in the first person, even if they do not have a special word to express this concept of 'I,'"[22] he notes:

> If Kant gives, to men and to languages that don't have a word for "I," credit for something for which he will never give credit to animals and their systems of signs, it is not just because the latter lack words in general . . . but because the "I" that is in thinking before being in language is nothing other than thinking itself, the power to think, the understanding that is lacking in the animal. (*Animal* 94)

The animal, in short, cannot think because it cannot utter the first-person pronoun, cannot say "I." In chapter 2, we saw Derrida and Agamben addressing similar questions, though without emphasis on the status of the animal. In "The Supplement of Copula," for instance, we saw that Derrida challenges Benveniste for having an insufficiently philosophical understanding of the word or concept of "being." In that piece Derrida argues that in "Categories of Thought and Language," Benveniste implicitly and unwittingly grants to the word "being" a special status as a sort of supershifter that provides the ontological grounding for the communication and translation between categories of thought and language. And yet, as I argued, a reading of Benveniste's other texts on deictics and demonstrative pronouns might have complicated Derrida's critique; indeed, Agamben's consistent attention to precisely this aspect of Benveniste's thought is one of the things that leads him to pursue a fundamentally divergent philosophical path. It is striking, then, that Derrida here reprises a reading of Benveniste in elaborating the linguistic deficiencies of the animal, though this time alluding to the power to utter the first-person pronoun and then recasting the figures for iterability/writing and self-presence/being as the animal and the human (*Animal* 94):

> But what is in dispute—and it is here that the functioning and the structure of the "I" count so much, even where the word *I* is lacking—is the power to make reference to the self in deictic or autodiectic terms, the capacity at least virtually to turn a finger toward oneself in order to say "this is I." For, as Benveniste has clearly emphasized, that is what utters and performs "I" when I pronounce or effect it. It is what says "I am speaking of me"; the one who says "I" shows himself in the present of his utterance, or at least of its manifestation. Because it is held to be incapable of this autodeictic or auto-referential self-distancing [*autotélie*] and deprived of the "I," the animal will lack any "I think," as well as understanding and reason, response and responsibility. The "I think" that must accompany every representation is this auto-reference as condition for thinking, as thinking itself; that is precisely what is proper to the human, of which the animal would be deprived. (*Animal* 94)

What this passage shows is that at a fundamental level Derrida's deconstruction of the human-animal distinction and its inherently anthropocentric biases is the same as his deconstruction of the phono-logo-centric biases inherent in the argumentation of, say, Saussure and Husserl. To be clear: *the two arguments are not merely similar (analogically, formally) to each other, but the same.* As Derrida states in a passage quoted above, the animal's unresponsive mechanical reaction "shares that irresponsibility with writing" (*Animal* 52), and any valorization of the human response is based on the vital self-presence that is held to be untainted by the contamination of iterability, mechanical reproducibility, and all of the characteristics that define the nature of the *gramma*. Again, this is not a mere analogy. In a tour de force of philosophical synthesis that grounds an extraordinarily wide range of reference upon his clearly demarcated first principles, Derrrida shows that the anthropocentrism of the human-animal distinction (in Descartes as well as Kant, Carroll, Husserl, and others) *is* phono-logo-centrism.

In this way, Derrida's reading of the human and animal in *The Animal That Therefore I Am* is no less programmatic than Agamben's critical survey of that same dividing line from the ancients to the moderns in the first half of *The Open*. While for Agamben the human and animal are continuously separated and articulated by the structure of the ban, the inclusive exclusion, in Derrida's reading we find the human defined by an untenable othering of "the animal" in an attempt to affirm and safeguard the coherence and purity of the human sphere—whether that be defined by reason, spirit, language, or some other criterion. In this sense, Agamben's and Derrida's texts on the animal appear to fall cleanly onto either side of the division between first principles that this book has been tracing, showing among other things how these first principles apply in specific contexts and with regard to particular questions, such as the human-animal distinction. These texts on the animal, however, also contain evidence of a more direct engagement between the two thinkers, or at least a more direct engagement with Agamben on the part of Derrida.

BIOS AND ZŌĒ

Early in *The Animal That Therefore I Am*, Derrida wonders whether "one can still confidently call *life* the experience whose limits come to tremble at the bordercrossings between *bios* and *zōē*, the biological, zoological, and anthropological, as between life and death, life and technology, life and history, etc." (*Animal* 24). Even though Agamben is not named at this—or indeed any other—point in that text, the reference to *bios* and *zōē* almost certainly alludes to Agamben's systemization of this split. And though in the pages of *The Animal That Therefore I Am*, *bios* and *zōē* are left without much more than a passing comment, in the few years following that lecture Derrida had arrived at a definite position on Agamben's biopolitical categories. Besides the fortunate attendees of Derrida's seminars for the 2000–2001 academic year, most of us had to wait until the publication of *The Beast and The Sovereign I* (French 2008, English 2009) to read what would prove to be his most direct and extended critique of Agamben, and in particular of his influential interpretation of the Greek terms *bios* (qualified or human life) and *zōē* (animal life). As Geoffrey Bennington notes, Derrida's reading of the passage in *The Politics* where Aristotle discusses the human as the *zōon politikon* (1278b 19) is intended at least in part as a critique of Agamben's claim that there is such a neat distinction to be drawn between these two terms; thus, by extension, Derrida suggests that Agamben's biopolitical thesis rests on unstable ground.[23]

Derrida first raises an objection to the *bios/zōē* distinction on logical and philological grounds. Agamben opens *Homo Sacer* with the now well-known statement that "The Greeks had no single term to express what we mean by the word 'life,'" and from there sets out the distinction between the senses attached to the two Greek terms: "*zoē*, which expressed the simple fact of living common to all living beings (animals, men, or gods), and *bios*, which indicated the form or way of living proper to an individual or a group" (*HS* 1). Agamben's very brief survey of the distinct usages of these terms in the Greek context culminates with a reading of a passage in Aristotle's *Politics* that appears to affirm just this distinction. In a key sentence, Aristotle writes that "If there is no great difficulty as to the way of life [*kata ton bion*], clearly most men will tolerate much suffering and hold onto life [*zōē*] as if it were a kind of serenity [*euēmeria*, beautiful day] and a natural sweetness" (1278b 29–31, qtd. in *HS* 2). Derrida, however, is skeptical, claiming that "on the basis of a single occurrence of the word *bios*, in the midst of many uses of *zōē* or *zēn* (to live) ... [Agamben] thinks he can find a distinction between *bios* and *zōē* that will structure his entire problematic" (*BS* 315). Derrida is surely overstating the case a bit in suggesting that Agamben draws this distinction on the basis of this single occurrence of the term *bios* (as he knows, and on the next page implicitly acknowledges, that Agamben also refers here to Plato's *Philebus* and Aristotle's *Nichomachean Ethics*, albeit in passing). Nevertheless, he does raise a critical question about the function of this lexical and conceptual distinction within Agamben's theory. Derrida writes: "What is unfortunate [for Agamben] is that this distinction is never so clear and secure, and that Agamben himself has to admit that there are exceptions, for example in the case of God, who, says Aristotle's *Metaphysics* [1072b 28, qtd. in *HS* 1], has a *zōē aristē kai aidios*, a noble and eternal life" (*BS* 316).

Agamben does in fact concede this usage of *zōē* in that passage, but he argues that the force of this phrase is that God, too, is a living being, rather than that nobility and eternity are "qualifications" or forms or ways of God's life, a claim that is indeed supported by the context of the Aristotelian text. More problematic, though, is the passage from the *Politics* in which Aristotle defines man as a "*politikon zōon*" (1253a 4). With regard to this usage, Agamben offers a much more cryptic explanation, which Derrida rejects out of hand. Agamben claims that "here (aside from the fact that in Attic Greek the verb *biōnai* is practically never used in the present tense), 'political' is not an attribute of the living being as such, but rather a specific difference that determines the genus *zōon*" (*HS* 2). Is there a logical difference between an attribute and a specific difference? Derrida argues that there is not (see *BS* 329), and that conceding this would "actually ruin everything that [Agamben] is saying" (*BS* 328). And there is no doubt that Agamben spends very little time explaining what precisely he means by this distinction, which is surprising given the importance that the *bios-zōē* split has for his argument. However, even though his discussion of this issue is rather laconic, it is not entirely illegible, and perhaps can be elucidated in such a way as to, if not answer all of Derrida's doubts, at least offer some initial response.

In the first place, *zōon*, the living being, which is derived from the verb *zēn*, has no common equivalent derived from *biōnai*, which in turn, as Agamben notes, is rarely used in the present tense. While this may go some way to explaining Aristotle's phrase, it is not in fact the argument Agamben actually offers. Rather, he says that *politikon* is a "specific difference" that determines the genus *zōon*. Agamben is alluding here to Aristotle's method of definition by division, later taken up in Scholastic logic, in which the key terms *genos* (genus, kind), *diaphora* (*differentia*, difference), and *idion* (property, attribute) are distinguished from one another. In *Topics*, Aristotle argues that (1) "A property is something which does not indicate the essence of a thing, but yet belongs to that thing alone, and is predicated convertibly of it" (102a 18), while (2) "A genus is what is predicated in what a thing is of a number of things exhibiting differences in kind" (102a 31).[24] In other words, a genus is determined by a predicate that is essential to it. This passage from the *Topics* goes on to explain the criteria of generic definition in terms that are directly pertinent to the debate at hand. Aristotle writes, "We should treat as predicates in what a thing is [i.e., essential predicates] all such things as it would be appropriate to mention in reply to the question, 'What is the object in question?'; as, for example, in the case of man, if asked that question, it is appropriate to say 'He is an animal' (102a 32–35).[25] Thus man belongs to the genus animal because being an animal is an essential predicate of being a human. By contrast, an attribute that may belong to the human (Aristotle's example is the capacity to learn grammar [see 102a 20]) may be unique to the human but it does not "indicate the essence" of the human.

If this schema is followed, Agamben's point appears to be that the human is indeed a *zōon*, that humans are part of the genus of living things, but that it is a living being that also has a distinctly "political" *way* of living, a *bios*. *Bios* would thus be the "specific difference" (*eidopoios diaphora*, the "difference that makes a species") of the *zōon* that is the human. There is no doubt that Agamben's wording is unclear, but perhaps the logic of the distinction he is making can be further illuminated by turning to another of his engagements with Aristotle's thought on the question of life. Indeed, even if he is invoking the difference between inessential and essential predicates, Agamben nevertheless appears to be very close to agreeing with the very argument he is critiquing here, namely, that the human is "a living animal with the additional capacity for political existence" (*HS* 3). For on such a reading the human would then be a member of the genus *zōon*, with additional capacities (politics, language) then defining its subgenus or species. This, however, assumes that the logic of Agamben's account is based on the *conjunction* and *addition* of elements and attributes, rather than on the "*mysterium disiunctionis*" that is at the center of the fourth chapter of *The Open*.

In "*Mysterium disiunctionis*," Agamben alludes to Aristotle's method of definition by division, though this time without evoking the terms "specific difference" and "genus." Nevertheless, the process by which one attribute becomes the essential characteristic for defining a genus (here called the "principle of foundation" [*O* 14]) can be observed in a passage on the various senses of the term "to live" from *De anima*. Using a phrase that could equally be applied to the distinction between *bios* and *zōē*, Agamben examines Aristotle's "strategic articulation of the concept of life" (*O* 13) and outlines the argumentation by which Aristotle arrives at the "nutritive power" (*threptikon*)—a rough equivalent of *zōē*—that is common to all living things. Aristotle writes:

> [The] term "to live" has more than one sense, and provided any one alone of these is found in a thing we say that the thing is living—viz. thinking, sensation, local movement and rest, or movement in the sense of nutrition, decay and growth. Hence we think of all species of plants also as living, for they are observed to possess in themselves a principle and potentiality through which they grow and decay in opposite directions.... This principle can be separated from the others, but not they from it—in mortal beings at least.... By nutritive power [*threptikon*] we mean that part of the soul which is common also to plants. (413a 20–413b 8, qtd. in *O* 13–14)

Agamben's interest here is not the way qualities and capacities are added onto this *zōē* or *threptikon* in order to arrive at higher living beings like animals and humans, but rather the way Aristotle must divide out and separate types of life in order to arrive at the most general and basic one. As he notes, Aristotle does not define what life is, but rather "limits himself to breaking it down, by isolating the nutritive function, in order then to rearticulate it in a series of distinct and correlated faculties or potentialities (nutrition, sensation, thought)" (O 14). The generic sense of "life," then, is arrived at by a strategic isolation and then rearticulation of its various senses, with one—*threptikon*, *zōē*—becoming the privileged and primary one on which all the others are then refounded. "In other words," Agamben writes, "what has been separated and divided (in this case nutritive life) is precisely what—in a sort of *divide et impera*—allows the construction of the unity of life as the hierarchical articulation of a series of functional faculties and oppositions" (O 14).

What Agamben observes at work here, in other words, is the logical structure of the ban as it is employed by Aristotle to define "life"—the very same logic that separates and at the same time relates *bios* and *zōē* in the argumentation of *Homo Sacer*. Though perhaps too obliquely presented in the opening pages of *Homo Sacer*, such a distinction among genus, attribute, and specific difference is indeed helpful in seeing a broader issue in Agamben's argument concerning *bios* and *zōē*, for this is not a division that indicates a clean and essential separation, but rather an imbeddedness; *zōē* is not autonomous and cleanly separated from *bios politikos*, but rather "inclusively excluded" from it. Derrida claims that in order for his biopolitical thesis to work, "Agamben is required to demonstrate that the difference between *zōē* and *bios* is absolutely rigorous" (BS 326), but this objection misses the point that Agamben is trying to make about the *kind* of difference or division that is established between the two terms, a difference that is precisely not "absolutely rigorous." The logic of Agamben's argument in the opening pages of *Homo Sacer*—oblique as it is on this point—is that the specific difference of *politikos* is an index precisely of the relation of ban that separates and binds the human and *zōē*. Even though, as Agamben notes, "to speak of a *zōē politikē* of the citizens of Athens would have made no sense" (HS 1), the *zōon politikon*, the living being that is "political" (i.e., the human), would not only make sense but indeed affirm the very claim that he is proposing, namely, that in man there is both *zōē* (in a removed, "banned" state) and *bios*. Or to put the point in another way, this distinction is not an example of what Agamben calls the "metaphysical mystery of conjunction" (*O* 16) (i.e., adding or joining the capacity for political existence to *zōē*), but rather of the "practical and political mystery of separation" (*O* 14).

Although Derrida rejects the notion that this is Aristotle's reasoning here, plausibly arguing instead that he "might very well have said, and in my opinion certainly did say, that 'the attribute of the living being as such' (and thus of bare life, as Agamben would say), the attribute of the bare life *of the being called man* is political, and that is his specific difference" (*BS* 329–30), Agamben reads Aristotle's logic in term of the ban-structure, which defines *zōē* (and produces it as bare life) by way of separation and inclusive exclusion:

> It is possible to oppose man to other living things, and at the same time to organize the complex—and not always edifying—economy of relations between men and animals, only because something like an animal life has been separated within man, only because his distance and proximity to the animal have been measured and recognized first of all in the closest and most intimate place. (*O* 15–16)

For Agamben, that measurement and recognition is a matter of imposing the ban on the *zōon* and creating the caesura within living things in order strategically to separate not only the human from the animal, but the human from its own animal life, its bare life, which nevertheless always remains exclusively included.

In fact, an excellent example of this logic at work can be found in Derrida's discussion of a key moment in Descartes's *Second Meditation* (a text that, perhaps surprisingly, Agamben does not directly address in *The Open*). In the course of arriving at the illustrious definition of the human as a thinking thing, Descartes actually rejects the idea that this being must be thought of as a "rational animal," arguing that if such a definition were accepted, "then I should have to inquire what an animal is, what rationality is, and in this way one question would lead me down the slope to other harder ones."[26] Over the next few pages, Descartes then goes on to eliminate all appeals to the physical, biological, and sensate body (in part because they are susceptible to deceit by the hypothetical "malicious deceiver, who is deliberately trying to trick me in every way he can") as criteria of self-definition, arriving finally, of course, at "thought."[27] As Derrida notes in his reading of this famous passage, Descartes's "'I am,' in the purity of its intuition and thinking, excludes animality, even if it is rational. In the passage that follows this bracketing of the rational animal, Descartes proposes abstracting from his 'I am,' if I can put it this way, everything that recalls life" (*Animal* 72). Or in other words, "in order to define access to a pure 'I am,' [Descartes] must suspend or, rather, detach, precisely as detachable, all reference to life, to the life of the body, and to animal life" (*Animal* 72). For Derrida, this opposition between the "I am" and the body in Descartes's argumentation constitutes a deconstructible opposition running through the middle of the most famous and influential Cartesian thesis. But it is easy to see how viewing this passage through the lens of the sovereign ban-structure would lead to an alternative, let us say Agambenian reading, wherein the exclusion of life from the sphere of the "I am" (which nevertheless still includes it) is the strategic ruse by which the construction of the Cartesian cogito can then found itself—an originary strategic separation, rather than conjunction.

This is to say, returning to the debate above, that Derrida's characterization of Agamben's distinction between *bios* and *zōē* as an (unsuccessful) "absolutely rigorous" difference (*BS* 326), "airtight frontier" (*BS* 321), and "strict opposition" (*Rogues* 24) provides an illustration of the different ways in which he and Agamben conceive of the logical and functional relation between polar terms. For Derrida, opposition implies and even requires a binary difference, two terms or poles separated by the space of difference or alterity. But in Agamben's schema, there is not an opposition between *bios* and *zōē* but a relation of ban, which is not a pure alterity but an inclusive exclusion. While for Derrida, "the human" and "the animal" are indeed opposite—and thus eminently deconstructible—terms, Agamben's paired terms stand in (fictional/mythic) relation to each other by way of the ban-structure, the "practical and political mystery of separation" that underlies his biopolitical argument much more fundamentally than the specific distinction between *bios* and *zōē*.

Such might serve as at least a preliminary response to Derrida's "logical-type observation" (*BS* 329) concerning Agamben's reading of the *bios-zōē* distinction in the opening pages of *Homo Sacer*. There is, however, another sense of Derrida's claim that Agamben cannot establish an "absolutely rigorous" difference between these two terms, and that is a historical-philological one. This critique is developed most fully not by Derrida himself, however, but by Laurent Dubreuil. In an oddly ad hominem attack—in truth, one that echoes a similar tone in Derrida's text—that seeks to "[divest] the crow of his peacock feathers," Dubreuil similarly questions Agamben's distinction between *bios* and *zōē*, and by extension his thinking on biopolitics more broadly.[28] Dubreuil, too, argues, not without force, that the terminological distinction is far more hazy than Agamben would have it, and that as clear as the line between these words might frequently seem in Aristotle, this would in any case not hold for the whole of the Greek linguistic world. Dubreuil's specific philological critique, however, quickly develops into a broader indictment of Agamben and, strangely, his readers. He states that Agamben's philology is presented so as to be mystifying and unchallengeable, that it is "*foremost* intended for the readers who do not possess the means of verification," that it is a "philology for show."[29] This is not the same as claiming—as one has every right to do—that some of Agamben's philological claims may be debatable (as are, say, some of Aristotle's, Heidegger's, or Derrida's). While Agamben's entry into the (semi-)popular consciousness has meant that his vocabulary (which Dubreuil also wants to claim is not even his)[30] is sometimes invoked in less than rigorous ways, it is nevertheless not clear whom exactly Dubreuil has in mind when he describes Agamben's audience as unable to verify (or even think critically about) this argument.

In any case, even someone who is not a classical philologist would be capable of opening Liddell and Scott and finding that *bios* is principally defined as "*life*, i.e. not animal life (*zōē*), but *a course of life, manner of living*," and thus be reassured both that the distinction is not entirely pulled out of Agamben's hat and that it is not the case, as Dubreuil (and to a lesser extent Derrida) claims, that "*zōē* has never uniquely signified bare or animal life."[31] Reading a little further, he or she can also find that *bios* is indeed sometimes used as a synonym for *zōē*, as in Aeschylus's *Bion ekpnein* ("he breathed out his life," i.e., "he breathed his last") and presumably many other places. With a little more initiative, the nonspecialist can also turn to a dictionary of Indo-European roots and discover that both *bios* and *zōē* appear to derive, as Agamben notes (*HS* 1), from the single Indo-European root **gweia*, which may or may not lead one to further reflection on the question of whether the Greek distinction historically inaugurates a conceptual difference that persists in Western thought. Or a nonspecialist can read Dubreuil's very interesting discussion of the Greek and Aristotelian usages and the grammarians' inconclusive debates over the meanings of the two terms. Though Dubreuil is just as correct as Derrida in pointing out that the precise significance of the two terms has varied over time (and place), Agamben is nevertheless—and perhaps even uncharacteristically—using them in their most widely accepted and historically consistent primary meanings. Indeed, while it is true that a great deal rests for Agamben on the distinction between *bios* and *zōē*, his reading of these terms is in truth much less idiosyncratic than, for example, his reading of *dunamis-adunamia*, as discussed in chapter 3. Far from offering an eccentric etymology and definition, Agamben's adoption of *bios* and *zōē* actually follows the first definition in every lexicon's entry for these terms.[32]

Another objection raised by Derrida in *The Beast and the Sovereign I*, however, has to do with Agamben's reading (or, by his account, lack of reading) of Heidegger in *Homo Sacer*, and this objection will return us to both *The Open* and *The Animal That Therefore I Am*. In the same session of the *Beast and the Sovereign* seminar that contains the polemic with Agamben, Derrida devotes some pages to a discussion of Heidegger aimed primarily at showing how a reading of his texts would have disrupted the presentation of biopolitics and biopower in the thought of both Agamben and Foucault (and even more pointedly, in the former's interpretation of the latter). Among the issues that Heidegger addresses in the passages Derrida selects for discussion is the relation between Dasein and its biological life, that is to say, Dasein and its animality.

The major point that Derrida makes in this discussion is that, rather than subscribing to the definition of the human as *rational animal*, Heidegger takes great pains to denounce "the biologism, the biologistic reduction of this definition of man" (BS 322). And to this effect he cites several long excerpts from the "Letter on 'Humanism,'" one of which includes this passage:

> Above and beyond everything else, however, it finally remains to ask whether the essence of man [*das Wesen des Menschen*] primordially and and most decisively lies in the dimension of *animalitas* at all [*in der Dimension der animalitas*]. Are we really on the right track toward the essence of man as long as we set him off as one living creature among others in contrast to plants, beasts, and God? . . . In principle [if we do this] we are still thinking of *homo animalis*—even when *anima* [soul] is posited as *animus sive mens* [spirit or mind], and this in turn is later

posited as subject, person or spirit [*Geist*]. Such positing is the manner of metaphysics. But then the essence of man is too little heeded and not thought in its origin, the essential provenance that is always the essential future for historical mankind. Metaphysics thinks of man on the basis of *animalitas* and does not think in the direction of his *humanitas*.[33]

Derrida quotes these passages as examples of Heidegger's denunciation of biologism (and of a particularly charged line of thought in the politics of the time). However, what is perhaps most striking about these pages of Derrida's seminar is their polemic with Agamben. Derrida writes of this passage (and the other key passages) that "Heidegger's propositions . . . are quoted neither by Foucault (who practically never talks about Heidegger, not even when he introduces his problematic of biopower), nor by Agamben, who, for his part, knows Heidegger well and of course quotes him, but not at all as he should have done in this context, recalling at least Heidegger's two major texts—as well known as they are accessible—on these questions" (*BS* 323–24). And a few lines down: "But on all these texts we have just read about the *logos*, about *zōē*, the zoological interpretation of man, about metaphysics and technology and Christianity as prevalent interpretations of *logos* and *zōē*, about the condemnation of biologism, absolute silence from Agamben" (*BS* 324). As noted at the beginning of this chapter, though *The Open* was published a month before this lecture was delivered (March 20, 2002), it is clear from this passage (which ironically reads like a précis of *The Open*) that Derrida had not at that point been aware of this material. Indeed, the sole text of which he makes mention in *The Beast and the Sovereign I* (as well as *The Animal* and *Rogues*) is *Homo Sacer*, which he clearly—and rightly—reads as a presentation of Agamben's biopolitical thesis, understanding the *bios-zōē* split as the centerpiece of that theory. Of course, the point of this observation is not to suggest that Derrida should have been aware of Agamben's text (and vice versa), but rather to note how closely their senses of the question of the animal in Heidegger parallel each other, as we will see in the next section.[34]

HEIDEGGER AND THE ANIMAL

In the book *Aporias*, which is the publication of his presentation at the Cerisy-la-Salle conference of 1992 (that is, five years before *The Animal That*

Therefore I Am), Derrida takes up the Heideggerian analysis of being-toward-death as the quality or capacity that distinguishes Dasein from other entities.[35] To be sure, the analysis of Dasein is not to be understood exactly as the analysis of "man," but of something previous to the "man" of humanism, something which Heidegger seeks to separate from the humanist concept of man by a rigorous analytical border. As Derrida writes: "[For Heidegger,] Dasein or the mortal is not man, the human subject, but it is that in terms of which the humanity of man must be rethought" (*Aporias* 35). And Heidegger's primary critique of the humanist tradition is that it conceives of man as the rational animal, the animal that has the capacity for thought or reason or language. Indeed, as Derrida notes, it is the ubiquity of this conception of the human that leads Heidegger to employ his most famous term: "If Heidegger uses the expressions Dasein and analysis of Dasein, it is because he does not yet allow himself any philosophical knowledge concerning what man is as *animal rationale*, or concerning the ego, consciousness, the soul, the subject, the person, and so forth, which are all presuppositions of metaphysics or of ontical knowledge, such as anthropo-thanatology or biology" (*Aporias* 29).

What, then, is it in *Being and Time* that distinguished the human from other living creatures? Many things, to be sure: Dasein is in-the-world, it is "there," it has foreknowledge and foreunderstading that discloses the world as world, and so forth. But in *Being and Time*, none of these capacities is presented and analyzed *in explicit contrast* to other living entities as openly as the capacity for being-toward-death. Indeed, as Derrida notes (*Animal* 144), one of the very few moments where the animal is mentioned at all in *Being and Time* is in the discussion of being-toward-death, where in truth it serves as a sort of straw man in the argument concerning Dasein's unique relation to its own finitude.

In §49, Heidegger defines and distinguishes several types of disappearance (or ceasing to be), and this is where he identifies "death" or "dying" as the type of disappearance proper only to Dasein. In *Aporias*, Derrida lingers on Heidegger's effort to differentiate the various types of disappearance and examines the stakes involved in Heidegger's assigning such a determinate function to "dying" as opposed to the other modes of disappearance, for example, the way mere animals cease to exist by "perishing." "The hierarchy of this order," Derrida writes, "is governed by the concern to think what the death proper to Dasein is, that is, Dasein's 'properly dying' (*eigentlich sterben*)" (*Aporias* 29–30). This line of demarcation between the types of disappearance (on the one hand *death*, which gives rise to Dasein and which defines its existential limit, and on the other hand, the sort of *perishing* characteristic of animals and their more or less purely biological—certainly not existential—nature) must be maintained at all costs if the Heideggerian analysis of Dasein is to remain intact; that is to say, even though it is translated into a language of "proper death" and "being-toward-the-end," the distinctive mortal-temporal structure of Dasein is founded on a recognizably "humanist" conception of the man-animal distinction. Or in other words, at a basic schematic level, the function of being-toward-death is roughly equivalent to that of the rational-linguistic criteria that, say, Descartes employs to distinguish the human from animals (and automatons). Derrida notes that the stakes of maintaining this border are extremely high, for "if the attestation of this 'properly dying' or if the property of this death proper to Dasein was compromised in its rigorous limits, then the entire apparatus of the edges would become problematic, and along with it the very project of an analysis of Dasein" (*Aporias* 30). And further: "If . . . the rigor of this distinction were compromised, weakened, parasited on both sides of what it is supposed to dissociate (*verenden / eigentlich sterben*), then . . . the entire project of the analysis of Dasein, in its essential conceptuality, would be, if not discredited, granted another status than the one generally attributed to it" (*Aporias* 31–32).

In *Aporias*, Derrida works at that weakening of this distinction by focusing on the idea of the "border." The range of reference in that book spans cultural, national, geographic, ethnologic, and anthropological notions of borders, among others, and reproducing its intricacies is beyond the scope of this chapter. But we can already see even in the above-quoted passages the affinities between Derrida's deconstruction of Dasein's constitutive being-toward-death and his deconstruction of the border between the human and the animal in *The Animal That Therefore I Am*, where his reading will again "consist, certainly not in effacing the limit, but in multiplying its figures, in complicating, thickening, delinearizing, folding, and dividing the line precisely by making it increase and multiply" (*Animal* 29).

Among the various engagements over the course of the Cerisy-la-Salle conference of 1997, Derrida's reading of Descartes is the most important, at least for our purposes, not only because it sets in motion the issues and problems structuring the seminar's other major readings of Kant, Levinas, and Lacan, but also, and most of all, because it is the starting point for the reading of Heidegger that Derrida had in preparation but presented only in an improvised and provisional form on the last day. As provisional as it may be, it nevertheless gives us very clear indications of the sort of argument Derrida would have presented, of the passages in *Fundamental Concepts* he would have scrutinized, and indeed of the key texts he would have had Heidegger confront. "I would have chosen," he says, "for reasons that you know, certain passages [in Heidegger's text] on Descartes, because what matters to me would be to show, in a provocative way, of course, that Heidegger's discourse is still Cartesian, whereas the prime target, in *Being and Time* but also here, is, of course, Descartes. Not only Descartes' mechanicism, but also Descartes' *cogito*" (*Animal* 146). As is well known, Heidegger puts the Cartesian cogito into question by suggesting that in his method of radical doubt Descartes nevertheless did not doubt the nature of the thinking I: "[With Descartes,] philosophizing begins with *doubt*, and it seems as though everything is put into question. Yet it only seems so [*Aber es sieht nur so aus*]. Dasein, the I (the ego), is not put into question at all [*Das Dasein, das Ich (das Ego) wird gar nicht in Frage gestellt*]."[36]

We saw earlier that Derrida similarly reproaches Descartes for not doubting his conviction that the animal was merely a reactive machine deprived of the capacity for true thought. Here it will be precisely the same reproach of insufficient doubt that will show how at base Heidegger remains within the Cartesian (and Cartesian-metaphysical) sphere, since his entire analytic is grounded on an underinterrogated assumption concerning a certain deprivation of the animal with respect to the human. Just as Heidegger, in other words, exposes a moment of credulity in Descartes, and from there proceeds to dismantle the Cartesian *cogito* (which becomes the Heideggerian Dasein), so, too, does Derrida show how Heidegger himself unwittingly assents to the Cartesian animal metaphysics precisely insofar as he continues to respect and observe the same determining division between human and animal. "[A]t this very moment," Derrida writes, "when Heidegger's gesture is to move forward in the direction of a new question, a new questioning concerning the world and the animal, when he claims to deconstruct the whole metaphysical tradition, notably that of subjectivity, Cartesian subjectivity, etc., insofar as the animal is concerned he remains, in spite of everything, profoundly Cartesian" (*Animal* 147).

But what for Heidegger is that lack and deprivation that separates the animal from the human (or Dasein)? It is, in the famous tripartite thesis of *The Fundamental Concepts of Metaphysics*, that while the stone is worldless and the human is "world-forming," the animal is "poor in world." Both Derrida's and, as we will see, Agamben's analyses center on what is at stake for Heidegger in this peculiar "poverty" that seems to lie uncertainly between having and not having world. What is the nature of this *Weltarmut*, which places the animal just on the border of Dasein's distinctive being-in-the-world and yet excludes it from fully having the world?

As this question implies, at stake in Heidegger's analysis of the animal in *The Fundamental Concepts of Metaphysics* is the question of *world* and of Dasein's distinctive and unique mode of being-in-the-world. As Derrida notes, in the beginning of §42 of *Fundamental Concepts*, where he introduces the tripartite thesis, Heidegger situates that text's discussion of the animal in relation to his previous investigations into the concept of world. On the one hand, in the 1928 essay "On the Essence of Ground," he had examined the "*history of the word* 'world' and the historical development of the concept it contains";[37] on the other, in *Being and Time* he had "attempted to provide a preliminary characterization of the *phenomenon of world* by interpreting the *way in which we at first and for the most part move about in our everyday world.*"[38] However, in *Fundamental Concepts* he informs us he will pursue a different strategy, "a *third path* . . . the path of a *comparative examination*" that will examine Dasein's having of world in relation to the animal's poverty in world.[39] As noted above, there is an important comparative element to Heidegger's original analysis of being-toward-death in *Being and Time*, though it consists in little more than an assertion that the animal does not properly die. Here however, the lengthy analysis of the animal's relation to its environment (*Umwelt*) in contrast to Dasein's relation to (or being in) the world (*Welt*) vastly expands the inquiry into animal life and behavior, and yet it still remains squarely within the parameters of the existential analytic of Dasein set out in the earlier text. That is to say, Heidegger's entire examination of the animal, which it must be said clearly entailed extensive reading in the biological, ethological, and zoological research of the time (as Derrida says: "a serious piece of work!" [*Animal* 143]) is at base an extension of his analysis of Dasein's mode of being-in-the-world; his inquiry has not shifted to an interest in the animal or animality for its own sake, but has rather simply shifted methodological gears in its pursuit of the concept of Dasein's world. The aporias and difficulties that Derrida will uncover in Heidegger's reading of the animal are, then, ultimately difficulties regarding the concept of world, which Derrida argues Heidegger will finally admit to be "a very obscure concept! At the point where he advances like an army, armed with theses, solid, positive theses, it buckles, and he says in the end: decidedly, this concept of world is obscure. At bottom he doesn't know what 'world' means" (*Animal* 151).

But what are these aporias and difficulties? In his concluding comments of the seminar, Derrida gestures toward a number of points that he would pursue in a reading of *Fundamental Concepts*. For example, since animals are neither *Vorhanden* nor *Zuhanden*, and yet not *Dasein*, what kind of beings are they? And more pointedly (and more poignantly), in what way do we share the world (*mitgehen? mitexistieren?*) with these beings—especially in the case of domestic animals (say, a cat) with whom we share our very home? (see *Animal* 145, 157–58). And since the question of home is raised, why does Heidegger denounce the modern city-dweller as the "ape of civilization," by which he means that the urbanite cannot truly feel the fundamental attunement (*Grundstimmung*) of homesickness? (see *Animal* 145–46).[40] And in denying the animal the *logos* (as part and parcel of denying the animal an existential relation to the world), how much of the argument depends of defining *logos* fundamentally as *propositional* language? (see *Animal* 141–43, 157).

All are paths worth pursuing, to be sure, but because it anticipates so closely Agamben's reading a few years later and because it is the most fully fleshed out in Derrida's text, I would like to focus briefly here on his outline for a deconstruction of Heidegger's deployment of the *weltarm* animal in the explication of the exclusively human possession of the "as such" (*die "als"-Struktur*). The reason for focusing on this issue is not simply because the "as such" is the definitive structure of Dasein's having of world—insofar as having world means being able to apprehend something *as* something, which for Heidegger the animal can never do (see *Fundamental Concepts of Metaphysics* 331; *Animal* 143, *O* 49)—but also because Derrida's sketch of a proposed reading at the end of *The Animal That Therefore I Am* can be filled out with a text to which he alludes but, in the context of these rushed closing comments, does not wish to return (see *Animal* 143), namely, the sixth chapter of 1987's *Of Spirit*.[41]

Ticks And Cats   197

I noted above that Derrida's outline in *The Beast and the Sovereign* of the way Agamben "should have" read Heidegger sounded uncannily like a précis of the reading that Agamben had in fact just published in *The Open*. In the case of *Of Spirit*, however, Derrida's text presents a reading of Heidegger on the question of the animal (and especially of the key sections of *Fundamental Concepts*) that, though brief, anticipates so closely the contours, if not the conclusions, of Agamben's reading that it is striking Agamben does not mention Derrida in the course of his exposition. Be that as it may, a review of this text will put into relief the different results obtained when Heidegger's texts on the animal are viewed through the lens of Derrida's deconstructive strategy and the lens of Agamben's analysis of the anthropological machine.

Derrida begins chapter 6 of *Of Spirit* with the question "What do we call the world?" (*OS* 47), lingering on Heidegger's evocations of the animal's attenuated or blocked relation to the world.[42] In answering—or deepening—that question "What do we call world?," Derrida provides a fairly thorough deconstructive critique of the human-animal distinction as it is deployed to support this central Heideggerian concept. Again, Heidegger approaches the question of world in *Fundamental Concepts* through a comparative examination that articulates itself in the tripartite thesis, the critical juncture of which is that between the animal's poverty in world and Dasein's having (or forming) of world. Obviously the animal is not simply without world like the stone or any other inanimate object that may, with regard to Dasein, be *vorhanden* or *zuhanden*. Rather, the animal participates in and interacts with the world in some way, and in this sense certainly shares something of the world with Dasein. But whatever this mode of impoverished relation to the world is, Heidegger insists that it is not the same as Dasein's having. For Derrida as well as Agamben, the precise nature or function of this distinction between poverty and wealth in world is the point on which everything rests. It is a nexus or pivot point that, as the reader will by now surely anticipate, carries different meanings for Derrida and Agamben: from Derrida's deconstructive position, which will "insist on the moments of vertigo and circularity in this text" (*Animal* 155), it will appear as an untenable and self-diffracting difference that cannot be maintained within Heidegger's contradictory argumentation; for Agamben, it is the nexus point in the inclusive-exclusive mechanism of the anthroplogical machine's ban-structure that will bind/separate/articulate the human and the animal in an ultimately biopolitical relation. Before examining Agamben's reading, however, let us conclude the discussion of Derrida.

In his closing comments at Cerisy-la-Salle in 1997, Derrida notes that "One of the most difficult places [in *Fundamental Concepts*] is where Heidegger, having to defend the thesis that the animal is *weltarm*, is keen to mark that that impoverishment is not caught in a hierarchy, that it is not simply a 'less'" (*Animal* 155). The stone, one presumes, has less of the world insofar as it has none (is *weltlos*), but the animal is not like the stone; it does not have no world, and therefore it does have world in some sense or to some degree. The animal, therefore, *does* have world, and yet not in the full way that Dasein does. This oscillation between having and not having is what Heidegger problematically names poverty, and it will be the point on which Derrida pushes most insistently in his reading. With respect to the worldless stone, he writes, "to say that the animal is poor in world is to demonstrate that it has world. And Heidegger consistently says deliberately contradictory things, namely that the animal has a world in the mode of 'not having.'" (*Animal* 156). An obscure statement to be sure: the animal has world in the specific way that is does not have world.[43] Such an explanation, of course, clearly begs the question yet again: "What does *weltarm* mean? What does this poverty of world mean?" (*OS* 48).

The question is not easy to answer, and Heidegger's contradictory statements about the animal's poverty at times suggest at least two possible readings. On the one hand, standing as it does between Dasein's wealth in world and the stone's total lack of world, the middle status of the animal's *Weltarmut* does suggest a "*difference of degree* separating indigence from wealth (*Reichtum*)" (*OS* 48) and thus that the animal's poverty is simply a "less." But on the other hand, according to Derrida, Heidegger also implies that

> [t]his poverty is not an indigence, a meagerness of world. It has, without doubt, the sense of privation (*Entbehrung*), of a lack: the animal does not have enough world, to be sure. But this lack is not to be evaluated as a quantitative relation to the entities of the world. It is not that the animal has a lesser relationship, a more limited access to entities, it has an *other* relationship.... [T]he difficulties are already piling up between two values incompatible in their "logic": that of lack and that of alterity. (*OS* 49)

As Derrida suggests (*OS* 48), of these two logics of poverty—one quantitative, one qualitative—Heidegger rejects the former and proposes that the animal's attenuated relation to the world is fundamentally different rather than lesser; and yet even this "choice" leaves the status of the animal's poverty uncertain. Poverty then becomes a kind of having, a kind of wealth, albeit a different kind, and if this is the case we must still allow that, in some strange way, "The animal *has* and *does not have* a world" (OS 50).

Poverty in world names a different kind of having of world, and the question then becomes what is the nature of this difference, which, no matter how strongly one might assert that it is not a hierarchical difference, nevertheless amounts to something that the human has which the animal doesn't? The key possession that the comparative examination is intended to bring to the fore, of course, is that what Dasein has of the world, or the way in which it has the world, is the "as such." The animal "has access to entities but, and this is what distinguishes it from man, it has no access to entities *as such*" (OS 51). That is the nature of *Weltarmut*: "The animal can have a world because it has access to entities, but it is deprived of a world because it does not have access to entities *as such*" (OS 51).

The importance of the *as such* structure in Heidegger's thought is well known, and need not be followed out in much detail here. Suffice to say that in apprehending something *as* something, that is, in apprehending the difference between being and beings (i.e., the ontological difference), Dasein opens the space for being to manifest itself. Higher stakes cannot be imagined in Heidegger's thought, and so a great deal is riding on the results of this comparative examination with the animal's *Weltarmut*, as Derrida repeatedly points out. Undermining this analysis of the "as such," then, would mean undermining the status and significance of world, and from there it is no great distance before the whole of the Hedeggerian project begins to tremble under deconstructive pressure. But what Derrida specifically focuses on in this chapter of *Of Spirit*, and indeed *The Animal That Therefore I Am*, is the way that this trembling is caused by an unwittingly "humanist teleology" (OS 56) that takes the human-animal divide to be firm and, in some sense, providential. At the level of Heidegger's more or less overt intentions, "The expression 'poor in world' or 'without world,' just like the phenomenology supporting it, encloses an axiology regulated not only upon an ontology but upon the possibility of the *onto-logical* as such, upon the ontological difference, the access to the Being of the entity" (OS 56). But insofar as Heidegger employs and deploys the animal as it has been generally conceived in the humanist tradition (i.e., as impoverished in some way), the comparative examination of Dasein's world opens itself to debilitating questions:

> Can one not say, then, that the whole deconstruction [in the Heideggerian sense] of ontology, as it is begun in *Sein und Zeit* and insofar as it unseats, as it were, the Cartesian-Hegelian *spiritus* in the existential analytic, is here threatened in its order, its implementation, its conceptual apparatus, by what is called, so obscurely still, the animal? Compromised, rather, by a *thesis*, on animality which presupposes—this is the irreducible and I believe dogmatic hypothesis of the thesis—that there is one thing, one domain, one homogeneous type of entity, which is called animality *in general*, for which any example would do the job. (OS 57)

Human exceptionality is founded on a presupposition of the animal's generality, something about which a good look at animals in their multiplicity—what indeed does an earwig have in common with a dolphin?—would give one pause. And this assumed generality of the animal in Heidegger's argumentation is the can of worms, so to speak, that Derrida would propose to open in a concerted reading of *Fundamental Concepts of Metaphysics*. With this tactic he would put into question not primarily the status of the animal's—or better, of animals'—poverty, but precisely the most coveted possession of the human:

> Hence the strategy in question would consist in pluralizing and varying the "as such," and, instead of simply giving speech back to the animal, or giving to the animal what the human deprives it of, as it were, in marking that the human is, in a way, similarly "deprived," by means of a privation that is not a privation, and that there is no pure and simple "as such." There you have it. (*Animal* 160)

Derrida questions whether Heidegger succeeds in carrying out the task he had set for himself as articulated in the "Letter on 'Humanism,'" that is, to think of man in the direction of his *humanitas* instead of beginning with *animalitas*.[44] What he finds is that the strategic and rhetorical separation of the animal creates a false and untenable structure that collapses under the intense pressure that it itself puts on the category of "the animal." Under Derrida's lens, this fault line between the human and the animal fractures and multiplies to the point where the entire Heideggerian project of a fundamental ontology begins to tremble.

This is also the fault line that Agamben surveys in Heidegger's thought, and as we now turn back to *The Open*, we will see once again the simultaneous proximity and distance between Derrida's and Agamben's methods. Chapter 12 of *The Open* is titled "Poverty in World," and it is, unsurprisingly, devoted to an examination of *Weltarmut* in *Fundamental Concepts*. On most of the key points regarding this concept, Agamben is in agreement with Derrida, as well as most commentators. For Agamben, too, *Weltarmut* occupies a strange middle ground between the total worldlessness of the stone and the world-building or being-in-the-world of Dasein. And indeed, as is suggested by the epigraph to the chapter ("The behavior of the animal is never an apprehending of something as something" [qtd. in *O* 49]), Agamben identifies the specific deprivation of the animal as lacking the "as such," although he does not use that precise term. Instead, he focuses the discussion on the closely related question of concealment and disconcealment. And he, too, asks what, in its poverty, is the precise nature of the animal's relation to the world? What is its mode of interacting with and behaving toward the objects with which it comes in contact? As is well known, with regard to its external environment the animal is, in Heidegger's terms, *benommen*, "captivated," and it is on this term that Agamben focuses his analysis.[45] Earlier we saw how Derrida questions the coherence of Heidegger's analysis by pushing on his claim that the animal "has a world in the mode of 'not having'" (*Animal* 156)—an apparently contradictory statement (among others) that Derrida underlines in Heidegger's text. Here, however, Agamben does not seek to intensify and multiply the fault lines in Heidegger's rhetoric so much as follow the development of his line of thought to the point where the human-animal divide (or nexus) reaches its most foundational articulation, which is also a zone of indistinction. Under Agamben's lens, this point of fundamental articulation, where the human primordially meets and separates itself from the animal, proves indeed to be captivation.

Heidegger characterizes *Benommenheit* as the animal's reaction and orientation to the "disinhibitors" that make up its *Umwelt* or environment. This environment, in turn, is a sort of analogue or impoverished version of Dasein's *Welt*. Thus the animal is exposed to, stimulated by, given over to, and captivated by its environment. It is fixed—or better, transfixed—in a direct relation of immediate stimulus and reaction with its disinhibiting ring. As Agamben notes, Heidegger gives some vivid examples of this captivated behavior, most notably the bee who continues to suck honey though its abdomen has been removed, and his interest in this absolutely transfixed behavior of the animal is evident. But what is most important about this "ceaselessly driven" behavior for Heidegger is that this ecstatic exposure and captivation is precisely the point where the question of "the open" arises. He writes:

> Because of this being ceaselessly driven the animal finds itself suspended, as it were, between itself and its environment, even though neither the one nor the other is experienced *as* a being. Yet this not-having any potentiality for revelation of beings, this potentiality for revelation as withheld from the animal, is at the same time a being taken by. . . . We must say that the animal is in relation with . . . , that captivation and behavior display an *openness* for. . . . For what?[46]

The openness of animal captivation is an openness toward the disinhibitor, but this is not experienced as a being, as anything "as such." The disinhibitor, whatever it may be, never appears to the animal as that which it is; it is never disconcealed as such. And yet, Heidegger argues that, for all that, it is not concealed either. The animal's openness to and captivation by its disinhibiting ring/environment is beyond the play of disconcealment and concealment, which is the exclusive domain of Dasein.

This description of captivation is, in fact, very much like the description of *Weltarmut* that Derrida had emphasized—in both, the animal in its poverty is deprived of the "as such." The terms in which Agamben presents this definition, however, are slightly different:

> The ontological status of the animal environment can at this point be defined; it is *offen* (open) but not *offenbar* (disconcealed; lit., openable). For the animal, beings are open but not accessible; that is to say, they are open in an inaccessibility and an opacity—that is, in some way, in a nonrelation. This *openness without disconcealment* distinguishes the animal's poverty in world from the world-forming which characterizes man. (*O* 55)

Is the animal, then, open? Is it in the open? The question is still not entirely decided, for though the animal does not have the "as such," it nevertheless appears to enjoy, in its captivation, an intense relation—even an immediacy—with its environment that could be considered a far richer experience than that enjoyed by Dasein in its "having" of world. Heideggger

Ticks And Cats 203

acknowledges this point and indeed some years later devotes a number of pages in his 1942–43 course on Parmenides to a discussion of the literary text that most forcefully imagines this wild gift of the animal precisely as a privileged experience to which man can never accede, namely, Rilke's eighth *Duino Elegy*.

As the opening lines of the elegy read: "With all its eyes the animal [*die Kreatur*] looks out / into the Open. Only *our* eyes are turned / backward, and surround plant, animal, child / like traps, as they emerge into their freedom."[47] For Rilke, the animal's experience is a richness compared to which our own reflective, rational, and representational experience can only appear as an extreme poverty indeed. And yet Heidegger forcefully rejects Rilke's valorization of the animal's "open" as being founded on the forgetting of the question of being and a misunderstanding of the ontological difference. For Rilke, the intensity of the animal's (and indeed the child's) experience of itself and its environment—which in a certain sense are one and the same—represents the highest prize conceivable. But this intensity, for Heidegger, is nothing but the experience of *Benommenheit*, the ontological limit beyond which the animal cannot move. For Heidegger, as Agamben puts it, "Only man, indeed only the essential gaze of authentic thought, can see the open which names the unconcealedness of beings" (O 58).

And yet, if this exposure is not truly the open as the unconcealedness of beings, it is nevertheless still something extraordinary and not to be dismissed or denigrated. In attempting to conceive of what this relation and experience of animal captivation is, Heidegger concludes that while captivation entails neither disconcealment nor concealment, when the disinhibitor comes into contact with the animal's sensory apparatus, it nevertheless "brings an *essential disruption* [wesenhafte Erschütterung] into the essence of the animal."[48] Akin to Dasein's *Weltbildung*, the essential disruption of *Benommenheit* is the point where man and animal become all but indistinguishable, and as Agamben will go on to argue, this is the place where we can see the operations of the anthropological machine at work most profoundly in Heidegger's thought.

On the one hand, "the essential disruption that the animal experiences in its being exposed in a nondisconcealment drastically shortens the distance that the course had marked out between animal and man, between openness and non-openness" (O 61), bringing the two to their closest proximity. At the same time, however, Heidegger insists that this "closest proximity of both essential constitutions is merely deceptive, and that an abyss lies between them that cannot be bridged by any mediation whatsoever."[49] Within the methodology of *Fundamental Concepts*, in which Dasein's having of world is to be examined by way of a comparative examination with the animal's poverty in world, Heidegger's argument has thus brought us to the point where the comparison reaches its critical juncture. As Agamben puts it, "the understanding of the human world is possible only through the experience of the 'closest proximity'—even if deceptive— to this *exposure without disconcealment*" (*O* 62).

The significance of this juncture for Agamben's reading can hardly be overestimated, for it is at this point in Heidegger's argumentation that anthropogenesis takes place. The animal's exposure without disconcealment is the site of the operation that will produce the human because it entails an anthropological operation on the animal *within* Dasein. Ecstatic exposure, consequently, is not only what Dasein and the animal appear (even if deceptively) to have in common; it is also what Dasein must "ban" or inclusively exclude in order to transform animal behavior and captivation into human comportment and ek-sistence. Agamben puts the point rhetorically:

> Perhaps it is not the case that being and the human world have been presupposed in order then to reach the animal by means of subtraction . . . ; perhaps the contrary is also, and even more, true, that is, that the openness of the human world (insofar as it is also and primarily an openness to the essential conflict between disconcealment and concealment) can be achieved only by means of an operation enacted upon the not-open of the animal world. (*O* 62)

With respect to the earlier modulations of the anthropological machine— say, Haeckel's *homo alalus*—there is a sort of reversal here, wherein it is no longer the human that is presupposed and subtracted to define the animal but the animal environment that is retracted to produce the human.

Eric L. Santner has noted that "Agamben's crucial contribution to [the] 'debate' between Rilke and Heidegger as to the meaning of 'the Open' in animal and human life has been to underline a profound ambiguity in Heidegger's own position."[50] While Derrida, as we saw above, puts pressure on a number of ambiguous and contradictory moments in Heidegger's argumentation, the ambiguity that Santner has in mind is a distinctly Agambenian one, having to do not with the question of alterity, undecidability, and multiplicity, but with the ambiguous logic of the ban-structure as it functions obscurely at the center of Heidegger's analysis. At the point of closest proximity between animal and human, animal captivation must be excluded from Dasein's ek-sistence; but this exclusion is also a gesture of capture which leaves an essential residue of animality within the structure of Dasein. As a product of the anthropological machine, Dasein is not an animal, but since this machine functions according to the ban-structure, Dasein *is* also an animal. As Santner puts it, "for Heidegger man's freedom and destiny as 'world-forming' include a dimension—I am tempted to say a traumatic dimension—that brings him into proximity to the animal, that renders him, in a certain sense, creaturely."[51] The "certain sense" that Santner evokes here can be more closely specified: it is precisely the way in which, in enacting the inclusive exclusion of the ban, or establishing a fictional state of exception, the anthropological machine creates a zone of indististinction or indifference between the two terms it means to separate, a zone in which one term blurs into the other. This, in short, is the locus of the "profound ambiguity of Heidegger's own position" that Agamben identifies.

In Heidegger's text we see this anthropogenetic operation and this proximity between captivation and comportment in *boredom*, the discussion of which takes up about one-third of *Fundamental Concepts of Metaphysics* and constitutes, as Agamben notes, the longest analysis Heidegger ever devoted to a *Stimmung* (attunement, mood) in his entire oeuvre. In the context of the present discussion, this stands to reason, since at stake in boredom is "nothing less than anthropogenesis, the becoming Da-sein of living man" (*O* 68). To best understand Agamben's investment in Heidegger's treatment of boredom, and to see how his reading of it is situated within his own philosophical system, it will be helpful to first make explicit a connection between the captivation of the animal, its enthrallment and exposure to its disinhibiting ring or environment, and the concept of potentiality that we examined in chapter 3. Where Heidegger—again, closely following Uexküll—describes the animal's mechanistic, instinctual reaction to its disinhibitors, what he is describing is a reactivity to a given stimulus; it is a foredetermined and compulsory reaction provoked by the contact between the disinhibitor and the animal's sensory apparatus. In short, given the fixity and automaticity of its reactions, we can say that the animal is a creature of *dunamis* or potentiality-to, but without any corresponding *adunamia* or potentiality-not-to. The animal cannot *not* react to the disinhibitor, is not free with respect to it, and thus is not—like the human—a "being of pure potentiality" (*WM* 2). I noted in chapter 3 how closely Agamben draws on Heidegger for his concept of pure potentiality, and indeed in his reading of Heidegger's pages on boredom in *Fundamental Concepts* the question of potentiality and possibility are the central issue once again. This background is essential for tracing the line of Agamben's reading here, for ultimately what occurs in the experience of boredom is an experience of *adunamia*, potentiality-not-to, *pure* potentiality.

In a well-known passage, Heidegger describes the experience of becoming bored while waiting at a train station. He paces up and down the platform, then up and down the road, stares blankly at the schedules, looks at the clock, cannot bring himself to read the book in his backpack. Nothing can break into or alleviate this feeling of emptiness that encompasses and saturates him. And yet, in an odd way, this boredom is profoundly compelling, so compelling, in fact, that in it Heidegger will see an analogue or echo of precisely that captivation that holds the animal riveted to its environment; he writes that "In becoming bored by something we are precisely still held fast [*festgehalten*] by that which is boring, we do not yet let it go [*wir lassen es selbst noch nicht los*], or we are compelled by it, bound to it for whatever reason."[52] Agamben explains this affinity between boredom and captivation in terms that will show both their proximity to each other and eventually their separation. He writes that "*In becoming bored, Dasein is delivered over* (ausgeliefert) *to something that refuses itself, exactly as the animal, in its captivation, is exposed* (hinausgesetzt) *in something unrevealed*" (*O* 65). Thus, in Dasein's experience of boredom, "something vibrates like an echo of that 'essential disruption' that arises in the animal from its being exposed and taken in an 'other' that is, however, never revealed to it as such" (*O* 65). But on the other hand, as Heidegger's analysis deepens, boredom is shown to hold within it an experience that is utterly unlike animal captivation, and this is because, unlike the animal in its *Benommenheit*, in the suspended state of boredom, Dasein comes to experience *potentiality*.

In boredom, Dasein is unable to have any relation to or engage with the *vorhanden* and *zuhanden* things of the world. Beings as a whole refuse themselves, allow no access and no *activity* on the part of Dasein. All of the things that Dasein might possibly do are held in suspense and withdrawn; and yet, for all this, of course, the world does not disappear and Dasein does not cease to exist. Instead, in this experience, something else obliquely appears: Dasein's potentiality-for-being in its pure state. As Heidegger writes: "This refusal tells of these possibilities of Dasein. . . . [T]here occurs the dawning of the possibilities that Dasein could have, but which lie inactive [*brachliegende*]. . . . [I]n refusal there lies a reference to something else. This reference is the *announcement of the possibilities which lie inactive*."[53] The reader at this point will see the significance for Agamben of this revelation of unrealized possibilities, of unrealized potentialities that nevertheless still *exist*, but in a modality of *adunamia*. It is none other than the

> experience of the disconcealing of the originary possibilitization (that is, pure potentiality) in the suspension and withholding of all concrete and specific possibilities.
>
> What appears for the first time as such in the deactivation (in the *Brachliegen*) of possibility, then, is the *very origin of potentiality*—and with it, of Dasein, that is, the being which exists in the form of potentiality-for-being [*poter-essere*]. But precisely for this reason, this potentiality or originary possibilitization constitutively has the form of a potential-not-to [*potenza-di-no*], of an impotentiality, insofar as it is *able to* [*può*] only in beginning from a *being able not to* [poter non], that is, from a deactivation of single, specific, factical possibilities. (O 67)

For Agamben, this crucial section of *Fundamental Concepts* tells the story of the revelation, and indeed the origin, of pure potentiality as the distinctive and constitutive structure of Dasein.

There are, of course, numerous moments in Heidegger's thought where potentiality-for-being is asserted as the distinctive structure of Dasein, but the crucial point here, in the context of the human-animal thematics that this chapter has been tracing, is that Heidegger's comparative examination establishes this structure not only in distinction to the animal, but also, on Agamben's reading, as a result of a certain operation enacted upon the animal, which Dasein must exclude and separate itself from. "The animal environment," Agamben writes, "is constituted in such a way that something like a pure possibility can never become manifest within it. Profound boredom then appears as the metaphysical operator in which the passage from poverty in world to world, from animal environment to human world, is realized" (*O* 68). About the structure of (im)potentiality as basis for a first philosophy, Agamben would more or less agree with Heidegger (from whom he primarily draws for this idea), but in the critical reading offered in *The Open*, Agamben seeks to show how Heidegger still sees potentiality in terms of a quasi-humanist teleology and most importantly (and more obscurely) of a biopolitical ban of the animal. Heidegger creates a story, a myth, about the origin of human potentiality that inscribes the animal as *sacer*, as bare life, and thus is still at some level operating within a biopolitical, sovereign, exceptional logic. In the argumentation of *Fundamental Concepts*, the human open "is opened only by means of a suspension and a deactivation of the animal relation with the disinhibitor. . . . [and] the wonder 'that beings *are*' is nothing but the grasping of the 'essential disruption' that occurs in the living being from its being exposed in a nonrevelation" (*O* 68). This "grasping"—this, so to speak, *capture*—of the animal's ecstatic captivation, which opens Dasein to the open, is at the same time and to the same degree an exclusion of *animalitas* from *humanitas*, from which it is separated by an "abyss." Dasein is produced by the inclusive exclusion of the animal at the point where captivation and boredom are articulated to each other across an empty space or zone of indistinction; anthropogenesis occurs in the space of the ban.

Agamben's reading of Heidegger in *The Open*, then, can certainly be said to be a "biopolitical" one, though here that biopolitical argument is modulated through the concept of the anthropological machine, which produces the ek-sistent human by effecting a "sovereign" ban on the living being and thus produces bare life in the form not only of "the animal" but also of the indispensable animality that is disavowed and yet retained in the animality of the human. For Agamben, Heidegger's argumentation in *Fundamental Concepts* is consistent with—and is perhaps the ultimate expression of—the anthropological machine of humanism that has informed the conception of the human since the ancients. As Agamben writes in a summary of his survey of the "anthropological" tradition: "Anthropogenesis is what results from the caesura and articulation between human and animal. This caesura passes first of all within man" (*O* 79). The establishment of this caesura is an ongoing and "political" act that must be reenacted every time the nature of the human is put into question, even in the case of Heidegger's attempt to conceive of man not beginning with his *animalitas* but in the direction of his *humanitas*. For even here,

> Being, world, and the open are not . . . something other with respect to animal environment and life: they are nothing but the interruption and capture of the living being's relationship with its disinhibitor. The open is nothing but a grasping of the animal not-open. Man suspends his animality and, in this way, opens a 'free and empty' zone in which life is captured and a-bandoned [*ab-bandonata*] in a zone of exception. (O 79)

That zone of exception, it must finally be noted, is the one established by the fictitious state of exception, which is defined primarily by its intention to reestablish the order that the anomic breach had made to tremble—the Schmittian rather than the Benjaminian emergency, which seeks to rearticulate the spheres of law and life, man and animal, rather than definitively separate them. The anthropological machine is an articulating machine. Halting the ceaseless, if shifting, articulations that the machine establishes between man and animal is what Agamben here identifies as the supreme political task. In the closing moments of *The Open*, he writes:

> As we have seen, in our culture man has always been the result of a simultaneous division and articulation of the animal and the human, in which one of the two terms of the operation was also what was at stake in it. To render inoperative the machine that governs our conception of man will therefore mean no longer to seek new—more effective or more authentic—articulations, but rather to show the central emptiness, the hiatus that—within man—separates man and animal, and to risk ourselves in this emptiness: the suspension of the suspension, Shabbat of both animal and man. (O 92)

It is no coincidence, of course, that this is an almost perfect repetition of the conclusion of *State of Exception*, the central concern of which is the articulation of law and life: "[I]f it is possible to attempt to halt the machine, to show its central fiction, this is because between violence and law, between life and norm, there is no substantial articulation" (SE 87).

The supreme concerns in Derrida's and Agamben's readings of the human and animal, then, are fundamentally different. Derrida focuses the question on the being of beings, the ontological difference, and how the effort to guarantee for Dasein the capacity to apprehend being as such by way of a comparison, and inevitable devaluation, of a monolithic animal Other collapses under its own multiple and multiplying fractures, fractures that are forced apart by the pressure of *différance*. For Agamben, on the other hand, the supreme stake is possibilitization, the origin of potentiality, and the way Heidegger cannot retrace the way back to this origin without recourse to the anthropological machine and the establishment of an inclusive exclusion of *animalitas* with regard to *humanitas*.

What, however, of the tick? We recall Uexküll's account of the tick that was kept alive in a Rostock laboratory for eighteen years "in a condition of absolute isolation from its environment" (*O* 47), that is to say, kept alive (if this is indeed the right term) in the total absence of that "essential disruption" (*wesenhafte Erschütterung*) that constitutes the animal's captivation, its impoverished, nondisclosive form of being-(almost)-in-the-world. In this limbo that is neither *weltbildend* nor *weltarm*, the tick persists and survives in a quasi-life as if the clock had stopped. Agamben notes that Uexküll offers little explanation of this strange experiment other than describing the tick's timeless life in the laboratory as a "period of waiting" and supposing that "without a living subject, time cannot exist" (*O* 47). "But what," Agamben asks, "becomes of the tick and its world in this state of suspension that lasts eighteen years? How is it possible for a living being that consists entirely in its relationship with the environment to survive in absolute deprivation of that environment? And what sense does it make to speak of 'waiting' without time and without world?" (*O* 47). If it is true that this tick "guards a mystery ... which neither Uexküll nor Heidegger was prepared to confront" (*O* 70), it is because under the privative conditions of the laboratory experiment it experiences no "essential disruption" that can be articulated, by means of an inclusive exclusion, to the boredom that is Dasein's fundamentally world-disclosive *Stimmung*. The tick is neither captivated nor bored; it obstinately dwells in a hidden, indistinct space within the topology of the anthropological machine, a space that is neither that of the human nor that of the animal. In its obscure suspension between the human world and the animal environment, the tick thus eludes the ban of "the animal" and refuses to articulate the two. Instead of maintaining the fiction of the anthropological machine's functioning, it marks and exposes the fracture that may definitively rupture its articulating, anthropogenetic mechanism.

Though it only appears briefly in the book, the tick in the Rostock laboratory might thus be seen not as an eccentric walk-on in the drama of *The Open*, but rather as its secret protagonist, who has already gone "beyond both disconcealing and concealing, beyond both being and the nothing" (*O* 91) and thus indicates the way toward the "Shabbat of both animal and man" (*O* 92). And perhaps this small and strange creature is also a messenger who, after eighteen years away, returns, as if from the dead, to tell us that within the chronological time of the calendar there is a different kind of time. This other kind of time—messianic time—is the subject of the next chapter.

6

A MATTER OF TIME

> Time present and time past
> Are both perhaps present in time future,
> And time future contained in time past.
> If all time is eternally present
> All time is unredeemable.
>
> —T. S. ELIOT, "BURNT NORTON"

In the last decade of the millennium, both Derrida and Agamben take up the question of "messianism" or "the messianic." As commentators have noted, few terms of this strong a religious provenance have received such heavy usage in recent philosophical debates, and certainly many of Agamben's and Derrida's texts of this period have been central to discussions of a supposed "religious turn" in contemporary philosophy.[1] While the issue of the messianic appears in a number of places in Derrida's work, the key text in which he addresses the question is, perhaps surprisingly, 1993's *Specters of Marx*; Agamben's central text on the messianic is, much less surprisingly, his "commentary on the Letter to the Romans," 2000's *The Time That Remains*. Both of these texts, however, take up and develop motifs that extend back to much earlier texts in which the messianic or religious issues are less pronounced, or indeed absent. Above all, the philosophical question that both Agamben's and Derrida's analyses of the messianic address, the context without which their considerations of the messianic are virtually unintelligible, is that of *time*. Thus for all their saturation with the language and conceptuality of theology, Derrida's and Agamben's discussions of messianism are most fundamentally considerations of the problem of temporality; for both, "the messianic" is above all a matter of time.

PROPHET OR APOSTLE

Agamben's central explication of "messianic time" in the fourth chapter of *The Time That Remains* is framed implicitly in contradistinction to Derrida's valorized notion of "the messianic" as the irreducible displacement and futurity of the "to come" [*à-venir*]. Indeed, one way to frame the basic difference between Derrida's and Agamben's conceptions of messianic time is precisely to ask: When, with respect to the present, does the messianic event happen? Is the messianic event yet to come or has it already occurred? It goes without saying that this question, perhaps more than any other, permeates the Judeo-Christian theological tradition. The properly theological implications of this issue, however, are beyond the scope of the present discussion, and though the vocabulary of the religious tradition will dominate the following pages, this is largely because of Derrida's and Agamben's frequent (though not exclusive) recourse to this vocabulary in their accounts of time and temporality.

In much the same way that Agamben dramatizes his differences with Derrida through his reconstruction of the debate between Benjamin and Schmitt, in *The Time That Remains* he sets in motion a polemic with deconstruction through an oblique allegorizing strategy that we must reconstruct here. Chapter 4 of the book opens with a consideration of Paul's description of himself in the Letter to the Romans as *apostolos*, an apostle, the literal meaning of which is "emissary" or "mandatory." "Why," Agamben asks, "does Paul define himself as an apostle and not, for example, a prophet? What difference is there between apostle and prophet?" (*TTR* 60). There is, it turns out, an absolutely critical difference. While Agamben discusses some philological issues related to these terms, such as their Hebrew equivalents (*shaliah* and *nabi*) and the usages of these terms in Judaism, his primary point is that "the prophet is essentially defined through his relation to the future" (*TTR* 61), while the apostle is an emissary sent forth by and speaking on behalf of the Messiah who has already come. He continues:

> [E]ach time the prophets announce the coming of the Messiah, the message is always about a time to come, a time not yet present. This is what marks the difference between the prophet and the apostle, The apostle speaks forth from the arrival of the Messiah. At this point prophecy must keep silent, for now prophecy is truly fulfilled. . . . The word passes

on to the apostle, to the emissary of the Messiah, whose time is no longer the future, but the present. This is why Paul's technical term for the messianic event is *ho nun kairos*, "the time of the now"; this is why Paul is an apostle and not a prophet. (*TTR* 61)

As the following pages will attempt to show, the line separating Derrida's and Agamben's fundamental philosophical programs—which the preceding pages have attempted to trace across their long careers—can also, and quite vividly, be seen in the difference between Derrida's insistence on the messianic "to come" and Agamben's valorization of the messianic "now."

If this is correct, and the passage just cited does contain a polemical characterization of Derrida's "*à venir*," it would not be the first time Agamben has implicitly characterized Derrida as something like a (false) prophet. As Adam Thurschwell has noted, in "*Pardes*," another theological allegory for his debate with Derrida, Agamben casts Derrida in the role of Rabbi Aher, who cuts the branches for Rabbi Akiba (Agamben) to enter the realm of divine knowledge while himself remaining stuck within the meshes of human language. As Thurschwell puts it: "Without saying so in quite so many words (although he comes very close elsewhere), Agamben's virtual charge here is the harshest that can be leveled: that Derrida, or rather deconstruction (there is nothing personal in any of this), is the false Messiah."[2] The "elsewhere" to which Thurschwell refers here is the 1992 essay "The Messiah and the Sovereign: The Problem of Law in Walter Benjamin," where Agamben characterizes deconstruction as a "petrified or paralyzed messianism that, like all messianism, nullifies the law, but then maintains it as the Nothing of Revelation in a perpetual and interminable state of exception, 'the "state of exception" in which we live'" (*P* 171). The debate over the Benjaminian and Schmittian states of exception has been discussed in chapter 4 and need not be reexamined here. But as we will see shortly, at a distance of roughly ten years from "*Pardes*" (and eight from "The Messiah and the Sovereign"), the allegory of *The Time That Remains*, while employing a different cast of characters, makes roughly the same argument and indeed repeats the charge: "Deconstruction is a thwarted messianism, a suspension of the messianic" (*TTR* 103).

For Agamben, a truly messianic time, a "time of the now," is what the apostle, rather than the prophet, announces. This is because the messianic event is not something to be awaited but something that has already occurred. While Paul's preterist conception of redemption—living in the time after the messianic event of Jesus's resurrection and thus living *in* messianic time—determines the entire discussion of *The Time That Remains*, it is also anticipated in Agamben's striking 1978 essay "Time and History: Critique of the Instant and the Continuum" and his brief but crucial discussion therein of the conception of time in Gnosticism, "that failed religion of the West" (*IH* 100). Just as with Paul, in Gnosticism "[t]he impetus toward redemption of Christian linear time is negated because, for the Gnostic, the Resurrection is not something to be awaited in time, to occur in some more or less remote future; it has already taken place" (*IH* 101).

Both Paul's "apostolic" relation to the messianic event and the Gnostics' analogously preterist view of redemption are examples of a conception of time that disrupts the notion of time as a line composed of successive points or instances leading either to a teleological end or simply to an ever-open future. This linear notion of time (and its disruption) can be further seen in a second distinction Agamben draws between messianic time and apocalyptic or eschatological time, the confusion of which he describes as the "most insidious misunderstanding" (*TTR* 62), more pernicious than even the confusion of apostolic announcement and prophecy. The *eskhaton* of time is the final point at which the line of time stops, the redemptive or wrathful culmination to which the apocalyptic thinker looks forward. By contrast, the apostle of the Messiah must negotiate the interstitial time *between* the messianic event and the future end. "The apocalyptic," he writes, "is situated on the last day, the Day of Wrath" while "[t]he time in which the apostle lives is . . . not the *eskhaton*, it is not the end of time" (*TTR* 62). Unlike the apocalyptic prophet, "[w]hat interests the apostle is not the last day, it is not the instant in which time ends, but the time that contracts itself and begins to end (*ho kairos sunestalmenos estin*; I Cor. 7:29), or if you prefer, the time that remains between time and its end" (*TTR* 62).

Another example of a heterodoxical conception of time that Agamben offers in that early essay "Time and History" is that of the Stoics. What is notable about the Stoic conception of time is not, of course, where it locates the moment of redemption along the chronological line, but rather rejection of the "geometry" of the chronological line itself. The Stoics' attempt to overcome the Greek concept of time, Agamben writes, appears as a refusal of the astronomical time of the *Timaeus*, image of eternity, and of the Aristotelian notion of the mathematical instant. For the Stoics, homogeneous, infinite, quantified time, dividing the present into discrete instants, is unreal time, which exemplifies experience as waiting and deferral. Subservience to this elusive time constitutes a fundamental sickness, which, with its infinite postponement, hinders human existence from taking possession of itself as something full and singular. (*IH* 101)

At this point, Agamben introduces what will prove to be a more or less exact synonym for messianic time in *The Time That Remains*: kairos.

> Against this, the Stoic posits the liberating experience of time as something neither objective nor removed from our control, but something springing from the actions and decisions of man. Its model is *kairos*, the abrupt and sudden conjunction where decision grasps opportunity and life is fulfilled in the moment. (*IH* 101; translation modified)

Gnosticism and Stoicism, then, with their fleeting glimpses into alternative conceptions of time and temporality, "emerge," in Agamben's formulation, "as the bearers of a message which is meant for us and which it is our task to verify" (*IH* 100).

What is striking about the essay "Time and History" is not only its uncanny anticipation of many of the arguments presented more than twenty years later in *The Time That Remains*—indeed, *The Time That Remains* is, in many ways, the fulfillment of the ideas initially presented in that essay—but the fact that it, too, is organized around a forceful, though somewhat implicit, polemic with Derrida. For example, in the passage cited above concerning the Gnostic rejection of the idea that the Resurrection is something that is to be "awaited in time," and in the passage concerning the Stoics' characterization of "waiting and deferral" and "infinite postponement" as a "fundamental sickness," one might—and should—hear an unflattering allusion to one of the most typical of deconstructive motifs. And one can equally hear an understated reference to Derrida's 1968 essay "*Ousia* and *Grammē*" in Agamben's assertion that "[w]hether it is conceived as linear or circular, in Western thought time invariably has the point as its dominating feature" (*IH* 100). As noted in the introduction to this book (see note 6), Agamben had almost certainly read "*Ousia* and *Grammē*" upon its publication in the collection *L'endurance de la pensée*, and there can be little doubt that this essay is very much on Agamben's mind when he writes "Time and History." It will therefore be worthwhile to spend some time here reviewing at least some of the salient features of Derrida's great essay in order to more fully illustrate the contesting position Agamben develops in "Time and History" and—much later, and much more fully—in *The Time That Remains*.

NUN, JETZT (1)

"*Ousia* and *Grammē*" is ostensibly a reading of an important late footnote in Heidegger's *Being and Time*. As is well known, Heidegger's magnum opus is, in fact, incomplete, and what we now read under that title is only the first of two projected parts of the work. The second half, the contents of which can be surmised from the material in Heidegger's lectures on *Kant and the Problem of Metaphysics* (1925–26), would have taken his project of fundamental ontology—and its "destruction" of classical ontology—further into the analysis of temporality gestured toward in the closing sections of the first (published) part of *Being and Time*. As Derrida notes in the opening sentence of his essay, this destruction required, first and foremost, that Heidegger "shake the 'vulgar concept' of time" (*M* 31) that governs the Western reflection on temporality from Parmenides and Aristotle to Husserl and Bergson. At the root of Heidegger's critique of this "vulgar concept" of time, and of the way it has often surreptitiously determined classical ontology, is an analysis of how it is grounded in an absolute valorization of the "present."

In Heidegger's formulation, this co-implication of a vulgar concept of time and classical ontology can be overtly seen in "the treatment of the meaning of Being as *parousia* or *ousia*, which signifies, in ontologico-Temporal terms, 'presence' (*Anwesenheit*). Beings are grasped in their Being as 'presence' (*Anwesenheit*); this means that they are understood with regard to a definite mode of time—the '*Present*' (*Gegenwart*)."[3] This determination of being as a both spatial and temporal present, with the former modeled on the latter, proves for Heidegger to be the presupposition from which Western ontology has never been able to escape. "From Parmenides to Husserl," Derrida writes, ventriloquizing Heidegger's position, "the privilege of the present has never been put into question. It could not have been.

218 *Strategy without Finality or Means without End*

It is what is self-evident itself, and no thought seems possible outside its element. Nonpresence is always thought in the form of presence . . . , or as a modalization of presence. The past and the future are always determined as past presents or as future presents" (*M* 34).

Heidegger's footnote concerning the vulgar concept of time occurs in a very late section of *Being and Time* titled "Temporality and Within-Timeness as the Source of the Ordinary Conception of Time," and the specific context of the note is a discussion of Hegel's analysis of time. While Heidegger's text (and indeed Derrida's reading of that text) opens out onto many spectacular vistas, for the purposes of the present discussion it will suffice to focus on the way the footnote claims that Hegel's analysis of time faithfully repeats the basic structures of Aristotle's exposition of time in *Physics IV*. Heidegger remarks, for instance, that

> Aristotle sees the essence of time in the *nun*, Hegel in the "now" (*jetzt*). Aristotle takes the *nun* as *horos*; Hegel takes the "now" as "boundary" (*Grenze*). Aristotle understands the *nun* as *stigmē*; Hegel interprets the "now" as a point. Aristotle describes the *nun* as *tode ti*; Hegel calls the "now" the "absolute this" (*das "absolute Dieses"*). Aristotle follows tradition in connecting *khronos* with *sphaira*; Hegel stresses the "circular course" (*Kreislauf*) of time.[4]

That is to say, there is an almost direct line that runs from Aristotle's concept of time to Hegel's (and beyond). And this continuity concerns not just one concept among others; rather, the conception of the "essence of time" as the "now," that is, as the present and as presence, provides the signal concept for virtually all philosophical thought in the tradition. "Has not," Derrida asks rhetorically, this time not merely ventriloquizing Heidegger, "the entire history of philosophy been authorized by the 'extraordinary right' of the present? Have not meaning, reason, and 'good' sense been produced within this right? . . . How could one think Being and time *otherwise* than on the basis of the present, in the form of the present, to wit a certain *now in general* from which no *experience*, by definition, can ever depart? The experience of thought and the thought of experience have never dealt with anything but presence" (*M* 38).

The Aristotelian *nun* and Hegelian *jetzt*, then, offer two exemplary instances of the Western reflection on time, and indeed on time conceived in terms of "the present." Because the temporal logic of the Hegelian

Aufhebung will prove to be crucial for Agamben's discussion of messianic time, we will direct our attention more toward Heidegger's and Derrida's treatments of Hegel than the parallel readings of Aristotle in which they are also engaged. Granted that frame, the first issue to clarify is the relation between the *jetzt* and the negating-preserving-raising action of the *Aufhebung*.[5]

As noted above, Heidegger suggests that Hegel's formulation of the problem of time is a near-perfect repetition of Aristotle's. Indeed, as Derrida notes (*M* 40), even though Hegel's key discussion of time in the *Jena Logic* never mentions Aristotle by name, it is such a self-evident allusion that any reference to Aristotle would be superfluous. As Derrida reconstructs the argument from *Physics IV* (*M* 39–40), Aristotle presents the aporetic status of the *nun* by asking two related questions: (1) does time belong to the sphere of beings or of nonbeings, and (2) what is its nature, its *phusis*? Aristotle claims that time is that which "is not" or "is barely, and scarcely," but he must paradoxically make this determination on the basis of a conception of the essence of time as the *nun* or "now," something like time's elementary particle. "The *nun*," Derrida argues, "is the form from which time cannot ever depart" (*M* 39), and out of this ambiguous element a number of difficult and inevitable aporias will arise concerning the nature of time.

In the first place, because the now is precisely what most obstinately eludes presence, Aristotle's conception of time as nonbeing is the necessary consequence of his having defined it as essentially constructed of an infinite series of nows. This is the source of a first paradox, for the fleeting *present instant* is what can never actually *be* present and always must experienced as nonbeing. In Derrida's words, "The now is given simultaneously as that which is *no longer* and as that which is *not yet*. It is what it is not, and is not what it is" (*M* 39). Time as such is conceived as a virtual series of "nows" that never individually achieve being insofar as they pass in the temporal flow from being to nonbeing in the very instant of their occurrence. Time itself, therefore, since it is composed of these infinite self-negating moments, is outside the realm of beings, it "belongs to nonbeings." As Derrida puts it, "that which bears within it a certain *no-thing*, that which accommodates nonbeingness, cannot participate in presence, in substance, in *beingness* itself (*ousia*)" (*M* 39–40).

And yet, according to Derrida, Aristotle also entertains the conflicting idea that the now is *not* the constitutive element of the nonbeing of time,

220   *Strategy without Finality or Means without End*

but is rather a nontemporal (i.e., substantial) element that is "affected" by time, which negates it by modalizing or "temporalizing" it, by turning it into either a past or future now. In this sense, "[e]ven if it is envisaged as (past or future) nonbeing, the now is determined as the intemporal kernel of time, the nonmodifiable nucleus of temporal modification, the inalterable form of temporalization" (*M* 40). Here Derrida alludes to the importance of the third-person present indicative "is" (which would be the intemporal medium in which beings "are") for the concept of "being" as such, and includes a reference to his own "The Supplement of Copula" as well as Heidegger's *Introduction to Metaphysics*, both of which were discussed in chapter 2 above. Most important for the purposes of the present discussion, however, is Derrida's illustration of the basic problematic out of which Aristotle formulates the "vulgar paradox" (*M* 43) that Hegel will repeat.

Hegel's repetition of this temporal problematic is not, however, a repetition without a difference. Indeed—and herein lies the salient point—it is "a *dialectical* repetition of the Aristotelian *aporia*" (*M* 41; Derrida's emphasis). Hegel has recast this aporetic structure as a key feature in—and in fact, as the driver of—the dialectic. Or to put this more precisely, the "now" (Hegel's *jetzt*) is the interval in which operates the *Aufhebung*. As Agamben notes in a passage from *The Time That Remains* to which we will return:

> In the *Phenomenology of Spirit*, the *Aufhebung* makes its appearance in the context of the dialectic of sense certainty and its expression in language via the "this" (*diese*) and the "now" (*jetzt*).... [The *Aufhebung*] transforms sense certainty into a negative and a nothingness and conserves this nothingness, converting the negative into being. In the "this" and the "now," the immediate is thus always already *aufgehoben*, lifted and preserved. Inasmuch as the "now" has already ceased to be once it has been uttered (or written), the attempt to grasp the "now" always produces a past, a *gewesen*, which as such is *kein Wesen*, nonbeing. (*TTR* 100)

Derrida's illustration of this dialectical process is taken from Hegel's somewhat less well-known analysis of the construction of geometrical space in the second part of the *Encyclopedia of the Philosophical Sciences*, also known as the *Philosophy of Nature*. Hegel's analysis here concerns how pure, undifferentiated space, "the abstract *universality of Nature's self-externality*, self-externality's mediationless indifference," comes to attain or receive determination or quality.⁶ As Derrida notes, "Differentiation, determination, qualification can only overtake pure space as the negation of this originary purity and of this initial state of abstract indifferentiation which is properly the spatiality of space" (*M* 41). That is to say, pure spatiality becomes phenomenal space by means of the dialectical negating-conserving process of the *Aufhebung*.

According to Hegel, spatiality unfolds itself into differentiated, phenomenal space by moving through a series of determinate negations (corresponding to the three dimensions) beginning with the point. We will focus on the first negation of the point in particular, but it may be worth citing all of Hegel's § 256, where we see the dialectical unfolding of phenomenal space as the *Aufhebung* of each dimension into the next, from point to line to plane. Hegel describes the process thus:

> The difference of space is, however, essentially a determinate, qualitative difference. As such, it is (α), first, the *negation* of space itself, because this is immediate *differenceless* self-externality, the *point*. (β) But the negation is the negation *of space*, i.e. it is itself spatial. The point, as essentially this relation, i.e. as sublating itself, is the *line*, the first other-being, i.e. spatial being, of the point. (γ) The truth of other-being is, however, negation of the negation. The line consequently passes over into the plane, which, on the one hand, is a determinateness opposed to the line and point, and so surface, simply as such, but, on the other hand, is the sublated negation of space. It is thus the restoration of the spatial totality which now contains the negative moment within itself, an *enclosing surface* which separates off a *single* whole space.⁷

In reviewing this paragraph, Derrida notes the way the point—insofar as it is the first determinate negation of abstract, indifferent space, and is yet itself necessarily caught up in (and in substance little more than the site of) the subsequent negation that gives us the line—constitutes something like that first "negative moment" that concrete space necessarily retains within itself in order to constitute itself.⁸ The function of the point, however, as the ambiguously positive and negating primary element of the dialectical construction of space, leads Derrida from the consideration of the construction of space to the "question of time" (*M* 42).

In this move from space to time, Derrida is directly following Hegel's line of argument. Indeed, Hegel moves almost directly from the paragraph quoted above to the section on time in the *Philosophy of Nature*. And with good reason, for as Derrida notes, in a certain sense we have already been talking about time. Time "has already appeared. The Being-no-longer and the Being-still which related the line to the point, and the plane to the line—this negativity in the structure of the *Aufhebung* already was time" (*M* 42). Because the constitution of space—or rather, the differentiation and phenomenalization of space—is a developmental process of negations and sublations, time is a "requisite" (*M* 42) for space; and the first negation of abstract spatiality is the point.

But again, the point is itself nothing more spatially substantial than the negation of itself into the line; it is, in other words, negativity itself. In a passage that Derrida cites, Hegel makes the triple identification of the point, negativity, and time in the following way: "Negativity, as point, relates itself to space, in which it develops its determinations as line and plane; but in the sphere of self-externality, negativity is equally *for itself* and so are its determinations."[9] That is to say that although punctual negativity relates itself to space, although it is, in the Hegelian terminology, "*for*" space, it is also *for itself* and can appear as "indifferent to the inert side-by-sideness of space."[10] This elemental negativity that, insofar as it is "for space," is constitutive of space but also, insofar as it is "for itself," indifferent to space draws us very near to the nucleus of the Aristotlelian problematic that, for Heidegger, Hegel is repeating albeit in a dialectical modulation. "Negativity," Hegel concludes, "thus posited for itself, is Time."[11] And as Derrida glosses this conclusion: "Time, therefore, is thought on the basis of, or looking toward, the point, and the point is thought on the basis of, or looking toward, time.... The *stigmē*, punctuality, therefore is the concept which, in Hegel as in Aristotle, determines nowness (*nun, jetzt*).... [T]he Hegelian dialectic is but the repetition ... the brilliant formulation of a vulgar paradox" (*M* 43).[12]

However, that paradox is based on only one of Aristotle's propositions concerning time—albeit the primary one—namely, that the now is a part (*meros*) of time, an insubstantial temporal nucleus, and that the being of time can be conceived on the basis of this constitutive minimal building block of the now or point. As noted above, however, Aristotle also allows for the possibility that the now is *not* a part of time and thus that the being—or more precisely the *phusis*—of time as such cannot be conceived according to this nexus point between being and time. As Derrida argues, the entire construction of the *phusis* of time in *Physics IV* proceeds without having actually decided on this fundamental question, and the thinking of time that Aristotle introduces to the Western tradition, and which lasts at least up until Hegel's dialectical repetition or reformulation of it, "evades" this undecided question. The stakes of this evasion are, for Derrida, as decisive for Western thought as any: "Metaphysics," he writes, "may be posited by this omission" (*M* 47).

In his critique of Hegel's repetition of the "vulgar" Aristotelian temporal problematic, Heidegger gestures, if implicitly, to this alternative conception of time that Aristotle clearly introduces but "leaves . . . in suspense" (*M* 47). Indeed, it must be recalled that Derrida's entire account of the Aristotelian *nun* and Hegelian *jetzt* is focalized through his reading of Heidegger's footnote in *Being and Time*, and that in addition to a reading of the history of the concept of time, what is at stake in this essay is the question of Heidegger's position vis-à-vis that tradition. Hegel has, for Heidegger (and Derrida), remained "*within* the first hypothesis of the Aristotelian aporetic" (*M* 46), but has Heidegger (for Derrida), either advanced beyond it or at least recovered its original ambivalence? It is difficult to say. Derrida writes:

> In repeating the question of Being in the transcendental horizon of time, *Being and Time* thus brings to light the omission which permitted metaphysics to believe that it could think time on the basis of a being already silently predetermined in its relation to time. If all of metaphysics is engaged in this gesture, *Being and Time*, in this regard at least, constitutes a decisive step *beyond or within metaphysics*. The question was evaded because it was put in terms of belonging to being or to nonbeing, being already determined as being-present. It is what the question evades that Heidegger puts back into play from the first part of *Being and Time* on: time, then, will be that on the basis of which the Being of beings is indicated, and not that whose possibility will be derived on the basis of a being already constituted. (*M* 47; my italics)

Derrida's intricate analysis of Aristotle, Hegel, Heidegger, and, to a lesser degree, Kant in this essay cannot be fully addressed here, but in the middle of this passage lies an index of one central point I would like to make. The Heideggerian project of a destruction of metaphysics by way of a reformulation of the relation between being and time constitutes, for Derrida, a "step beyond or within metaphysics." Is this an opposed pair of possibilities, or an identification of the two? Again it is difficult to say, but the argumentation of the piece, especially with regard to Heidegger's "decisive step," appears to suggest not only that this is a step *within* metaphysics, but that this step is already predetermined or at least preannounced in Aristotle's foundational text. As Derrida writes, "What Aristotle has set down [in introducing and then not resolving this dual possibility regarding the being of time] is both traditional metaphysical security, and, in its inaugural ambiguity, the critique of this security" (*M* 49). Or in other words, the destruction of metaphysics, insofar as it excavates a possibility that is there already in one of the inaugural texts of metaphysics, also constitutes a repetition of the Aristotelian concept of time—albeit not the traditional "vulgar" one. What Heidegger's text does, Derrida suggests, is reveal—if not actually decide on—a possibility that has lain dormant within that concept from its origins:

> Aristotle furnishes the premises of a thought of time no longer dominated simply by the present (of beings given in the form of *Vorhandenheit* and *Gegenwärtigkeit*). There is here both an instability and several possibilities of overturning; and we may wonder whether *Sein und Zeit* has not, in a way, arrested them. Whatever elements of the transcendental imagination that seem to escape the domination of the present given in the form of *Vorhandenheit* and *Gegenwärtigkeit* doubtless have been foreshadowed in *Physics IV*. The paradox would be the following, therefore: the originality of the Kantian breakthrough, such as it is repeated in *Kant and the Problem of Metaphysics*, transgresses the vulgar concept of time only by making explicit something hinted at in *Physics IV*. (*M* 49–50)

But even though the Heideggerian reformulation makes an implicit appeal to this undeveloped possibility in Aristotle's text, the point that Derrida goes on to make here is not simply that Heidegger, too, is "repeating" Aristotle (though he does suggest that), but also that in truth even the alternative conception of time as not belonging to beings surreptitiously depends on a metaphysics of presence insofar as it nonetheless argues from a conception of the *nun* as present. Derrida argues that since time is excluded from being on the grounds that it includes past and future "nows" that are obviously not present—that *are* not—this necessarily implies an assumption concerning the nature of the current or present "now," namely, that it *is*. Arguing for the nonbeing of time, therefore, "supposes that I have somehow anticipated *what* time *is*, to wit, the nonpresent in the form of the now that is past or to come. The current now is not time, because it is present; time is not (a being) to the extent that it is not (present). . . . Being has been determined temporally as being-present in order to determine time as nonpresent and nonbeing" (*M* 50–51). That is to say, before Heidegger's destruction of metaphysics by way of, at least in this case, the reformulation of being's relation to time, there is a, so to speak, earlier undeconstructed aporia in the formulation of Aristotle's question concerning whether time is or is not a part of *onta*.

The consequences of this undeconstructed tension are significant. The metaphysical assumption of an always anterior being-present structures not only any consideration of time, for Derrida, but indeed any consideration of *meaning*, including (and especially) the basic Heideggerian question concerning the "meaning of Being." This therefore encloses Heidegger's project within the sphere of the very metaphysics that it had sought to "destroy." "The *meaning* of time," Derrida writes,

> is thought on the basis of the present as nontime. And this could not be otherwise; *sense* (in whatever sense it is understood: as essence, as the meaning of discourse, as the orientation of the movement between *arkhē* and *telos*) has never been conceivable, within the history of metaphysics, otherwise than on the basis of presence and as presence. . . . To put it quite summarily, one seeks in vain to extract the question of meaning (the meaning of time, or of anything else) as such from metaphysics, or from the system of so called "vulgar" concepts. Such also would be the case, therefore, for a *question of Being* determined, as it is at the beginning of *Being and Time*, as a question of the *meaning of Being*, whatever the force, necessity, and value (irruptive as well as fundamental) of such a question. (*M* 51–52)

What is asserted here is more than simply a critique of a supposed failing on Heidegger's part. Rather, in this passage one can recognize a version of what might be called a deconstructive methodological principle: that one seeks "in vain" to cleanly escape from the metaphysics of presence and that therefore one must work at a deconstruction of metaphysics from *within* metaphysics, the "epoch of meaning" (*WD* 268).

Such a deconstruction is not only necessary but is made possible by the movement of *différance* within that system, and in the context of "Ousia and Grammē," the index of that *différance*—and perhaps a near-synonym for that *différance*—is time.[13] In the concluding pages of "*Ousia* and *Grammē*," Derrida suggests that "perhaps there is no 'vulgar concept of time'" (*M* 63) for Heidegger to destroy and thus accede to an authentic temporality. "The concept of time, in all its aspects, belongs to metaphysics, and it names the domination of presence" (*M* 63), and for this reason "an *other* concept of time cannot be opposed to it, since time in general belongs to metaphysical conceptuality" (*M* 63). However, Derrida asserts that there is another gesture possible here, one that "announc[es] itself in certain calculated fissures of the metaphysical text" (*M* 65), and this gesture consists of "inscribing a trace" in that text. The place of that inscription in the texts that Derrida deconstructs in "*Ousia* and *Grammē*" (Aristotle's, Hegel's, Heidegger's) is the sign of "time." While Heidegger gets caught up in a repetition of the inherently metaphysical conceptuality of being and time, attempting to arrive at the *meaning* of the former by way of an *authentic* experience of the latter, Derrida proposes here, albeit "from afar and in a still quite undecided way" (*M* 34), another possibility for unravelling that metaphysical fabric from within its interior stitching. "In order to exceed metaphysics," he writes, "it is necessary that a trace be inscribed within the text of metaphysics, a trace that continues to signal not in the direction of another presence, or another form of presence, but in the direction of an entirely other text" (*M* 65). The entirely other text alluded to here can be identified as the arche-text, written by the arche-trace, which, for Derrida, would be precisely that "writing without presence and without absence, without history, without cause, without *arkhia*, without *telos*, a writing that absolutely upsets all dialectics, all theology, all teleology, all ontology" (*M* 67).

Let us return, then, to the discussion of temporality, and indeed to two of the categories that Derrida mentions in this last list of metaphysical concepts, namely dialectics and theology—or more specifically, the *Aufhebung* and messianic time.

AUFHEBUNG (1)

Though Hegel's conception of time is a repetition of Aristotle's, it is a repetition with a difference, and that difference is the dialectical machine that is driven by the motor of the *Aufhebung*. The Hegelian *Aufhebung* is not only a temporal process, but also, perhaps above all, a synthesizing mechanism. In the temporal passage from, say, abstract spatiality through point, line, and plane, what is crucial is not only the idea that time has always already "occurred" in the constitution of space, but that the punctual, linear, and planar stages in that temporal development of space are all negated and preserved. The same logic not only informs every individual step that spirit takes along its "stations of the cross" in the *Phenomenology of Spirit*—for example, the negation and retention of "sense certainty" in the movement to "perception" (I–II) or the negation and preservation of our dependency on (and identification with) "life" in the slave's progress into free self-consciousness (IV)—but also accounts for the way in which absolute spirit, at the end of that journey, retains within it every stage through which it has passed.

The logic of the Hegelian *Aufhebung* is the object of extended critique in Derrida's 1967 essay "From Restricted to General Economy: A Hegelianism without Reserve." This essay, in truth, is a rather sympathetic reading of Georges Bataille's critique of the Hegelian dialectic and the way it relentlessly and unfailingly appropriates all forms of negativity into the grand dialectical unfolding of history and the absolutization of spirit (the *telos* of the *Phenomenology*). Against this conception of a purely and exclusively "productive" negativity, Bataille famously proposes—through a series of concepts such as loss, expenditure, sacrifice, potlatch, laughter, ecstasy, and so forth—a "negativity with no use" that would constitute a breach in the omnicomprehensive, omnivorous system of the dialectic. For Bataille, this unappropriable, entirely "wasteful" negativity does not lend itself to the supersession of the *Aufhebung*, and thus would not only threaten to bring the motor function of the dialectic to a halt (or at least cause it to run inefficiently) but also offer the possibility of a wholly other "sovereign" experience outside of metaphysics, phenomenology, and phenomenality; it would be, in Derrida's words, "a negativity that never takes place, that never *presents* itself, because in doing so it would start to work again. A laughter that literally never *appears*, because it exceeds phenomenality in general, the absolute possibility of meaning" (*WD* 256).

That Bataille evidently gestures toward such an *other* experience and toward a sovereign freedom that purely exceeds or escapes the metaphysical-Hegelian system, is a fact for which Derrida takes him to task. Indeed, for all his sympathy with Bataille's thought, one point at which Derrida overtly distinguishes his position from Bataille's is where he asserts that though Bataille may seek to offer a series of counterconcepts to those of the Hegelian system (the prime example here being his nonrelational concept of sovereignty against Hegel's lordship), his terminology and conceptual repertoire nevertheless remains intrinsically bound to the metaphysical lexicon. He writes: "[T]his displacement [of lordship into sovereignty] is powerless to transform the nucleus of predicates. All the attributes ascribed to sovereignty are borrowed from the (Hegelian) logic of 'lordship.' We cannot, and Bataille neither could, nor should dispose of any other concepts or any other signs, any other unity of word and meaning. The sign 'sovereignty' itself, in its opposition to servility, was issued from the same stock as that of 'lordship.' Considered outside of its functioning, nothing distinguishes it from 'lordship'" (*WD* 267). Thus in a gesture analogous to the point made above about Heidegger's use of the sign/term "time," Derrida reveals (or redraws) a metaphysical limit on the far side of Bataille's lexicon.

Nevertheless, for Derrida, Bataille (like Heidegger) is thinking right up against that limit. Bataille's great intervention is to isolate the play of negativity in the grand speculative system of the dialectic and to attempt to radicalize it, thus bringing to light its determinative function. Even though Derrida is skeptical of Bataille's attempt to identify a pure negativity in the form of what he calls "sovereignty," Bataille nevertheless provides the framework for understanding the architectonic—one might even say, geometric—function of the negative. Bataille, however, does this not in order to reaffirm the dialectical construction of positivity and phenomenality, but rather, in order to perversely affirm the negative as such. Above we noted how the negativity of the *jetzt* constitutes the elusive *point* of negation in the temporal-geometric construction of space, and here, too, Derrida observes a similar operation in the construction of meaning. He argues that for Bataille the

> blind spot of Hegelianism, *around* which can be organized the representation of meaning, is the *point* at which destruction, suppression, death and sacrifice constitute so irreversible an expenditure, so radical a negativity—here we would have to say an expenditure and a negativity *without reserve*—that they can no longer be determined as negativity in a process or a system. . . . Now, the sovereign operation, the *point of nonreserve*, is neither positive nor negative. It cannot be inscribed in discourse, except by crossing out predicates or by practicing a contradictory superimpression that then exceeds the logic of philosophy. (*WD* 259; italics in original)

Bataille's negativity with no use wrenches away this hypernegativity (which can no longer be identified with the useful negativity that is simply the flip side of positivity in the dialectical logic) and seeks to follow it where it may lead, sure only that this path leads somewhere beyond philosophical logic.

Unwilling or unable to see the radicality of this negativity without reserve, Hegel sees it as a "resource," seeks to put it to work, to turn it wholly toward the productivity of the dialectical machine, and has thus "blinded himself to that which he had laid bare under the rubric of negativity" (*WD* 259). Thus, in a way that works both with and against Hegel's text, the Bataillean-deconstructive reading of this hypernegativity seeks

> convulsively to tear apart the negative side, that which makes it the reassuring *other* surface of the positive. . . [and to] exhibit within the negative, in an instant, that which can no longer be called negative. And can no longer be called negative precisely because it has no reserved underside, because it can no longer permit itself to be converted into positivity, because it can no longer *collaborate* with the continuous linking-up of meaning, concept, time and truth in discourse; because it literally can no longer *labor* and let itself be interrogated as the "work of the negative." (*WD* 259–60)

Commenting on this passage, Rodolphe Gasché identifies in it an emblematic gesture of deconstruction, writing that "Instead of determining negativity as only a facet, a moment, or a condition of meaning—as work—Derrida's philosophy, like Bataille's, pushes the negative to its logical end, to that point where the negative seems an afterimage of something that resists all salvage by the system of meaning."[14] Gasché would thus define

Derridean alterity as "not even a negative" and both "more and less than negativity," but we might in the context of this discussion of the Hegelian *Aufhebung* describe it rather as a nondialectical negativity, a negativity that cannot be appropriated, determined, and put to work in the mechanism of the dialectic.[15]

While the issue of play will be taken up at some length in the conclusion following this chapter, it is worth noting here that in giving way to this hypernegativity, the dialectic gives way to play. Or to put this another way, in revealing its subordination to *différance*, the steady and sober progress of the dialectic is equally revealed to be contained within a larger field of play and chance. Whether Hegel is unaware of this and has simply assumed that spirit labors its way toward its singular end, or is instead aware of the possibility that the dialectic rests on play and chance and simply places a wager on the teleology of spirit's forward unfolding, the Hegelian dialectic—the grand work that the *Aufhebung* performs—amounts to a denial of the irreducible play of *différance* in the system. To this effect, Derrida writes:

> In interpreting negativity as labor, in betting for discourse, meaning, history, etc., Hegel has bet against play, against chance. He has blinded himself to the possibility of his own bet, to the fact that the conscientious suspension of play (for example, the passage through the certitude of oneself and through lordship as the independence of self-consiousness) was itself a phase of play; and to the fact that play *includes* the work of meaning or the meaning of work, and includes them not in terms of *knowledge*, but in terms of *inscription*: meaning is a *function* of play, is inscribed in a certain place in the configuration of a meaningless play. (*WD* 260)

Meaninglessness before meaning; meaninglessness as the (non)ground of meaning; expenditure and dissemination before accumulation and consolidation; pure chance against a rigged game; work as a function of play. These are the claims that Derrida extracts from his reading of Bataille's—and Heidegger's—readings of Hegel.

MESSIANIC (1)

It is helpful to keep in mind Derrida's critiques of the accumulative-synthetic mechanism of the Hegelian *Aufhebung* (in both the temporally oriented presentation in "*Ousia* and *Grammē*" and the "speculatively" oriented presentation in "From Restricted to General Economy") when considering his presentation of "the messianic," which is also, above all, a temporal concept and a wager on chance. Before turning to Agamben, let us finally examine the temporal logic of Derrida's notion of the messianic, though as noted above, this discussion (as well as the following pages on Agamben) will largely veer away from theological questions and stick to primarily temporal and logical ones. As Martin Hägglund notes in his book on the temporal dimension of Derrida's thought, "more than any other term in Derrida's vocabulary, the messianic has invited the misconception that Derrida harbors a religious hope for salvation."[16] Notwithstanding their great interest, Hägglund's polemics with readers of Derrida—such as John Caputo and Richard Kearney—who see in Derrida's thought a more or less nondogmatic negative theology ("a 'good' religion that welcomes others" as opposed to "a 'bad' religion that excludes others")[17] are less relevant to the present discussion than his concise definition of the Derridean messianic as "another name for the relation to the undecidable future."[18] Indeed, as the opening discussion of this chapter has already proposed, it might be said that herein lies the basic difference between the Derridean and Agambenian notions of the messianic, for as Hägglund's gloss implies, the Derridean "prophetic" messianic (as opposed, as we will see, to the Agambenian "apostolic" messianic) is fundamentally a matter of the aleatory "to come."

The analysis of *Specters of Marx* is organized around a reading not only of Marx but also of *Hamlet*. And for Derrida's reading perhaps the single most important line from that play is Hamlet's assertion that "the time is out of joint," which Derrida tellingly chooses as the epigraph to the book. The function of this assertion within Derrida's analysis is to identify and affirm a breach in the supposed closure and completion of the Hegelo-Marxist dialectic that is, if not unambiguously asserted, at least rhetorically valorized in a number of the texts (by Fukuyama, by Kojève) he engages here. Among these specific engagements, that with Kojève and his *Introduction to the Reading of Hegel* can provide the best illustration of the irreducible futurity of Derrida's messianic "to come."

Focusing in on a particular imperative phrase in the description of "post-historical man" that Kojève added in a footnote to later editions of the *Introduction*, Derrida asks about the meaning of the verb "devoir," *must*. In this footnote, after describing the state of man after the closure and completion of the dialectical unfolding of history, Kojève make certain "prescriptive utterance[s]" (*SM* 73) about what posthistorical man must (*doit*) continue to do (he "must remain a 'Subject *opposed* to the Object'" and he "must continue to *detach* 'form' from 'content'").[19] In fact, the specific imperatives of these Kojèvian prescriptions are not important for Derrida; rather he focuses on the form of the prescription itself, and on the way the futurity of this *devoir* constitutes a disjointedness in Kojève's supposedly posthistorical condition. Derrida argues that

> [w]hatever may be the case concerning the modality or the content of this "devoir," whatever may be the necessity of this prescription, even if it calls for eternities of interpretation, there is an "it is necessary" for the future. Whatever may be its indetermination, be it that of "it is necessary [that there be] the future" ["*il faut l'avenir*"], there is some future and some history.... We must insist on this specific point precisely because it points to an essential lack of specificity, an indetermination that remains the ultimate mark of the future. (*SM* 73)

Kojève's passing use of the verb "*devoir*" in this passage, then, opens up for Derrida a glimpse into the temporal fissure of the historical dialectic, even—and especially—once that dialectic has supposedly come to a rest.

Again, the specific content of Kojève's prescription (whether we take him seriously here or not) is a matter of indifference.[20] It is instead the formal temporal-grammatical logic of the imperative "devoir" itself that is at stake for Derrida, for within the fissure opened by the syntax of Kojève's prescription, we can see the messianic. Indeed the messianic *is* that fissure. He continues:

> Apparently "formalist," this indifference to the content has perhaps the value of giving one to think the necessarily pure and purely necessary form of the future as such, in its being-necessarily-promised, prescribed, assigned, enjoined, in the necessarily formal necessity of its possibility—in short, in its law. It is this law that dislodges any present out of its contemporaneity with itself. Whether the promise promises this or that, whether it be fulfilled or not, or whether it be unfulfillable, there is necessarily some promise and therefore some historicity as future-to-come. It is what we are nicknaming the messianic without messianism. (*SM* 73)

Another way to put this is that even after time, the time is out of joint. The spacing that opens and breaches that joint is the same futurity and promissory structure of *différance* that here bears that nickname "the messianic."

Commenting on this passage in the context of his polemic with religious readings of Derrida, Hägglund notes that "Derrida can thus be seen to invert the logic of religious eschatology. Instead of promoting the end of time, Derrida emphasizes that the coming of time exceeds any given end."[21] His reading is persuasive. But in the present context, we might further inquire about the "eschatology" at issue here, since it will lead us directly to Agamben's equally "anti-eschatological" (though for slightly different reasons) conception of messianic time. Indeed, Agamben precisely does not suggest that Derrida promotes the end of time; rather, he argues that deconstruction places an injunction on conceiving time differently, and thus bars the arrival or experience of what he, in contradistinction to the deconstructive messianic, calls messianic time. Let us return to the now.

NUN, JETZT (II)

Derrida shows how the spacing of the punctual now, the elusive constitutive element of any geometric representation of space and/or time, requires that time already have taken place. This means not merely that we are always "too late" to experience this spacing but that—insofar as this temporal spacing is identified with *différance*—there *is* nothing there to be experienced in the first place. Herein lies, for Derrida, the originary and irreducible paradox within the Western reflection on time, out of which he derives the messianic futurity of the *à-venir*. In his own explication of messianic time, Agamben addresses the same set of questions, but as we will see, he draws significantly different conclusions from the paradoxes of the temporal "now" that the tradition has tended to think of as a point lying along a linear continuum of chronological time. As he writes in a phrase that refers precisely to the argument of "*Ousia* and *Grammē*," "It has often been noted that these spatial representations—point, line, segment—generate a kind of falsification that makes unthinkable the lived experience of time" (*TTR* 64). Agamben's reading of messianic time in the Pauline letters is aimed at cutting through that aporetic impasse.

What is messianic time? Agamben proposes the following definition: "messianic time is *the time that time takes to come to an end*" (*TTR* 67). The phrasing of this definition, while evocative, is rather cryptic, but it can be clarified if we recall his claims concerning the incongruity between the lived experience of time and the (linear) representation of time as well as his rejection of the prophetic/apocalyptic view of time as progressing toward and ultimately arriving at its teleological end point. The "time that time takes to come to an end" is emphatically not the time that it takes to arrive at a final *eskhaton* or end point; it is, rather, *the time that it takes for a representation of time to be constructed*. "Time" in this phrase has, then, a very specific meaning: not linear, represented time, but the unrepresented, lived experience of time that almost instantly comes to an end in the construction of its own representation. Thus "time" has two senses that must be kept distinct from each other. On the one hand, a *time$_1$*, which is the linear, let us say "vulgar" notion of time, to which Agamben also give the name *khronos*, and on the other, a *time$_2$*, which is this time within time, a time$_2$ that takes a certain amount of time$_2$ to come to an end in the process of constructing a representation of itself (time$_1$) and which Agamben also identifies as *kairos*. In the definition of messianic time offered in this first formulation, "the time that time takes to come to an end," the term "time" must be understood as signifying time$_2$.

Drawing on the work and terminology of the linguist Gustave Guillaume, Agamben also gives the name "operational time" to this time within time. For Guillaume, the mind experiences time in two distinct ways that can be mapped onto the schema of time$_1$ and time$_2$ proposed above; on the one hand, we have our more or less spatial and linear conception, but on the other we have a much more elusive, anterior experience of the time that it takes to form such a representation. In another gloss, Agamben defines operational time as *"the time the mind takes to realize a time-image"* (*TTR* 66). In this formulation, the "realization" or construction of the chronological time-image is part and parcel of the "coming to an end" of operational/kairological time; the realization of time$_1$ is the coming to an end of time$_2$. The "operation" of operational time, then, is precisely the construction of chronological time. Thus accepting Guillaume's argument here, Agamben therefore proposes yet another synonym for this type of time: "chronogenetic time."

One of the merits of this concept of chronogenetic time, Agamben argues, is that it allows us to think about temporal modality and tense (time's extension into the past and the future) in a way other than simply the absence (the *no-longer* and the *not-yet*) of a "now" passing along the linear chronological continuum or time-image. Indeed, it enables us to think of the temporal instant itself in terms other than the presence or absence of any realized actuality at all. "The schema of chronogenesis," he writes, "thus allows us to grasp the time-image in its pure state of potentiality (time *in posse*), in its very process of formation (time *in fieri*), and, finally, in the state of having been constructed (time *in esse*), taking into account all of the verb forms of a language (aspects, modalities, and tenses) according to a unitary model" (*TTR* 66).

Chronogenetic time gives rise to the representation of time, to *khronos*, by effacing or withdrawing itself from that linear representation. It is not the line, and is not even the point on that line. It is not even the space between two points on that line. It stubbornly resists representation in any such time-image. Is there, then, any index of the chronogenetic time to which we might appeal? Agamben offers one that relates this temporal problematic to a linguistic one with which we are familiar, namely, the question of enunciation.

In truth, this relation between chronogenetic time and linguistics is not one that Agamben simply invents or intuits, for Guillaume is, after all, a linguist himself and develops the idea of operational time in order to pursue a properly linguistic problem. For Guillaume, linguistic inquiry is incomplete if it considers language only in its "constructed or achieved state" (*TTR* 65)—let us say, as an already existing *langue*, or even as an already achieved utterance. Instead, in order to fully understand the nature of language, "you also have to represent the phases through which thought had to pass constructing it" (*TTR* 65), and this passing, of course, involves the passage of some sort of time. While the idea of operational time "allow[s] Guillaume to restore time in a spatial representation that is completely deprived of time, as are all images" (*TTR* 66), it also, according to Agamben, allows for the development of Benveniste's theory of enunciation, the focal point of which, as we have previously discussed, is the linguistic deictic or shifter. Insofar as the shifter has as its reference only the instance of the taking place of discourse itself—that is to say, the construction of a statement—it is equally an index of precisely this infinitesimally brief "coming to an end" of chronogenetic time. To this effect, Agamben writes: "Through shifters, what Benveniste calls *indicateurs de l'énonciation*, language refers to its own taking place, to a pure instance of discourse in action. This capacity to refer to the pure presence of the enunciation goes hand in hand, according to Benveniste, with *chronothèse*, time-positing (literally 'chronothesis'), itself the origin of our representation of time. In this way, an axial point of reference is established with regard to our representation of time" (*TTR* 66). The now of chronothesis is therefore a now that is "more" now than any punctual instant along the representational-chronological line. It is, however, important to note, as Agamben does here, that this self-referentiality of the linguistic shifter does not constitute any sort of subjective immediacy with the instance of discourse, any sort of "presence" to the present of enunciation. Indeed, he makes quite the opposite claim: the chronogenetic now insinuates a temporal disjointedness *within* the disjointedness constituted by the nonpresence of the now-point on the chronological line. This notion develops and deepens Agamben's earlier accounts of enunciation by identifying the kairological gap that inheres in the realization of language in discourse. Chronothesis "contain[s] within itself another time that introduces a disjointedness and delay in the 'pure presence' of the enunciation," and this "lapse and delay would then be a part of the structure of the subject" (*TTR* 66–67). That lapse and delay within the structure of the subject is an interval that is not locatable along the chronological continuum, even in the minimal form of the point or the space between points. It is a kairological time that must pass and "come to an end" in the process of spatializing time into a thinkable representation, and thus might be conceived of as belonging to another dimension than the linear-temporal continuum. Indeed, Agamben makes just such claim when he suggests that chronogenetic time is "no longer linear but three-dimensional" (*TTR* 66).

Analogous to the dual structure of signification discussed in chapter 3, wherein there is necessarily an *intentio prima* and an *intentio secunda* in any signifying act, so, too, there is a dual temporal structure—there are two "times"—at stake in Agamben's conception of time, and the intimate tension between the, so to speak, "*tempus primum*" and "*tempus secundum*" proves to be the central problematic of his analysis of messianic time. *Kairos* or operational time is, on the one hand, "not entirely consumed by representation" (*TTR* 67), but on the other neither is it "another time, . . . a supplementary time added on from the outside to chronological time" (*TTR* 67). From the perspective of chronological time, kairological time has always already passed, but it is not the chronological past. It is not a present, punctual "now" that has by virtue of temporal modalization been absented and exceeded along the forward march of *khronos*. Instead, it is "something like a time within time—not ulterior but interior" (*TTR* 67). From the perspective of chronological time *kairos* is, to invoke a well-known phrase, "a past that was never present"; yet from the messianic perspective, we might say that, insofar as it is operative in all our representations of time, past, present, and future, this time is "a present that is never past."

This dual structure of time informs Agamben's reading of two key concepts in Paul (and indeed in the Christian theological tradition), namely, *parousia* and typology. With regard to the first, Agamben notes that for Paul, since the Messiah has already arrived, we are now living in the time of the Messiah; the Messiah *has come*. However, we are also awaiting the *parousia*. On Agamben's reading, for Paul, both of these moments together, in their disjuncture, constitute the messianic event in its entirety. He writes: "Paul decomposes the messianic event into two times: resurrection and *parousia*, the second coming of Jesus at the end of time. Out of this issues the paradoxical tension between an *already* and a *not yet* that defines the Pauline conception of salvation" (*TTR* 69). For Agamben, however, it is a misunderstanding of the term *parousia* to see the "second coming" as merely a *chronologically* second, that is to say, future event (even one that inherently remains always to come). Indeed, the *parousia* is simultaneous with the present. Or rather, insofar as "*par-ousia* literally signifies to be next to" and thus indicates that "being is beside itself in the present" (*TTR* 70), it names the dual structure of the present. In a passage that obviously invokes the Derridean logic of supplementarity, Agamben writes:

> *Parousia* does not signal a complement that is added to something in order to complete it, nor a supplement, added on afterward, that never reaches fulfillment. Paul uses this term to highlight the innermost unidual structure of the messianic event, inasmuch as it is comprised of two heterogeneous times, one *kairos* and the other *khronos*, one an operational time and the other a represented time, which are coextensive but cannot be added together. (*TTR* 70)

A reading of the second coming or *parousia* as a future event, or indeed as a pure principle of undecidable futurity depends, for Agamben, on taking chronological time for temporality as such, for the entirety of time. But chronological time is not the entirety of time; it is only the static, formal "time-image," the representation of time, its "text." And "as an image devoid of time, it is itself impossible to seize hold of, and, consequently, tends to infinitely defer itself" (*TTR* 70). Or in other words, the error of such a reading "lies in changing operational time into a supplementary time added onto chronological time, in order to infinitely postpone the end" (*TTR* 70). Agamben's "uni-dual" reading of Pauline *parousia*, by contrast, leads to rather different consequences. "The Messiah," he writes, "has already arrived, the messianic event has already happened, but its presence contains within itself another time, which stretches its *parousia*, not in order to defer it, but, on the contrary, to make it graspable" (*TTR* 71).

The same conception of the dual nature of time informs Agamben's interpretation of typology in the Pauline text. Famously analyzed by Erich Auerbach in his essay "Figura" (to which Agamben refers in passing), the aim of early and medieval Christian typological reading "was to show that the persons and events of the Old Testament were prefigurations of the New Testament and its history of salvation."[22] Thus, for example, Tertullian reads Moses's naming of Joshua (Num 13:16) as a prefiguration of Jesus, and Augustine reads Noah's Ark as a prefiguration of the Church.[23] Agamben finds a similar typological interpretation already at work in Paul's evocation of certain episodes in Israel's history, most notably the passage in 1 Corinthians 10:1–11 in which Paul recalls the way God rejected most of the Israelites who had passed through the Red Sea and cast them out into the desert to die (Num 14:29–30). Paul comments on this episode thus (in Agamben's rendering): "Now these things happened unto them by way of figure [*tupikōs*]; and they were written for us, for our admonition, upon whom the ends of the ages are come to face each other [*ta telē tōn aiōnōn katentēken*; *antaō*—from *anti*—means 'to be face to face, to confront each other']" (*TTR* 73).[24]

It is well known that typology becomes a dominant mode of biblical exegesis by the Middle Ages, but what is most important for Agamben is not typology as a hermeneutic method, or even "the fact that each event of the past—once it becomes figure—announces a future event and is fulfilled in it," but rather "the transformation of time implied by this typological relation" (*TTR* 74). In seeing every moment of the past as a "type" that corresponds to an "antitype" in the messianic present, Paul provides, in yet another modulation, a model for thinking time in its dual structure, now conceived in terms of a "tension that clasps together and transforms past and future, *tupos* and *antitupos*, in an inseparable constellation. The messianic is not just one of two terms in this typological relation, *it is the relation*

A Matter of Time 239

itself" (*TTR* 74). That is to say that both the "figural" announcement of a coming fulfillment *and* the, so to speak, "memorial" recapitulation (Paul's *anakephalaiōsis*) of that announcement in the messianic present are requisite components of messianic time. This is also why

> the widespread view of messianic time as oriented solely toward the future is fallacious. We are used to hearing that in the moment of salvation one has to look to the future and to eternity. To the contrary, for Paul recapitulation, *anakephalaiōsis*, means that *ho nun kairos* is a contraction of past and present, that we will have to settle our debts, at the decisive moment, first and foremost with the past. (*TTR* 77–78)

It is clear, then, why the distinction between apostle and prophet is so critical for Agamben's conception of messianic time and for the critique of the Derridean messianic contained therein. For Agamben, the time to which we must direct our attention is not something that, from a chronological-representational perspective, is forever "to come," but rather something that has already happened and is always already happening in the present. "Just as the apostle differs from the prophet, so does the temporal structure implied by his *euaggelion* [literally 'joyful message'] differ from the temporal structure of prophesy. The announcement does not refer to a future event, but to a present fact" (*TTR* 89). In this sense, for all of its hypersaturation by the Pauline language through which it is focalized, the entire apostolic-messianic framework of Agamben's analysis—that is to say, the entire religious-theological framework—can be read as a model for conceiving a temporal-logical problematic, a model for conceiving the present, the "time of the now."

AUFHEBUNG (II)

Let us return, then, to the key temporal-logical operator of the Hegelian system, although such a "return" hardly leaves behind the theological frame, for as Agamben is by no means the first to suggest, "Hegel's dialectic is nothing more than a secularization of Christian theology" (*TTR* 99). As noted in the opening of this chapter, Agamben overtly polemicizes with Derrida in the book's fifth chapter, but that polemic, to which we will turn in a moment, is prepared for by a discussion of three key terms, *katargein*, *astheneia*, and *Aufhebung*. Let us briefly review how Agamben's engagement with these concepts (the first two Pauline, the last, of course, Hegelian) prepare the way for his critique of deconstruction as a "thwarted messianism" (*TTR* 103).

Katargein is the term Paul uses to describe the transformation of the law in the messianic state, for example, in Romans 7:5–6, which Agamben renders as "For when we were in the flesh, the passions of sin were enacted [*enērgeito*] through the law in our members to bring forth fruit unto death. But now we are de-activated [*katergēthēmen*, 'made inoperative'] from the law" (*TTR* 96).[25] What does it mean to be "de-activated from the law," and what is the status of the law in such a deactivation? For Agamben, Paul's intention here can be discerned straightaway from the etymological meaning of the verb, which comes from "*argos*, meaning 'inoperative, not-at-work (*a-ergos*), inactive" (*TTR* 95). The messianic transformation of the law through *katargēsis*, therefore, is a matter of rendering it inoperative, suspending its "work." In terms that correspond directly to his theory of (im)potentiality discussed at length in chapter 3 above, Agamben writes that in this process of Pauline *katargēsis*

> potentiality passes over into actuality and meets up with its *telos*, not in the form of force or *ergon*, but in the form of *astheneia*, weakness. Paul formulates this principle of messianic inversion in the potential-act relation in a well-known passage. Just as he asks the Lord for liberation from the thorn lodged in his flesh, he hears "Power [or potentiality] realizes itself in weakness [*dunamis en astheneia teleitai*]" (2 Cor 12:9). This is repeated in the next verse: "when I am weak, then I am powerful." (*TTR* 97)

Agamben thus argues that Paul's theory of potentiality and act is virtually identical to his own. Again, this theory was discussed in detail in chapter 3, but it may be worth recalling here how, for Agamben, the salient point about potentiality—and specifically human potentiality—is that it is essentially inseparable from impotentiality, the capacity *not* to pass over into any given act, and that any human act must therefore be thought of not merely as the realization of a potentiality-to (be or do) but also, paradoxically, as the realization of the distinctively human potentiality-not-to (be or do). On Agamben's reading, this conception of the way (im)potentiality passes over into act, and thus of the way the "act" (or indeed being itself) is fundamentally a precipitate of that (im)potentiality, is precisely what is

A Matter of Time 241

at stake in Paul's—or more precisely God's—assertion that "potentiality realizes itself in weakness." The restoration of this constitutive *adunamia* to every human *ergon* is the operation of messianic *katargēsis*.

Agamben's reading of *katargēsis* and *astheneia*, and his appropriation of these terms into his own conceptual system, however, does not stop there. Indeed, in keeping with his suggestion that Hegel's dialectic is a "secularization of Christian theology," he offers a historical-philological account of how the Hegelian *Aufhebung* is not only the secularized version of the concept of *katargēsis*, but also, by way of translation from Paul's Greek to Luther's German, the *very same word*. Luther translates *katargēsis* in the Pauline letters as *Aufhebung*, seeing in this term that peculiar messianic dynamic of cancellation and preservation that brings fulfillment, and it is from Luther that Hegel adopts his key term. The difficult logic of Paul's paradoxically antinomian fulfillment of the law hinges on the function of this strange Greek term that Paul adopts as the messianic verb par excellence. And it is therefore by way of a direct line of descent that this messianic operator, *katargēsis*, surreptitiously becomes what could legitimately be called the central concept of philosophical modernity.

The Hegelian adoption of *katargēsis*/*Aufhebung*, however, entails an elision of an important part of Paul's messianic conception of temporality that, for Agamben, will lead to a persistent and stubborn aporia in modern philosophical thought. If his philological reading of the term *Aufhebung* is correct, Agamben claims, "then not only is Hegelian thought involved in a tightly knit hermeneutic struggle with the messianic . . . but this also holds for modernity, by which I intend the epoch that is situated under the sign of the dialectical *Aufhebung*" (TTR 100). To evoke once again Derrida's discussion of the Aristotelian-Hegelian "now," we might ask: What, then, is "evaded" in Hegel's dialectical repetition of the Pauline conception of messianic time? And how does this evasion produce these seemingly intractable aporias?

Let us return to a passage cited earlier. Agamben notes that,

> the *Aufhebung* makes its appearance in the context of the dialectic of sense certainty and its expression in language via the "this" (*diese*) and the "now" (*jetzt*). . . . In the "this" and the "now," the immediate is thus always already *aufgehoben*, lifted and preserved. Inasmuch as the "now" has already ceased to be once it has been uttered (or written), the

attempt to grasp the "now" always produces a past, a *gewesen*, which as such is *kein Wesen*, nonbeing. (*TTR* 100)

At the point where the *Aufhebung* is introduced as the fundamental driver of the dialectic in the *Phenomenology*, it produces a negativity as the anterior and constituent element of every positivity (even if—especially if—that positivity is an always provisional one in the steady progress of Spirit along its itinerary toward its self-absolution). Indeed, as discussed at some length in chapter 2 above, the structure of this dialectical *Aufhebung* of sense certainty into "perception" (see *Phenomenology* sections I–II) mirrors the structure of linguistic deixis, which Agamben analyzes at greatest length in *Language and Death*. Taking the argument of that book up again at this point in *The Time That Remains*, he writes:

> The "Eleusinian mysteries" of sense certainty—the exposition of which initiates the *Phenomenology of Spirit*—show themselves to be nothing more than an exposition of the structure of linguistic signification in general. To use the language of modern linguistics, as language refers to its own taking place via shifters, the "this" and the "now," language produces the sensible expressed in it as a past and at the same time defers this sensible to the future. In this fashion, it is always already caught up in a history and a time. In each case what is presupposed by the *Aufhebung* is that what has been lifted is not completely eliminated, but rather persists somehow and can thus be preserved. (*TTR* 100)

Hegel has thus incorporated a key element of the function of Pauline *katargēsis* into the function of the dialectical *Aufhebung*, namely, the nonelimination of the negated in the movement of supersession. And as noted above, Agamben identifies this persistence of the negated within the produced positivity (that is, its persistence as an essential structural component of any positivity) with the persistence of impotentiality within every realized actuality (making every passage from potentiality to act equally an "act of impotentiality" [see chapter 3]). But he also argues that there is an important element of the original Pauline messianic-temporal problematic that has not been transferred into the Hegelian dialectic, and this has to do with what I above characterized (again following Agamben's analysis of the dual structure of language) as the "*tempus seuncdum*" of operational time. In short, the Hegelian dialectical conception of time is limited to the time-image of linear chronology, and thus cannot comprehend the "now" as anything but an infinitely receding anteriority or blind spot.

Another way Agamben puts this is that, in its simultaneous obsession with and inability to grasp the origin or foundation of chronological time, this thinking misses the true implications of Paul's messianic temporality, and thus conceives of the irreducible dialectical displacement of the *jetzt* as a constitutive nonclosure and futurity in every present. "While messianic time (as operational time) also introduces a disconnection and delay into represented time," he writes, "this cannot be tacked onto time as a supplement or as infinite deferment. To the contrary, the messianic—the ungraspable quality of the 'now'—is the very opening through which we may seize hold of time, achieving our representation of time, making it end" (*TTR* 100). Again, this coming to an end of time is not to be understood as a sort of end point or culmination of the chronological temporal continuum, nor indeed as any sort of future event. It is, rather, the reintegration of *tempus primum* with *tempus secundum*, a *restitutio in integrum* that occurs in the messianic *katargēsis* or *désoeuvrement* (Agamben suggests that this would also be a "good translation of Pauline *katargein*" [*TTR* 101]) of "actual" (i.e., chronological) time.

These are the precise terms in which Agamben presents his overt critique of deconstruction in *The Time That Remains*. The problem can be roughly identified as taking *intentio prima* as the whole of language and *tempus primum* as the whole of time. In each case, deconstruction assumes that the level of "representation" (whether that be the linguistic signifier and the signifying chain or the time-image) is irreducible and insuperable. With nowhere else to go, the aporias that are produced at the limit—or margins—of these representational systems, which Agamben always credits Derrida with having limned most profoundly, are what necessitates an "ontology of the trace and originary supplement" (*TTR* 102):

> The concept of the "trace" names the impossibility of a sign to be extinguished in the fullness of a present and absolute presence. In this sense, the trace must be conceived as "before being," the thing itself, always already a sign and *repraesentamen*, the signified always already in the position of signifier There is no nostalgia for origins since there is no origin. The origin is produced as a retroactive effect of nonorigin and a trace, which thus becomes the origin of the origin. (*TTR* 102–3)

But this ontology of the (non)originary trace is necessary only if those aporetic limits of representation are taken as absolute, only if language (or time) in its entirety consisted of *intentio prima* (or *tempus primum*). For Agamben, Derrida's concepts (or nonconcepts) "call into question the primacy of presence and signification for the philosophical tradition, yet they do not truly call into question signification in general" (*TTR* 103). This last point has at least two valences.

(1) Insofar as the trace, while not being any sort of presence, is nevertheless not totally insignificant, this means that even beyond the metaphysics of presence (and absence) that Derrida assails, there is nevertheless still semiological signification. This arche-signification is located in the "arche-trace," which Agamben describes as "a sort of archiphoneme between presence and absence" (*TTR* 103) that supports and drives the differential play of signs anterior even to being and nonbeing. Thus, what is irreducible is not presence, but the differential play of semiological signification itself. For all its antinostalgia, deconstruction nevertheless has recourse to a sort of structural memory of the origin in the form of the trace's "zero degree" of signification, which is not pure nonsignification and which is the true unextinguishable of deconstruction. "In order for deconstruction to function," Agamben writes, "what must be excluded is not the fact that presence and origin are *lacking* but that they are purely insignificant" (*TTR* 103). And it is for this reason that, for Agamben, Derrida's thought can be described as an "ontology of the trace."

(2) The second valence of Agamben's assertion can be discerned by recalling the discussion of the first chapter of this book and Agamben's figure, in the last section of *Stanzas*, of a "semiology from the point of view of the Sphinx." There, the absolutization of the Saussurian-structural model of linguistics constituted as a sort of trap that forced us to remain within what was described as an "Oedipal" semiology, an understanding of language as essentially semiological code (or riddle) to be deciphered. As discussed in chapter 2 above, this reading, in which another experience of language "from the point of view of the Sphinx" is introduced, is the subject of Agamben's work on the "human voice" and the *experimentum linguae* in the late 1970s and early 1980s. In claiming here, albeit in a rather condensed formulation, that deconstruction does not call into question signification in general, Agamben is thus alluding to that decades-long critique of deconstruction.

What the assertion that Derrida does not "truly call into question signification in general" means most precisely in the present context, however, is that in reading the *Aufhebung* in terms of originary *différance* rather than the operation of *katargēsis*, deconstruction has jettisoned the messianic from the range of its thought. In a key passage, Agamben puts the point this way:

> [On Derrida's reading] the movement of the *Aufhebung*, which neutralizes signifieds while maintaining and achieving signification, thus becomes a principle of infinite deferment. A signification that only signifies itself can never seize hold of itself, it can never catch up with a void in representation, nor does it ever allow anything to be an in-significance; rather, it is displaced and deferred in one and the same gesture. In this way, the trace is a suspended *Aufhebung* that will never come to know its own *plērōma*. Deconstruction is a thwarted messianism, a suspension of the messianic. (*TTR* 103)

Unlike the prophet, however, the apostle of the Messiah sees the time of the now in its double structure. Messianic time is precisely the incorporation of operational time into the experience of time; this is what distinguishes it from mere chronological time or the time of the time-image. The thwarted messianic may indeed see the irreducible displacement and futurity of the punctual instant on the timeline, but the true messianic also gazes "backward" upon the kairological "now" that is always already happening in the production of *khronos*. This incorporation of *kairos*/operational time into our *experimentum temporis* is the messianic operation itself.[26] Without this "apostolic" point of view, we are left with the "homogeneous, infinite, quantified time" (*IH* 101) of *khronos*, and messianism is thwarted. Or as Agamben puts the point: "If we drop the messianic theme and only focus on the moment of foundation and origin—or even the absence thereof (which amounts to the same thing)—we are left with empty, zero degree, signification and with history as its infinite deferment" (*TTR* 104). This is why Paul is an apostle and not a prophet.

MESSIANIC (II)

In addition considering himself an apostle of the Messiah, Paul also describes himself as a "slave" or "servant" (*doulos*) to the Messiah. As Agamben notes in a brief review of the word's meaning and etymological provenance, *doulos* is a properly juridical term. Paul is, moreover, completely aware of the technical meaning of the word, and employs it in order precisely to invert or modify the term's legal significance. Or better, Paul's phrase is intended to indicate the inversion or modification of the status of the *law itself* in the messianic condition. As a slave to the Messiah, Paul is no longer a slave to law as it is understood before the Messianic event (the resurrection), and this is because the Messianic event has transformed the status and standing of the law as such. For Agamben, Paul's term *doulos* "is used to express the neutralization that the divisions of the law and all juridical and social conditions in general undergo as a consequence of the messianic event.... [T]he syntagma 'slave of the Messiah' defines the new messianic condition for Paul, the principle of a particular transformation of all juridical conditions" (*TTR* 13).

In chapter 4, we viewed the debate between Benjamin and Schmitt as an allegory for Agamben's and Derrida's views concerning the law, with Agamben arguing that deconstruction maintains the law in a virtual and purely formal state, while his own aim is to definitively neutralize the law and move beyond what he sees as the deconstructive impasse. Another way to say this is that for Agamben, Derrida's (and Schmitt's) legal thought is not messianic, for rather than endlessly "negotiat[ing] with the law" (*SE* 88), the messiah "cut[s] the Gordian knot" (*HS* 48) of the law and neutralizes it. Schmitt appears once again in *The Time That Remains* as a figure of antimessianism, but one who nevertheless provides the theoretical tools for conceiving of a truly messianic experience.

In answer to the question, "What is a law that is simultaneously suspended and fulfilled?" (*TTR* 104), Agamben appeals to the logic of the Schmittian state of exception and the inclusive exclusion that is the means by which law articulates itself with life, bringing it under its control. As he recapitulates the argument here,

> the exception is not a mere exclusion, but an *inclusive exclusion*, an *ex-ceptio* in the literal sense of the term: a seizing of the outside. In defining the exception, the law simultaneously creates and defines the space in which juridical-political order is granted value. In this sense, for Schmitt, the state of exception represents the pure and originary form of the enforcement of the law, and it is from this point

only that the law may define the normal sphere of its application. (*TTR* 105)

On Agamben's reading, Paul's conception of the law in messianic time (under messianic *katargēsis*) can be aligned with this conception of the law in the state of exception—but only up to a point. He explains that in Schmittian terms, three things can be said about the law in the state of exception: (1) There is an absolute indeterminacy between the inside and the outside of the law. The sovereign suspension of the law blurs the border between the legal and the extralegal spheres, and it does so precisely in order to articulate the two by means of the *fictio iuris* of their nexus. That nexus is the legal fiction par excellence. (2) In the state of exception, it is impossible to tell if any human action is in observance or in transgression of the law. Any action might be permissible and any action may be punished. (3) In the state of exception, the statutes of the law cannot be positively formulated. The law has no positive content.

Now, all three of these characteristics of the law in the state of exception have precise equivalents in Paul's account of the law in the time of the Messiah. As a corollary to (1), Agamben refers to Paul's erasure of the distinction between Jews and non-Jews. Rather than a gesture toward a tolerant universalism (as in Alain Badiou's reading of Paul; see *TTR* 49ff.), the effect of this "splitting" of the division between those inside and outside the law is to generate a new type of messianic subject. Paul's intent here is to describe (or produce) a human agent that exists in a sphere of action no longer subject to the law.[27] Agamben describes this postjuridical humanity in terms of a remnant left after the process of the messianic *katargēsis* of the law. "This remnant—the non-non-Jews—is neither properly inside nor outside, neither *ennomos* nor *anomos* (according to the way Paul defines himself in I Cor 9:21); it is the cipher of messianic deactivation of the law, the cipher of its *katargēsis*. The remnant is an exception taken to its extreme, pushed to its paradoxical formulation" (*TTR* 106).

As a corollary to the closely related points (2) and (3), Agamben refers to Paul's formulation of the new law of faith and its indifference to its observance in the sphere of works. Indeed, he writes that "[t]he entire critique of the *nomos* in Romans 3:9–20 is no more than a clear-cut enunciation of a real messianic principle of the unobservability of the law" (*TTR* 107). The passage in question reads as follows (in the NEB): "What then? Are we Jews any better off? No, not at all! For we have already drawn up the accusation that Jews and Greeks alike are all under the power of sin. This has scriptural warrant:"—at which point Paul invokes (in the Greek of the Septuagint) Psalm 14: "There is no just man, not one; / no one who understands, no one who seeks God. / All have swerved aside, all alike have become debased [ēkhreōthēsan] (Rom 3: 9–12). While the general Pauline intention of erasing the distinction between Jew and non-Jew is clear enough from the opening of this passage, the last phrase is of particular importance for Agamben's interpretation of Pauline *katargēsis*. According to Agamben, "[t]he particular expression Paul uses in verse 12, 'all ēkhreōthēsan,' which Jerome translates as *inutiles facti sunt*, literally means (*a-khreioō*) 'they were made unable to use,' and perfectly conveys the impossibility of use, the unobservability that characterizes the law in messianic time, which only faith may restore in *khrēsis*, in use" (*TTR* 107).[28]

It is at this point that the decisive difference between the Pauline and the Schmittian states of exception can be seen, for the point at which the two diverge is the point where the law is either reaffirmed (the Schmittian/antimessianic position) or definitively deactivated and rendered inoperative (the Agambenian/Pauline/Benjaminian position). As an "apocalypticist of counterrevolution" (*TTR* 104), Schmitt seeks to bring the legal order back from the brink of catastrophe and reaffirm its rule. In chapter 4, I discussed this reaffirmation of the juridical order in terms of the "fictitious state of exception" (the ultimate *fictio iuris* that grounds the law). In the present context, however, Agamben reads the counterrevolutionary antimessianism of Schmitt's thought through Paul's obscure reference, in 2 Thessalonians 2:3–9, to the *katekhōn*, the force that holds back and delays the apocalyptic revelation of the *parousia* at the end of time. In Agamben's rendering of this cryptic passage, Paul writes:

> You know what it is that now holds back [*to katekhōn*], so that he [i.e., the man of lawlessness, *ho anthrōpos tēs anomias*] will be revealed when his time comes. For the mystery of anomy (*anomia*) is already at work, but only until the person now holding him back [*ho katekhōn*] is removed. Then the lawless one [*ho anomos*] will be revealed, whom the Lord will abolish with the breath of his mouth, rendering him inoperative [*katargēsei*] by the manifestation of his presence [*parousia*]. (2 Thes 2: 6–8) (*TTR* 109; translation modified)

This passage presents a number of interpretive difficulties, not least of which is the identification of the "man of lawlessness" or "lawless one," which has generally been identified as the antichrist, even though Paul does not use the term ("*antikhristos*" only appears in the Letters of John). Even if this identification is accepted, however, the identity of the *katekhōn* (whether as an impersonal force, as in the first occurrence in the passage, or as a person, as in the second) remains unclear. As Agamben notes, there is a tradition, beginning as early as Tertullian, that identifies the *katekhōn* with the Roman Empire, which as long as it remains in power staves off the apocalyptic end of time, and thus "in this sense, has a positive historical function" (*TTR* 109). Most important, however, is that this conception of the *katekhōn* as the force holding back catastrophe is the basis for Schmitt's Christian theory of the state.

In *The Nomos of the Earth*, Schmitt writes that "The decisive historical concept of [the Christian Empire's] continuity was that of the restrainer: *katechōn*. 'Empire' in this sense meant the historical power to *restrain* the appearance of the Antichrist and the end of the present eon; it was a power that withholds (*qui tenet*), as the apostle Paul said in his Second Letter to the Thessalonians" (qtd. in *TTR* 109).[29] For Schmitt, the *katekhōn* is the power that staves off catastrophe, the Christian state that restrains and retards the coming of the "lawless one," and it is for this reason that Paul's *katekhōn* appears to Schmitt as the decisive concept of Christian political empire.[30] Agamben notes that, among other things, this translation of a theological concept into a political one exemplifies the Schmittian theory of secularization and political theology ("All significant concepts of the modern theory of the state are secularized theological concepts").[31] But more importantly, and far more strikingly, he suggests that this notion of the katekhontic state fundamentally misses the point Paul wants to make about the *katekhōn*, and it does so by not reading Paul as a truly messianic thinker.

On Agamben's reading, not only does this passage from 2 Thessalonians "not harbor any positive valuation of *katekhōn*" (*TTR* 110), but the *anomia* referred to there is precisely "the condition of the law in messianic time, when the *nomos* is rendered inoperative and is in a state of *katargēsis*" (*TTR* 110). That is to say, Paul is calling here for a real, rather than fictitious, state of emergency in which the law is definitively deactivated and fulfilled.[32] He writes:

> The *katekhōn* is therefore the force—the Roman Empire as well as every constituted authority—that clashes with and hides *katargēsis*, the state of tendential lawlessness that characterizes the messianic, and in this sense delays unveiling the "mystery of lawlessness." The unveiling of this mystery entails bringing to light the inoperativity of the law and the substantial illegitimacy of each and every power [*potere*] in messianic time. (*TTR* 111)

The connection between the deferring, delaying, antimessianic *katekhōn* and Derridean *différance* is evident, if implicit, here. Agamben, however, makes that connection explicit in a passage from his introduction to a 2005 collection of Schmitt's writings. In terms that we have already encountered in his engagement with Derrida's reading of Kafka's "Before the Law," Agamben writes:

> The *katekhōn*, suspending and holding back the end, inaugurates a time in which nothing can truly happen [*avvenire*], because the sense [*senso*, also "direction"] of historical becoming, which has its truth only in the *eskhaton*, is now indefinitely deferred. What happens [*avviene*] in the suspended time of the *katekhōn* is, in this sense, an undecidable, which happens, so to speak, without truly happening because its coming [*avvenire*], the *eskhaton* that alone could give it sense [*senso*], is ceaselessly deferred and adjourned. Schmitt's katekhontic time is a thwarted messianism: but this thwarted messianism shows itself to be the theological paradigm of the time in which we live, the structure of which is none other than Derridean *différance*. Christian eschatology had introduced a sense and a direction in time: *katekhōn* and *différance*, suspending and delaying this sense, render it undecidable.[33]

Thus, though the specific terms are slightly different, the discussion of Pauline messianism in *The Time That Remains* is fundamentally a perfectly coherent continuation of Agamben's presentation of both the Benjamin-Schmitt gigantomachy concerning the fictitious and real state of exception and, at the same time, the gigantomachy between Agamben and Derrida, between an antinomian messianism and a katekhontic thwarted messianism.

Indeed, the intention of Schmitt's entire theory of the *Ausnahmezustand* is to affirm the rule of law by looking squarely at its true foundation,

A Matter of Time 251

the exception, and acting as the *katekhōn* to hold back the end of the time. The intention of Paul's "theory" of messianic *katargēsis*, on the contrary, is to deactivate the law and step into a new sphere of human action that has left the juridical order behind. This, however, is no nostalgic restoration of a supposedly pure prelegal originary state, nor is it a deconstructive volatilization of that irretrievable origin; rather, it is the messianic fulfillment of the law in its definitive supersession. As Agamben writes, "The messianic is not the destruction but the deactivation of the law, rendering the law inexecutable [*l'ineseguibilità della legge*]" (*TTR* 98). And in the messianic state that obtains after the deactivation/inexecutability/unusability of the law, a new dimension of human action opens up. Understanding, establishing, and entering into this dimension is the ultimate desideratum of Agamben's political thought.

What, then, can be said about this alteration of the nature of human action as it moves from the juridical to this postjuridical sphere? If, as Agamben claims, "from a legal standpoint it is possible to classify human actions as legislative, executive, or transgressive acts" (*SE* 50), then how might be classified the human action that occurs under the deactivation of the law, after the Benjaminian "real state of exception" has been brought about? In *State of Exception*, one model Agamben proposes for conceiving of this anomic sphere is the Roman *iustitum*, the suspension of law in the periods of emergency (that is, roughly the same legal phenomenon as the *Ausnahmezustand*—"a kenomatic state, an emptiness and standstill of the law" [*SE* 48]). But Agamben's most evocative and vivid analogy for this sort of "purified" human action (in the sense of "purification" discussed in chapter 4) is one that, perhaps not coincidentally, is a homonym for one of Derrida's central concepts: *play*.

Agamben makes the association—or identification—between the postjuridical action and play by way of Benjamin's reading of Kafka. In a letter to Scholem of 1934, Benjamin states that "the Scripture without its key is not Scripture but life," and in the essay "Franz Kafka" of the same year, he writes, "The law which is studied but no longer practiced is the gate to justice" (qtd. in *SE* 63). Commenting on these two passages, Agamben writes: "The Scripture (the Torah) without its key is the cipher of the law in the state of exception.... According to Benjamin, this law—or, rather, this force-of-law—is no longer law but life.... Kafka's most proper gesture consists not (as Scholem believes) in having maintained a law that no longer has any meaning, but in having shown that it ceases to be law and blurs at all points with life" (*SE* 63). Kafka would thus be another antinomian messianic, looking forward—or better, looking directly at—the deactivation of law and its blurring with life, that is, its blurring with a human action purified of law. For Agamben, who has his critique of the Derridean *katekhōn* very much in mind here, the point of Kafka's (and Benjamin's) imagery of a defunct, idling, inoperative law is not a matter of "a transitional phase that never achieves its end, nor of a process of infinite deconstruction that, in maintaining the law in a spectral life, can no longer get to the bottom of it. The decisive point here is that the law—no longer practiced, but studied—is not justice, but only the gate that leads to it. What opens a passage toward justice is not the erasure of the law, but its deactivation and inactivity [*inoperosità*]—that is, another use of the law" (*SE* 64). This other use is rendered possible not by the total destruction and erasure of the law and a return to a pure, originary essence, nor certainly by the endless maintenance of the law in a sort of zero-degree state. Rather it is the possibility opened by a deactivating operation enacted on the existing apparatuses—the law in particular—that capture life *now*. And Agamben's privileged figure for the way postjuridical humanity "uses" those deactivated apparatuses is *play*.

CODA
Play

Over the last three chapters of this book, we've seen Agamben call for the neutralization and deactivation of a number of apparatuses that govern and determine human action—law, "anthropology" or anthropogenesis, and even chronological time. What all of those apparatuses have in common is that they are machines for creating separations and articulations between life and the structural forms in which that life is lived, between life and the forms imposed on that life. In the most general sense, this division is the function of what Agamben calls biopolitics, that is, the fundamental separation/articulation of *zōē* and *bios*; and the act of separating these two (and surreptitiously capturing the former as "abandoned" bare life) is the action of sovereignty. "Political power [*potere*] as we know it," Agamben writes in the 1993 essay "Form-of-Life," "always founds itself—in the last instance—on the separation of a sphere of naked life from the context of the forms of life" (*MWE* 4).

In a later essay titled "The Work of Man," Agamben notes that the term *energeia*—which is derived from the word *ergon* ("work") and literally means "being at work"—"was, in all probability, created by Aristotle, who uses it in functional opposition to *dunamis*" (*WM* 1). In the *Nicomachean Ethics*, Aristotle considers the way certain "works" or activities provide the criteria for defining certain types of beings. For example, the flute player is defined by playing the flute, the sculptor by making sculptures. But problems arise when we ask about the human as such. The sculptor clearly produces *agalmata*, but what is the "work of man" as man? Is there no distinct *ergon* into which the potentiality of the human realizes itself? Is man as such *argos* (without work)? This quandary in the Aristotelian argument provides Agamben (via later commentators such as Averroës and Dante) with the basis for his account of the human not as a being endowed with this or that particular potentiality or capability (or any corresponding "work" or form), but as a being of "pure potentiality." Because of the impossibility of "identifying the *energeia*, the being-at-work of man as man, independently of and beyond the concrete social figures that he can assume" (*WM* 2), Agamben suggests that in Aristotle we can discern "the idea of an *argia*, of an essential inactivity [*inoperosità*] of man" (*WM* 2).

For Agamben, this means that the human as such has no "form of life"—no predefined work or act—toward which its potentialities are rigidly directed. The human is thus a being defined not by any particular act or form but precisely by the pure potentiality not to pass over into any given act or form. This being of pure potentiality, and the action of this potential being, are the subject and the praxis of Agamben's "coming politics," the inaugural task of which is to halt the mechanisms of the biopolitical machine that seek to capture that potentiality in actualized works. "If there is today a social potentiality," he writes, "it must see its own impotentiality through to the end, it must decline any will to either posit or preserve law [*diritto*], it must break everywhere the nexus between violence and law, between the living and language that constitutes sovereignty" (*MWE* 113; translation modified).

In this image of a human action that neither posits nor preserves law, one can certainly hear an echo—in truth, an anticipation—of Agamben's reading of Benjamin's "Critique of Violence" in *State of Exception*, which was discussed in chapter 4 above. There, as we saw, Agamben identifies the ultimate desideratum of Benjamin's legal thought to be not precisely justice (which is set aside quite early in the essay) or even a legal *Gewalt* that leads to just ends, but rather "violence as 'pure medium,' that is, as the figure of a paradoxical 'mediality without ends'—a means that, though remaining such, is considered independently of the ends that it pursues" (*SE* 62). The essential point about this pure violence—the "purity" of which has nothing to do, we recall, with originariness and uncorruptedness—is that in withholding itself from being appropriated by the apparatuses of law, in its "passive resistance" to any juridical instrumentalization, it disruptively exposes the fact that the law has no dominion over life and that there is no vital core to the legal order. The law is a fiction—like all the ultimately fictitious apparatuses that parcel out and define human action—that falters in the face of an anomic, pure violence that refuses to be converted into a means toward an end. As Agamben puts it, "pure violence is that which does not stand in a relation of means toward an end, but holds itself in relation to its own mediality.... [And it] is attested to only as the exposure and deposition of the relation between violence and law" (*SE* 62). Pure violence is not "absolute" violence, but a violence that, as pure means, has absolved itself of its ends.

Pure means, or means without end, is Agamben's figure for human action in the real state of exception, *after* the apparatuses of law (and of economics, anthropology, government, etc.) have been definitively deactivated. And bringing about this real state of exception, as Benjamin exhorts us to, is what Agamben repeatedly, though perhaps in varied terms, calls "the political task of the coming generation" (*Prof* 92). What is pursued in this undertaking is not a lost purity but rather a new condition in which a postjuridical human action has detached itself from any juridical ends it might have once served. As he writes in the paragraph that concludes his chapter on the Benjamin-Schmitt gigantomachy: "One day humanity will play with law just as children play with disused objects, not in order to restore them to their canonical use but to free them from it for good.... This liberation is the task of study, or of play" (*SE* 64). In the context of the present discussion, this last term must resonate especially strongly, since in choosing "play" as one of his privileged images of this postsovereign politics of the coming community, Agamben has provocatively (whether intentionally or not) chosen a homonym for one of Derrida's most influential and distinctive concepts. And I have chosen the term "homonym" carefully here, since "play" in Agamben's lexicon does not carry the same meaning as it does in Derrida's.

Among the many places where Derrida elaborates his concept (and valorization) of play, the first that comes to mind for many readers will be "Structure, Sign, and Play in the Discourse of the Human Sciences." This essay's discussion of play is particularly relevant for our purposes here because it throws into relief at least two ways in which the Derridean notion of play is unlike the Agambenian notion. In the first place, for Derrida, the primary overtones of the word include the definitions "free and unimpeded movement" and, above all, "freedom or room for movement; the space in or through which a thing can or does move" (*OED*). In fact, Derrida even proposes play as a synonym, or near-synonym, for *différance*: "*Différance* is the systematic play of differences, of the traces of differences, of the *spacing* by means of which elements are related to each other" (*Pos* 27). The play of differences, the play that worries the hairline fractures and fissures of every structure, the unstoppable play that fatally undermines any appeal to a solid, pure presence, these are the well-known valences of this key term of the deconstructive lexicon, as can be seen in Derrida's employment of it in his critique of Lévi-Strauss in "Structure, Sign, and Play."

But as important as it is to pin down that particular usage of the term, it is perhaps even more crucial to note here how for Derrida the identification of this "differantial" play is the key gesture in undermining any and all appeals to—and ultimately all desires for—an origin or originary state or being:

> Play is the disruption of presence. . . . Play is always play of absence and presence, but if it is to be thought radically, play must be conceived of before the alternative of presence and absence. Being must be conceived as presence or absence on the basis of the possibility of play and not the other way around. (*WD* 292)

If understood correctly, the acknowledgment of a play of differences before any determinations of presence or absence combats, in Derrida's view, all nostalgias for the origin whose loss is precisely marked by that always-anterior play. Indeed "loss" is not even the right term here, since there never was any origin to lose—only the illusion of this imaginary homeland and of the possibility of returning to it. But having awakened from that illusion and having unreservedly affirmed the originless open-endedness and pure promise of undecidable play, man shakes off his metaphysical baggage and forgets about the lost home he never had—forgets, even, himself. Such an affirmative, antinostalgic deconstructive thought, Derrida says, is "no longer turned toward the origin, affirms play and tries to pass beyond man and humanism, the name of man being the name of that being who, throughout the history of metaphysics or of ontotheology—in other words, throughout his entire history—has dreamed of full presence, the reassuring foundation, the origin and the end of play" (*WD* 292). This antinostalgia is, of course, one of the hallmarks of deconstruction, and stands as the (non)basis for the "strategy without finality" and "blind tactics" of Derrida's philosophical and political thought.

The significance of "play" in Agamben's usage, however, leads beyond an affirmation (whether resigned or joyous) of the impossibility of an original purity and presence. Agamben's concept of play has a number of obvious antecedents. Certainly he refers to Benveniste's studies of the relation between games and sacred rites, and his 1978 essay "In Playland" is largely a reading of Lévi-Strauss (to whom it is dedicated). The thinker whose conception of play, however, most closely resembles Agamben's, though Agamben does not refer to him in this context, is perhaps Hans-Georg Gadamer. In a section of *Truth and Method* titled "Play as the Clue to Ontological Explanation," Gadamer gives a sort of phenomenology of play that not only provides a vivid description of the total absorption of players into the game, but also anticipates Agamben's argument concerning the "deactivation" of human behavior as it becomes play and of instrumental objects (such as tools) as they become toys. For example, he notes that "in playing, all those purposive relations that determine active and caring existence have not simply disappeared, but are curiously suspended."[1] And furthermore, he argues that in this playful deactivation of the mean-and-ends relations, playful behavior enters into a sphere of pure self-manifestation: "Play is really limited to presenting itself. Thus its mode of being is self-presentation. . . . First and foremost, play is self-presentation."[2]

Two points here are most important to note about Gadamer's phenomenology of play. First, it does not seek to describe a merely subjective condition or orientation. Rather, the player and the played (that is, the object the player encounters or uses—or in Heideggerian terminology, the *vorhanden* or *zuhanden* object) assume a different mode of being in the game. Subject and object are equally taken up and transformed in the sphere of play. Second, play is not conceived as an originary condition or an experience of an originary, pure, or "authentic" mode of being. Instead, it is the result of a transformation worked on that object and subject. The "player" and the "toy" are not figures for a lost Adamic condition or "natural" state; they become these things by means of a process that detaches them from their instrumental ends and opens them up for this new, playful use. This is the process that Agamben calls *désoeuvrement* or deactivation, and the condition or mode of being of everything that is "in play" after this deactivation is "inoperativity."

At the end of chapter 6, we saw how for Agamben the deconstruction of origins is but one-half of the messianic project, and how as long as we neglect the other half we remain in an interminable space of deferral and postponement, the undecidable state of suspense that is the thwarted

Coda   259

messianism of the prophet. Deferral and *différance* are perhaps necessary concepts for initiating the critique of a certain metaphysics, but *deactivation* is the indispensable counterpart to this opening gesture, a counterpart without which we remain caught up in the irreducible negativity of the metaphysical problematic. From the Agambenian perspective, Derridean play and deconstructive "strategy without finality" entail the maintenance of the fictitious state of exception and the logic of sovereignty in their most crystalline form. Deconstruction rigorously identifies this form and in doing so comes exceedingly close to the messianic event, but as the *katechōn*, which maintains the apparatus in virtual and endlessly deferred form, Derridean "play" holds back the entry into the time of the Pauline Messiah, wherein human action becomes a means without end. Agambenian "play" is precisely the cipher for this human action after the definitive *katargēsis* of those structures in the real state of exception.

Agamben discusses the link between play and the "messianic" disruption of chronological time as early as the essay "In Playland," where he claims that "In play, man frees himself from sacred time and 'forgets' it in human time" (*IH* 70).³ Though in this early piece the temporal terms are not quite the same as those presented in *The Time That Remains*, it would not be misleading to suggest that in Agamben's lexicon of 1978, "human time" or "human temporality" (*IH* 72) is an anticipation—would it be too much to say the typological prefiguration?—of his later concept of the messianic "time of the now." And the toy, or play, is the messianic operator that brings this temporality to fruition. Perhaps the key point to make here, however, is not merely that human action in "Playland" (the reference is to the *Paese dei balocchi* in chapter 31 of *Pinocchio*) unfolds in an altered temporality, but also that both play and toys become such only by way of an alteration of existing behaviors and objects and not a return to an original state. "The toy is what belonged—*once, no longer*—to the realm of the sacred or of the practical-economic" (*IH* 71). While Agamben does not insist on this point in "In Playland" as much as he will later do, he nevertheless clearly envisions the mechanism of deactivation and inoperativity that turns tools into toys, retaining their functions but evacuating their instrumental uses: "What the toy preserves of its sacred or economic model, what survives of this after its dismemberment or miniaturization, is nothing other than the human temporality that was contained therein: its pure historical essence" (*IH* 71), that is to say, "*history; in other words, human time*" (*IH* 75).

The alignment of chronological or calendrical time with "sacred time" in "In Playland" anticipates another near-synonym for deactivation or *katargēsis*, namely, "profanation," which is the deactivation of the sacralizing apparatus of ritual. Agamben writes that "we can hypothesize a relation of both correspondence and opposition between play and ritual, in the sense that both are engaged in a relationship with the calendar and with time, but this relationship is in each case an inverse one: ritual fixes and *structures* the calendar; play, on the other hand, though we do not yet know how and why, changes and *destroys* it" (*IH* 69). This point is emphasized in the 2005 text "In Praise of Profanation," where Agamben urges us to "recall that profanation does not simply restore something like a natural use that existed before being separated into the religious, economic or juridical sphere" (*Prof* 85). At this point, Agamben makes a surprising, and somewhat puzzling, analogy to the animal sphere. As I have argued is the case with nearly the entire discussion of animals in *The Open*, this analogy, too, must be read not as a claim about animals, or even about a particular animal, but rather as a claim about the human and as an illustration or "symbol"—as he says of another analogy—"of what has been separated and can be returned to common use" (*Prof* 87):

> The cat who plays with a ball of yarn as if it were a mouse—just as the child plays with ancient religious symbols or objects that once belonged to the economic sphere—knowingly uses the characteristic behaviors of predatory activity (or, in the case of the child, of the religious cult or the world of work) in vain. These behaviors are not effaced, but, thanks to the substitution of the yarn for the mouse (or the toy for the sacred object), deactivated and thus opened up to a new, possible use. (*Prof* 85)

As noted at the end of chapter 4 above, this is not a call for the end of predation in the animal kingdom (and the impracticability of such a call shows the nature of the analogy) but rather an illustration of the way that in becoming play, human action "thus becomes a pure means . . . and can now show itself as such, as a means without an end" (*Prof* 86).

Play transforms actions and objects into something new; it does not restore them to an original state. And as with the cat or the child who in play turns a tool into a toy, so, too, does the deactivation of the law open human action to a truly postjuridical condition animated by a pure *Gewalt*, a *Gewalt purified* of the law. "One day," Agamben, writes,

> humanity will play with law just as children play with disused objects, not in order to restore them to their canonical use but to free them from it for good. What is found after the law is not a more proper and original use value that precedes the law, but a new use that is born only after it.... This liberation is the task of study, or of play. And this studious play is the passage that allows us to arrive at that justice that one of Benjamin's posthumous fragments defines as a state of the world in which the world appears as a good that absolutely cannot be appropriated or made juridical. (SE 64)

In such a postjuridical and truly anomic space there may still be the remnants of the juridical machine (as well as other machines); there is, however, no longer any need to endlessly "negotiate with the law" (SE 88), but rather the possibility for a human action or praxis that—conceived along the lines of a child's "play," the new attorney's "study," and a noninstrumental "use"—Agamben, following Benjamin, defines as a pure means. As a figure for a human action, a "truly political action," that has freed itself from the apparatuses of power, pure violence turns what was once a tool into a toy, effecting that slight shift in which, as Benjamin said of the world to come, "[e]verything will be the same as here—only a little bit different."[4] Or as he also writes, in a 1928 essay titled "Toys and Play," "[W]hen a modern poet says that everyone has a picture for which he would be willing to give the whole world, how many people would not look for it in an old box of toys?"[5] Agamben asks us to see the world to come, which is nothing other than the world that is already here, as that old box of toys.

NOTES

INTRODUCTION

1. Martin Heidegger, *"Mein liebes Seelchen": Breife Martin Heideggers an seine Frau Elfride, 1915–1970*, ed. Gertrud Heidegger (Munich: Deutsche Verlags-Anstalt, 2005) 358.

2. In addition to Agamben's numerous evocations of these events, see Leland de la Durantaye's account in *Giorgio Agamben: A Critical Introduction* (Stanford: Stanford UP, 2009) 1–4.

3. Agamben, "L'albero del linguaggio," *I Problemi di Ulisse* 21.9 (September 1968): 112.

4. Agamben, "L'albero del linguaggio," 112. The internal quotation is from *G* 14.

5. Agamben, "L'albero del linguaggio," 113.

6. In addition to the critique contained in "L'albero del linguaggio," the chapter of Agamben's first book, *The Man without Content* (1970), titled "The Melancholy Angel," which was also published in *Nuovi Argomenti* 19 (July-September 1970), contains a footnoted reference to "the most penetrating analysis of Kafka's relationship with history," Beda Allemann's "Kafka et l'histoire," which was published in the 1968 volume *L'Endurance de la pensée: Pour saluer Jean Beaufret*. This volume, edited by René Char, also contained Derrida's essay "*Ousia* and *Grammē*: Note on a Note from *Being and Time*," which the young student of Heidegger could not have failed to read. The publication history of *L'Endurance de la pensée* is quite interesting in itself, involving charges of anti-Semitism leveled at Beaufret and Derrida's and Blanchot's near-withdrawal of their contributions from the collection (see Dominique Janicaud, *Heidegger en France*, vol. 2 [Paris: Éditions Albin Michel, 2001] 96–100).

7. In response to a question from Lorenzo Fabbri in 2006 about the striking lack of reference to Agamben in Derrida's work, especially in the later work that touched on themes concerning which Agamben's thought had become an important touchstone, Jean-Luc Nancy reticently says:

> You are touching on a rather difficult and painful subject for me as a friend of both Derrida and Agamben. For Agamben began at a certain point to reject Derrida in a radical way, which was of course his right, all the while taking back up many of Derrida's themes (such as messianism and, yes, the animal). He showed himself in this respect to be extremely unjust—I mean philosophically speaking. To speak, as he did, of *différance* as a perpetual delay is to deliberately refuse to read the texts. Or else to write about messianism after Derrida without mentioning him is aggressive and unscholarly (and I know that this was intentional). One could make a whole case here, but it would be rather petty and uninteresting. In any case, I cannot and do not want to say anything more about it; this has been a subject of discussion and even disagreement between Agamben and me. (Jean-Luc Nancy and Lorenzo Fabbri, "Philosophy as Chance: An Interview with Jean-Luc Nancy," trans. Pascale-Anne Brault and Michael Naas, *Critical Inquiry* 33.2 [Winter 2007]: 435)

The intention of the present study is not to make a "whole case" of this in the sense Nancy intends. But there is an important history to be recounted by following the intersecting intellectual paths of these major thinkers of the postwar continental tradition. And the chapters that follow will offer a reading of that intellectual history that does not quite correspond to—or that at least complicates—the personal one that Nancy sketches here.

8. Derrida's first published reference to Agamben is equally esoteric in its way. It comes in a text he wrote to accompany a photographic project by Marie-Françoise Plissart titled *Droit de regards* (Paris: Éditions de Minuit, 1985) xxv. In this text, Derrida cites a passage not from one of the four books Agamben had published up to that point, but rather from a slim and obscure pamphlet titled *La fine del pensiero/La fin de la pensée*, trans. Gérard Macé (Paris: Le Nouveau Commerce, 1982).

9. For Derrida's comments on the systematicity of his thought, see the opening pages of Derrida and Maurizio Ferraris, *A Taste for the Secret*, trans. Giacomo Donis (Cambridge: Polity, 2001) 1ff., where he asserts:

> If by "system" is meant—and this is the minimal sense of the word—a sort of consequence, coherence and insistence—a certain gathering together—there is an injunction to the system that I have never renounced, and never wished to. This can be seen in the recurrence of motifs and references from one text to another in my work, despite the differing occasions and pretexts—a recurrence that, having reached a certain age, I find rather striking.

10. While there is a truly voluminous body of criticism on Derrida, the work of Rodophe Gasché, especially his book *The Tain of the Mirror: Derrida and the Philosophy of Reflection* (Cambridge: Harvard UP, 1986), remains the canonical account of Derrida as a philosopher within the continental philosophical tradition. For an incisive systematic account of Agamben's thought, see Catherine Mills's *The Philosophy of Agamben* (Montreal: McGill-Queen's UP, 2008).

11. For an expansive discussion of Agamben's thought as it relates to questions of literature, see William Watkin, *The Literary Agamben* (New York: Continuum, 2010).

12. Here and throughout this book, I use the "untranslated" and italicized term "*différance*," which has become the standard convention in translating Derrida's nonword. I agree, however, with Jonathan Rée that David B. Allison's earlier rendering as "differance" better preserves the sense and effects of the term in Derrida's text (see Jonathan Rée, "The Translation of Philosophy," *New Literary History* 32.2 [2001] 237–38).

13. Agamben, "La 121ᵃ giornata di Sodoma e Gomorra," *Tempo Presente* 9.3–4 (1966): 60. For a discussion of this essay and of Agamben's very early "Artaudian" period more generally, see Kevin Attell, "Agamben's Artaud," *Giorgio Agamben: Legal, Political and Philosophical Perspectives*, ed. Tom Frost (London: Routledge, 2013) 175–88.

1. AGAMBEN AND DERRIDA READ SAUSSURE

1. Franz Kafka, *The Trial*, trans. Breon Mitchell (New York: Schocken, 1998) 224.

2. See Gasché, *The Tain of the Mirror*, esp. 142–54.

3. Agamben is also, to a lesser extent, responding in this chapter to the reading of the parable offered by Massimo Cacciari, who, among other things, traces (via Gershom Scholem) the possible source of the story to a passage from Origen (see Cacciari, *Icone della legge* [Milan: Adelphi, 1985] 66–67). As Scholem summarizes it: "In his commentary on the Psalms, Origen quotes a 'Hebrew' scholar ... as saying that the Holy Scriptures are like a large house with many, many rooms, and that outside each door lies a key—but it is not the right key. To find the right key is the great and arduous task.... The Rabbi whose metaphor so impressed Origen still possessed the Revelation, but knew that he no longer had the right key and was engaged in looking for it" (*On the Kabbala and Its Symbolism*, trans. Ralph Mannheim [New York: Schocken, 1965] 12–13). Agamben briefly takes up this passage from Origen in *The Time That Remains*, trans. Patricia Dailey (Stanford: Stanford UP, 2005) 92.

4. "*Venire a capo*," which Heller-Roazen translates as "to master" and I have elsewhere translated as "to get to the bottom of," is something like a technical term in Agamben's vocabulary. It occurs with some frequency throughout his work, and when it does, it is most often used to describe the aporetic limit that he argues deconstructive thought is unable to think beyond, the difficulty that it cannot master, the problematic that it cannot get to the bottom of.

5. "L'albero del linguaggio," *I Problemi di Ulisse* 21.9 (September 1968): 104–14.

6. For recent reevaluation of the early and lasting influence of Husserl on Derrida's thought, see Joshua Kates's formidable study *Essential History: Jacques Derrida and the Development of Deconstruction* (Evanston: Northwestern UP, 2005).

7. For a sort of snapshot of the debate concerning structuralism and a nascent poststructuralism in the mid-1960s, see the collection *The Structuralist Controversy: The Languages of Criticism and the Sciences of Man*, ed. Richard Macksey and Eugenio Donato (Baltimore: Johns Hopkins UP, 1972). Consisting of papers presented and discussions held during the famous symposium at the recently founded Humanities Center at Johns Hopkins University in 1966, this volume includes Derrida's essay "Structure, Sign, and Play in the Discourse of the Human Sciences."

8. Rodolphe Gasché, "Deconstruction as Criticism," *Inventions of Difference: On Jacques Derrida* (Cambridge: Harvard UP, 1994) 26.

9. The corpus of deconstructive literary criticism—even if limited to that of the 1970s and early 1980s—is large and varied and far beyond the scope of the present discussion. For an authoritative examination of that work, which takes into account Gasché's polemic as well as much else, see Jonathan Culler, *On Deconstruction: Theory and Criticism after Structuralism* (Ithaca: Cornell UP, 1982), esp. chaps. 2.5 and 3.

10. Heidegger, "Letter on 'Humanism,'" trans. Frank A. Capuzzi, *Pathmarks*, ed. William McNeill (Cambridge: Cambridge UP, 1998) 250.

11. For further comment on this argument, as well as a discussion of Derrida's use of the phrase *"s'entendre parler* (to hear/understand oneself)" to indicate the way the vocal sign seems to erase itself, see Culler, *On Deconstruction*, 107–9.

12. Gasché, "Deconstruction as Criticism," 38.

13. "It is the domination of beings that *différance* everywhere comes to solicit, in the sense that *sollicitare*, in old Latin, means to shake as a whole, to make tremble in entirety" (*M* 21).

14. Gasché, "Deconstruction as Criticism," 39. Derrida also describes this strategy of redirecting the terms we have inherited from the tradition as a matter of *paleonymy*. In his 1971 interview with Jean-Louis Houbedine and Guy Scarpetta, Derrida explains his "occasional maintenance of an *old name* in order to launch a new concept" thus:

> Taking into account the fact that a name does not name the punctual simplicity of a concept, but rather a system of predicates defining a concept, a conceptual structure *centered* on a given predicate, we proceed: (1) to the extraction of a reduced predicative trait that is held in reserve, limited in a given conceptual structure (limited for motivations and relations of force to be analyzed), *named* X; (2) to the delimitation, the grafting and regulated extension of the extracted predicate, the name X being maintained as a kind of *level of intervention*, in order to maintain a grasp on the previous organization, which is to be transformed effectively. Therefore, extraction, graft, extension: you know that this is what I call, according to the process I have just described, *writing*. (*Pos* 71)

15. These publications on the anagrams culminate in Starobinski's book *Les mots sous les mots* (Paris: Gallimard, 1971). In the counterportrait that he develops here,

Agamben offers what might be thought of as yet a *third* Saussure, distinct from the "two Saussures" (the Saussure of the *Course* and that of the anagrams) proposed by the editors of *Semiotext(e)* as the subject of a 1974 conference. The proceedings of the conference were published in *Semiotext(e)* 1.2 (Fall 1974) and 2.1 (Spring 1975).

16. Derrida would also have been aware of Saussure's crisis through his reading of Robert Godel's *Les sources manuscrites du cours de linguistique générale* (Geneva: Droz, 1957), which he cites in *Of Grammatology*, 329n38. The doubts and hesitations of Saussure that Derrida does occasionally mention in *Of Grammatology* are those associated with the work on the anagrams (see, for example, *Of Grammatology*, 72, 245, and 329n38).

17. "[H]ere at least, . . . caring very little about Ferdinand de Saussure's *very* thought *itself*, I have interested myself in a *text* whose literality has played a well-known role since 1915" (*G* 329n38). From a perspective very different from Agamben's, in a reading of Saussure that seeks to bring his thought closer to Derrida's than Derrida's own engagements with Saussure might seem to promise, Jonathan Culler, too, returns to the students' course notes in Engler's critical edition to find that Saussure is far less insistent on the arbitrariness (and absolute unmotivatedness) of the linguistic sign than the published text of the *Course* suggests. For Culler, this implies that Saussure had more or less already allowed for the contamination, relative motivation, and recombinatory play of linguistic marks that the canonical version of his thought would seem to resist. Instead, he writes, "Saussure's conception of the mechanisms of the linguistic system—the play of differences, the operation of analogy, the series that generate units of indeterminate status and, above all, grammar as a process of motivation—precludes a theory based on signs purified of motivation or a theory that does not permit a structural 'openness' of this 'système interne de la langue'" ("The Sign: Saussure and Derrida on Arbitrariness," *The Literary in Theory* [Stanford: Stanford UP, 2007] 133–34). Though he persuasively suggests that Derrida's intuition was correct when he "suspected something was wrong [with the text of the *Course*]" (123), and that Saussure's own thought points toward the deconstruction of the purity of *la langue*, Culler's argument, nevertheless, also centers on the implications of Derrida's use of the influential though problematic published text of the *Course*, noting among other things that the examples of the quasi-onomatopoetic words *fouet* and *glas* appear not to have been Saussure's but an addition by the editors (123–24).

18. Quoted in *M* 10–11; the cited passage can be found in Ferdinand de Saussure, *Course in General Linguistics*, trans. Wade Baskin (New York: McGraw-Hill, 1966) 117–20. Part of this passage is also cited by Derrida in *Of Grammatology*, 326n16, in the context of a discussion of how in his argumentation Saussure—against his own intention of a phonologically oriented linguistics (*G* 29)—"contradicts the allegation of a naturally phonic essence of language" (*G* 53) and must "borrow all his pedagogic resources from the example of writing" (*G* 52).

19. For a meticulous critique of this gesture, from a perspective informed by Merleau-Ponty's thought, see M. C. Dillon, *Semiological Reductionism: A Critique of the Deconstructionist Movement in Postmodern Thought* (Albany: State University of New York Press, 1995), esp. chaps. 1–3.

20. The passage Agamben cites can be found in Émile Benveniste, *Problems in General Linguistics*, trans. Mary Elizabeth Meek (Coral Gables: U of Miami P, 1971), 34; and in Godel 31.

21. The passage Agamben cites can be found in Ferdinand de Saussure, *Cours de linguistique générale*, ed. Rudolph Engler (Wiesbaden: Otto Harrassowitz, 1968), xi; and in Godel 30.

22. For an illuminating discussion of *différance* as spacing, see Gasché, *The Tain of the Mirror*, 198–202.

23. See Saussure, *Cours*, ed. Engler, 272. Though the letter to Meillet is written thirteen years before the first course on general linguistics, Godel (who notes the "interesting and surprising confidences" [31] contained in the letter) reviews the evidence of Saussure's preoccupation with general (synchronic) linguistics in the decades before the course (see Godel 23–35).

24. In *Glas*, Derrida similarly presents Saussure as a strident defender of the thesis of the arbitrary and unmotivated nature of the sign. Derrida focuses here on Saussure's discussion of the quasi-onomatopoeic words *fouet* and *glas* and shows how his attempt to rescue the purity and arbitrariness of *la langue* from the "dangerous" contamination of onomatopoeia collapses under pressure. As mentioned above, however, the discussion of *fouet* and *glas* appears to have been added to the *Course* by the editors (see Derrida, *Glas*, trans. John P. Leavy Jr. and Richard Rand [Lincoln: U of Nebraska P, 1986] 90–97).

25. This quote is taken from the preface Agamben wrote in 1988–89 for the French translation of this 1978 book.

26. See Saussure, *Course*, xix.

27. As Charles Segal notes: "Sophocles' play, unlike the modern versions of Jean Cocteau, Hugo von Hofmannsthal, and Pier Paolo Pasolini, for example, omits any detailed account of this mythical episode.... When Oedipus, frightened by Jocasta's story of Laius' death, tells about his journey from Corinth to Thebes, he makes no mention of meeting the Sphinx on the way" (Segal, *Sophocles' Tragic World* [Cambridge: Harvard UP, 1995] 171). The question of the role of the Sphinx in the Oedipus legend is an interesting and complicated one, about which much, of course, has been written. For a brief overview of a number of arguments regarding the history and narrative function of the episode in the Oedipus story, see Lowell Edmunds, *The Sphinx in the Oedipus Legend*, Beiträge zur klassischen Philologie 127 (Königstein/Ts.: Anton Hain, 1981). Given that, as is well known, Agamben appeared as the apostle Philip in Pier Paolo Pasolini's 1964 film *Il vangelo secondo Matteo*, it may also be relevant to note that in Pasolini's 1967 film *Edipo re*, the

Sphinx does not ask Oedipus the famous riddle; rather, the monster says: "There is an enigma in your life. What is it?" Oedipus responds, "I don't know. I don't want to know," and attacks the Sphinx, who, being hurled down, cries, "It is useless. The abyss into which you push me is inside of you." Pasolini, furthermore, was co-editor (with Alberto Carocci and Alberto Moravia) of the journal *Nuovi Argomenti*, which published a number of pieces by Agamben between 1968 and 1970.

28. This argument also constitutes a critique of the "Oedipal" nature of Freudian thought concerning the symbolic. Unlike, for example, Jean-Pierre Vernant's historically-anthropologically oriented critique of the anachronistic and selective adoption of the ancient Oedipus myth into the modern Freudian "complex" (see "Oedipus without the Complex," in Jean-Pierre Vernant and Pierre Vidal-Naquet, *Myth and Tragedy in Ancient Greece*, trans. Janet Lloyd [New York: Zone, 1990] 85–111), Agamben, drawing on Jacques Lacan, argues that the Oedipal misunderstanding of the Sphinx's "archaic" and enigmatic language as a code to be deciphered (and the repetition of this misunderstanding in the Western tradition from that point forward) determines the structural model of the psyche as split between the conscious and the unconscious, where the former is the sphere of proper meaning and the latter the sphere of repression, concealment, and dissimulation. See especially Agamben, *Stanzas*, 145–49. Vernant's essay appeared in Italian translation in *Nuovi Argomenti* 12 (October-December 1968). This issue also contained Agamben's piece "L'uomo senza contenuto," which consisted of the chapters "The Man of Taste and the Dialectic of the Split," and "The Cabinet of Wonders" from *The Man without Content*.

29. Martinez includes the quite legitimate glosses "story, fable" (and, on page xviii, "tale") of the term *ainos*, but perhaps more to the point would be Gregory Nagy's suggestion that "it is better to think of the *ainos* as a mode of speech, not as a genre" (*Pindar's Homer* [Baltimore: Johns Hopkins UP, 1990] 150). While Nagy's analysis of the *ainos* in archaic Greek poetry does not ultimately coincide with Agamben's claim (he reads it precisely as a code bearing a message that will be intelligible only by its intended audience and misunderstood or garbled by everyone else, hence the noun *ainigma*, which derives from it), they would nevertheless agree that the *ainos* is to be understood as a particular mode of speech rather than a generic form. Nagy furthermore suggests that the unattested verb **aínomai*, from which the noun *ainos* presumably derives, "must have meant 'say [in a special way]'" (*The Best of the Achaeans* [Baltimore: Johns Hopkins UP, 1979] 241).

30. See Derrida's comments on "monstrosity" in *Of Grammatology*, 5, and in the closing lines of "Structure, Sign, and Play in the Discourse of the Human Sciences," *Writing and Difference*, trans. Alan Bass (Chicago: Chicago UP, 1978) 293.

31. That Agamben's is at base a linguistic first philosophy—and one that identifies *logos* most fundamentally as the "taking place" of human language—is a point critically examined by Jenny Doussan in *Time, Language, and Visuality in Agamben's*

Philosophy (Basingstoke: Palgrave Macmillan, 2013), in which she argues that Agamben's own logocentrism leads him, in various modulations over the course of his career, to assimilate the visual—and cognition itself—to the linguistic.

32. The possibility of such a "non-Oedipal" experience or conception of language is something Derek Attridge excludes in his affirmation of the Derridean position against Agamben's critique. Citing (only) Agamben's acknowledgment that "Even if it were possible to reveal the metaphysical inheritance of modern semiology, it would still be impossible for us to conceive of a presence that, finally freed from difference, was only a pure and undivided station in the open" (*S* 156), Attridge asserts that "Derrida has shown, in many different readings, just this: attempts from Plato to Husserl to conceive of such a form of presence always break down, always reveal that presence is divided from the start" (*Reading and Responsibility: Deconstruction's Traces* [Edinburgh: Edinburgh UP, 2010] 10). The counter-questions here (and throughout much of what is to follow) would include whether Derrida's claims have been definitively "shown" and where we locate "the start." Attridge finds it "odd" that Agamben critiques Derrida for "fail[ing] to transcend metaphysics" because, in his words, "the impossibility of transcending metaphysics is a key point in Derrida's readings of the tradition" (10), but his argument is circular.

33. Agamben, "L'albero del linguaggio," 112.

2. "THE HUMAN VOICE"

1. The quote from Servius is taken from his commentary on Donatus's *Ars grammatica*, which can be found in Heinrich Keil, ed., *Grammatici Latini*, vol. 4 (Leipzig: B. G. Teubner, 1864) 405.

2. This text has recently been retranslated by Leonard Lawlor under the title *Voice and Phenomenon* (Evanston: Northwestern UP, 2010). I will nevertheless continue to refer to the earlier translation since it has been the text used by English-speaking readers for the last forty years.

3. As Paola Marrati notes: "It is the Living Present that allows Husserl, in the last instance, to gloss over the possibility of an empirical destruction of sense and to consider death ... as inessential and external to the trajectory of truth. This trajectory will lead Derrida to elaborate the notion of *arche-writing* through that of writing in the usual sense of the term. ... Something like a 'transcendental sense of death' ... will need to be read as haunting the 'life' of the Living Present" (Paola Marrati, *Genesis and Trace: Derrida Reading Husserl and Heidegger*, trans. Simon Sparks [Stanford: Stanford UP, 2005] 38).

4. It also, of course, has a prehistory. Leonard Lawlor carefully excavates the origins of Derrida's argument in the *Introduction* (and the early development of several key Derridean concepts such as *différance*, trace, and supplement) back to

his reading of texts by Jean Hyppolite, Tran-Duc-Thao, and Eugen Fink (see his *Derrida and Husserl* [Bloomington: Indiana UP, 2002], esp. chaps. 1, 4, and 5).

5. Husserl's formulation of the "principle of all principles" is found in §24 of *Ideas I* and is as follows: "*that every originary presentive intuition is a legitimizing source of cognition,* that *everything originarily* (so to speak, in its 'personal' actuality) *offered* to us *in 'intuition' is to be accepted simply as what it is presented as being,* but also *only within the limits in which it is presented there*" (Edmund Husserl, *Ideas Pertaining to a Pure Phenomenology and to a Phenomenological Philosophy, First Book,* trans. F. Kersten [The Hague: Martinus Nijhoff, 1982] 44).

6. A second critical problem that the figure of the voice seeks to address in Husserl's thought is that of temporality, which is analyzed in *SP* primarily in chapter 5, "Signs and the Blink of an Eye." For a discussion of Derrida's reading of Husserl's *Augenblick*, see Marrati, *Genesis and Trace*, 69–77. The question of temporality in Derrida's and Agamben's work will be addressed in chapter 6 of this book.

7. Derrida discusses the problems involved in translating the terminology of "meaningful" and "meaningless signs" from German into French (and English) on pages 17–18.

8. For Derrida's comments on this juxtaposition, see *SP* 46n5.

9. For such a discussion, see Lawlor, *Derrida and Husserl*, 180–88.

10. For a fine discussion of the contaminations this irreducible auto-affection introduces into Husserl's logic of identity, see Martin Hägglund, *Radical Atheism: Derrida and the Time of Life* (Stanford: Stanford UP, 2008) 50–75.

11. Edmund Husserl, *Cartesian Meditations*, trans. Dorion Cairns (The Hague: Martinus Nijhoff, 1977) 38–39.

12. Hamann's claim for "the 'genealogical primacy' of language over pure reason" (*IH* 44) is found in his "Metacritique on the Purism of Reason," *Writings on Philosophy and Language,*" ed. and trans. Kenneth Haynes (Cambridge: Cambridge UP, 2007) 211.

13. Oddly, Derrida alludes to the ambiguity of the first-person pronoun in Husserl's thought in the first epigraph to *Speech and Phenomena*: "'When I read this word "I" without knowing who wrote it, it is perhaps not meaningless, but is at least estranged from its normal meaning'—*Logical Investigations*." Given the analyses presented in that book, the importance Derrida appears to be assigning this passage here has less to do with the nature of pronouns as such than with the iterability of the written inscription, its ability to be read in the absence—or death—of the speaker (see, for example, *SP* 54).

14. Émile Benveniste, *Problems in General Linguistics*, trans. Mary Elizabeth Meek (Coral Gables: U of Miami P, 1971) 224.

15. Martin Heidegger, "Letter on 'Humanism,'" trans. Frank A. Capuzzi, *Pathmarks*, ed. William McNeill (Cambridge: Cambridge UP, 1998) 240; qtd. in *M* 179.

16. As Derrida himself suggests when he writes, "This is why, above all, we are not trying to gainsay the question asked by Benveniste, quite the contrary; we are, rather, attempting to analyze certain of its presuppositions, and perhaps to pursue, however minimally, its elaboration" (*M* 187).

17. Benveniste, *Problems*, 61; qtd. in *M* 196.

18. Benveniste, *Problems*, 62; qtd. in *M* 197.

19. Martin Heidegger, *An Introduction to Metaphysics*, trans. Ralph Manheim (New Haven: Yale UP, 1959) 82; qtd. in *M* 199.

20. Benveniste, *Problems*, 163; qtd. in *M* 200.

21. It would be right to point out here, as Agamben does in *Remnants*, that an even better-known—and, Agamben claims, contiguous—analysis of the enunciative function is to be found in Foucault's theory of statements (*énoncés*). Agamben's debt to Foucault is well known, and acknowledged frequently enough in his own writings. However, it is generally understood that this debt is primarily to Foucault's later work and his analysis of biopower, which of course has become one of Agamben's central concerns over the last twenty years or so. Agamben's early analysis of the signifying event, however, also finds an analogue in Foucault's earlier thought (as Agamben implicitly indicates in his introduction to the recent reprint of Enzo Melandri's magisterial 1968 study *La linea e il circolo* [Macerata: Quodlibet, 2004], which Agamben presents as a necessary, and long-neglected, complement to Foucault's *Archaeology of Knowledge*, published one year later). The problematic we have been describing here—that of the relation of the signifier and structure to sense or expression, and the Derridean absolutization of the former—is to be found in Foucault's work from what is frequently called his Heideggerian period, and can be seen lying behind his polemical response to Derrida's "Cogito and the History of Madness" (the response was included as an appendix in the 1972 edition of *Histoire de la folie*, and is found in English as "My Body, This Paper, This Fire" in Foucault, *Aesthetics, Method, and Epistemology*, ed. James D. Faubion, trans. Robert Hurley et al. [New York: New Press, 1998] 393–417). Foucault, it is generally believed, abandoned this problematic and moved toward a structuralist or poststructuralist one in the "archaeological" period, while Agamben remains faithful, so to speak, to the Heideggerian endeavor. Nevertheless, the shift in Foucault's focus at this stage in his career, and his polemics with Derrida, serve to illustrate further the division between the Heideggerian anthropo-ontological problematic and the structuralist/poststructuralist one. While it is beyond the scope of this study, it would surely be interesting to examine whether Agamben's explicit incorporation of Foucault's late work on biopower into his own post-Heideggerian thinking would in turn reveal certain continuities between Foucault's early and late work, and perhaps better enable us to understand Foucault's famous comment: "For me Heidegger has always been the essential philosopher" (Foucault, *Politics, Philosophy, Culture: Interviews and Other Writings 1977–1984*, ed. Lawrence D. Kritzman, trans. Alan

Sheridan et al. [New York: Routledge, 1988] 250). For a relevant discussion of Foucault's early work, see Simon During, *Foucault and Literature* (New York: Routledge 1992) 15–31.

22. The lines Agamben quotes from Benveniste are found in *Problèmes de linguistique générale*, vol. 2 (Paris: Gallimard, 1974) 66.

23. The chapters in *Language and Death* (like those of *The Time That Remains*) are given as "days" to reflect the seminar format in which they were originally presented and developed.

24. Martin Heidegger, *Being and Time*, trans. John Macquarrie and Edward Robinson (New York: Harper and Row, 1962) 171; qtd. in *LD* 4.

25. See Catherine Mills, *The Philosophy of Agamben* (Montreal: McGill-Queen's UP, 2008) 17. In truth, this analogical scheme of capitalization does not apply to Heidegger's German text, or even the standard Italian translations of Heidegger (which generally use "essere" and "ente"), but it does neatly map onto this convention used in many English translations.

26. Heidegger, *Being and Time*, 329–30; qtd. in *LD* 56.

27. Heidegger, *Being and Time*, 318 (modified); qtd. in *LD* 58.

28. Heidegger, "Postscript to 'What Is Metaphysics?,'" trans. William McNeill, *Pathmarks*, ed. William McNeill (Cambridge: Cambridge UP, 1998) 236; qtd. in *LD* 60–61. The capitalization of "Voice" and the German interpolations in this passage reproduce Agamben's Italian rendering.

3. POTENZA AND DIFFÉRANCE

1. Leland de la Durantaye cites portions of this parable in the context of a discussion of Agamben and Derrida, quite rightly pointing out that the question of nihilism it evokes is a central element in Agamben's long engagement with deconstruction. Though de la Durantaye sees the parable as being "not directed explicitly at Derrida" (*Giorgio Agamben* 191), I would suggest that, though certainly elliptical, this chapter of *Idea of Prose* indeed is more than implicitly directed at deconstruction, and in fact provides an indirect though very illuminating self-characterization of Agamben's position on the relation between his thought and deconstruction in the period of the 1980s. The last sections of this chapter intend to demonstrate that claim.

2. As Adam Thurschwell has commented, Agamben always makes a point of praising the rigor and acuteness of Derrida's readings and occasionally, for example in the essay "*Pardes*," presents Derrida as holding a position identical—or at least assimilable—to his own, a presentation that I think Thurschwell rightly argues to be strategically deceptive (see Thurschwell, "Cutting the Branches for Akiba," *Politics, Metaphysics, and Death: Essays on Giorgio Agamben's "Homo Sacer,"* ed. Andrew Norris [Durham: Duke UP, 2005] 177).

3. Aristotle, *The Metaphysics, Books I–IX*, trans. Hugh Tredennick (Cambridge: Harvard UP, 1933) 439.

4. For reasons that will be explained below, page references to this essay will be given to both the American and Italian editions (*Potentialities* and *La potenza del pensiero*, abbreviated *P* and *PP* respectively). Where reference is given only to one edition, that passage is missing from the other version. I have also modified passages from the English translation in accordance with the Italian version.

5. See Heidegger, *Aristotle's "Metaphysics" Θ 1–3*, trans. Walter Brogan and Peter Warnek (Bloomington: Indiana UP, 1995) 189–90.

6. Pierre Aubenque, *Le problème de l'être chez Aristote* (Paris: PUF, 1962) 453n1; Aristotle, *Metaphysics*, ed. W. D. Ross, vol. 2 (Oxford: Oxford UP, 1924) 245.

7. Aristotle, *Metafisica*, ed. Giovanni Reale, vol. 3 (Milan: Vita e Pensiero, 1993) 439–40.

8. Aubenque's translation of the lines is: "On appelle *possible* ce à quoi, lorsque aviendra l'acte dont il est dit avoir la puissance, n'appartiendra aucune impossibilité." Ross's translation is: "And a thing is capable of doing something if there is nothing impossible in its having the actuality of that of which it is said to have the capacity." Reale's translation is: "Una cosa è in potenza, se il tradursi in atto di ciò di cui essa è detta aver potenza non implica alcuna impossibilità." Reale also notes the comments of Hermann Bonitz and Franz Brentano on this "vicious circle," which Heidegger might have had in mind.

9. Cf. "There are many senses in which a thing is said to 'be' (*to de on legetai men pollakhōs*) but they are related to one central point, one definite kind of thing, and are not [merely] homonymous (*kai oukh homōnumōs*)" (1003a 32–34). The "elsewhere" to which Aristotle refers in the passage above is the discussion of the various senses of term in book *Delta* 12. There is considerable debate over whether *pollakhōs legomenon* (multivocal) and *homōnumōs* (homonymous) are equivalent or whether Aristotle is exploiting a difference between them. The logic of the two sentences cited here seems to require a difference, as is noted by Terence Irwin in "Homonymy in Aristotle," *Review of Metaphysics* 34.3 (1981): 531. For an extensive discussion of homonymy in Aristotle, see Christopher Shields, *Order in Multiplicity: Homonymy in the Philosophy of Aristotle* (Oxford: Clarendon, 1999) 22–28, 42, who takes the position that multivocity and homonymy are ultimately equivalents.

10. For an account of this distinction, as well as complications in maintaining it throughout Aristotle's text, see Jaakko Hintikka, *Time and Necessity: Studies in Aristotle's Theory of Modality* (Oxford: Carendon, 1973) 1–26. Michael Frede suggests that a further complication may be that not only is Aristotle attempting to describe *dunamis* itself, but he is grappling with the insufficient vocabulary at his disposal; that is to say, part of Aristotle's difficulty, and hence ours in reading this text, arises out of the need to use a single term—*dunamis*—that is not adequate ("Aristotle's Notion of Potentiality in *Metaphysics* Θ," *Unity, Identity, and*

Explanation in Aristotle's "Metaphysics," ed. Theodore Scaltsas et al. [Oxford: Carendon, 1994] 175). What we would have here, then, is a treatise in part on the uses and meanings of the term *dunamis*.

11. One important definitional distinction within the latter of these two types of *dunamis* is that between proximate and remote potentialities (e.g., the builder's capacity to build and the child's capacity to grow up to be a builder). For a discussion of the degrees of potentiality, see Terence Irwin, *Aristotle's First Principles* (Oxford: Clarendon, 1988) 230–33. Agamben distinguishes between proximate and remote potentialities as "existing" and "generic" potentialities, and states that the latter sense "is not the one that interests Aristotle" (*P* 179; *PP* 276). For Agamben, what distinguishes existing or proximate potentiality (potentiality proper, potentiality as capacity) is that it "belongs to someone who, for example, has knowledge or an ability." Unlike someone who may "suffer an alteration (a becoming other) through learning" and thus acquire a proximate potentiality, a person is potential "thanks to a *hexis*, a 'having,' which he can also *not* bring into act or actualize, passing from a not being in act to a being in act (*ek tou . . . mē energein de, eis to energein* [417a 32–b 1]). Potentiality, then, is defined essentially by the possibility of its not being exercised" (*P* 179; *PP* 276–77).

12. Irwin, *Aristotle's First Principles*, 563n11. Irwin further justifies this reading on precise philological grounds: "'Capable' (rather than 'possible') for *dunaton* is supported by (i) *hōste*, 1047a20, drawing a conclusion from his previous remarks about the potentialities of substances, 1047a10–17; and (ii) by the fact that the subject of *dunaton* is also the bearer of *dunamis*, i.e. a substance with a potentiality. 'Impossible' in the last clause is justified by 1047b12, referring clearly to the impossibility of a state of affairs (*to metreisthai*), and relying on the definition in ix 3" (563–64n11).

13. Irwin, *Aristotle's First Principles*, 229.

14. Irwin, *Aristotle's First Principles*, 229.

15. Though Aristotle says in 1046a 5 that *dunamis* has equivocal senses, if Harry Ide's analysis is correct it appears he never (or at least in the texts under consideration here) actually uses the noun *dunamis* to mean "possibility." While he uses adjectival derivatives (*dunatos*, etc.) to describe states of affairs as possible, or as possibilities (*dunata*), dunamis is always reserved for potentiality in its "first meaning," the "authoritative definition" (see Ide, *Possibility and Potentiality from Aristotle through the Stoics*, diss., Cornell University, 1988, 20–21).

16. In *Ways of Being: Potentiality and Actuality in Aristotle's "Metaphysics"* (Ithaca: Cornell UP, 2003), Charlotte Witt has made a very similar claim about the basic goal of book *Theta*, in which, she argues, "being X potentially and being X actually distinguish two ways of being rather than adding two new kinds of entities to Aristotle's ontological inventory" (44). She has also argued that Aristotle subtly draws on the modal significance of *dunamis* or *dunaton* in order to bolster

his ontological analysis of *dunamis* as capacity or existing-yet-inactive potentiality (30–37). As the title of her book suggests, Witt essentially reads book *Theta* as an ontological treatise on the nature of potential being as opposed to actual being, and suggests that the burden of the argument in *Theta* is to introduce a "new, ontological meaning of *dunamis*" (40). On this basic point, for which she more or less implicitly draws on Heidegger's lectures on *Theta*, Agamben would presumably agree, though Witt argues that in the end Aristotle shows certain "Megarian tendencies" (19) and proposes a "kind of Aristotelian actualism" (15) in granting primacy to actuality (see especially her chapter 4). This latter interpretation is, not without reason, widely accepted; as will be noted below, however, Agamben claims that the position of primacy in Aristotle's text is less easily decided.

17. Martin Heidegger, *Basic Problems of Phenomenology*, trans. Albert Hofstadter (Bloomington: Indiana UP, 1988) 308.

18. Heidegger, *Being and Time*, 183. See also Heidegger's comments on *Möglichkeit* in the "Letter on 'Humanism,'" in *Pathmarks* 242.

19. *Impotenza* as the potentiality-not-to is defined, for Agamben, by a "*hexis*," a having. To have a potentiality means to be able and be able not to exercise a potentiality. As noted above, this corresponds to the distinction between proximate and remote potentialities. The latter are not subject to a "having" (see *P* 178–80; *PP* 275–77).

20. And see, in general, his discussion of potentiality, 14–18.

21. On modal negation, see also "Bartleby" in *P* 261–65.

22. This passage would roughly replace the last paragraph on page 183 of *Potentialities*.

23. As is well known, Agamben studied law at university, but turned to philosophy soon thereafter. His legal training, however, served him well in his research for *Homo Sacer*, as he noted in a 2001 interview: "For a long time [after turning to philosophy], I thought it was a mistake to have studied law. That is something, however, that I no longer think because without this familiarity I would probably never have been able to write *Homo Sacer*" (qtd. in de la Durantaye, *Giorgio Agamben*, 203–4). It is, further, on the basis of his having "caught sight" of the inclusive-exclusive ban structure that Agamben distinguishes his thought from the political traditions to which it is probably closest, namely, anarchism and Marxism (*HS* 12).

24. Witt, *Ways of Being*, 23.

25. In "*Ousia* and *Grammē*: Note on a Note from *Being and Time*," Derrida writes: "From Parmenides to Husserl, the privilege of the present has never been put into question. It could not have been. It is what is self-evident itself, and no thought seems possible outside its element. Non-presence is always thought in the form of presence, . . . or as a modalization of presence. The past and the future are always determined as past presents or as future presents" (*M* 34). For Derrida, Heidegger's thought, too, even though it seeks to conceive "the possible [as] higher

than everything actual," fails to escape this privilege of actuality or the inherently privileging relation between *dunamis* and *energeia*, and thus "still remains within the grammar and lexicon of metaphysics" (*M* 63).

26. See Saussure, *Course*, 65–67.

27. Saussure, *Course*, 112.

28. John Edwin Sandys, *A History of Classical Scholarship*, vol.1, *From the Sixth Century B.C. to the End of the Middle Ages* (Cambridge: Cambridge UP, 1903) 253.

29. In the "Bartleby" essay, Agamben writes: "There is only one text in the entire Aristotelian *corpus* that contains a similar image [i.e., 430a 1], which may have furnished Cassiodorus or an unknown writer with the basis of this metaphor" (*P* 244). There is some slippage between the two images, however, since on the one hand we have an ink-filled quill and on the other a stylus that scratches the wax *epitedeiotes*. Agamben briefly discusses the historical transformation of the wax tablet and stylus into the white sheet and pen on pages 244–45.

30. As it happens, the passage Agamben cites from page 61 of the *Grammatology* does not appear in the original article "*De la grammatologie (II)*" published in *Critique* 224 (January 1966): 21–53 (it would have fallen on page 32) and belongs to Derrida's extraordinary revision and expansion of the text for the book.

31. See Thomas Dutoit's comments on how this ambiguity is rendered in the English translation (*K* xii).

32. English translation of *Timaeus* by Donald J. Zeyl in *Plato: Complete Works*, ed. John M. Cooper (Indianapolis: Hackett, 1997).

33. To take just two recent commentators on either side of this debate, John Sallis (on the Derridean side) claims that "Given the decisiveness and even the manifestness of the difference between *khōra* and *hulē*, one cannot but suspect that their identification serves to transpose into the economy of Aristotle's thought a moment of the Timaean discourse that otherwise would simply be lost or else would disrupt that economy" (*Chorology* [Bloomington: Indiana UP, 1999] 153), while Thomas Kjeller Johansen (on the Agambenian side) argues that "Aristotle's claim that Plato identified *khōra* with matter reflects quite accurately on the way in which Plato uses *khōra* in the *Timaeus*, though this is not sufficient reason for saying that *khōra* plays the full role of Aristotelian matter" (*Plato's Natural Philosophy* [Cambridge: Cambridge UP, 2004] 132).

34. Adam Thurschwell, "Cutting the Branches for Akiba," *Politics, Metaphysics, and Death: Essays on Giorgio Agamben's "Homo Sacer,"* ed. Andrew Norris (Durham: Duke UP, 2005) 181.

35. It is worth noting also that in this passage, matter is a sort of substrate of both of *lingua* and of *parola*, but not of *linguaggio*, which is in a sense coterminous with it.

36. Agamben's allusion in the passage is further obscured by his spelling of the word as "selva" rather than "silva," which would tend to lead readers into Dante's

dark wood, which is perhaps where the English translators of *Idea of Prose* derived their gloss, "wildwood."

37. For a discussion of this transmission that takes up issues that are relevant though not explicitly linked to Agamben's thought on potentiality and matter (and on the classical background to the poetry of the troubadours), see Daniel Heller-Roazen, "The Matter of Language: Guilhem de Peitieus and the Platonic Tradition," *MLN* 113.4 (1998), esp. 859–67.

38. Martin Heidegger, *On the Way to Language*, trans. Peter D. Hertz (New York: Harper and Row, 1971) 59.

39. Heidegger, *On the Way to Language*, 59.

40. Heidegger, *On the Way to Language*, 57. In his introduction to the English translation of *Idea of Prose*, Alexander García Düttmann notes the importance of Heidegger's 1958 lecture "Words" (also collected in *On the Way to Language*) to the pieces that make up the volume.

41. Agamben's appeal here to Plotinus and neo-Platonism is only deceptively a turn back from Aristotle to Plato; in truth, it is rather an implicit affirmation of the Aristotelian reading of *khōra-hulē* and of an Aristotelianized Platonism. As Judith Butler notes, "It is only once Aristotle provides an explicit philosophical discourse on matter that Plotinus writes a reconstruction of the Platonic doctrine of matter" (*Bodies That Matter* [New York: Routledge, 1993] 253n22).

42. For an elaboration of the issue Agamben identifies here, see Daniel Heller-Roazen's *The Inner Touch: Archaeology of a Sensation* (New York: Zone, 2007).

43. *Timaeus* 52b. For further discussion of this phrase in a distinctly Agambenian mode, see Daniel Heller-Roazen's *The Inner Touch*, 299, as well as his "The Matter of Language," 856–59.

44. Thurschwell, "Cutting the Branches," 183.

45. See Thurschwell, "Cutting the Branches," 181.

46. Thurschwell, "Cutting the Branches," 173.

47. See Thurschwell, "Cutting the Branches," 181–83.

48. Thurschwell, "Cutting the Branches," 185.

4. SOVEREIGNTY, LAW, AND VIOLENCE

1. Jean-Luc Nancy, *The Birth to Presence*, trans. Brian Holmes et al. (Stanford: Stanford UP, 1993) 43–44.

2. Nancy, *Birth*, 44.

3. Carl Schmitt, *Political Theology*, trans. George Schwab (Chicago: U of Chicago P, 2005) 5. Simon Morgan Wortham has noted how, for Agamben, the foundational political concept in Schmitt is not the friend-enemy distinction but the state of exception, which shifts the focus from that of Derrida's reading of Schmitt in *The Politics of Friendship* (see *Derrida: Writing Events* [London: Continuum, 2008]

60–61). Among other things, this recasts the political as a matter of sovereign decision and the ban rather than of alterity and *différance*. Agamben writes: "The fundamental categorial pair of Western politics is not that of friend/enemy but that of bare life/political existence, *zōē/bios*, exclusion/inclusion. There is politics because man is the living being who, in language, separates and opposes himself to his own bare life and, at the same time, maintains himself in relation to that bare life in an inclusive exclusion" (*HS* 8). While the friend-enemy distinction is thus explicitly demoted among political categories in Agamben's thought, Wortham also recalls Agamben's brief essay "The Friend" (in *"What Is an Apparatus?" and Other Essays*, trans. David Kishik and Stefan Pedatella [Stanford: Stanford UP, 2009] 25–37) and his puzzling comments on Derrida's *The Politics of Friendship*, in which Agamben is named as one of the friends who has helped with Derrida's philological research on Diogenes Laertius's disputed and enigmatic phrase *o philoi, oudeis philos* ("O my friends, there is no friend"), which is a sort of leitmotif in Derrida's book (see *The Politics of Friendship*, trans. George Collins [New York: Verso, 1997] 225n10). What is puzzling is that Agamben, while claiming to have discovered and informed Derrida of the correct version of this phrase (which would be translated as "He who has many friends does not have a single friend"), asserts that in Derrida's book there is no trace of either this alternative reading or their conversation on the matter. Both assertions are simply incorrect.

4. Thanos Zartaloudis, *Giorgio Agamben: Power, Law and the Uses of Criticism* (Abingdon: Routledge, 2010) 134.

5. Agamben mentions here that this lecture was delivered at the Cardozo School of Law, though in fact the reading of "Critique of Violence," which makes up the second half of the piece ("Prénom de Benjamin") was not read aloud but simply distributed in print among the participants. "First Name of Benjamin" was first presented aloud in April 1990 at the conference "Nazism and the 'Final Solution': Probing the Limits of Representation" at UCLA (see *FL* 230).

6. Leo Strauss, "Natural Law," *International Encyclopedia of the Social Sciences*, ed. David L. Sills, vol. 11 (New York: Macmillan, 1968) 80.

7. Walter Benjamin, "Critique of Violence," trans. Edmund Jephcott, *Selected Writings*, vol. 1, *1913–1926*, ed. Marcus Bullock and Michael W. Jennings (Cambridge: Belknap/Harvard UP, 1996) 236.

8. Though Benjamin asserts that natural law is "the main current of legal philosophy" ("Critique" 236), what may have been true of legal-philosophical culture in 1921 was on the verge of change. Reviewing these changes in 1968, Leo Strauss will be able to write that "Natural law, which was for many centuries the basis of the predominant Western political thought, is rejected in our time by almost all students of society who are not Roman Catholics" ("Natural Law" 80). I note this simply to indicate another element of the historical context of Benjamin's essay, namely, that the tension between natural and positive law that constitutes

the dual impediment to thinking of violence without regard to its legal ends is not an anachronism or purely a matter of legal history. It is, rather, one of the central issues of legal debates of the time.

9. Hans Kelsen, *General Theory of Law and State*, trans. Anders Wedberg (Cambridge: Harvard UP, 1945) 5.

10. Kelsen, *General Theory*, 14.

11. Benjamin, "Critique," 237.

12. Benjamin, "Critique," 237.

13. Benjamin, "Critique," 239.

14. "To resolve this question a more exact criterion is needed, which would discriminate within the sphere of means themselves, without regard for the ends they serve." Benjamin, "Critique," 236.

15. Benjamin, "Critique," 243.

16. Derrida repeats this observation at various junctures in the reading, showing how with virtually every set of terms Benjamin adopts there arise irresolvable contradictions. Some examples: "[I]s not tautology the phenomenal structure of a certain violence of the law that lays itself down, by decreeing to be violent, this time in the sense of outlaw [*hors-la-loi*], anything that does not recognize it?" (*FL* 267); "How to interpret this contradiction? [i.e., of the right to strike]" (*FL* 268); "[The law of war] involves the same contradictions as the right to strike" (*FL* 273); "Here [i.e., with the difficulty of critiquing military violence on pacifist principles] we are dealing with a *double bind* or a contradiction" (*FL* 274).

17. Benjamin, "Critique," 245, 239.

18. Benjamin, "Critique," 246.

19. Benjamin, "Critique," 243.

20. Benjamin, "Critique," 243.

21. Benjamin, "Critique," 242; qtd. in *FL* 273.

22. Within that chapter, a long historical excursus (*SE* 11–22) concretely and specifically traces the way emergency law—or more accurately, the suspension of law in the face of emergency—has been employed in Europe and the United States from the period of the French Revolution up through implementation of the "USA Patriot Act" in the wake of the terrorist attacks of 2001. Among the most striking things that emerge from this account is the consistency and continuity of emergency measures employed by states across relatively disparate historical moments and constitutional types. That continuity—which, of course, is precisely what Agamben intends to emphasize—is given its legal-theoretical rationale in the argumentation that makes up the bulk of this opening chapter.

23. See section 16 of *Being and Time*.

24. Carl Schmitt, *Political Theology*, 15; qtd. in *HS* 16.

25. In *State of Exception*, Agamben obviously reads "Critique of Violence" with Derrida's text in mind, but he had been grappling with Benjamin's essay as early

as 1969–70 and his piece "On the Limits of Violence." The twenty-eight-year-old Agamben sent a copy of this essay, along with a letter of general gratitude, to Hannah Arendt. An image of Agamben's letter can be found as an addendum to the translation of "On the Limits of Violence" in *diacritics* 39.4 (2009): 111.

26. In "Force of Law," Derrida refers to a "letter of congratulations" that Schmitt is supposed to have sent to Benjamin upon the publication of "Critique of Violence" (*FL* 263). He does not cite is source for this allusion, and it in fact appears to be an error (perhaps a misremembered reference to Benjamin's letter to Schmitt of December 1930). Certainly, if such a letter existed (or does exist), Agamben could have included it in his discussion of the "exoteric dossier" of the debate between Benjamin and Schmitt, and would have had to work much less hard to support his supposition that Schmitt had read and been influenced by "Critique of Violence" while writing *Political Theology*.

27. For Agamben, these are more or less synonyms in Benjamin's essay. As he writes, "Benjamin calls this other figure of violence 'pure' (*reine Gewalt*) or 'divine,' and, in the human sphere, 'revolutionary'" (*SE* 53).

28. Walter Benjamin, "On the Concept of History," trans. Harry Zohn, *Selected Writings*, vol. 4, *1938–1940*, ed. Howard Eiland and Michael W. Jennings (Cambridge: Belknap/Harvard UP, 2003) 392; translation modified; qtd. in *SE* 57.

29. Benjamin, "Critique," 252.

30. Benjamin, "Critique," 252.

31. For a highly critical account of Agamben's antinomian critique of deconstructive graphocentrism, see Jeffrey Librett, "From the Sacrifice of the Letter to the Voice of Testimony," *diacritics* 37.2-3 (2007): 11–33. While Librett draws out a number of pertinent elements of Agamben's engagement with deconstruction (for example, his account of the way Agamben identifies metaphysics with graphocentrism itself [12–17]), his condemnation of Agamben's thought ultimately boils down to the charge that Agamben's antinomianism is, consciously or unconsciously, in league with a (crypto-)Christian antinomianism that, according to Librett, was the primary motivation of Nazi ideology and the Holocaust. While Librett seems to want to limit his attack to Agamben, the logical upshot of his argument is that *any* antinomic critique of graphocentric metaphysics and of the law (and its letter) is in collusion with Nazi ideology. Once one grants this untenable premise, the cards are stacked.

32. Benjamin, "Critique," 236.

33. Walter Benjamin, *The Correspondence of Walter Benjamin*, ed. Gershom Scholem and Theodor W. Adorno, trans. Manfred R. Jacobson and Evelyn M. Jacobson (Chicago: U of Chicago P, 1994) 138; qtd. in *SE* 61.

34. Walter Benjamin, "Karl Kraus," trans. Rodney Livingstone, *Selected Writings*, vol. 2, *1927–1934*, ed. Michael W. Jennings et al. (Cambridge: Belknap/Harvard UP, 1999) 455; qtd. in *SE* 61.

35. See, for example, Thurschwell, "Cutting the Branches" and "Specters of Nietzsche."

36. Walter Benjamin, "Franz Kafka," trans. Harry Zohn, *Selected Writings*, vol. 2, *1927–34*, ed. Michael W. Jennings et al. (Cambridge: Belknap/Harvard UP, 1999) 815; qtd. in *SE* 63.

5. TICKS AND CATS

1. "L'animal que donc je suis (à suivre)," *L'animal autobiographique: Autour de Jacques Derrida*, ed. Marie-Louise Mallet (Paris: Galilée, 1999); "Et si l'animal répondait?," *Cahier de L'Herne*, no. 83, *Jacques Derrida*, ed. Marie-Louise Mallet and Ginette Michaud (Paris: L'Herne, 2004).

2. These seminars were first published as *Séminaire: La bête et le souverain, Vol. 1 (2001–2002)*, ed. Michel Lisse et al. (Paris: Éditions Galilée, 2008).

3. Dominick LaCapra, *History and Its Limits: Human, Animal, Violence* (Ithaca: Cornell UP, 2009) 168.

4. See, for example, Agamben's very brief comments on the "complex—and not always edifying—economy of relations between men and animals" (*O* 15), and Derrida's sketch of the "*unprecedented* . . . subjection of the animal" (*Animal* 25) over the last two centuries (*Animal* 25–27).

5. Matthew Calarco, "Jamming the Anthropological Machine," *Giorgio Agamben: Sovereignty and Life*, ed. Calarco and Steven DeCaroli (Stanford: Stanford UP, 2007) 170.

6. A more detailed account of these debates is found in Agamben's essay "The Glorious Body," *Nudities*, trans. David Kishik and Stefan Pedatella (Stanford: Stanford UP, 2011) 91–103.

7. He also suggests that Linnaeus's later addition of *sapiens* to the name of the species is nothing but a simplification or gloss of the phrase *nosce te ipsum* (see *O* 25).

8. The most famous case of these *enfants sauvages* is perhaps Victor of Aveyron (subject of the 1970 film by François Truffaut), who was found in 1797, but there were many such cases and many accounts written of them.

9. See Wills's "Translator's Note," *Animal* 162.

10. As David Wills notes, the English translation of the *Meditations* generally follows the Latin text, and it renders this sentence as "But what shall I now say that I am" (René Descartes, *Meditations on First Philosophy*, trans. John Cottingham, *The Philosophical Writings of Descartes*, vol. 2 [Cambridge: Cambridge UP, 1984] 18). The French sentence is *Mais moi, qui suis-je?* (see *Animal* 167).

11. Descartes, *Meditations*, 19.

12. Descartes, *Meditations*, 18.

13. See, for example, the last extant passage of the *Treatise on Man*, in which Descartes is describing the fictional humans that he has, over the course of the treatise,

hypothetically constructed from scratch on purely mechanical principles: "I should like you to consider that these functions [i.e., digestion, circulation, growth, sense perception, appetites, passions, memory, etc.] follow from the mere arrangement of the machine's organs every bit as naturally as the movements of a clock or other automaton follow from the arrangements of its counter-weights and wheels. In order to explain these functions, then, it is not necessary to conceive of this machine as having any vegetative or sensitive soul or other principle of movement and life, apart from its blood and its spirits, which are agitated by the heat of the fire burning continuously in its heart—a fire which has the same nature as all the fires that occur in inanimate bodies" (René Descartes, *Treatise on Man,* trans. Robert Stoothoff, *The Philosophical Writings of Descartes,* vol. 1 [Cambridge: Cambridge UP, 1985] 108).

14. René Descartes, *Discourse on the Method,* trans. Robert Stoothoff, *The Philosophical Writings of Descartes,* vol. 1 (Cambridge: Cambridge UP, 1985) 140.

15. Descartes, *Discourse,* 139.

16. Descartes, *Discourse,* 139–40.

17. Descartes, *Discourse,* 140.

18. Descartes, *Discourse,* 140.

19. Descartes, *Discourse,* 140.

20. Descartes, *Discourse,* 140; qtd. in *Animal* 81.

21. Lewis Carroll, *Through the Looking Glass, The Complete Works of Lewis Carroll* (New York: Modern Library, 1936) 269; qtd. in *Animal* 8.

22. Immanuel Kant, *Anthropology from a Pragmatic Point of View,* ed. and trans. Robert B. Louden (Cambridge: Cambridge UP, 2006) 15; qtd. in *Animal* 93.

23. See Geoffrey Bennington, "Political Animals," *diacritics* 39.9 (2009): 21. Derrida also gestures toward this critique pointedly in *Rogues*: "In [Aristotle's *Politics*], as in so many others of both Plato and Aristotle, the distinction between *bios* and *zōē*—or *zēn*—is more than tricky and precarious; in no way does it correspond to the strict opposition on which Agamben bases the quasi totality of his argument about sovereignty and the biopolitical in *Homo Sacer* (but let's leave that for another time)" (*Rogues* 24).

24. Aristotle, *Topics,* trans. W. A. Pickard-Cambridge, *The Complete Works of Aristotle,* vol. 1, ed. Jonathan Barnes (Princeton: Princeton UP, 1984) 170.

25. Aristotle, *Topics,* 170.

26. Descartes, *Meditations,* 17.

27. Descartes, *Meditations,* 18.

28. Laurent Dubrueil, "Leaving Politics: *Bios, Zōē,* Life," *diacritics* 36.2 (2006): 88.

29. Dubrueil 88.

30. See Dubrueil 84.

31. Dubrueil 88

32. Kalpana Rahita Seshadri notes that this distinction is also evoked by Heidegger in *Basic Concepts of Aristotelian Philosophy* and by Hannah Arendt in *The*

Human Condition (though, in truth, Arendt does not actually name *zōē* there). *HumAnimal: Race, Law, Language* (Minneapolis: U of Minnesota P, 2012) 269n9.

33. Heidegger, *Pathmarks*, 246–47; qtd. in *BS* 322–23.

34. When Derrida returns to this question a year later, in the *Beast and the Sovereign II*, especially in the seventh, eighth, and ninth sessions (February 26, March 5, and March 12, 2003), he makes no reference to *The Open* (or to any other text by Agamben). A distant, almost imperceptible echo, however, may be heard (if it is even there) at the beginning of the seventh session, where Derrida reads from a letter from Timothy Bahti on the Veil of Veronica, which is one of final images of *The Open* (*O* 92) (see Derrida, *The Beast and the Sovereign, Vol. 2*, ed. Michel Lisse et al., trans. Geoffrey Bennington [Chicago: U of Chicago P, 2011] 172).

35. The title of the 1992 conference was "Le Passage des frontiers (autour de Jacques Derrida)."

36. Martin Heidegger, *The Fundamental Concepts of Metaphysics: World, Finitude, Solitude*, trans. William McNeill and Nicholas Walker (Bloomington: Indiana UP, 1995) 20; qtd. in *Animal* 146.

37. Heidegger, *Fundamental Concepts*, 176.

38. Heidegger, *Fundamental Concepts*, 177.

39. Heidegger, *Fundamental Concepts*, 177.

40. Heidegger, *Fundamental Concepts*, 5.

41. Derrida also notes that, in addition to *Aporias* and *Of Spirit*, he has taken up related texts and questions in "The Ends of Man" (1968), "Geschlecht" (1983), "Heidegger's Hand" (1985), and "Heidegger's Ear" (1993).

42. While much of the analysis of this chapter concerns the issue of spirit (*Geist*) in Heidegger's thought, which is, after all the central question of the book as a whole, for the purposes of the present discussion that issue will have to be left to the side.

43. And, in fact, the contradictory statements are even most extreme if one includes Heidegger's comments from *Introduction to Metaphysics* in the discussion, as Derrida does in *Of Spirit*. There, not more than five years after the lectures of *Fundamental Concepts* and the comparative examination of the concept of world, Heidegger flatly states that "the animal has no world nor any environment [*Das Tier hat keine Welt, auch keine Umwelt*]" (Heidegger, *Introduction to Metaphysics*, 45; qtd. in *OS* 47). It is worth noting that Agamben does not introduce this complication into his analysis in *The Open*.

44. "Metaphysics thinks of the human being on the basis of *animalitas* and does not think in the direction of his *humanitas*" (Heidegger, *Pathmarks*, 246–47).

45. In a reading that cannot be followed here, Agamben traces the intricate etymological play in Heidegger's terminology, noting how a number of his key terms in this text derive from a common root in the verb *nehmen*, "to take" (see *O* 52).

46. Heidegger, *Fundamental Concepts*, 248; translation modified; ellipses in original; qtd. in *O* 54.

47. *The Selected Poetry of Rainer Maria Rilke*, trans. Stephen Mitchell (New York: Random House, 1982) 193; translation modified to reflect Agamben's reading.
48. Heidegger, *Fundamental Concepts*, 273; qtd. in O 61.
49. Heidegger, *Fundamental Concepts*, 282; qtd. in O 62.
50. Eric L. Santner, *On Creaturely Life* (Chicago: U of Chicago P, 2006) 10.
51. Santner, *On Creaturely Life*, 10.
52. Heidegger, *Fundamental Concepts*, 92; qtd. in O 64.
53. Heidegger, *Fundamental Concepts*, 140–41; translation modified; qtd. in O 66.

6. A MATTER OF TIME

1. See, for example, Colby Dickinson, *Agamben and Theology* (London: T&T Clark, 2011) 86ff.
2. Thurschwell, "Cutting the Branches for Akiba," 174.
3. Heidegger, *Being and Time*, 47; translation modified; qtd. in M 31.
4. Heidegger, *Being and Time*, 500nxxx; translation modified; qtd. in M 37. The note goes on to identify similar analogies between Bergson's analysis of time and Hegel's.
5. Alan Bass discusses Derrida's ingenious translation of the *Aufhebung* as *la relève* in M 19n23, 43n15, and 88n16.
6. G. W. F. Hegel, *Hegel's Philosophy of Nature*, trans. A. V. Miller (Oxford: Oxford UP, 1970) 28.
7. Hegel, *Philosophy of Nature*, 31.
8. Derrida also notes here that the construction of space through the point, line, and plane could be conceived in reverse and thus the point would be the end of the backward progression from concrete space to abstract spatiality.
9. Hegel, *Philosophy of Nature*, 33–34; qtd. in M 43.
10. Hegel, *Philosophy of Nature*, 34.
11. Hegel, *Philosophy of Nature*, 34.
12. "As soon as being and present are synonymous, to say nothingness and to say time are the same thing. Time is indeed the discursive manifestation of negativity, and Hegel, mutatis mutandis, will only make explicit what is said of *ousia* as presence" (M 51).
13. In *Of Grammatology*, Derrida writes: "That which is not subjected to the process of differance is *present*. The present is that from which we believe we are able to think time, effacing the inverse necessity: to think the present from time as differance" (G 166).
14. Gasché, *The Tain of the Mirror*, 103.
15. Gasché, *The Tain of the Mirror*, 103.
16. Martin Hägglund, *Radical Atheism: Derrida and the Time of Life* (Stanford: Stanford UP, 2008) 132.

17. Hägglund, *Radical Atheism*, 135.

18. Hägglund, *Radical Atheism*, 132.

19. Alexandre Kojève, *Introduction to the Reading of Hegel*, trans. James H. Nichols Jr. (Ithaca: Cornell UP, 1969) 162.

20. On the question of the seriousness of this note, see Agamben's discussion of this passage in *O* 9–12.

21. Hägglund, *Radical Atheism*, 134.

22. Erich Auerbach, "Figura," *Scenes from the Drama of European Literature* (Gloucester, MA: Peter Smith, 1973) 30.

23. See Auerbach, "Figura," 29, 38.

24. The New English Bible renders the passage thus: "All of these things that happened to them were symbolic, and were recorded for our benefit as a warning. For upon us the fulfillment of the ages has come" (1 Cor 10:11).

25. The NEB renders it thus: "While we lived on the level of our lower nature, the sinful passions evoked by the law worked in our bodies, to bear fruit for death. But now, having died to that which held us bound, we are discharged from the law."

26. David E. Johnson is right, in a sense, to see Agamben's valorization of the messianic "time of the now" as an appeal a certain "present." However, the deconstruction of Agamben to which the title of his piece lays claim does not fully acknowledge the underlying critique of the "metaphysics of the negative" on which Agamben's affirmation of messianic time is based. If one accepts the Derridean notion of Western thought as a metaphysics of presence, then a valorization of the "time of the now" might appear as a rather retrograde and traditionalist gesture. But if one accepts Agamben's critique of Western thought as being a metaphysics of the negative, a critique which, as we have seen, places Derrida at the most extreme point in the tradition, then the deconstructive account of the messianic "to come" will appear to be just as Agamben characterizes it: a pushing to the limit, a revealing of the limit, but a remaining within the limit, of the logic of negative metaphysics, a logic which it will in turn, and perhaps against its intentions, reaffirm in its injunction against attempting to think beyond or before that limit (see Johnson, "*As If* the Time Were Now: Deconstructing Agamben," *South Atlantic Quarterly* 106.2 [2007]: 265–90).

27. The text Agamben is discussing here is Alain Badiou, *Saint Paul: The Foundation of Universalism*, trans. Ray Brassier (Stanford: Stanford UP, 2003). For further comment on the differences between Agamben's and Badiou's readings of Paul, see Eleanor Kaufman, "The Saturday of Messianic Time (Agamben and Badiou on the Apostle Paul)," *South Atlantic Quarterly* 107.1 (2008) 37–54.

28. Agamben might have further emphasized this point by noting that the word in the Hebrew Psalm is *alach* ("filthy," "corrupt," "rotten to the core") and has no connotations regarding use.

29. In the English version of *The Time That Remains*, this citation is unclear. It comes from Schmitt, *The Nomos of the Earth*, trans. G. L. Ulmen (New York: Telos Press, 2003) 59–60.

30. For a fine discussion of Agamben's and Schmitt's readings of the Pauline *katekhōn*, see Sergei Prozorov, "The Katechon in the Age of Biopolitical Nihilism," *Continental Philosophy Review* 45.4 (2012): 483–505. Among other things, Prozorov notes that Schmitt's elision of the difference between the Roman Empire (to which Paul may be referring) and the Holy Roman Empire leads him to read the *katekhōn* in neutral and general terms and that "In this neutral and general sense the katechon refers to any constituted authority, whose function is to delay the social catastrophe while simultaneously withholding a radical redemption from it" (487).

31. Schmitt, *Political Theology*, trans. George Schwab (Chicago: U of Chicago P, 1985) 36.

32. In a recent text, Agamben further investigates the heterodox tradition (which begins with Ticonius in the fourth century) that the *katekhōn* is to be identified with the institutionalized church itself, which has lost its original messianic vocation. "The *katekhōn*," he writes, "is the power [*potenza*]—the empire, but also the church as well as every juridically constituted authority—that hinders and hides the anomie that defines messianic time and in this way delays the revelation of the 'mystery of anomie.' The disconcealment of this mystery coincides with the manifestation of the inoperativity of the law and the essential illegitimacy of every power [*potere*] in messianic time" (Agamben, *Il mistero del male: Benedetto XVI e la fine dei tempi* [Rome: Laterza, 2013] 35).

33. Giorgio Agamben, "Introduzione" to Carl Schmitt, *Un giurista davanti a se stesso: Saggi e interviste*, ed. Agamben (Vicenza: Neri Pozza, 2005) 16–17.

CODA: PLAY

1. Hans-Georg Gadamer, *Truth and Method*, 2nd rev. ed., trans. Joel Weinsheimer and Donald G. Marshall (New York: Crossroad, 1989) 102.

2. Gadamer, *Truth and Method*, 108.

3. And, in fact, there are clear anticipations of this analysis of play in Agamben's slightly earlier discussion of commodity fetishism in *Stanzas*, especially the chapter titled "Mme Panckoucke; or, The Toy Fairy" (*S* 56–60).

4. Walter Benjamin, "In the Sun," trans. Rodney Livingstone, *Selected Writings, Vol. 2*, 664; qtd. in *CC* 53.

5. Walter Benjamin, "Toys and Play," trans. Rodney Livingstone, in *Selected Writings, Vol. 2*, 120.

WORKS CITED

Agamben, Giorgio. "La 121ª giornata di Sodoma e Gomorra." *Tempo Presente* 9.3–4 (1966): 59–70.
——. "L'albero del linguaggio." *I Problemi di Ulisse* 21.9 (September 1968): 104–14.
——. *The Coming Community*. Trans. Michael Hardt. Minneapolis: U of Minnesota P, 1993.
——. *La fine del pensiero / La fin de la pensée*. Trans. Gérard Macé. Paris: Le Nouveau Commerce, 1982.
——. *Homo Sacer: Sovereign Power and Bare Life*. Trans. Daniel Heller-Roazen. Stanford: Stanford UP, 1998.
——. *Idea of Prose*. Trans. Michael Sullivan and Sam Whitsitt. Albany: State U of New York P, 1995.
——. *Infancy and History*. Trans. Liz Heron. New York: Verso, 1993.
——. *Language and Death*. Trans. Karen Pinkus. Minneapolis: U of Minnesota P, 2006.
——. *The Man without Content*. Trans. Georgia Albert. Stanford: Stanford UP, 1999.
——. *Means without End*. Trans. Vincenzo Binetti and Cesare Casarino. Minneapolis: U of Minnesota P, 2000.
——. *Il mistero del male: Benedetto XVI e la fine dei tempi*. Rome: Laterza, 2013.
——. "On the Limits of Violence." Trans. Elisabeth Fay. Ed. Lorenzo Fabbri. *diacritics* 39.4 (Winter 2004): 103–11.
——. *Potentialities: Collected Essays in Philosophy*. Trans. Daniel Heller-Roazen. Stanford: Stanford UP, 2000.
——. *La potenza del pensiero: saggi e conferenze*. Milan: Neri Pozza, 2005.
——. *Profanations*. Trans. Jeff Fort. New York: Zone, 2007.
——. *Remnants of Auschwitz*. Trans. Daniel Heller-Roazen. New York: Zone, 2002.
——. *Stanzas*. Trans. Ronald L. Martinez. Minneapolis: U of Minnesota P, 1993.

———. *State of Exception*. Trans. Kevin Attell. Chicago: U of Chicago P, 2005.
———. *The Time That Remains*. Trans. Patricia Dailey. Stanford: Stanford UP, 2005.
———. *"What Is an Apparatus?" and Other Essays*. Trans. David Kishik and Stefan Pedatella. Stanford: Stanford UP, 2009.
Aristotle. *Metafisica*. Vol. 3. Ed. Giovanni Reale. Milan: Vita e Pensiero, 1993.
———. *Metaphysics*. Vol. 2. Ed. W. D. Ross. Oxford: Oxford UP, 1924.
———. *The Complete Works of Aristotle*. Vol. 1. Ed. Jonathan Barnes. Princeton: Princeton UP, 1984.
———. *The Metaphysics, Books I–IX*. Trans. Hugh Tredennick. Cambridge: Harvard UP, 1933.
Attell, Kevin. "Agamben's Artaud." *Giorgio Agamben: Legal, Political and Philosophical Perspectives*. Ed. Tom Frost. London: Routledge, 2013.
Attridge, Derek. *Reading and Responsibility: Deconstruction's Traces*. Edinburgh: Edinburgh UP, 2010.
Aubenque, Pierre. *Le problème de l'être chez Aristote*. Paris: PUF, 1962.
Auerbach, Erich. *Scenes from the Drama of European Literature*. Gloucester, MA: Peter Smith, 1973.
Badiou, Alain. *Saint Paul: The Foundation of Universalism*. Trans. Ray Brassier. Stanford: Stanford UP, 2003.
Benjamin, Walter. *The Correspondence of Walter Benjamin*. Ed. Gershom Scholem and Theodor W. Adorno. Trans. Manfred R. Jacobson and Evelyn M. Jacobson. Chicago: U of Chicago P, 1994.
———. *Selected Writings*. Vols. 1–4. Ed. Michael W. Jennings. Cambridge: Belknap/Harvard UP, 1996–2003.
Bennington, Geoffrey. "Political Animals." *diacritics* 39.9 (2009): 21–35.
Benveniste, Emile. *Problèmes de linguistique générale*. Vol. 2. Paris: Gallimard, 1974.
———. *Problems in General Linguistics*. Trans. Mary Elizabeth Meek. Coral Gables: U of Miami P, 1971.
Butler, Judith. *Bodies That Matter*. New York: Routledge, 1993.
Cacciari, Massimo. *Icone della legge*. Milan: Adelphi, 1985.
Calarco, Matthew. "Jamming the Anthropological Machine." *Giorgio Agamben: Sovereignty and Life*. Ed. Calarco and Steven DeCaroli. Stanford: Stanford UP, 2007.
Culler, Jonathan. *The Literary in Theory*. Stanford: Stanford UP, 2007.
———. *On Deconstruction: Theory and Criticism after Structuralism*. Ithaca: Cornell UP, 1982.
De la Durantaye, Leland. *Giorgio Agamben: A Critical Introduction*. Stanford: Stanford UP, 2009.
Derrida, Jacques. *The Animal That Therefore I Am*. Ed. Marie-Louise Mallet. Trans. David Wills. New York: Fordham UP, 2008.

———. *Aporias*. Trans. Thomas Dutoit. Stanford: Stanford UP, 1993.

———. *The Beast and the Sovereign, Vol. 1*. Ed. Michel Lisse et al. Trans. Geoffrey Bennington. Chicago: U of Chicago P, 2009.

———. *The Beast and the Sovereign, Vol. 2*. Ed. Michel Lisse et al. Trans. Geoffrey Bennington. Chicago: U of Chicago P, 2011.

———. "Before the Law." Trans. Avital Ronell. *Acts of Literature*. Ed. Derek Attridge. New York: Routledge, 1992.

———. *Droit de regards*. Paris: Éditions de Minuit, 1985.

———. *Edmund Husserl's "Origin of Geometry": An Introduction*. Trans. John P. Leavey Jr. Lincoln: U of Nebraska P, 1978.

———. "Force of Law: The 'Mystical Foundations of Authority.'" Trans. Mary Quaintance. *Acts of Religion*. Ed. Gil Anidjar. New York: Routledge, 2002.

———. *Glas*. Trans. John P. Leavy Jr. and Richard Rand. Lincoln: U of Nebraska P, 1986.

———. "Khōra." *On the Name*. Trans. David Wood, John P. Leavey Jr., and Ian McLeod. Ed. Thomas Dutoit. Stanford: Stanford UP, 1995.

———. *Margins of Philosophy*. Trans. Alan Bass. Chicago: U of Chicago P, 1982.

———. *Of Grammatology*. Trans. Gayatri Chakravorty Spivak. Corrected ed. Baltimore: Johns Hopkins UP, 1997.

———. *The Politics of Friendship*. Trans. George Collins. New York: Verso, 1997.

———. *Positions*. Trans. Alan Bass. Chicago: U of Chicago P, 1981.

———. *Rogues; Two Essays on Reason*. Trans. Pascale-Anne Brault and Michael Naas. Stanford: Stanford UP, 2005.

———. *Specters of Marx*. Trans. Peggy Kamuf. New York: Routledge, 1994.

———. *Speech and Phenomena: And Other Essays on Husserl's Theory of Signs*. Trans. David B. Allison. Chicago: Northwestern UP, 1973.

———. *Of Spirit: Heidegger and the Question*. Trans. Geoffrey Bennington and Rachel Bowlby. Chicago: Chicago UP, 1989.

———. *Writing and Difference*. Trans. Alan Bass. Chicago: Chicago UP, 1978.

Derrida, Jacques, and Maurizio Ferraris. *A Taste for the Secret*. Trans. Giacomo Donis. Cambridge: Polity, 2001.

Descartes, René. *Discourse on the Method*. Trans. Robert Stoothoff. *The Philosophical Writings of Descartes*. Vol. 1. Cambridge: Cambridge UP, 1985.

———. *Meditations on First Philosophy*. Trans. John Cottingham. *The Philosophical Writings of Descartes*. Vol. 2. Cambridge: Cambridge UP, 1985.

———. *Treatise on Man*. Trans. Robert Stoothoff. *The Philosophical Writings of Descartes*. Vol. 1. Cambridge: Cambridge UP, 1985.

Dickinson, Colby. *Agamben and Theology*. London: T&T Clark, 2011.

Dillon, M. C. *Semiological Reductionism: A Critique of the Deconstructionist Movement in Postmodern Thought*. Albany: State University of New York Press, 1995.

Doussan, Jenny. *Time, Language, and Visuality in Agamben's Philosophy.* Basingstoke: Palgrave Macmillan, 2013.
Dubrueil, Laurent. "Leaving Politics: *Bios, Zōē,* Life." *diacritics* 36.2 (2006): 83–98.
During, Simon. *Foucault and Literature.* New York: Routledge, 1992.
Edmunds, Lowell. *The Sphinx in the Oedipus Legend.* Beiträge zur klassischen Philologie 127. Königstein/Ts.: Anton Hain, 1981.
Foucault, Michel. *Aesthetics, Method, and Epistemology.* Ed. James D. Faubion. Trans. Robert Hurley et al. New York: New Press, 1998.
———. *Archaeology of Knowledge.* Trans. Rupert Sawyer. New York: Vintage, 2010.
———. *Politics, Philosophy, Culture: Interviews and Other Writings 1977–1984.* Ed. Lawrence D. Kritzman. Trans. Alan Sheridan et al. New York: Routledge, 1988.
Frede, Michael. "Aristotle's Notion of Potentiality in *Metaphysics* Θ." In *Unity, Identity, and Explanation in Aristotle's "Metaphysics."* Ed. Theodore Scaltsas et al. Oxford: Clarendon, 1994.
Gadamer, Hans-Georg. *Truth and Method.* 2nd rev. ed. Trans. Joel Weinsheimer and Donald G. Marshall. New York: Crossroad, 1989.
Gasché, Rodolphe. *Inventions of Difference: On Jacques Derrida.* Cambridge: Harvard UP, 1994.
———. *The Tain of the Mirror.* Cambridge: Harvard UP, 1986.
Godel, Robert. *Les sources manuscrites du cours de linguistique générale.* Geneva: Droz, 1957.
Hamann, J. G. *Writings on Philosophy and Language.* Ed. and trans. Kenneth Haynes. Cambridge: Cambridge UP, 2007.
Hegel, G. W. F. *Hegel's Philosophy of Nature.* Trans. A. V. Miller. Oxford: Oxford UP, 1970.
Heidegger, Martin. *Aristotle's "Metaphysics"* Θ *1–3: On the Essence and Actuality of Force.* Trans. Walter Brogan and Peter Warnek. Indianapolis: Indiana UP, 1995.
———. *Being and Time.* Trans. John Macquarrie and Edward Robinson. New York: Harper and Row, 1962.
———. *The Fundamental Concepts of Metaphysics: World, Finitude, Solitude.* Trans. William McNeill and Nicholas Walker. Bloomington: Indiana UP, 1995.
———. *An Introduction to Metaphysics.* Trans. Ralph Manheim. New Haven: Yale UP, 1959.
———. *"Mein liebes Seelchen": Breife Martin Heideggers an seine Frau Elfride, 1915–1970.* Ed. Gertrud Heidegger. Munich: Deutsche Verlags-Anstalt, 2005.
———. *Pathmarks.* Ed. William McNeill. Cambridge: Cambridge UP, 1998.
Heller-Roazen, Daniel. *The Inner Touch: Archaelogy of a Sensation.* (New York: Zone, 2007).
———. "The Matter of Language: Guilhem de Peitieus and the Platonic Tradition." *MLN* 113.4 (1998): 851–80.

Hintikka, Jaakko. *Time and Necessity: Studies in Aristotle's Theory of Modality*. Oxford: Clarendon, 1973.

Husserl, Edmund. *Cartesian Meditations*. Trans. Dorion Cairns. The Hague: Martinus Nijhoff, 1977.

———. *Ideas Pertaining to a Pure Phenomenology and to a Phenomenological Philosophy, First Book*. Trans. F. Kersten. The Hague: Martinus Nijhoff, 1982.

Ide, Harry. "Possibility and Potentiality from Aristotle through the Stoics." Diss. Cornell University, 1988.

Irwin, T. H. *Aristotle's First Principles*. Oxford: Oxford UP 1989.

———. "Homonymy in Aristotle." *Review of Metaphysics* 34.3 (1981): 523–44.

Janicaud, Dominique. *Heidegger en France*. Vol. 2. Paris: Éditions Albin Michel, 2001.

Johansen, Thomas Kjeller. *Plato's Natural Philosophy*. Cambridge: Cambridge UP, 2004.

Johnson, David E. "*As If* the Time Were Now: Deconstructing Agamben." *South Atlantic Quarterly* 106.2 (2007): 265–90.

Kafka, Franz. *The Trial*. Trans. Breon Mitchell. New York: Schocken, 1998.

Kates, Joshua. *Essential History: Jacques Derrida and the Development of Deconstruction*. Evanston: Northwestern UP, 2005.

Kaufman, Eleanor. "The Saturday of Messianic Time (Agamben and Badiou on the Apostle Paul)." *South Atlantic Quarterly* 107.1 (2008): 37–54.

Keil, Heinrich, ed. *Grammatici Latini*. Vol. 4. Leipzig: B. G. Teubner, 1864.

Kelsen, Hans. *General Theory of Law and State*. Trans. Anders Wedberg. Cambridge: Harvard UP, 1945.

Kojève, Alexandre. *Introduction to the Reading of Hegel*. Trans. James H. Nichols Jr. Ithaca: Cornell UP, 1969.

LaCapra, Dominick. *History and Its Limits: Human, Animal, Violence*. Ithaca: Cornell UP, 2009.

Lawlor, Leonard. *Derrida and Husserl: The Basic Problem of Phenomenology*. Bloomington: Indiana UP, 2002.

Librett, Jeffrey. "From the Sacrifice of the Letter to the Voice of Testimony." *diacritics* 37.2–3 (2007): 11–33.

Macksey, Richard, and Eugenio Donato, eds. *The Structuralist Controversy: The Languages of Criticism and the Sciences of Man*. Baltimore: Johns Hopkins UP, 1972.

Marrati, Paola. *Genesis and Trace: Derrida Reading Husserl and Heidegger*. Trans. Simon Sparks. Stanford: Stanford UP, 2005.

Melandri, Enzo. *La linea e il circolo*. Macerata: Quodlibet, 2004.

Mills, Catherine. *The Philosophy of Agamben*. Montreal: McGill-Queens UP, 2008.

Nagy, Gregory. *The Best of the Achaeans*. Baltimore: Johns Hopkins UP, 1979.

———. *Pindar's Homer*. Baltimore: Johns Hopkins UP, 1990.

Nancy, Jean-Luc. *The Birth to Presence*. Trans. Brian Holmes et al. Stanford: Stanford UP, 1993.

Nancy, Jean-Luc, and Lorenzo Fabbri. "Philosophy as Chance: An Interview with Jean-Luc Nancy." Trans. Pascale-Anne Brault and Michael Naas. *Critical Inquiry* 33.2 (Winter 2007): 427–40.

Plato. *Timaeus*. Translated by Donald J. Zeyl. *Plato: Complete Works*. Ed. John M. Cooper. Indianapolis: Hackett, 1997.

Prozorov, Sergei. "The Katechon in the Age of Biopolitical Nihilism." *Continental Philosophy Review* 45.4 (2012): 483–505.

Rée, Jonathan. "The Translation of Philosophy," *New Literary History* 32.2 (2001): 223-257.

Rilke, Rainer Maria. *The Selected Poetry of Rainer Maria Rilke*. Trans. Stephen Mitchell. New York: Random House, 1982.

Sallis, John. *Chorology*. Bloomington: Indiana UP, 1999.

Sandys, John Edwin. *A History of Classical Scholarship*. Vol. 1, *From the Sixth Century B.C. to the End of the Middle Ages*. Cambridge: Cambridge UP, 1903.

Santner, Eric L. *On Creaturely Life*. Chicago: U of Chicago P, 2006.

Saussure, Ferdinand de. *Cours de linguistique générale*. Ed. Rudolph Engler. Wiesbaden: Otto Harrassowitz, 1968.

———. *Course in General Linguistics*. Trans. Wade Baskin. New York: McGraw-Hill, 1966.

Schmitt, Carl. *The Nomos of the Earth*. Trans. G. L. Ulmen. New York: Telos Press, 2003.

———. *Political Theology*. Trans. George Schwab. Chicago: U of Chicago P, 1985.

Scholem, Gershom. *On the Kabbala and Its Symbolism*. Trans. Ralph Mannheim. New York: Schocken, 1965.

Segal, Charles. *Sophocles' Tragic World*. Cambridge: Harvard UP, 1995

Seshadri, Kalpana Rahita. *HumAnimal: Race, Law, Language*. Minneapolis: U of Minnesota P, 2012.

Shields, Christopher. *Order in Multiplicity: Homonymy in the Philosophy of Aristotle*. Oxford: Clarendon, 1999.

Starobinski, Jean. *Les mots sous les mots*. Paris: Gallimard, 1971.

Strauss, Leo. "Natural Law." *International Encyclopedia of the Social Sciences*. Vol. 11. Ed. David L. Sills. New York: Macmillan, 1968. 80.

———. *Natural Right and History*. Chicago: U of Chicago P, 1953.

Thurschwell, Adam. "Cutting the Branches for Akiba: Agamben's Critique of Derrida." *Politics, Metaphysics, and Death: Essays on Giorgio Agamben's "Homo Sacer."* Ed. Andrew Norris. Durham: Duke UP, 2005. 73–197.

———. "Specters of Nietzsche: Potential Futures for the Concept of the Political in Agamben and Derrida." *Cardozo Law Review* 24.3 (2003): 1193–260.

Vernant, Jean-Pierre, and Pierre Vidal-Naquet. *Myth and Tragedy in Ancient Greece*. Trans. Janet Lloyd. New York: Zone, 1990.
Watkin, William. *The Literary Agamben: Adventures in Logopoiesis*. New York: Continuum, 2010.
Witt, Charlotte. *Ways of Being: Potentiality and Actuality in Aristotle's Metaphysics*. Ithaca: Cornell UP, 2003.
Wortham, Simon Morgan. *Derrida: Writing Events*. London: Continuum, 2008.
Zartaloudis, Thanos. *Giorgio Agamben: Power, Law and the Uses of Criticism*. Abingdon: Routledge, 2010.

INDEX

abandonment, Nancy's concept of, 127–28
adunamia, 93–95, 120, 133, 191, 207–8, 242
Aeschylus, 190
ainos (story, fable), 36, 37, 269n29
"L'albero del linguaggio" (Agamben), 1–2, 19, 22, 39
Allemann, Beda, 263n6
alterity, 8, 9, 118, 137, 168, 189, 199, 206, 231, 279n3
anagrams, Saussure's work on, 29, 266–67nn15–16
animal-human distinction, 4, 8–9; and Agamben's *Homo Sacer*, 131–34, 183–84, 186–87, 190; and Agamben's *Infancy and History*, 57; and Agamben's *Language and Death*, 75–82; and Agamben's *The Open*, 8, 168–75, 202–12, 282n4; and anthropological machine of humanism, 8, 168–69, 171–75, 198, 204–6, 209–11; and ban-structure, 168, 173–74, 189, 209; and bare life, 169, 174, 188, 209; and being-toward-death, 193–94, 196; and biopolitics, 169, 183, 187, 189–92, 198–99, 209; and *bios*/*zōē* distinction, 131–34, 173, 183–92, 283n23; and Dasein, 72–73, 76–78, 91–92, 193–98, 202–8; and Derrida's *Animal That Therefore I Am*, 8, 167–68, 175–83, 188–89, 191, 192–93, 194, 195, 197–202, 282n4; and Derrida's *Aporias*, 192–94; and Derrida's *Beast and The Sovereign I*, 183–85, 187–89, 191–92; and Derrida's *Of Spirit*, 197–201; and Descartes's work, 175–81, 188–89, 194–95; and exceptionality, 173–74, 201, 206, 210; and feral children, 171–72; and Haeckel's work, 172–73, 205; and Heidegger's work, 76, 77, 78, 174, 191–211, 284n44; and language, 57, 172–73; and Linnaeus's work, 170–71, 177, 282n7; and *logos*, 192, 197; and missing link, 172–73; and poverty, 196, 198–205, 209, 211; and resurrected body, 170; and sovereign ban, 168, 174, 189, 209; and Uexküll's work, 174–75, 211; and voice, 75–82, 133

The Animal That Therefore I Am (Derrida), 8, 167–68, 175–83, 188–89, 191, 192–93, 194, 195, 197–202, 282n4
anthropocentrism, 8, 182
anthropological machine, Agamben's concept of, 8, 168–69, 171–75, 198, 204–6, 209–11
antinomianism, 126, 157, 242, 251, 253, 281n31

apocalyptic time, Agamben's concept of, 216, 249
Aporias (Derrida), 192–94
apostle *vs.* prophet, in Agamben's work, 214–16, 232, 235, 240, 242, 246
Aquinas, Thomas, 170
arche-trace, Derrida's concept of, 22, 27, 30, 227
arche-writing, Derrida's concept of: and Husserl's work, 270n3; and Saussurian semiology, 25–26
Arendt, Hannah, 281n25, 283–84n32
Aristotle, 60, 61, 62, 79–81, 83, 274–75nn9–10; and Agamben's concept of potentiality, 86, 87–100, 106–7, 114, 116, 120, 133, 255–56; and *bios/zōē* distinction, 183–84, 186–88, 283n23; and concept of *hulē* (matter), 112–14, 117, 277n33, 278n41; and concept of time, 217, 218–21, 223–28, 242; and Derrida's critique of Agamben, 183–84, 188, 283n23; Heidegger on, 88, 274n8, 283n32
Attridge, Derek, 270n32
Aubenque, Pierre, 88, 90, 274n8
Auerbach, Erich, 239
Aufhebung, 220–23, 227–28, 231, 240, 242–43, 246, 285n6

Badiou, Alain, 248
Bahti, Timothy, 284n34
ban, Agamben's concept of: and animal-human distinction, 168, 173–74, 189, 209; and *bios/zōē* distinction, 187; and Derrida's work, 130; and Kafka's "Before the Law," 13, 15–16, 17; and Nancy's concept of abandonment, 127–28, 129; and potentiality, 98, 134; and sovereignty, 8, 17, 18, 130–34, 162, 163, 168, 174, 189, 209

bare life, Agamben's concept of, 7, 17, 86, 127, 130, 132–34, 157, 164, 169, 174, 188, 209, 255, 279n3
"Bartleby, or On Contingency" (Agamben), 87, 107–8, 277n29
bastard reasoning, 110, 117–20
Bataille, Georges, 228–30
Baudelaire, Charles, 13
The Beast and The Sovereign I (Derrida), 183–85, 187–89, 191–92
The Beast and The Sovereign II (Derrida), 284n34
Beaufret, Jean, 72, 263n6
"Before the Law" (Kafka), 13–19, 135, 144–45, 251
being: and Agamben's reading of Benveniste's work, 67, 68; and being-toward-death, 193–94, 196; and Derrida's critique of Benveniste's work, 61–66, 181; and Heidegger's work, 64, 78, 193–94, 196; and temporality, 218–21, 223–26; transcategoriality of, 61, 62, 64, 66, 67, 68
Being and Time (Heidegger), 72, 76–78, 92, 193, 195–96, 218–19, 224–27
Benjamin, Walter, 3, 4, 7, 8, 215, 247, 249, 252–53; "Critique of Violence" by, 135–66, 256–57, 262, 279n8; "Toys and Play" by, 262
Bennington, Geoffrey, 183
Benveniste, Émile: Agamben on, 29, 54–56, 65–68, 74, 154, 236–37, 259; Derrida on, 59–66, 181
biblical exegesis, 239
biopolitics, 7, 8, 86, 127, 130–34, 157, 169, 183, 187, 189–92, 198–99, 209, 255, 256
biopower, 191, 192, 272n21
bios/zōē distinction, 131–34, 173, 183–92, 255, 283n23
Bonitz, Hermann, 274n8

298 Index

boredom, Heidegger's concept of, 206–7, 208
Brentano, Franz, 274n8
Brisson, Luc, 110
Buddhism, 84–85
Butler, Judith, 278n41

Cacciari, Massimo, 265n3
Calarco, Matthew, 169
Calcidius, 114
Cassiodorus, 106, 277n29
catachresis, 25, 30, 104, 110, 111, 119, 120
Char, René, 1
China, 126
Chomsky, Noam, 2
chronogenetic time, 134, 235–37
close reading, 21
The Coming Community (Agamben), 7, 85, 93, 125
Course in General Linguistics (Saussure), 5, 23, 26–35, 104, 267nn17–18, 268n24
Culler, Jonathan, 267n17

Dante Alighieri, 256, 277–78n36
Dasein, Heidegger's concept of, 72–73, 76–78, 91–92, 193–98, 202–8
death: and Derrida's concept of writing, 44–45; and Heidegger's concept of being-toward-death, 193–94, 196; and Heidegger's concept of Dasein, 73, 193–94; and Heidegger's "The Nature of Language," 69–70
decipherment, Derrida's practice of: and Kafka's "Before the Law," 18
deconstruction, Derrida's theory of: and Agamben's antinomianism, 281n31; and Agamben's concept of messianism, 215, 244–46, 251, 259–60; and Agamben's concept of potentiality, 7, 85–86, 100, 107; and Agamben's concept of reference, 101, 102; and Agamben's *Homo Sacer*, 16–17, 18, 127; and Agamben's *Idea of Prose*, 273n1; and Agamben's "Pardes," 7, 100, 101, 102, 105–6; and Agamben's *Stanzas*, 19–20, 21–22, 26–27; and Agamben's *The Time That Remains*, 22; and Agamben's work in general, 3–5; and Benjamin's "Critique of Violence," 136, 137; Gasché on, 21, 24, 25–26; and justice, 158–59; and Kafka's "Before the Law," 16–17, 18–19; and literary criticism, 20–21; and play, 258, 260; and reinscription, 24–25, 26; and Saussurian semiology, 30–31; as thwarted messianism, 215, 241, 246, 251, 259–60
deictics, 66, 70, 73–74, 76, 102, 181–82, 236, 243
De la Durantaye, Leland, 273n1
de Man, Paul, 5
Descartes, René, 53, 175–81, 188–89, 194–95, 282–83n13, 282n10
dialectics, Hegelian, 221–24, 227–33, 240, 242–44
différance, Derrida's concept of: and Agamben's concept of (im)potentiality, 7, 100, 116; and Agamben's concept of reference, 103–5; and Agamben's work in general, 6–7, 264n7; as antimessianism, 251; and Benveniste's work, 65; and Husserl's *Origin of Geometry*, 45; and Husserl's phenomenology, 45, 52–53; and justice, 158–59, 162; and Kafka's "Before the Law," 14–16, 18, 135; and play, 231, 257–58; and

Index 299

Saussurian semiology, 29–34, 104; and temporality, 9, 227, 234, 285n13
Diogenes Laertius, 279n3
Doussan, Jenny, 269–70n31
Dubois, Eugen, 172
Dubreuil, Laurent, 189–91
dunamis: and *adunamia*, 93–95, 120, 133, 191, 207–8; and Agamben's concept of potentiality, 83, 87–94, 96, 98, 99, 255, 275–76n16, 275n11; and *energeia*, 83, 86–87, 91–94, 99, 255, 277n25

Eliot, T. S., 213
energeia, 83, 86–87, 91–94, 97, 99, 255–56, 277n25
Engler, Rudolph, 33, 267n17
enigma of the Sphinx, 19, 35–37, 39, 245, 268–69nn27–28
enunciation, theory of, 56, 58, 66–67, 68, 154, 236–37, 272n21
epistemological break, 24
erasure: of the law, 163, 253; and self-erasure, 103
eschatology, 9, 216, 234, 251
ethics: and Agamben's work in general, 40, 119, 120–21; and Derrida's reading of Plato, 118–19; Levinasian, 118, 120
euporias, 16, 17, 37, 117
event, Derrida's concept of, 143, 144
exception, state of, 128–29, 135, 149–53, 155–58, 160, 163, 165, 256, 257, 260; and animal-human distinction, 173–74, 201, 206, 210; and messianic time, 247–49, 251–52
experimentum linguae, 38, 83, 86, 101, 106, 115–17, 120, 161, 245
exteriority: and Derrida's concept of arche-writing, 25, 26; and Derrida's critique of Husserl's phenomenology, 49, 50, 51

feral children, 171–72, 282n8
"Force of Law" (Derrida), 136–37, 139, 141–48, 152, 158, 280n16, 281n26
"Form-of-Life" (Agamben), 255
Foucault, Michel, 131, 272n21
Fourcade, Dominique, 1
Frede, Michael, 274n10
Frege, Gottlob, 103
Freud, Sigmund, 108, 269n28
"The Friend" (Agamben), 279n3
Fundamental Concepts of Metaphysics (Heidegger), 195–99, 201–2, 205–9, 284n43

Gadamer, Hans-Georg, 259
Gasché, Rodolphe, 15, 20–21, 24, 25–26, 230, 264n10
geometry, Husserl's work on, 41, 42–46
Glas (Derrida), 268n24
Gnosticism, 216, 217
Godel, Robert, 267n16, 268n23
gramma, 70, 74, 79–83, 86, 182
grammatology, Derrida's concept of: Agamben on, 21, 102, 105, 107, 120; and Benveniste's work, 59, 63, 65, 66; and Husserl's work, 43; and Saussure's work, 23, 24, 31
graphocentrism, 106, 107, 281n31
Greece, ancient: philosophy in, 60–61, 216–17; politics in, 131
Guillaume, Gustave, 235–36

Haeckel, Ernst, 172–73, 205
Hägglund, Martin, 232, 234
Hamann, J. G., 54
Hamlet (Shakespeare), 232
hauntology, Derrida's concept of, 148–49
Hegel, G. W. F., 70, 219–24, 227–32, 240–43
Heidegger, Martin: Agamben

influenced by, 1, 2, 8, 21, 22, 99, 115; and Agamben's *Infancy and History*, 115; and Agamben's *Language and Death*, 69–73, 75–78; and Agamben's *The Open*, 174, 198, 202–11, 284n45; and Agamben's "The Work of Man," 207; and animal-human distinction, 76, 77, 78, 174, 191–211, 284n44; on Aristotle, 88, 274n8, 283n32; *Being and Time* by, 72, 76–78, 92, 193, 195–96, 218–19, 224–27; and boredom, 206–7, 208; and Cartesian *cogito*, 195; and concept of being-toward-death, 193–94, 196; and concept of Dasein, 72–73, 76–78, 91–92, 193–98, 202–8; and concept of time, 218–21, 223–27, 229, 231; critique of Sartre by, 22, 82; Derrida influenced by, 19; and Derrida's *Animal That Therefore I Am*, 192–93, 194, 195, 197–202; and Derrida's *Aporias*, 192–94; and Derrida's *Margins of Philosophy*, 276–77n25; and Derrida's *Of Spirit*, 197–201, 284n43; and Derrida's "*Ousia* and *Grammē*," 218–21, 223–27, 229, 231; and Derrida's reading of Benveniste, 59–60, 62–64; Foucault influenced by, 272n21; *Fundamental Concepts of Metaphysics* by, 195–99, 201–2, 205–9, 284n43; *Introduction to Metaphysics* by, 221, 284n43; *Kant and the Problem of Metaphysics* by, 218, 225; "Letter on 'Humanism'" by, 22, 82, 191–92, 201; "The Nature of Language" by, 69, 114, 115; and Rilke's work, 204; and seminars at Le Thor, 1

Heller-Roazen, Daniel, 94

Homer Sacer: Sovereign Power and Bare Life (Agamben): and Aristotle's work, 87, 91, 93, 95, 98, 99–100; and ban-structure, 13, 98, 127, 130–34, 276n23; and bare life, 7, 17, 86, 127, 130, 132–34, 157, 164, 169, 174, 188, 209, 255, 279n3; and *bios/zōē* distinction, 131–34, 183–84, 186–87, 190, 191–92, 283n23; and deconstruction, 16–17, 18, 127; and Kafka's "Before the Law," 13, 15–19; and sovereignty, 98, 128–34, 149

hulē, 112–14, 117, 277n33

humanism, 8, 22, 171, 193, 194, 200, 209, 258; anthropological machine of, 168–69; and Heidgger's "Letter on 'Humanism'", 22, 82

"The Human Voice" project, Agamben's, 6, 40–41, 85, 120, 245

Husserl, Edmund: and Agamben's *Infancy and History*, 53–55, 58; and Derrida's critique of "living present," 45–46, 270n3; and Derrida's critique of *Origin of Geometry* by, 6, 41, 42–46; and Derrida's critique of phono-logocentrism, 41; and Derrida's *Of Grammatology*, 20; and Derrida's *Speech and Phenomena*, 6, 20

Ide, Harry, 275n15

"The Idea of Matter" (Agamben), 113, 115, 121

Idea of Prose (Agamben), 84–85, 113, 273n1

impotentiality, Agamben's concept of, 93–97, 99, 116, 120, 208, 241, 243, 256

Infancy and History (Agamben), 9, 20, 38, 40, 86; and critique of transcendental subject, 54–58; and Heidegger's work, 115; and Husserl's work, 53–55; and messianic time, 216–17; and play, 260–61; and speech, 68–69, 83

Index 301

"In Playland" (Agamben), 9, 259, 260
"In Praise of Profanation" (Agamben), 165–66, 261
intentio prima vs. intentio secunda, 102–5, 237, 244–45
interiority: and Derrida's critique of Husserl's phenomenology, 49, 50, 51
Irwin, Terence, 90
iterability, Derrida's concept of, 45, 137, 145–48, 181, 182, 271n13

Jakobson, Roman, 2, 55, 74
Jesi, Furio, 168
Jews *vs.* non-Jews, in Pauline doctrine, 248–49
Johansen, Thomas Kjeller, 277n33
Johnson, David E., 286n26
justice, 138–39, 158–59, 162

Kafka, Franz: Allemann's essay on, 263n6; "Before the Law" by, 13–19, 135, 144–45, 147, 251; Benjamin's essay on, 164–65, 252
kairos, 9, 215–17, 235, 237–38, 240, 246
Kant, Immanuel, 54, 181
katargēsis, 241–44, 246, 248–52, 260–61
katekhōn, 249–53, 287n30
Kelsen, Hans, 138
"Khōra" (Derrida), 108, 110–12, 118–19
khōra, Platonic concept of, 108–13, 117–21, 277n33
khronos, 9, 219, 235–38, 246
Kojève, Alexandre, 232–33
Kraus, Karl, 161

LaCapra, Dominick, 168
language: and Agamben on animal-human distinction, 172–73; and Agamben's concept of potentiality, 114; and Agamben's critique of Husserl's work, 53–55; and Agamben's critique of transcendental subject, 54–58; and Agamben's legal theory, 153–54; and Agamben's reading of Aristotle, 79–81, 83, 113–14; and Agamben's theory of infancy, 56–58; and Derrida's critique of Benveniste's work, 60–66; and Derrida's critique of Husserl's work, 42–43, 47; and Derrida's legal theory, 153–54; and Heidegger's work, 69, 114–15; and linguistic shifters, 55, 56, 66, 67–68, 70–73, 75–76, 181, 236–37, 243; and prelinguistic experience, 43, 49, 53, 55, 58, 160; and temporality, 236–37. *See also* semiology; sign; speech; voice; writing
Language and Death (Agamben), 20, 40; and Aristotle's work, 79–81, 83; and concept of the *gramma*, 79–83; and concept of the Voice, 6, 69–70, 74–82; and critique of negativity, 6, 69–70, 73–75, 77–79, 81–82; and Derrida's work, 74, 79, 81–82; and Heidegger's work, 69–78; and linguistic shifters, 70–71, 243
"Language and History" (Agamben), 85
langue, 23, 56–57, 58, 67, 71, 82, 83, 153, 154, 236, 267n17, 268n24
law: and Agamben's concept of exception, 128–29, 135, 149–53, 155–58, 160, 163, 165; and Agamben's concept of potentiality, 86; and Agamben's concept of sovereignty, 8, 129–30, 136–37, 149, 151–53, 155–58, 162–63; and Benjamin's essay on violence, 135–66, 256; and Derrida's concept of *différance*, 158–59, 162; and Derrida's concept of iterability, 137, 145–48; and Derrida's "Force

of Law," 136–37, 139, 141–48, 158, 280n16, 281n26; distinguished from justice, 138–39; erasure of the, 163, 253; and *fictio iuris,* 152, 157, 158; and Kafka's "Before the Law," 13–19, 135, 144–45, 147, 251; and messianic time, 241, 247–53; and Nancy's concept of abandonment, 127–28; natural, 137–39, 150, 159–61, 279n8; positive, 137–40; and Saussurian linguistics, 153–54; and violence, 136, 137, 140–49, 256–57
Lawlor, Leonard, 270nn2,4
"Letter on 'Humanism'" (Heidegger), 22, 82, 191–92, 201
Levinas, Emmanuel, 118
Lévi-Strauss, Claude, 20, 258, 259
Librett, Jeffrey, 281n31
linguistics, Sausurrean. *See* semiology, Sausurrean
Linnaeus, Carl, 170–71, 177, 282n7
literary criticism, 20–21
logocentrism, Derrida's critique of: and Agamben's "The Human Voice" project, 6, 41; and Agamben's "Pardes," 105, 106; and Agamben's work in general, 269–70n31; and Derrida's *Animal That Therefore I Am,* 179, 182; and Derrida's *Speech and Phenomena,* 41, 46, 49, 51, 52, 53; and Husserl's work, 41, 46–53; and Saussurian semiology, 29
logos, 2, 38, 39, 40, 192, 197, 269n31
Luther, Martin, 242

Mallet, Marie-Louise, 167
The Man without Content (Agamben), 86, 263n6, 269n28
Margins of Philosophy (Derrida), 30, 45, 59–65, 158–59, 218–27, 266n13, 272n16, 276–77n25

Marrati, Paola, 270n3
Martinez, Ronald L., 269n29
Marxism, 125, 232, 276n23
matter: in Aristotelian philosophy, 98–99, 112–14, 277n33, 278n41; intelligible, 119–20
Means without End (Agamben), 255
mechanistic worldview, 177–80, 283n13
Megarians, 90–91, 93, 98–99, 276n16
Melandri, Enzo, 272n21
"The Messiah and the Sovereign" (Agamben), 215
messianic time: and Agamben's *Infancy and History,* 216–17; and Agamben's *The Time That Remains,* 213–18, 234–52, 260; and apostolic view, 246; and Derrida's *Specters of Marx,* 9, 233–34; distinguished from apocalyptic time, 216; dual structure of, 237–39, 246; and *kairos,* 9, 215–17, 235, 237–38, 240, 246; and *katargēsis,* 241–44, 246, 248–52, 260–61; and *katekhōn,* 249–53, 287n30; and language, 236–37; and law, 241, 247–53; and negativity, 243, 286n26; and Pauline interpretation, 9, 238–44, 246–52, 260, 287n30; and play, 260–61; and potentiality, 241–43; and state of exception, 247–49, 251–52; and *tempus primum* vs. *tempus secundum,* 237, 243–45
messianism, 9, 38, 126, 213, 215, 233–34, 251, 264n7
metaphysics: and Agamben's critique of negativity, 69–70, 78, 82, 286n26; and Agamben's *Language and Death,* 69–70, 78, 82; and Agamben's *Stanzas,* 19, 21, 22, 26, 37, 82; and Aristotle's work, 99; and Derrida's critique of Husserl's work, 46, 51; and Derrida's

practice of reinscription, 26; and Derrida's reading of Plato, 112; and Heidegger's critique of Sartre, 22; and Kafka's "Before the Law," 16, 18
Mills, Catherine, 75
missing link, in human evolution, 172–73
Monboddo, Lord, 172
muteness, 50, 54, 55

Nagarjuna, 84–85, 113
Nagy, Gregory, 269n29
Nancy, Jean-Luc, 16, 127–28, 129, 130, 263–64n7
natural law, 137–39, 150, 159–61, 279n8; vs. positive law, 137–40
"The Nature of Language" (Heidegger), 69, 114, 115
Nazism, 156–57, 281n31
negativity: and Agamben's concept of messianic time, 243, 286n26; and Agamben's *Language and Death*, 6, 69–70, 73–75, 77–79, 81–82; and Bataille's work, 228–30; and Derrida's concept of arche-writing, 25, 26; and Derrida's "Force of Law," 144; and Hegel's work, 228–31; and temporality, 223, 228–32
New Criticism, 21
Nietzche, Friedrich, 27, 59, 60, 62
nihilism, 70, 84, 85, 113, 273n1
now, temporal. *See* present

objectivity: and Derrida's critique of Husserl's *Origin of Geometry*, 42–46
O'Brien, Flann, 40
Oedipus, story of the Sphinx and, 35–37, 245, 268–69nn27–28
Of Grammatology (Derrida): and Agamben's "L'albero del linguaggio," 2; and Agamben's *Stanzas*, 5, 19, 21–22, 26–28, 31–35; and present time, 285n13; and Saussurian semiology, 2, 5, 19–21, 23–34, 38, 267nn16–18
Of Spirit (Derrida), 197–201, 284n43
"On Potentiality" (Agamben), 87, 94–95, 116
"On the Limits of Violence" (Agamben), 281n25
ontology: and Agamben's concept of potentiality, 99–100, 134; and Agamben's *Language and Death*, 69–73; and Agamben's theory of enunciation, 56; and Derrida's work, 112, 118, 244, 245; and Heidegger's work, 21, 63, 69–73, 112
ontotheology, 70, 258
The Open (Agamben), 167–68, 191–92; and animal-human distinction, 8, 168–75, 202–12, 282n4; and anthropological machine of humanism, 8, 168–69, 171–75, 198, 204–6, 209–11; and Aristotle's work, 186–88; and *bios/zōē* distinction, 186–88; and bodily resurrection, 169–70; compared to Agamben's *Infancy and History*, 57; and feral children, 171–72; and Haeckel's work, 172–73; and Heidegger's work, 174, 198, 202–11, 284n45; and Linnaeus's work, 170–71, 177, 282n7; and missing link, 172–73; and sovereign ban, 168, 173–74; and Uexküll's work, 174–75, 211; and Veil of Veronica, 284n34
operational time, 235–39, 243, 244, 246
Origen, 265n3
Origin of Geometry (Husserl), 41, 42–46
otherness, 25, 30, 69, 118–19
"*Ousia* and *Grammē*" (Derrida), 108, 217–27, 231, 234, 263n6, 276n25, 285n12

"*Pardes:* The Writing of Potentiality" (Agamben), 7, 85, 100–108, 113, 116–17, 120, 121, 215, 273n2
parole, 57, 58, 67, 71, 82, 83, 113, 153, 154
parousia, 218, 238–39, 249
Pasolini, Pier Paolo, 268–69n27
Paul, Saint, 9, 38, 214, 216, 238–52
phenomenology: and Derrida's critique of Husserl's work, 45, 46, 47, 49, 50, 51
phōnē, 40, 52, 61, 75, 77, 79–80, 82–83, 133
phonocentrism, Derrida's critique of, 23–24; and Agamben's "The Human Voice" project, 41; and Agamben's *Language and Death,* 69, 73, 78–79, 82; and Derrida's *Animal That Therefore I Am,* 179, 182; and Derrida's *Speech and Phenomena,* 41, 51; and Husserl's work, 41, 51
Pico della Mirandola, 171
Plato, 39, 58, 184, 278n41, 283n23; *Timaeus* by, 108–11, 113–14, 117–19, 277n33
play: Agamben's concept of, 9, 166, 252–53, 257, 258–62, 287n3; Derrida's concept of, 9, 231, 257–58, 260; Gadamer's concept of, 259
Plissart, Marie-Françoise, 264n8
Plotinus, 116, 278n41
politics: and Agamben's *The Coming Community,* 7, 125–26; and Agamben's "Form-of-Life," 255; and Agamben's *Homo Sacer,* 7, 125–34, 187–88, 276n23, 279n3; and Agamben's *State of Exception,* 149, 162–63, 164; and bare life, 127, 130, 132–34, 157, 164, 255; and *bios/zōē* distinction, 131–34, 187–88; and Derrida's *Specters of Marx,* 125; and play, 9, 257, 262; and potentiality, 256; revolutionary, 9, 140–44, 150, 152, 155, 157; and sovereign ban, 17, 18, 130–34, 162, 163, 168, 174, 189, 209. *See also* biopolitics
The Politics of Friendship (Derrida), 278–79n3
Positions (Derrida), 23, 24, 41, 46, 258, 266n14
positivity, in Saussurian semiology, 33
Potentialities (Agamben), 9, 87, 91, 94, 95
potentiality, Agamben's concept of, 39, 86–100; and *adunamia,* 93–95, 133; and Aristotle's work, 86, 87–100, 106–7, 114, 116, 133, 255–56, 275–76n16, 275n11; and ban-structure, 98, 134; and Derrida's work, 85–86, 100, 106; and *différance,* 7, 100, 116; and *dunamis,* 83, 87–94, 96, 98, 99, 133, 255; and *energeia,* 83, 86–87, 91–94, 97, 99, 255–56, 277n25; and form of life, 256; and Heidegger's work, 88, 91–92, 207, 208–9; and impotentiality, 93–97, 99, 116, 120, 208, 241, 243, 256; and messianic time, 241–43; and Plotinus's work, 116; and politics, 256; and sovereignty, 8, 98, 134; and voice, 133; and writing, 106, 107
La potenza del pensiero (Agamben), 87, 91, 95–97
poverty, of animal being, 196, 198–205, 209, 211
prelinguistic experience, 43, 49, 53, 55, 58, 160
presence, Derrida's critique of: and Agamben's *Language and Death,* 69; and Agamben's *Stanzas,* 21, 22, 38, 39; and Attridge's defense of Derrida against Agamben, 270n32; and Derrida's *Of Grammatology,* 23,

Index 305

38; and Derrida's "*Ousia* and *Grammē*," 218–20, 225–27, 276n25; and Derrida's *Positions,* 23; and Derrida's *Speech and Phenomena,* 50–53; and Derrida's *Writing and Difference,* 258; and Kafka's "Before the Law," 16; and play, 258
presence, fracturing of, Agamben's concept of, 19, 33–34, 38
present: and Agamben's concept of messianic time, 237–40, 244, 286n26; and Derrida's critique of Husserl, 45–47, 52–53, 270n3, 276n25; and Derrida's *Of Grammatology,* 285n13; and Derrida's "*Ousia* and *Grammē*," 218–21, 225–26, 233
Profanations (Agamben), 38, 257, 261
pronoun, personal, 55–56, 70–71, 74, 180–82, 271n13
prophecy, Agamben's concept of, 214–16, 232, 235, 240, 242, 246, 260
Protagoreans, 98, 99
Prozorov, Sergei, 287n30

Reale, Giovanni, 88, 90, 274n8
reinscription, Derrida's practice of, 24–25, 26; and Agamben's *Stanzas,* 26–27; and deconstructive literary criticism, 21; Gasché on, 21, 24; and Kafka's "Before the Law," 18; and Saussurian semiology, 26–27
Remnants of Auschwitz (Agamben): and Benveniste's work, 66–68
resurrection of the body, 169–70
revolution, social, 9, 140–44, 150, 152, 155, 157
Rilke, Rainer Maria, 204
Rivaud, Albert, 110
Rogues (Derrida), 283n23
Roman Empire, 250–51, 287n30

Ross, W. D., 88, 90

Sallis, John, 277n33
Santner, Eric L., 205
Sartre, Jean-Paul, 22, 82
Saussure, Ferdinand de, 2, 23, 26–35, 48, 104, 153; correspondence of, 32–33, 268n23; unpublished work by, 28–29
Schmitt, Carl, 98, 128, 149, 151, 153–59, 165, 210, 214, 215, 247–51, 257, 278n3, 281n26, 287n30
Scholem, Gershom, 252, 265n3
Sebald, W. G., 84
Segal, Charles, 268n27
self-referentiality, 67, 71, 102–7, 117, 121, 237
semiology, Saussurian: and Agamben's "L'albero del linguaggio," 2, 19, 22, 39; and Agamben's concept of fracture, 33–34; and Agamben's *Stanzas,* 2, 5–6, 19, 21–22, 26–28, 31–35, 38, 41; and Culler's work, 267n17; and Derrida's concept of *différance,* 29–34, 104; and Derrida's critique of Husserl's work, 48; and Derrida's *Glas,* 268n24; and Derrida's *Of Grammatology,* 2, 5, 19–21, 23–34, 38, 267n16–18; and Derrida's practice of reinscription, 26–27; and Saussure's *Course in General Linguistics,* 23, 26–35, 267nn17–18, 268n24; and Saussure's unpublished work, 28–29
Seshadri, Kalpana Rahita, 283–84n32
shifters, linguistic, 55, 56, 66, 67–68, 70–73, 75–76, 181, 236–37, 243
sign: and Agamben's "L'albero del linguaggio," 2; and Agamben's "*Pardes,*" 102–3; and Agamben's *Stanzas,* 21–22, 27, 32–39;

arbitrariness of, 23, 59, 267n17, 268n24; and Derrida's concept of *différance*, 29–30, 37; and Derrida's concept of Husserl's work, 46–53; Husserl's concept of expressive vs. indicative, 47–51; and *intentio prima* vs. *intentio secunda*, 102–5, 237, 244–45

"Signature Event Context" (Derrida), 45

Sorel, Georges, 141

sovereignty, Agamben's concept of: and Benjamin's "Critique of Violence," 136–37, 149, 151–53, 155–58, 162–63; and exceptionality, 7, 128–30, 149, 151–52, 155–57; and Kafka's "Before the Law," 13, 15, 16, 17, 18; and Nancy's concept of abandonment, 128; and potentiality, 8, 98, 134; and Schmitt's work, 155–56; and sovereign ban, 8, 17, 18, 130–34, 162, 163, 168, 174, 189, 209

Soviet Union, 125, 126

spatiality, in relation to temporality, 222–23, 228, 234, 285n8

Specters of Marx (Derrida), 9, 125, 148, 213, 232–34

spectrality, Derrida's concept of, 148–49

speech: and Agamben's *Infancy and History*, 68–69, 83; and Derrida's concept of arche-writing, 25; and Derrida's critique of phonocentrism, 23–24, 25

Speech and Phenomena (Derrida), 6; and Husserl's phono-logocentrism, 41; retranslation of, 270n2

Sphinx, enigma of the, Agamben on, 19, 35–39, 245, 268–69nn27–28

Stanzas (Agamben): and Derrida's *Of Grammatology*, 5, 19, 21–22, 26–28,

31–35, 245; and disjuncture of the sign, 32–34, 37; and enigma of the Sphinx, 19, 35–39, 269n28; and fracturing of presence, 19, 33–34, 38; and metaphysics, 19, 21, 22, 26, 37, 82; and play, 287n3; and Saussurian semiology, 5–6, 19, 21–22, 26–28, 31–35, 38, 41

Starobinski, Jean, 29, 266n15

State of Exception (Agamben), 3, 135–36, 149–65, 210, 256–57, 280n22

Stoicism, 216–17

Strauss, Leo, 279n8

strike, general, 141–42

structuralism: and Lévi-Strauss's work, 20; and Saussure's work, 20, 28–29, 35

"Structure, Sign, and Play" (Derrida), 9, 257–58

subjectivity: Agamben's critique of transcendental, 54–58; and Benveniste's work, 55–56

"The Supplement of Copula" (Derrida), 29, 59, 65–66, 68, 181, 221

Taubes, Jacob, 155

Tertullian, 239, 250

theology, 158, 169–70, 213, 214, 215, 227, 232, 238, 240, 242, 250–51; and ontotheology, 70, 258

"The Thing Itself" (Agamben), 85

Thurschwell, Adam, 113, 118–19, 120, 215, 273n2

Tiananmen Square protests, 126

Timaeus (Plato), 108–11, 113–14, 117–19, 217, 277n33

time: Aristotelian concept of, 217, 218–21, 223–28, 242; chronogenetic, 134, 235–37; and Derrida's concept of *différance*, 227, 234, 285n13; and Derrida's "*Ousia* and *Grammē*,"

Index 307

217–27; dual structure of, 237–39, 246; and Hegel's work, 219–24, 227–32, 240–43; and Heidegger's work, 218–21, 223–27, 229, 231; as *kairos,* 9, 215–17, 235, 237–38, 240, 246; as *khronos,* 9, 219, 235–38, 246; operational, 235–39, 243, 244, 246; and spatiality, 222–23, 228, 234; Stoic concept of, 216–17. *See also* messianic time

"Time and History" (Agamben), 9, 216–18

The Time That Remains (Agamben), 22, 213; and apocalyptic time, 216; and apostle-prophet distinction, 214–16; and messianic time, 213–18, 234–52, 260

topology: and Agamben's concept of signification, 37, 38–39; differantial, 16–17

trace, Derrida's concept of: and Agamben's concept of messianic time, 244–45; and Agamben's concept of potentiality, 100, 107, 116, 120; and Agamben's concept of reference, 103–4; and Agamben's "Pardes," 100–103, 106, 119–20; and Derrida's *Of Grammatology,* 26, 34, 37, 38; and Husserl's phenomenology, 52

transcategoriality of being, 61, 62, 64, 66, 67, 68

transcendence: and Agamben's critique of Husserl's work, 54–55; and Agamben's reading of Heidegger, 71; and Derrida's critique of Husserl's work, 42–46, 48–53

Tredennick, Hugh, 87, 89, 90

The Trial (Kafka), 14

Truffaut, François, 282n8

typology, in biblical exegesis, 238–39, 260

Uexküll, Jakob von, 174–75, 206, 211

undecidables, Derrida's concept of, 22, 158

Veil of Veronica, 284n34

venire a capo, 18–19, 265n4

Vernant, Jean-Pierre, 108

violence: and Agamben's reading of Benjamin, 135–37, 149–66, 256, 262, 280–81n25; and Derrida's reading of Benjamin, 135–49, 152, 280n16; extrajuridical, 129, 139–42, 150–51, 154–57; lawmaking *vs.* law-preserving, 136, 137, 140–49; and natural *vs.* positive law, 137–40; pure, 140, 146, 149, 152, 155–57, 160–66, 256–57; revolutionary, 140–44, 150, 152, 155, 157; and Schmitt's work, 151, 153–59, 165

voice: and Agamben's *bios*/*zōē* distinction, 133; and Agamben's concept of (im)potentiality, 133; and Agamben's critique of Husserl's work, 53–54; and Agamben's "The Human Voice" project, 6, 40–41, 53; and Agamben's *Language and Death,* 6, 69–70, 74–82; and Agamben's reading of Heidegger's work, 69–70, 74, 75–78; and animal being, 75–82, 133; and Derrida's critique of Husserl's work, 46, 48, 49, 50, 51, 53; and Derrida's *Of Grammatology,* 23; and Derrida's *Speech and Phenomena,* 46, 48, 49, 50, 51, 53; muteness of, 50, 54, 55. *See also* phonocentrism; speech

Weimar Germany, 8, 154, 155, 156

Wills, David, 282n10

Witt, Charlottte, 99, 275–76n16

"The Work of Man" (Agamben), 207, 255

Wortham, Simon Morgan, 278n3
writing: and Agamben's concept of potentiality, 106, 107, 120; and death, 44–45, 177–80; and Derrida's *Animal That Therefore I Am*, 177–80; and Derrida's critique of Husserl's *Origin of Geometry*, 44–46; and Derrida's critique of phonocentrism in general, 23–26; and Derrida's *Of Grammatology*, 23–26, 27–28, 33; and Saussurian semiology, 23–26, 27–28, 33

Writing and Difference (Derrida), 227, 229, 230, 231, 258

Zartaloudis, Thanos, 129

COMMONALITIES

Timothy C. Campbell, series editor

Roberto Esposito, *Terms of the Political: Community, Immunity, Biopolitics.* Translated by Rhiannon Noel Welch. Introduction by Vanessa Lemm.

Maurizio Ferraris, *Documentality: Why It Is Necessary to Leave Traces.* Translated by Richard Davies.

Dimitris Vardoulakis, *Sovereignty and Its Other: Toward the Dejustification of Violence.*

Anne Emmanuelle Berger, *The Queer Turn in Feminism: Identities, Sexualities, and the Theater of Gender.* Translated by Catherine Porter.

James D. Lilley, *Common Things: Romance and the Aesthetics of Belonging in Atlantic Modernity.*

Jean-Luc Nancy, *Identity: Fragments, Frankness.* Translated by François Raffoul.

Miguel Vatter, *Between Form and Event: Machiavelli's Theory of Political Freedom.*

Miguel Vatter, *The Republic of the Living: Biopolitics and the Critique of Civil Society.*

Maurizio Ferraris, *Where Are You? An Ontology of the Cell Phone.* Translated by Sarah De Sanctis.

Irving Goh, *The Reject: Community, Politics, and Religion After the Subject.*

Kevin Attell, *Giorgio Agamben: Beyond the Threshold of Deconstruction.*

J. Hillis Miller, *Communities in Fiction*

www.ingramcontent.com/pod-product-compliance
Lightning Source LLC
Chambersburg PA
CBHW022033290426
44109CB00014B/848